When the Going Gets Weird

Hunter S. Thompson

The Twisted Life and Times of

A Very Unauthorized Biography

When the Going Gets Weird

Peter O. Whitmer

HYPERION

New York

The author gratefully acknowledges permission from these sources to print the following:

Atlantic Monthly Press, for excerpts from *The Ginger Man* by J.P. Donleavy, © 1965 by J. P. Donleavy.

High Times, for excerpt from interview with Hunter Thompson by Ron Rosenbaum © 1977.

The Eglin AFB *Command-Courier,* for excerpts from sports columns by Hunter Thompson.

Patti Roberts-Nelson for Art Linson, Knickerbocker Films, Inc., for excerpt from *Where the Buffalo Roam.*

Bantam, Doubleday, Dell Publishing Group, Inc., for excerpts from *Even Cowgirls Get the Blues* by Tom Robbins © 1976.

Random House, Inc., for excerpts from "Barn Burning," from *Collected Stories* by William Faulkner; and for excerpts from *Hell's Angels* by Hunter S. Thompson © 1967.

Harold Ober Associates, for excerpts from *Babylon Revisited and Other Stories* by F. Scott Fitzgerald.

The Nation, for excerpts from "The Nonstudent Left" and "The Hell's Angels" by Hunter S. Thompson © 1965.

Grove Weidenfeld, for excerpts from *Freewheelin' Frank* by Frank Reynolds and Mike McClure © 1965.

John Lombardi of *The Los Angeles Free Press,* for excerpts from "The Ultimate Freelancer" by Hunter Thompson © 1967.

Tony Lukas, for excerpts from article on Hunter Thompson in *MORE* magazine © 1972.

Playboy and Craig Vetter, for excerpts from article on Hunter Thompson © 1974.

Library of Congress Cataloging-in-Publication Data

Whitmer, Peter O.
When the going gets weird : the twisted life and times of Hunter S. Thompson / by Peter O. Whitmer.—1st ed.
p. cm.
ISBN 1-56282-856-8
1. Thompson, Hunter S.   2. Journalists—United States—20th century—Biography.   I. Title.
PN4874.T444W45   1993
070'.92—dc20
[B]

92-31507
CIP

Design by Richard Oriolo

First Edition

10 9 8 7 6 5 4 3 2 1

Again, for the Great Habeeb, for The Water Queen,
and, still, the view to the West.

It's a shame that the only thing a man can do for eight hours a day is work. He can't eat for eight hours; he can't drink for eight hours; he can't make love for eight hours. The only thing a man can do for eight hours a day is work.

—William Faulkner

... the only people for me are the mad ones, the ones who are mad to live, mad to talk, mad to be saved, desirous of everything at the same time, the ones who never yawn or say a commonplace thing . . .

—Jack Kerouac
On the Road

"Bartender, give me five for the road."

—Sebastian Dangerfield, in J. P. Donleavy's
The Ginger Man

I wouldn't recommend alcohol and drugs to anyone. But they have always worked for me.

—Hunter S. Thompson

Acknowledgments

The process of writing is like no other, involving protracted periods of monk-like solitude, punctuated by manic social flailings to interview people, suck dry their information, then scurry back to the quiet of the cave, light the candle, and try to make sense of it all.

Sometimes it works better than others, and often this is because of the help provided by people, above and beyond the author's expectations. These people deserve to be acknowledged in some way, especially given the thin-ice task of writing a biography about an individual who is still both very much alive, and has a reputation for pinpoint accuracy at long range.

First credits go to Jill Kneerim and Ike Williams at the Palmer and Dodge Agency for having the guts to entertain my idea of this book, then actually to go forth and sell it. That took vision and persuasiveness, commodities I found lacking in numerous other agents.

The various members of the Louisville Athenaeum Literary Association, that now sadly defunct organ of intellect and outlet of talent that provided Hunter Thompson with his initial audience and encouragement, provided me with rich and telling vignettes of those early days of Gonzo, in the land that once was Louisville, "caught under amber." Of special note are Gerald Tyrrell, Stewart Smythe, Neville Blakemore, Larry Jelsma, Porter Bibb, Paul Semonin, and George Logan. Another ALA member, Ralston Steenrod, helped with a variety of matters that ranged from the historical and literary to the litigious. I thank him and my 215-pound American attorney, Joe Mincberg, for helping me to word properly the legal stipuation that forever precludes me from delivering flowers to Hunter's mother. Sorry, Virginia; there is no Flower Power any more.

I am extremely indebted to Alan Rinzler, who used his own literary Lamaze procedures to birth so much of Thompson's work. (I find it perfectly fitting that Alan has gone from being an editor to being a psychotherapist, for books, too, are life, and they should both be allowed to live as fully as one's potential allows.) He allowed me to look at the evolution of Thompson's creativity, to see how and why it has changed over the years.

For the chapter material on the 1960s, and the San Francisco–Berkeley swirl, I thank everyone who made an appearance in my earlier book, *Aquarius Revisited,* especially William Burroughs, Tim Leary, Allen Ginsberg, Ken Kesey, Norman Mailer, Tom Robbins, and Hunter himself. Those were seminal times; those are seminal people.

George Plimpton was encouraging and enlightening; he supported my notion that the works of Thompson will be taught in universities in the next century, he regaled me with tales from the heart of Zaire, and he showed me the infamous Black Hand.

George McGovern surprised and pleased me by writing back to this anonymous person, saying "I would *love* to talk about Hunter Thompson," and following through with vividness and detail, as did Frank Mankiewicz, of the days on the campaign trail.

Philip Caputo and Nick Proffitt helped me turn comic-strip myth into factual reality about Hunter's days (and nights) in Vietnam. Jo Hudson and Mike and Dennis Murphy were invaluable in helping reconstruct the Brigadoon-like ethos that used to be Big Sur, as it was evolving into the Esalen Institute. Roxanne Pulitzer helped add truth to the Palm Beach scene.

Each individual whose name appears in the list of interviewees is to be thanked for their contributions.

There is a long list of people in Aspen who shall go nameless, as I don't want them to be refused a beer at the W. C. Tavern. And in matters that formed the nuts and bolts of doing a book, I wish to thank my editor, Leslie Wells, and the entire crew at Hyperion for incredible human contact and understanding during the process. And: Jill Krementz for her cover photograph; Tim Leary for his quote; Pat Lawton for her amazing alacrity in turning around interview transcriptions, and my Packard Bell Legend 720X and GeoWorks software for neither exploding, imploding, or otherwise acting dysfunctional over the long strange trip it's been on. And its important to note the value added due to due diligence and patient understanding of Ted Bililies for both proofreading and encouragement.

Contents

When
the
Going
Gets
Weird

1.

Eight Balls

and

Lipstick

Success in this country is worshipped to a point where it is a
frenzied renown. You are swarmed over. Made crazy. It's
hard to be gracefully successful and remain a human being.
It's almost a contradiction of terms. You don't realize that
until you've reached that point. The air! It is hard to find air
anymore. It gets real difficult to breathe. There is so much
clamping around you. So many things . . .
—HUNTER S. THOMPSON

Tires screeched, car doors slammed, and the boom of
"Dunhills! Dunhills!" bounced off the wet Seattle
street and into the quiet, mannerly department
store like a clap of thunder. Clerks folding Hermès
scarves turned to see Hunter S. Thompson leading
a charge right at their doors. He stormed the entrance to Frederick & Nelson's like a zealot in the

heat of battle followed by his troops—a handful of students assigned to transport him from Seatac Airport. No one had promised a non-stop journey, yet no one expected Thompson to run out of cigarettes and explode like fireworks with a passionate nicotine fit.

Shaking off water from the rain, Thompson stopped dead still, just inside the store. The students bumped into one another, then watched in amazement as Thompson rummaged through an array of women's handbags. He looked them over with care; he appeared to know what he was doing. After careful inspection, he selected one and headed for the counter, rendering the clerk mute. "People don't think I know this," he told the stunned woman behind the glass case, all the while tearing out the paper stuffing from inside the $85 bag and flinging it to the floor, "but this is the finest craftsmanship. . . . Yes! We must have this!" The students looked around in vain for the plurality of Thompson's "we" but found no one.

The handbag was the beginning of a scavenger hunt for the unimaginable. The Dunhill cigarettes seemed forgotten. "Bath oil," he demanded of a male employee, while waving his recently purchased purse. "Chanel Number Five . . . where is it?" The clerk located bath gel. Thompson put the container on the floor and prodded it gently with his foot, like a camper stirring embers in a dying fire. "No. This gel most certainly will not do. We must have the oil." The clerk eyed Thompson as if he were a moon rock, but kept his composure adequately to extol the virtues of the gel. "You're breaking my heart," Thompson said to the clerk, taking the gel and handing him a leather-gloved fistful of dollars.

The small band of scavengers seemed outward bound, the hunt completed, when suddenly Thompson stopped dead again and said, "Lipstick! We should try the samples at the cosmetics counter!" Who were they to argue with such logic? The University of Washington's finest stood scratching their heads, exchanging conspiratorial looks of disbelief as Thompson selected a sample lipstick with a square base, smeared it back and forth across his lips, and looked in the small round mirror and pronounced, "Not my color." After stuffing his purchases into his handbag, he led the troupe out the door and through the rain, looking like a tall, balding transvestite. At least the students knew with whom they were dealing, and to expect something unexpected; inside Frederick & Nelson's, a group of clerks had gathered. Watching and listening, they remained stock-still.

Amerrican West flight 435 whined to a stop at Seattle's Seatac Airport. It was Tuesday morning in March of 1987, and it was a moment of some import. The welcome for Hunter S. Thompson was warm; Timothy Leary had arrived a half hour earlier, after a long night, an early alarm, and a two-hour flight from Los Angeles. In spite of Leary's irrepressible energy at sixty-seven years of age, this Social Security recipient was intending to take a nap before the afternoon press conference, and then the 8 P.M. "tribate" with Abbie Hoffman and Thompson at the University of Washington. The presentation was billed as "Children of the Sixties; Relics of the Eighties," and right now Leary felt more like the latter.

A handful of students had met his plane. They encouraged Leary to stay with them a few minutes to meet Thompson's plane; then they could all drive to the hotel together. Leary, never one to dissuade the youth of America, agreed. Besides, strange as it might seem, Timothy Leary and Hunter Thompson had never met. It was strange only in the sense that the two leap out of the memories and off the pages of the era of angst and illumination. If Leary was the professor with the vision to inspire the youth to remake themselves, and then the system, then Thompson was the scribe with the Remington Selectric typewriter to document the results while participating in the process. But when it came down to their relationship, there had been a tension of long standing.

Long before their first and only meeting, Thompson had reviewed his changing sentiments toward, as he referred to Leary, "the Dope Doctor." He had known of Leary early in his career as a journalist, "long before Berkeley or Kesey, or the Hell's Angels. As a matter of fact, I liked Tim earlier more than later on." The change came when Leary's following burgeoned, and his name became the international lightning rod for everything that was counter to culture. "I came to see him as a huckster, really, for his own interests. At first it sounded like an honorable case of rebellion. You know—one of us. I began to think, after a while, that he was less one of 'us.' Not one of 'them.' Just not one of 'us.' "

For Thompson, there seemed to have been a flavor of status in his opinion of Leary, and also an inflection of humor. "If I had had a wreck on my motorcycle, with a head full of acid, maybe I would have blamed it on Leary. But it would have been a joke, like when I attributed Melville's quotation 'Genius round the world stands hand in hand, and one shock of recognition runs the whole circle round' to Art Linkletter. But I have to draw a distinction. If there was an outlaw club on the top of a fantastic building in L.A., Leary would join it. It is a mentality, a mind-set. And I consider my position as pretty pure. But I distrust Leary's credentials as an outlaw. He is far too eager to join whatever mainstream there is around him. An outlaw is not some 'thing.' I don't think it is spelled with a capital *O.*"

Before that rainy day in Seattle, Leary's view had been equally bitter. If there had been a "shock of recognition" in his awareness of Thompson, it had not been energizing. "Hunter Thompson I have no respect for at all," he had said just two years earlier. "I suppose to many people we are seen as very similar, like troublemaking freaks. But I find running through most of Hunter's books a meanness; he makes fun of everybody. Sure, you can take drugs, and get drunk and not show up, or you can get stoned and watch district attorneys, and they are fools and so forth, but there is no warmth, no vision, no humor, and there is a lot of violence. He is like the Grateful Dead. Like the Hell's Angels, who, by the way, helped him get started."

With old age, buildings, politicians, and whores each gain respect. Perhaps anarchists as well. When Hunter Thompson and Timothy Leary were within eyesight, all animosity was forgotten. They embraced as if at a class reunion. They appeared respectful.

However, "He was coked, zooming," Leary recalled. "When Hunter Thompson stepped off the flight, he was already drunk," said Bruce Taylor, a writer for the University of Washington's newspaper. As he came down the stairway, Thompson waved a purple bottle of Chivas Regal in his hand. It was empty.

"Free drinks! I've never been on a flight like that before! Where's the bar?" shouted Thompson, who seemed oblivious to the fact that it was 10:30 in the morning. Dressed in a heliotrope aloha shirt, shorts, and tennis shoes, his energy overflowing, he insisted Leary have a drink to celebrate the long-overdue, momentous occasion. Within the context of the '60s counterculture, this was analogous to Leonardo da Vinci meeting Chuck Yeager. Thompson, who always moves in a hyperkinetic series of jerks and shakes, spun in tight circles, looking for a watering hole. Instead, he found an Official State of Washington Apple Booth.

"Where's the bar and restaurant?" he asked the clerk, who was barricaded behind a mound of gleaming red and yellow orbs. The speechless clerk held up a bag labeled "Golden Delicious."

"You know," Thompson shouted at the attendant, "drinks

. . . whiskey! If we can't find a bar, apples are not going to do us much good. I've never seen such a fucked-up airport." He swung manically in an arc around the baggage carousel, spotted a sign for the lounge, and headed for it as Leary turned to one of the students.

"Listen, do you have two cars? Drive me to the hotel. Tell Hunter that I look forward to a big party with him tonight." Leary left with one of the students. Hunter, followed like a mother goose by her goslings, headed toward the empty lounge, mumbling, "People hate me . . . I've noticed this more and more these days. . . . God . . . this place is spread out . . . the bar is thirteen miles down here."

In an otherwise empty bar, three students watched Thompson line up four Chivas-on-the-rocks, and briefly invert the open end of each glass in the palm of his hand—yet another Thompson trademark. He talked, without provocation, for the duration, touching on lawyers, Lyndon LaRouche, Wobblies, "the yuppie disease," and drugs. "Crack!" he said in a boom. "Who the hell is selling crack? I mean, I have tried every drug in the world, and nobody has offered me any crack! I'd like to try some." They nodded. They observed. Thompson talked. Thompson drank. Then, with some non-verbal signal—like the end of the last glass of Chivas—it seemed time to drive to the hotel.

There were only two commitments for Thompson all day, the 4 P.M. press conference and the 8 P.M. tribate at Meany Hall, and he was late for each. When he appeared a half hour late for the press conference, now dressed in a horizontally striped T-shirt, yellow aviator's glasses, and a baseball cap reading "San Francisco Marina Asst. Harbormaster," he brought with him his well-known rumpled brown paper bag. No traces of lipstick were evident. The bottle of Wild Turkey came out of the bag, and someone put extra drinking glasses down, one in front of Tim Leary, one in front of Hoffman.

Thompson uncorked the whiskey, poured, sipped, and then lit up a Dunhill. He began a low mumble in response to questions about his writing, the politics of Ronald Reagan, and ways of thinking about current events, all the time knowing that what they said this afternoon would appear as tomorrow's bannerline. All three had learned during the '60s—television's second full decade of existence—that the medium really was the message. TV had made Vietnam "the living-room war" and propelled each of these men to such heights that here they were again, back by popular demand, in front of the cameras and microphones.

He had been drinking since shortly after boarding his early morning flight, and showed no indication of letting up. Actually, Thompson had been drinking for a lot longer than that. "He was an alcoholic by the time he was sixteen. There's no doubt about it," commented Sam Stallings, Jr., a high-school classmate of Hunter's. Leary and Hoffman both wondered silently about their colleague's conspicuous consumption. But Hunter Thompson without alcohol would be like Leary without a vision, or Hoffman without an opinion.

The press conference seemed to focus on Hunter and Abbie, and Ronald Reagan's recent admission that he had, in fact, allowed arms to be sold to Iran. "What's so 'intelligent' about the CIA?" Hoffman barked. "To mention free speech in the same breath with the CIA is like talking about affirmative action in the Mafia. It's obscene. The CIA wants to destroy free speech."

"We're ten years past Watergate and the press hasn't learned anything," Thompson barked. "Irangate is a conscious network, a far-reaching conspiracy of people all through the government." The microphones migrated to a spot in front of him like a school of fish being fed his words. This was the man who dedicated his biggest book, *The Great Shark Hunt,* "To Richard Milhous Nixon, who never let me down," and was now finding yet another Republican President as a target for his wrath. He seemed rejuvenated, energized to be able once again to spit out firecrackers and have an appreciative audience hanging on his every word. Hoffman raged. Thompson raged. Leary left. "I just quietly walked out because it was in such good hands, and my presence was not necessarily missed."

Making points with a jab of his Dunhill, Thompson was in his medium. In front of the electronics, yet behind his tinted glasses, he was in control and in his glory: Hunter S. Thompson was a rock star trapped in the mind of a journalist, a man drawn narcissistically to the illumination of the limelight, and this was his sell-out concert.

Serious matters were being dealt with back at the Camlin Hotel. After the press conference, Tim Leary had finally taken a nap. At 7:30 he received a call from the student organizers waiting in the hotel lobby to take the three to Meany Hall. Leary called Thompson's room. He heard a background noise of a mob scene gone haywire. Over the din, Thompson said, "Come on down!" Leary did, only to find Abbie with Hunter, who was dressed in only his underwear. "He was definitely not ready to leap onto the lecture platform," Leary observed. "He and Abbie had placed a hundred-dollar bet on the televised basketball game between the Seattle Sonics and the Houston Rockets. It was the beginning of the third quarter, and obvious to me that they were not going to leave their hundred-dollar bet for anything as unimportant as a public appearance. Hunter was on the phone talking to somebody named Tony—about an eight ball. I said to them, 'Listen you guys, I'll go over to the auditorium and be your warm-up.' "

Leary began his talk by telling the crowd a reality of the times: "The main reason the three of us are together tonight is that we all have the same agent. It's too bad we live in a culture where the highest aspiration is the bottom line." Much of his message fell on the deaf ears of a group that had recently raised Ivan Boesky to the level of a cult hero. "I am waiting with great anticipation to see what the fuck is going to happen tonight," Leary told them, knowing full well that antics were waiting in the wings, and back at the hotel.

Hunter's team was losing badly, and he refused to cough up the hundred dollars, locking himself in his room while Hoffman tried to kick the door down. From inside, Hunter hurled obscenities. In the lobby, a Thompson groupie worked the telephones. "I need a quarter up to an eight ball!" the groupie shouted into the pay phone. "Don't do anymore of it . . . I need it . . . Don't cut the shit" was one side of the conversation. "Do you know who this is for? It's for Hunter Thompson. . . . You've got to meet me backstage at Meany Hall. . . . No . . . I've only got one ticket. . . . Leave now, man . . . meet me at the back door."

Hoffman, wearing a red bandanna, kicked one last time, and turned down the hall toward his room. The door to Thompson's room jerked open; he drenched Hoffman with a bucketful of water and bellowed, "You slimy pig! See what you learned in politics?" Thompson seemed genuinely pleased to be reunited with his old friend.

While Thompson and Hoffman engaged in a water fight, more than an hour past the scheduled show, Leary's "warm-up" exercises were getting drenched by crowd noise. Back at the hotel, Thompson proceeded to lock himself in his room, refusing to come out until the students slid the payment for his appearance under his door. He could not be budged. "I'm not going anywhere until I get my fucking check!" he shouted through the wood. Guests must have wondered. Finally, one student lured him out, saying that the check was in the car waiting to take him to the auditorium. He relented and headed for the show.

"GONZO . . . GONZO . . ." was quickly countered from the other side of the auditorium by the growing volume and sharper cadenced pulsing of "DUKE-DUKE-DUKE." It was clear that if there was a favorite among the three, the crowd preferred America's quintessential outlaw journalist over the psychology professor or the political anarchist—probably by three to one.

Most of the crowd understood the meaning of "Gonzo"—a balls-to-the-wall, accelerator-to-the-floor style of life for which Hunter Thompson was revered as the founding father and ace practitioner. For them, Gonzo meant an excess of adolescence, like jumping naked into the swimming pool, or driving thirty-six hours non-stop to some Spring Break salt lick. Gonzo, for them, was something situational, a brief phase of life, a window of carefree zaniness you could pass through, then joke about later when you were older and saddled with maturity. For Thompson, it was a projection of the very core of his existence, of the energies that moved him, for a half century now, along the jet streams of the American Experience.

The half of the audience chanting "Duke" was too young to be aware of the heated rankling that boiled toward the surface in Thompson whenever he heard that word. To Thompson, any reference to Duke, the cartoon character, elicited a response like a Romanian peasant hearing "vampire." In the mid-1970s—when most of the audience was in pre-school—there had been a hostile takeover of the persona of Hunter Thompson. It had been carried out, with considerable popular and financial success by Garry Trudeau, in the "Doonesbury" cartoon character Duke. In 1977, in Los Angeles promoting his new book, *The Great Shark Hunt*, Thompson had vented his anger, writing two long, scathing letters to Trudeau. He told his old friend from the Big Sur days in the early '60s Dennis Murphy, "Do you have any idea what it is like to wake up, look in the mirror . . . and see a cartoon? My God; I'm not even forty years old yet, and I've been MYTHOLOGIZED!"

Anger filled the air until it hummed like a tuning fork. The standing-room-only crowd in the auditorium, and the overflow crowd in the adjoining room with the video monitors were sucking it up like a drug. The people were too packed in to hit anyone, or even poke someone in the eye.

Hoffman came out, and then when Thompson walked on stage, there was a thunderous cheering. To many, this entrance was a surprise; they had fully expected him to materialize from a huge fireball. Perhaps he *was* human.

Up on stage were two bald men in their fifties, and another nearing seventy, with a shock of white hair. Two felons and a hillbilly. Leary, once an Irish-Catholic altar boy, placed in the silence of Coventry as a West Point plebe, excommunicated as a professor of psychology from Harvard for his LSD experimentation, and imprisoned for five years as one of the FBI's Ten Most Wanted. There was another of the FBI's Ten Most Wanted; Abbie Hoffman, a Jew, a Brandeis graduate who studied under Abraham Maslow before doing graduate work at Berkeley. He had nominated a pig for President, been convicted for "crossing state lines with intent to riot" during the 1968 Democratic Convention in Chicago, then later fled to live underground for seven years.

Hunter S. Thompson's family background was Fundamentalist Christian, from a town in Kentucky whose only reason for existing was a vast subterranean labyrinth of connected caverns that spat bats and sucked in tourists. As far as credentials were concerned, Thompson never finished high school before he changed the style of journalism to fit the times. But he remained the only person to have ridden with both the Hell's Angels and Richard Nixon: the perfect outlaw résumé.

While the mediums might have differed, the message of the three men on stage was shared—those three little words guaranteed to age a parent quickly, to send a college administrator around the bend: FUCK THE SYSTEM.

In a display of masterful staying power, the three men were going transgenerational. The parents of tonight's audience had, twenty years before, watched, read, and listened to the same persons, who had then used slight variations on tonight's themes. Twenty years before—1967—it had been "Turn on, tune in, and drop out," Tim Leary's mantra for a generation, his blueprint for higher consciousness through LSD. Tonight, the second generation was listening to the same man react to Nancy Reagan's anti-drug message by telling the students to "Just say know," and encourage them to use their computers to get smarter electronically. Tonight, it was "Turn on, tune in, and boot up."

For Abbie Hoffman, it was hyperbole, Round 2. This was the man about whom the civil rights attorney William Kunstler had said, "I use publicity as an adjunct to the law. The one who taught me that was Abbie Hoffman at the Chicago conspiracy trial." Tonight's variation on the theme of "civil disobedience as theater" was Hoffman's recent response to the government's incursion into individual rights by mandating drug testing. He was pitching his new book, *Steal This Urine Test*.

And then there was Hunter S. Thompson, always marching to a different drummer, even when the only others marching were distinctly one of a kind. Thompson, by comparison, seemed a purist, in that his bile was untempered; no signs of mellowing with age were apparent.

It had always been the passion of his bile that set him apart— from Leary and Hoffman, and from all other individuals, writers, and traditions. To some, he carried on the tradition of social satire begun by Jonathan Swift, mixed with the personalized, crystal-clear reportage of Stephen Crane. Many picked him as the next Mark Twain, but he proved that he was not the next anybody; he was the first Hunter S. Thompson, and his life-style was his writing.

Hoffman was speaking: "Telling an addict to 'just say no' is like telling a chronically depressed person to 'just cheer up.' "

Under cover of the applause, Hunter leaned over to Leary and said, "Listen, would you go backstage and see if Tony is there. If he is, get an eight ball from him."

"It was very elegant backstage," Leary observed. "It was like an opera house, with maybe a dozen people in it, and I said, 'Is there anybody named Tony?' Someone said 'Yeah, I'm Tony.' So I said, 'Do you have anything for Mr. Thompson?' He handed me a vial. So, out of scientific interest and protection of my friend—I would not want to be guilty of handing out something that might be deleterious to the young fellow—I went into the men's room. I found some white powder in the vial. I put just a little bit in my nose just to see what would happen, and it did indeed give me a real jolt of energy. So I bounded back on stage and said to Hunter, 'Yeah, Tony's here,' and I reached over and put the vial in his pocket."

Thompson leaped to the microphone, picking up where Hoffman had left off, accusing the country and the audience of being "a generation of swine! It is pitiful, like a person who has hurt himself and doesn't know what to do about it. The saddest thing, I think, is that this is a generation without a sense of possibility. In the '60s, we may have been foolish, but we thought we could change the world. It was fun to be in a world where there were possibilities. The eloquence and passion of it all is when you decide that there is one thing to do that's right, and you go ahead and do it."

The crowd cheered his energy, knowing neither its source nor that his reference to a generation of swine was actually a plug, the title of his first book in five years, in galley proofs as he spoke. They didn't care; what was important was that he had insulted them, and they loved it. A body slam from the Father of Gonzo Journalism was an anointment, and tonight his audience glowed in it.

They reveled in everything Thompson did that night. When Hoffman told the students, "Every good idea I ever had, I had when I was seventeen years old. Young people today have creativity, moral outrage, energy—and personal computers," Thompson noisily clanked his now empty whiskey bottle and glass together in applause, then rolled the bottle off the stage. A dozen kids swarmed for it as they would have a shirt tossed by Mick Jagger. Then someone in the audience launched a rubber shark that bounced across the stage with spastic jerks. Thompson raced to it like a sled dog to food, tearing it open, looking for drugs: The Great Rubber Shark Hunt. It came up empty, but the effort pleased all.

Dr. Thompson had never warmed his stethoscope before taking the pulse of America. He tapped a different nerve than did his colleagues that night. While all three were connective tissue to that decade of protest and tie-dye, the decade that refuses to go away, Thompson's presence was different. The students would go out and see Oliver Stone's movie, *The Doors,* and then communicate their thoughts to one another over electronic mail on their computer network, the tool of Tim Leary. Others would show their moral outrage and chain themselves to a redwood tree filled with spotted-owl nests; for that they were indebted to Abbie Hoffman.

But Thompson had acted out every one of their fantasies. They all had '60s posters on their dorm walls, had watched the specials on TV, and had asked their parents the tough questions: the ones about their involvement with sex, drugs, and rock and roll. Parents are strangely mute on these points, but for every mute parent there is a page of Hunter Thompson to be read. Ride with the Hell's Angels. Arm-wrestle with Ken Kesey and the Merry Pranksters. Talk football with Richard Nixon, and drive at 97 miles an hour in your convertible with the top down, with the trunk so full of drugs it looks like a mobile police lab, and head straight for Las Vegas in search of the American Dream.

For the parents of the audience, the shock of Hunter Thompson had exploded off the pages of *Rolling Stone,* and in his *Fear and Loathing* books. Both what Thompson said and how he said it were things they had never before experienced. He was outrageous, yet those were outrageous times. Castrate Hubert Humphrey? John Chancellor taking LSD? Weekly inside coverage of the George McGovern Presidential campaign? Thompson seemed to be in the midst of every corner of the American scene, at the hottest places in the most explosive times. He had been an unavoidable dimension to life in the '60s, '70s, and even in the early '80s. In the last few years, he had been quiet, but he was certainly not forgotten. Tonight's audience wanted to compare myth with reality. They wanted to see just what kind of beast had so many lives.

Hunter S. Thompson is the Gutenberg Bible of '60s excess, and there he is, up on stage, lurching full speed ahead toward the '90s, clanking his whiskey bottle, zooming on Tony's eight ball, and making $5,000 in the process. The average college student who harbors ambivalence over being forced to bear the weight of adult responsibility, and who fears the very real danger of becoming part of the process that he now abhors, can look to the tall man on stage for career guidance. He has Peter Pan's invincibility; he is James Dean in aviator glasses, Marlon Brando in top physical shape. When they read Hunter Thompson, when they see him on stage, they all say silently in the back of their minds, "Maybe I don't have to grow up after all!" But if they were to look more closely, to roll back the years to when Thompson was their age, they would find a different story, a saga that may be all-American, but is also all weird machine.

2.

Horse

Cave

n the center of the flag of Kentucky are two men shaking hands, surrounded by the slogan "United We Stand—Divided We Fall." One man is dressed in rough, country buckskin. The other wears nineteenth-century formal wear. The two men on the flag are Daniel Boone and Henry Clay. Neither was born in Kentucky. The two never met.

Over the years, the state flag has been modified. Originally the two were hugging, but that was considered unmanly, and anachronistic. Regardless, the confrontation between frontiersman Boone and Clay, the educated, upper-class, three-time Presidential candidate, has existed through the years. It is an institutionalized metaphor for the huge historical and cultural gaps that form an odd, yet integral dimension of this state.

Kentucky is cusp country; a quarter-million miles of contrast and paradox that do not seem to fit together, yet still manage. As the history of Kentucky has worked its way through four centuries, the Thompson family has been there for every step.

In the mid-1700s, when the populations of the large East Coast cities hemorrhaged, they coagulated in Kentucky. To the east, neighboring Virginia was the most heavily populated colony in America, more so than New York and Pennsylvania combined; the power of territorial imperative pushed people south and west. Thousands flowed through the arteries and capillaries of the wall of the Appalachian Mountains, through Cumberland Gap, Scuttle Hole, and the Doubles. The newcomers were the illiterate, the untamed, the dross of English urban population explosions; skilled artisans remained behind. The original population of Kentucky was composed of social outcasts, debtors, orphans, and indentured servants. Many escaped into the Blue Ridge Mountains, then down the western valleys to the flatlands of Kentucky, where they existed in total isolation for nearly a century. Harry Caudill, Kentucky state senator and social reformer, referred to them as "human refuse." They were penniless, angry, resentful of any form of imposed government, and filled with a penchant for untrammeled freedom.

They were frontiersmen. They followed the setting sun across the mountains. They fought, then mated, with Indians. They settled and established an order of human existence never known before. It became Kentucky, the first area west of the Appalachians to be settled by American colonists, a former county of the state of Virginia, the fifteenth state of the Union, a land hell-bent on developing a tradition of contrast, dissension, feudal anarchy, and bloodshed that exists through the past to the present.

The origins of Hunter Thompson's family can be traced to the 1500s in England. The Thompson family tree can be climbed for nine generations. Then, beyond the ca. 1600 marriage of John

Jennings and Mary Joyce Wearner, whose great-granddaughter would marry a Thompson, the lineage branches out and disappears into medieval mists. But very quickly some characters appear: the Duke of Marlborough, and Tyrconnel, the Lord Lieutenant of Ireland, were married to sisters of Thompson's seventh-generation forebear, William Jennings.

The Duke of Marlborough married Sarah Eddington Jennings, Hunter Thompson's aunt, seven generations removed. Sarah's younger sister, Fannie, married Richard Talbot, Earl of Tyrconnel, who in 1689 attempted to reestablish a Catholic king in Ireland. But it was Sarah and her husband who drew the attention of the day, and the place in the history books.

In the language of the times, Sarah Jennings Churchill was referred to as "a beautiful termagant," and the Duke of Marlborough as "the English Caesar." Together they formed a political team that not only pulled diplomatic levers and fought important battles, but set the tone for freedom of the press, and helped sponsor the careers of Pope, Swift, Defoe, and Voltaire. This means Hunter Thompson's ancestral home is the stately Blenheim Palace, and that his relations are buried in Westminster Abbey; their portraits hang in the National Portrait Gallery. Further, this relates Hunter S. Thompson to Winston Churchill and Douglas MacArthur.

Another legacy of the Thompson family lives on in Manchester, England. In the late 1700s, a nephew of the Duke and Duchess of Marlborough, also known as William Jennings, built a phenomenal financial empire on an invention, the Jennings loom. It was an improvement on the standard weaving machinery of the day, the Jacquard loom, and it created a financial empire that still exists. The puzzling question, fought in the courts for centuries, is who are the rightful heirs? William Jennings the inventor never married, had no children, and died with an incredible amount of wealth, factories, and valuable patents, but without a will. In the 1920s it was estimated by a family member that over half a million dollars had been spent in lawyers' fees—with no results. As recently as 1940, Sterling Thompson, Hunter Thompson's uncle, remarked that "we have a detective in London working on it now."

The first Thompson relative who came to the United States arrived as an Indian fighter. The Duchess of Marlborough's brother, William Jennings, was known as "the British officer," and received three land grants in Amelia County, Virginia, for his efforts. One of his grandsons, William Thompson, felt the pull of the sun setting to the west over the mountain range, and pushed his way into Kentucky in 1800. In succeeding generations, other family members would follow their original paths. To this day, in the small area around Horse Cave, Kentucky, there are 168 Thompsons in the phone directory.

When William Thompson made the move, the name of the land to the west of the mountains carried a powerful mixed message. Both names were from the Indians, who called their hunting grounds either Ken-To-Kah, meaning "Land of Tomorrow," or Ken-Tuh-Key, translated as "A Dark and Bloody Ground." The truth seemed to swing from one to the other with the pendulum of time.

In the 1820s, when the Thompson family was scratching out a living in the Horse Cave area, an Austrian writer visited Kentucky, and fired a shot warning others of the randy character of the people. Kentucky could not be recommended to new settlers, he stated, as their mix of sociology offered "serious warnings to every lover of peace and tranquillity." He concluded by describing their level of civilization as "emetic" and their temperament as marked by "the most lawless arrogance, and an untameable spirit of revenge."

The Thompsons' "untameable spirit" can be seen in their collection of family names, some given to children generation after generation. Over the years, the alternatives included Memory, Hook, Pearl, Ruby, Garnet, Wathal, Smiser, Bagby, and Waddy. The name Stockton appears both on Hunter S. Thompson's mother's Louisville side of the family and on his father's side. Hunter was the maiden name of Thompson's maternal grandmother. But there had been other colorful options hanging from the family tree. One relative was born in Ireland, but named America. Pocahontas, the legendary Indian, was a relation, and the name Lawless was used for many members, including an uncle of Hunter's. Given the tradition of naming children after their ancestors, had the family picked another set of names, the quintessential outlaw journalist could have been known as Lawless America.

Until April 12, 1861, the Thompsons lived relatively uneventful lives as farmers, some wealthy enough to own slaves. Then came radical, enduring change. The Civil War split Kentucky like an ax. The wound festered, refusing to heal for the next seventy-five years. In the state of Kentucky, like no other state in the country, the war became one of patricide and fratricide. While Kentucky officially remained "neutral," the Thompson family, like the state, sent soldiers to fight on both sides. In the wake of the Civil War, fighting continued. Old issues of social stratum, relative wealth, and slave ownership would be carried forward in the form of the archetypal Kentucky morality play, the family feud. The destructive synergy of envy, class division, religious differences, as well as an endless, senseless list of long-standing arguments between families, was now fuel on the fire.

For years, the Thompson family lived near Horse Cave. This was still an "area"; known for the hole in the ground, it would not be recognized officially as a one-square-mile "town" for another seven years. This was a town of coincidence, where the first settlers stumbled upon refuge in the underground caverns, and all the land above stayed as barren as it had been when the buffalo roamed and the Indians hunted. It was an area to which change came infrequently.

Horse Cave was surveyed by a former military officer in the Mexican-American War, Major Robert Anderson, using the only measuring device he had—a 100-foot linen tape measure. The narrow streets and strangely angled intersections, still very much a part of the small town, are blamed on him: "If only he had gotten a longer tape measure" is an old joke in town.

Hunter Thompson's grandfather, John Donand Thompson, was born in Horse Cave in 1857, the same year that the Louisville & Nashville Railroad was born. Life there from then on would never be the same after the ground crew came to survey and grade for the L&N's railbed. With them came a mini-boom for the area in employment, supplies, lodging, and all the many-headed creatures that travel along with civilization. In that year, Horse Cave contained six families, one trading post (hides, tallow, wool, feathers, bacon, beeswax; eggs at five cents a dozen), 280 pigs, and one cave.

By 1893, when Hunter's father, Jack Robert, was born, Horse Cave had grown: nine families, two stores, four churches, two schools, a depot, a tobacco "factory," fairgrounds, and one cave. With the railroad had come growth, pollution, bribery, fashion, wealth, and poverty. In essence, the future of Horse Cave had arrived on steel rails and wooden ties, but it was Louisville where the railroad built great fortunes and created the kind of culture that Hunter Thompson would find intolerable.

During the time of Hunter Thompson's grandparents, a cosmopolitan atmosphere pervaded Louisville. Isaiah Rogers, designer of Boston's Tremont House, came and built Louisville's Galt House. Charles Dickens stayed there while researching *Martin Chuzzlewit* and *American Notes.* Audubon came and painted his first American bird—the wild turkey. Washington Irving sketched the town while George Keats, brother of the poet, settled there and became the director of a bank, and a city council member helping to establish Louisville's school system.

As late as 1937—the year Hunter Thompson was born— Louisville was described in a *Harper's* article as "an American Museum Piece . . . under glass . . . [where] the curious may see memorials of the 'American Spirit' in its purest form, monuments of individual enterprise." The article captured the spirit of intrigue and tight-knit control that seemed a gentrified extension of the strange-breed Mountain Man mentality of fierce independence and an abhorrence of imposed, outside controls.

Horse Cave, like dozens of other rural, agrarian spots, was linked to Louisville by the *L&N* as if by a metal umbilical chord. For the John Donand Thompson family, entering the twentieth century with four sons—Hunter's father, Jack Robert, and three brothers—it was, indeed, a lifeline. To safeguard goods shipped on the railroad, an insurance brokerage was formed. When the freight rates skyrocketed and local farmers shipped less, the brokerage was transplanted to Louisville, where it continues to operate.

Hunter Thompson's paternal grandmother's family was the first involved in insurance in that area. Colonel William Wheeler, CSA, developed a career in insurance. Then, attracted to the vigor of Louisville, he took his insurance company there.

John Donand Thompson, Hunter's grandfather, was born and raised within the sound of the *L&N* train whistle. It would wail in the middle of baptisms; it blasted its approval at the turn of a double play on the ball field just off the tracks. John Thompson became a "drummer." To drum was to travel; to travel was to ride the *L&N*; to ride the *L&N* was to see and smell and feel the excitement of the larger cities on the river, especially Louisville. A natural salesman, he was an outgoing, handshaking pure extrovert of a man. His wife, Corrie Lee, "never knew how many to expect for dinner." He traveled the L&N first for a Louisville wholesale shoe manufacturer, then sold fertilizer mined from bat dung in the local caves. He was known as "Clever Jack Thompson" and "Genial Jack Thompson" in the local press, where his sales talents were vaunted with the accolade that "no [more] clever gentleman or better salesman ever extended the glad hand to the merchants."

John and Corrie Lee Thompson's four sons were exuberant boys, and enjoyed their childhoods in Horse Cave to the fullest. Each had his signature prank. One prank they would pull together, much to the entertainment of the townsfolk. One day, Mr. Shirley Gossett, whose family sharecropped on the Thompson family's farm, saw the oldest brother, Jean, in action: "They had a big pond on the side of the barn, and they had a black saddle horse, a fine horse, slick and black. And I seen Jean take this horse one day, and they just had a little halter thing and the one little line near as I remember, and he stood up on that horse's back and swum him across that pond." The true risk of this particular acrobatic act was less in standing bareback atop a swimming horse than in the pond on the Thompson property. Horse Cave, Kentucky, is karst country, an area of geographical formations found only there and to the west of Trieste, in Yugoslavia. The ponds that dot the landscape are quite shallow and perfectly symmetrical. At the very bottom of each pond is a thin membrane of limestone that is gradually leached away into the endless caverns that run just underground until the membrane becomes paper-thin. With surprising regularity, the people of Horse Cave have gone into their fields only to see the kicking hind legs of a hog or a prize bull—or a family member—who has broken through to the underworld, leaving behind a drained sinkhole. The Thompson brothers were skilled in assessing such risks— perhaps that is why they all ended up in the insurance business.

Their group trick involved "a big Jersey bull. They would ride him to town, all four of them—Jean, Jack Robert, Lawless, and Sterling—and that bull would just come along like a saddle horse, right up to the general store. It created a big excitement with a lot of the people. But the people who knew them knew they weren't crazy; they were smart," Gossett observed.

Horse Cave was a small town, a place where adolescent energies can take an odd turn or two. Corrie Lee Wheeler Thompson, the boys' mother, whose family background was said to contain considerable Indian blood (probably more than her husband's, whose relation to Pocahontas was direct but distant), was zealously religious, a trait that seemed to start and end with her. Her zeal of preference was the Fundamentalist Christian Church, and she had attended Science Hill, a women's seminary in Shelbyville, Kentucky, before marrying and moving to Horse Cave. There, and later in Louisville, she became an integral part of the church. One day when she saw that her church's lawn needed mowing, she commanded her sons to do the work. They did. It was summer. Summer in Horse Cave can be unbearable; finishing the lawn, all four brothers jumped into the huge ten-by-twelve-foot baptismal. Their splashing brought the pastor, and his wrath, but it was tempered knowing that he had baptized Hunter's father and his brothers in the same pool. He had written into the records that "Jack Robert Thompson obeyed the Gospel and joined the Christian Church on the night of 15 December, 1904, at the age of 10 years."

Another prank, one with a wider impact on the community, involved the blacks' Baptist church, a simple wooden structure set off the ground on four-foot stilts. During Sunday night prayer meeting, the four brothers quietly removed the front steps before shouting in the windows, "Fire! Fire! Everyone out!" It was a long, hungry day in Horse Cave that Monday: "There was not a cook in town," explained Gossett.

But even this carefree country life was to come to an end. On the last Friday of December, 1911, John Donand Thompson was extending his salesman's glad hand to Horse Cave Mayor Branstetter when he dropped dead of a heart attack. The papers described this as "apoplexy" and in his death as having "instantly passed to the great Beyond . . . when he fell and expired instantly heart trouble being the cause. It was known that Mr. Thompson was effected [sic] with this malada [sic] and his friends, while greatly shocked, were not much surprised at the end. He leaves four sons,: Lawless, Eugene, Sterling, and [Jack] Robert." With the death of Genial Jack, his wife packed the four boys onto a train and headed for Colonel Wheeler's Louisville townhouse. Jack Robert was nineteen.

When Jack Robert made the quantum leap with his family from tiny Horse Cave to the metropolis of Louisville, he took with him memories of small-town baseball. Horse Cave—all four hundred people—had for years produced championship ball clubs, and had regularly played Louisville's American Association team known as the Kentucky Colonels. Further, the Horse Cave Cave Men had regularly stomped the Colonels, as the schedule of the small town's team always included a spring season filled with the best competition available: major-league teams moving north along the L&N Railroad from warm-weather training.

Baseball would become a constant in Jack Robert's life. The rest of the world could easily disappear when he sat in Parkway Field, or after 1922 when the radio station WHAS began to broadcast and even the away games could be heard. He would be glued to the radio every spring through to the fall. Baseball was therapy, a respite. Neither his career, his family, nor life in general ever seemed to grant him the right opportunities to put everything together and achieve his dreams. When it came to success, it was his younger brother, Sterling, who made things happen. In the years before World War I, the Thompson boys had moved out of Colonel Wheeler's townhouse, but worked in the same building as the Colonel, who was now approaching seventy. A Thompson family story relates the young boys' first day at work when they happened to find themselves in the same crowded elevator as their grandfather, a head taller and probably fifty years older than everyone else. The others in the elevator all removed their hats, mumbling on exit, "Good morning, Colonel," until only Wheeler and the Thompsons remained. Then the Colonel turned to them, looked them up and down, silently acknowledging their presence before asking, "And who might you all be?" Sheepishly, they replied, "Your grandsons, Colonel." The family was never close, either between generations or between brothers.

When the United States finally entered World War I, the only state where the draft did not have to be mandated in every county was Kentucky. Many called it patriotism. Some assessed it as just a bunch of guys who liked to shoot people and wanted to get out of the mountains for a while at someone else's expense.

Jack Robert Thompson was already out of the mountains; he volunteered anyway. He joined the U.S. Army as a private in July of 1918, and mustered out as a corporal with an honorable discharge from the Park Battery Artillery Unit. Getting in the service was no problem for the 24-year-old, nor was getting out: Camp Zachary Taylor had been built hastily in Thompson's back yard. It housed 50,000 trainees after the War Department selected Louisville as the regional training center in June, 1917. For recruits from all over the Midwest and South there was ease of access along the rail lines. While thousands of doughboys poured into Louisville, riding Pullman cars painted "TO HELL WITH

THE KAISER," all Jack Robert had to do was hop a streetcar.

The twelve months of duty in between were not so easy. Although they were in different units, both Jack Robert and his older brother, Jean, saw the countryside of France framed within the gunsights of a 155-mm. Schneider Howitzer as they fought their way from the Argonne to the Marne to Vesle; just before the Armistice, they were put onto a boat and sent back home.

Thompson's war years carried interesting literary overtones. When Jack Robert mustered in at Camp Zachary Taylor, F. Scott Fitzgerald was in training; at Saint-Mihiel and in the Champagne sector in France, he had fought with William Faulkner's brother Jack. Both Fitzgerald and Faulkner would be profound influences on Hunter Thompson.

As if trying to make up for lost time, Jack Robert married less than three months after his discharge, and soon fathered a son, Jack Robert, Jr. His wife, Garnett Sowards, was from Greenup, Kentucky, near Ashland. Immediately after their marriage, his insurance business transferred them to Pikeville, Kentucky. This town of a few thousand was the county seat for Pike County, the center of the Appalachian Plateau, heart of coal country, twenty miles from Virginia, twenty-five from West Virginia, and a million miles from civilization. The sport here was danger; the players were from a league like no other.

Horse Cave had been populated by people who years before had trekked through or moved out of Pikeville because of its inherent hostility. Jack Robert had heard from friends and relatives the folklore of feuds and strange barefooted men who took the law into their own hands. During high school in Horse Cave, he had read bits and pieces about this part of the state in the textbook *History of Kentucky,* written by his cousin Captain Edward Porter Thompson. But to actually go to Pikeville in the 1920s was to go backward in time, to enter a feudal war zone. This was land untouched by law, where cousins married cousins, "doctors" required no licensing, and the recent intrusion of the railroads to rape the land of its essence had brought entire "coal towns" of eastern European laborers who could not speak English and lived in fealty to the large corporations. Pikeville contained the McCoy side of the flagrantly brutal Hatfield-McCoy feud, a savage clan war that took at least sixty-five lives and branded the area with a nefarious reputation that could never be shed.

On the heels of the Hatfield-McCoy era, like a tag team from Hell, came the relentless "moonshine wars," a constant deadly skirmish between government revenue collectors and operators of stills. Pike County had been legally dry decades before the 1920 Volstead Act, as a way of cornering the market to sell their own home-grown liquor; the area was dirt poor, and this was a traditional source of income. However, with the passage of Prohibition, things heated up. During Jack Robert's stay in Pikeville, a nearby newspaper, the Hazard, Kentucky, *Herald,* was constantly running bannerlines such as: "FRANK SPENCER, 'KING OF THE MOONSHINERS,' KILLED BY DEPUTY SHERIFF," "MAN SHOT RESISTING ARREST AT LOTHAIR," "SEVEN STILLS, THREE MEN CAPTURED IN COUNTY."

It was tough duty selling insurance on a battlefield; no one was interested in life policies. But the big railroads paid well to insure their cargo, and it was Jack Robert's duty to set the rates. By the time the great union battles of the United Mine Workers took over where the moonshine wars left off, Jack Robert was on his way back to Louisville. He took with him an ailing wife. Garnett was dying of pneumonia, a common disorder in coal-dust-soaked Pikeville. She died just before Christmas of 1923.

Jack Robert left his infant son with his in-laws in Ashland, Kentucky, and returned to Louisville. It had been eleven years since his family left Horse Cave, filled with wide-eyed expectation and optimism. Thompson had had a budding insurance career interrupted by the war, a son born, and a wife die. At the age of thirty, he found himself back in Louisville with no family, doing the tedious work of an insurance rate-setter. It was a new decade with a new mentality, one of peace, prosperity, and jazz, yet his life seemed an extension of a number 2 pencil.

3.

Louisville

Sluggers

ven in the Depression years, the insurance business went on; businesses that had little left to lose wanted to make sure that small part was protected. Since Louisville was a crossroads of rail lines, with some shipping still going on over the Ohio River, Jack Thompson stayed employed. Again, baseball provided a diversion

from work. In a curious blend of fan and fanatic, Jack Robert and his mother, Corrie, carefully watched the opening day of the Louisville team, as future Yankee and Hall of Famer, Earle "the Kentucky Colonel" Combs, a local product, made the first and last out of the game, while in the stands was former baseball player Billy Sunday. After the game, Corrie attended Billy Sunday's evangelic tent show, where the entire audience was mesmerized by his unique bombastic delivery.

In 1934, Jack Robert was introduced by mutual friends to Virginia Davidson Ray, a 26-year-old Louisville native.

Virginia was born on New Year's Day, 1908; she was fifteen years younger than Jack Robert. Her father, Presley Stockton Ray, had come to Louisville from the smaller town of Springfield, "as soon as he was able to get out of there," Virginia recalled. He decided to start a company to manufacture horse-drawn carriages. Presley Stockton Ray & Company, Inc., Carriage Manufacturers, was its uninspired name, and the offices were at 1337 South Second Street. The secretary and treasurer was H. C. Hunter—a relative of Virginia's mother, whose maiden name was Lucile Cochran Hunter. The idea was good—hooking together a quality supply of local horses with locally produced carriages— but the timing was horrible. The company existed for two years, 1903 to 1905, then was quite literally driven out of business by the horseless carriage. Presley Stockton Ray went into the insurance business.

Virginia was bright and articulate; she attended the University of Michigan from 1925 through 1927. She pledged and became a member of Alpha Gamma Delta sorority, but did not graduate, returning to Louisville during the trough of the Depression. Through mutual friends, she met Jack Robert. A year later they were married, on November 2, 1935. Almost two years later, they were expecting a child.

In the history of Louisville, the spring of 1937 is used as a milestone in time; the entire city was flooded and two earthquakes hit. The recovery from the natural disater was slow, but it was thorough, and included both political and cultural reformations that would eventually bring Louisville out of its antebellum mentality. Progress was slow but noticeable.

In the summer of 1937, days after the appearance of a new July moon, Virginia Ray and Jack Robert Thompson were delivered of their first son, Hunter S. Thompson, at ten o'clock on Sunday night, the 18th, at Louisville's Norton Infirmary. After Hunter's birth, Jack Robert and Virginia moved twice before settling into what would become their family home at 2437 Ransdell Avenue. It was a solid two-story wooden house in the pleasant, modest neighborhood known as Cherokee Triangle. They bought the house in February of 1943 with a six-percent loan for $4,100, and moved in the next month. It would be the only house that Jack Thompson ever owned.

The Cherokee Triangle neighborhood was originally forest and farmland owned by the parents of President Zachary Taylor. It booame one of the original suburbs of old Louisville, but by World War II most of the old money had moved farther out, and most of the large estates had been subdivided and built on. It still remained a pleasant community; one of the old estates became the Louisville Collegiate Girls School, a private school to which the Binghams, owners of the *Courier-Journal,* sent their daughters. While the area was not triangular, there had been Cherokees: eight blocks from the house where Hunter Thompson was raised, Sunday afternoons would find Cherokee Indians riding their horses and performing at Doctor Ira Newhall's Cure-All Medicine Show, at Zendher's Garden Restaraunt. Of greater interest to Jack Robert was the nearby residence of John Hillerich, founder of the Hillerich-Bradsby Company, makers of the Louisville Slugger baseball bat.

The neighborhood was quiet and peaceful, with milk bottles on the front porches in the early morning, cars parked at night out of sight in the alleyway behind. Fifty-year-old oak trees, planted as saplings when the roads were laid out, provided ample shade in the summer, and piles of colorful leaves each fall. It was a comfortable place to live.

The house at 2437 Ransdell was a picture of symmetry. A paved walk equally divided the front lawn and went up seven lucky steps to the front door. The entrance to the house was placed exactly in the middle of the two front windows, and directly below the center of the narrow second-floor porch. Only the chimney was off to one side, and that by just a half-foot. The first floor was dominated by a grand brick fireplace, with an arched hearth and a tapered chimney. The living room, kitchen, and dining areas were all on this floor. The fireplace was large enough to heat the entire house; from the inside it would be easy to imagine the whole Thompson clan gathered around a snapping fire, enraptured by Jack Robert spinning tales of his impressions of Paris, the woods of Argonne, or the ways of the hill people around Pikeville.

But Jack Robert never spoke much of his war involvement,

nor did Hunter to his friends. Only Duke Rice, a neighbor the same age as Hunter, had any recollection of this: "I can remember during World War II that Hunter said his dad had been in World War I, and had been in Europe. But that was it. The only reason it ever came up was because of sports. All our baseball heroes had left to fight the war; at the end of the war it was like we had gotten all of our old friends back again—Ted Williams, Pee Wee Reese, Phil Rizzuto—especially the ones we knew because we'd seen them play in Louisville. As kids, that was our real big connection to the war. We wanted our heroes back!"

In the corner to the right of the fireplace, solid wooden stairs go up, then make a 90-degree turn to the left. Hunter's room was the second on the right. At a snug ten-by-fourteen feet, it was just enough for a bed, a desk, and a dresser. Its one window looked out over the steam radiator to the back yard and the alley. That was where all the action took place, especially after the basketball hoop was put up. Even at night, people would park their cars in the alley to light up the never-ending games: basketball, baseball, street hockey, football. In the early going, Hunter seemed headed for athletic fame of some degree. And, like his father, baseball was his consuming passion and his best sport.

With the move to Cherokee Triangle, and the onslaught of World War II, Hunter Thompson's formal education began. The I. N. Bloom Elementary School was the neighborhood school, and Hunter would make friends who stayed with him all the way through high school—Bill Smith, Duke Rice, and Gerald Tyrrell. All three went to the same three schools—I. N. Bloom, Highland Junior High, and Louisville Male High School. Along the way, they joined the same clubs: first the Hawks, a neighborhood sports group they created before they were old enough to join the teenagers' Castlewood Athletic Club. At the high-school level, several of the boys, including Hunter, were asked to join the venerable Athenaeum Literary Association, an elite organization whose roots were deeply entrenched in the Louisville of the 1860s.

The first year of school can be tough enough; when it coincides with a year of your nation at war, the impressions are deeply etched. Duke Rice, in the same class as Hunter, recalled the reactions of a six-year-old to a world at war. "We collected tin cans in our wagons for the war effort. I can remember the air-raid drills, the black-out curtains, the wardens in the street who would come knock on your door if you didn't black out all your lights. We grew a Victory Garden of vegetables at the I. N. Bloom School, which was kind of fun because it got us outdoors. Inside it was old and dark and all the teachers were women." Larry Jelsma, who also grew up in this period, recalls a constant sense of "being worried. People were always worried something serious was going to happen. It was way beyond rationing gas, or sending away twenty-five cents and a box-top of Wheaties for model fighter planes. I grow up with what I thought was a fear of invasion. We went to the movies and saw the Pathé News clips of the war—guns and flames. Every day you watched the front page of the newspaper, and the Axis and Allied lines were in bold black-and-white, with arrows pointing to show the advances."

All across Louisville, people hung stars in their windows: one color for a family member in the service, another for one killed in action. But for kids six to eight years old, the sense of tense urgency was occasionally broken by what appeared to be a circus atmosphere along the downtown streets of Louisville. At Bowman Field there was a training school for glider pilots, and Standiford Field was the staging area for final production of Curtiss-Wright cargo planes, used by nations around the world. "Fort Knox was also close—you would go to downtown Louisville and it was like the United Nations in uniform" was the way Duke Rice described the city during wartime. "Towns like Louisville had never seen people like that before . . . Australians, Gurkha troops with their heads wrapped . . . you'd see a cross section of troops that were in training in the greater Louisville area."

Exactly one month before his third birthday, Hunter became an older brother on June 18, 1940, when Davidson Wheeler Thompson was born. Davidson developed into a virtual mirror image of his older brother's looks: tall, lean, a thick head of dark, almost Indian hair, high cheekbones, intense black eyes, and a tightness around the mouth that appeared menacing. He did become a menace, but he confined it to the football field where he developed into one of the best linebackers in the history of Kentucky high-school football. He excelled at sports, joined the Castlewood Athletic Club, then the Athenaeum Literary Association as his older brother did, and in many ways walked the same path. But for every act of anger-fueled defiance or resentment that got his older brother into trouble, Davidson seemed to work at conforming. He got good grades and a scholarship to Vanderbilt, did his time in the service, married, stayed married, and worked for the same company for the rest of his life. Hunter and Davidson grew up in the same household, the same neighborhood, the same city. People remarked how much they looked alike—right down to the rachet-like rumbling delivery of their speech, and the awkward, shuffling style of walking—but their lives were as different as one could imagine.

Toward the end of World War II, Hunter came face-to-face with the strange reality that he was, in fact, not the oldest Thompson boy: Jack Robert Thompson, Jr., the child of Jack's first marriage, came to Louisville for a visit. He was twenty-three, and an officer in the Navy, stationed at Key West. He made a lasting impression. "Jack, Jr., served in World War II in the Navy," recalled Duke Rice. "I have memories of him in a Navy officer's uniform. He'd come over to the house, but only occasionally. He was much older than we were, of course." And Hunter's father was much older than that. These age discrepancies, coupled with both being "Jack Robert Thompson," were confusing for many of Hunter's friends; some confused Jack Robert, Jr., for Hunter's father. During Thompson's fourth birthday party, when the family was living at 1277 Bassett Avenue, his neighbor Peter Lanham bugged Hunter about the actual age of his father. Hunter himself was curious, but at first refused to ask. This was a ploy, intended to whip Lanham's curiosity to a frenzy. It worked. Hunter then started the interrogation, imploring his father to reveal his age. His father refused to answer. Finally, the two got through to him, and he answered the youngsters with his characteristic sly wit. "I'm four hundred and twenty-four years old," said the forty-eight-year-old father. "Oh, baloney. He doesn't look it," Lanham said.

Hunter spent his first six school years at the I. N. Bloom school, and his classmates remember a kind of budding leadership quality, a sort of indescribable charisma that Hunter exuded from an early age. There was a dimension to Hunter's presence that others picked up when they first met him, and it set him apart from the herd. The precise "read" one had on Hunter varied considerably. Friends from the Athenaeum were consistent in recognizing his unique sense of humor. "He made an impression because he was noisy, self-confident, and funny," was how T. Floyd Smith put it. "He never told jokes. Some guys tell jokes, but Hunter never did. He was an incredibly witty guy, and had his own way of looking at things. I think everyone recognized that about Hunter immediately." The Thompson aura was tough to articulate, in part because it seemed to change from person to person. For Susan Peabody, who first knew him as a young teen, "Hunter was very polite. Very polite to the point of being courtly." The recollection of George Logan was close to that of Smith's. "You knew you had met a different kind of guy. He was an outspoken, dominating figure with a quick lip, the ability to turn a phrase, and his own brand of humor." Logan's last description—"I don't know anyone who didn't like Hunter on first meeting him"—was in stark disagreement with the opinion of one of the teachers at I. N. Bloom School. "A little dictator" was her way of putting it, as he consistently showed defiance from an early age. No matter how difficult it was to put words on Hunter's actions, all through school he was easy to spot: he was the only one with a can of Mace in his lunchbucket.

In 1946, when Hunter was nine, the Boston Red Sox, owners of the Louisville minor-league team, played the St. Louis Cardinals in the World Series. Emotions were split in Louisville; many of the big-league Red Sox players had spent their early years with the Louisville club, and the newspapers paid close attention to how the parent club was doing. On the other hand, St. Louis was an easy drive. Hunter and his father had been to watch both the Cardinals and the Reds in Cincinnati; radio broadcasts from each could be picked up easily in Louisville. Hunter had endeared himself to his friends by bringing back extra programs from each ball club for them to pin up on their bedroom walls, just as he did. But, putting things in perspective, it didn't matter if you rooted for Schoendienst, Musial, and Garagiola with St. Louis, or Williams, DiMaggio, and Pesky with Boston, for there was a World Series going on right in Louisville, and the Thompson men were riveted with interest.

The Kentucky Colonels had won the American Association Championship and were to play in the Junior World Series. Hunter, his father, and Davidson, now six, had great entertainment in their own back yard. Parkway Field was a bike ride away, and the Louisville YMCA sponsored the Knot Hole Gang for kids. Hunter, Duke Rice, and other neighborhood boys would pay fifty cents and enter the stadium through a large round knothole painted on the outfield fence. It was wholesome, all-American fun—until the first home game of the Junior World Series, when things turned ugly, revealing a side of their home town that Hunter and his friends knew of only in the abstract, but had never seen so vividly.

The Colonels were hosting the champions of the International League, the Montreal Royals, for two games. Parkway Field before the first game was standing room only; red, white, and blue bunting hung everywhere, and the voice of announcer Don Hill worked the crowd and all who listened on radio into a good pre-game frenzy. Then came the unexpected: as the Royals took the field, the entire Colonels team, led by their manager, Harry Leibold, walked out of the dugout. Then they kept going, and walked right out of the park. The crowd was stunned. Although reported by the newspapers as a conflict between manager and umpire, it was forever remembered as a symbolic protest against Jackie Robinson, the Royals' black infielder. It was also a form of Louisville tradition, and an old one. The local club had done the exact same thing in 1881, when the Cleveland team brought Moses Fleetwood Walker, a black catcher out of Oberlin College. The Colonels-Royals game was delayed for twenty minutes until the owners of the teams convinced the manager and players to go ahead and play ball. But the point had been made, in a very public way, to all those watching, listening, or reading about it in the papers the next day: the year 1946 might have been the dawn of a new era, but the social barriers of old Louisville society were very much a part of life.

The appearance of Early Gonzo can be dated from the sports season that covered the fall of 1948 and the spring of 1949. The *Southern Star* was the name, and it was a two-paged, well-organized piece of journalism written by the eleven-year-old Hunter and his friends for the neighborhood. It cost four cents, and covered the Cherokee Triangle gang's involvement with basketball, the Chicago Railroad Fair, stamp collecting, poetry, and even a few advertisements paid for by local small businesses. In many ways, it demonstrated Hunter and his crowd's budding intelligence, energy, and sense of industry. Hunter's writing style was linear and to the point ("let's go over last season. Hawks first beat Taylorsville at Tyler Park 15 to 6. But two weeks later in a night game . . . Let's hope Kentucky gets back in first place . . . and that U. of L. beats Western in the return game soon"), and showed a clear enjoyment of competition. There was no fear, no loathing yet in Louisville in 1948.

He did show a touch of ego by listing the lineup of the Hawks basketball team, with Hunter at one forward, and Duke Rice, then just an inch taller, at center. One of the columns written by another youngster hinted toward the future. It carried a banner line of WE THE PEOPLE PROTEST, and contained a message to the Mayor asking for help repairing the local streets. But whether it was urging their readers to BUY WAR BONDS or advertising for Myra's Grill on Ray Avenue or Forbes Drugstore on Bardstown Road, it all seemed to work smoothly. No one involved recalled any problems with deadlines or with censorship.

From the outside looking in, the Thompson household in the late 1940s seemed idyllic. Jack Robert had over thirty years' experience in the insurance business, and Virginia Thompson had two handsome, bright, athletic sons to be proud of. They lived in a comfortable, picture-postcard neighborhood of neat houses with trim lawns. Their place was a magnet for socializing; all the neighborhood kids were drawn to the Thompsons' house. "That was the place. In every neighborhood there is a place where people congregate. We congregated in Hunter's front yard. That is where we planned our activities, and did our things from," said Gerald Tyrrell. Whether it was digging entrenchments for toy soldiers in the back yard, taking a bicycle trip to the Sleepy Hollow resort area, or catching the bus downtown to shoot beans at each other in the Rialto Theater, there was always a buzz of energy around 2437 Ransdell Avenue. At times, the crowd was so thick that a person could vanish for a year without being noticed. Gerald Tyrrell's father was with the British Foreign Service, and his family spent the year of 1948 to 1949 in Canton, China. While Tyrrell and his family dodged bullets and tanks in the Orient, Ransdell Avenue was business as usual. "I had gone down to Hunter's the day before I left for China," recalled Tyrrell, "and a year later, the day after I got back, I got up, put on my play clothes, and went down to Hunter's house. It was just the same. Same guys doing the same things. Nobody really missed me. Somebody might have said, 'Where have you been—you missed a really good thing last month.' We just dealt in longer time frames then."

In fact, some things had changed in the Thompson household by the time Tyrrell returned, but from the outside looking in not all of them were obvious. Not yet visible was the level of nagging fatigue that Jack Robert must have begun to experience daily by 1949. His insurance career had humbled him slightly; he had left his long-standing position at First Kentucky Fire Insurance, spent a brief time at another agency, then went to work for his younger brother, Sterling. The youngest of the four Thompson brothers, Sterling had shown considerable consistency and ability, and had formed Sterling Thompson & Company. They dealt not just in insurance, but in land development and construction. In the great wave of postwar urban growth, Sterling Thompson was riding the crest; he pulled his older brother in his wake.

The first problems Jack Robert must have felt were initially so minor as to be ignored; they grew slowly in intensity. Problems with his vision and fatigue—a draining, sapped feeling that left him with little energy to play catch with his sons after work. He was sick and did not know it. His health was declining on the installment plan, a tiny bit every day.

By 1949, Jack Robert was fifty-five and getting close to retirement age, yet he had one son in junior high and another just starting the first grade. He had always been perceived as an optimistic, intelligent man. He had an encyclopedic mind. One family member was impressed by his style and his ability "to answer your questions, and then tell you more and more about whatever it was. The topic didn't matter. He was a trivia expert. Just ask him a question, and he could go on and on. He seemed to know the most incredible details about everything." But overall, he was a back-seat man. He spoke quietly, kept his war medals in a box, and never went with his fanatical mother, Corrie Lee—now eighty and going strong—to her Christian Church. He was not distant or aloof; he was a low-key person, more content to watch and listen than to participate actively. He took pride in showing saddle horses at local state fairs, going and coming from work with regularity, and always listening to baseball.

"I clearly remember Mr. Thompson at night when I was over at the house," said Duke Rice. "He'd sit there by his radio and listen to a baseball game. The Colonels had a very popular radio announcer, Don Hill. Or he'd pick up the Cards on KMLX, or the Reds. Baseball was his dad's passion. That is my only recollection of him—that he was a big baseball fan. When I hear the name 'Mr. Thompson,' I see him sitting there by that radio listening to baseball games in the evening. That is my most vivid recollection of him."

Jack Thompson's age and, by 1949, his pernicious fatigue were part of Gerald Tyrrell's observations from that time. "I never had the feeling that Hunter's father was that big an influence. His father was just sort of 'the old man who sat on the porch.' Every so often he'd look at us playing catch or whatever, and grunt or yell a little bit. But he was definitely not like a young or more active father, taking Hunter places.''

At the age of forty-one, Virginia Thompson became pregnant for the third time. On the 2nd of February, 1949, Hunter and Davidson greeted their baby brother, James Garnett Thompson. Twelve years younger than Hunter—essentially a generation apart, given the rate at which the world was beginning to change—Jim was never part of the same social crowd as his two older brothers'. Like the other two, Jim would develop a fanatic interest in sports, and, like Hunter, he never followed through on early interests, never even tried out for a high-school team. In his development, he was to become as ground-breaking in his individuality as his oldest brother. As Hunter set off to rebel against every form of authority, and as Davidson toed the line of conformity, Jim grew up headed in a third direction. Jim knew from an early age that there was something about him that was different from both his family and his community. From an early age, he knew he was gay.

During the two summers after Jim was born, Hunter spent weeks at a Presbyterian church camp on the grounds of the Kentucky Military Institute, in Lyndon, a few miles east of Louisville. It was a sprawling series of three-story, white-pillared buildings that had graduated five Union and two Confederate generals in its time. These summers its curriculum changed, graduating Hunter into the world of smoking, Bible classes, bullwhips, and women. "It was a nice camp. Nice people went there," said Evelyn Laurent, who had attended as a girl, hinting of the social classes from which the camp drew. The days were filled with sports competition between teams named after Indian tribes, and each day began with the blare of bugles. In Laurent's memory, Hunter's courtly side showed again. "He was a nice boy, outstandingly nice. He had a polite side to him. He was a gentlemen, you could tell that. I think he was kind of admired by some of the little girls. He was kind of silly and he tried to be brusque, but underneath you could tell he was a very nice person."

"Hunter and I got in all the trouble, except smoking," Gerald Tyrrell recalled. "We'd sneak out, cut Bible classes, have gatherings in our rooms when we were not supposed to. But none of it was serious." The two made friends with and later visited some teens from Shelbyville, home of an annual county fair. "We saw our first naked woman, who did disgusting things with cigarettes" was one experience that stayed with Tyrrell. The guys from Shelbyville also introduced them to bullwhips. Hunter, on the border-line between kid's stuff and tough stuff, was so taken with this new weapon that he sold his army of toy soldiers to Tyrrell and used the money to buy his own bullwhip. "It was just fantastically lucky we didn't put anybody's eyes out, because we were cracking those whips, trying to take cigarettes out of people's mouths . . . every so often we'd accidentally whip one of the little guys."

There were times when Hunter wished he could have used his bullwhip on the bigger guys as well. "In 1951, Hunter was riding his bike to my house with a Christmas present," Susan Peabody, a former girlfriend, recalled. "It was an I.D. bracelet with my name on the front and his on the back. It was puppy love." Susan had an older, bigger brother who knew of Hunter, bullwhips and all. He and another big boy stopped Hunter on the street. "They took his bike," Peabody continued, "and they put it in a tree. Then they de-pantsed him—that was the thing to do in those days. So there was poor Hunter with no pants on, and his bike in a tree. Even in those early times, Hunter was nervous and ditsey and very bright—a darling, really cute boy—but he always had a touch of craziness in him, even back then. I always blamed my brother for everything that happened to Hunter after that."

T o live in Louisville in the first half of the 1950s was to live in a mecca of sports heroes. There were so many as to seem com-monplace, yet they loomed in mythical proportion. To impres-sionable kids feeling the confusion of hormones and body hair, becoming an athlete seemed a compelling and honorable way to go. To become a star athlete seemed the fire behind the dream, to become a professional athlete heaven on earth.

Everyone in the Hawks or in the Castlewood Athletic Club knew the story of Pee Wee Reese. He was from just down the road in Ekron, Kentucky, and had played high-school ball for Louis-ville's Dupont Manuel High. Then he had been signed by the Bos-ton Red Sox, and assigned to play for the Colonels. Most of Hunter's friends were too young to remember clearly the Colo-nels' dream season of 1939, but it was the stuff of legend. They knew the story of the Colonels' fourth-place finish that season, then their series of improbable victories to win the American Association Championship, and then the Junior World Series. They had galvanized Louisville baseball fans when something was sorely needed to divert their attention from the dregs of the Depression, and the threat of war.

The Colonels were the only team in the history of professional baseball to leap from fourth place to Series Champs, and Pee Wee Reese was the spark plug. After that season, Reese was traded to the Dodgers—player-manager Joe Cronin of the Red Sox evidently did not want competition at his position—and immediately half of Louisville became Dodger fans. During the summer of 1952, all the Castlewood Athletic Club members followed Reese, his .272 average and his league-leading 30 stolen bases all the way to the World Series, which the Dodgers lost to the Yankees. The local Red Sox fans were mildly disappointed when Ted Williams spent nearly the entire season fighting in the Korean War. Consequently, to Hunter and his friends, the thought of becoming an athlete of some level of achievement was not an impossibility. The real challenge was how to harness that energy and head it in the proper direction. "Hunter wanted to be a big athlete at that time," Tyrrell stated. "I thought baseball was his strong suit," said Duke Rice. "He was very competitive. He was a leader. We would cover our rooms with pictures cut out of sports magazines."

Baseball was not the only game in town. At the University of Kentucky, two legends coached at the same time. Adolph Rupp created a basketball dynasty, winning their first NCAA Championship in 1948, while Bear Bryant headed the football program. At the University of Louisville, on the same field where the Colonels played during the summer, Hunter and his friends trooped down regularly to watch Johnny Unitas quarterback the Cardinals. At the same time, across town at Flaget High School, Paul Hornung was rewriting every Kentucky schoolboy quarterback record, on his way to Notre Dame, the Heisman Trophy, and five NFL and two Super Bowl Championships. (Between 1958 and 1969 there was only one year when Unitas or Hornung did not play for the NFL championship game.)

Some future greats were right there in the Castlewood Athletic Club, a sports organization set up in the 1920s by Lee Reed, Jr., as a way of instilling positive moral fiber, team awareness, and the ethic of self-discipline in young teenagers. The club also served as a "feeder" for the three local high schools, whose coaches scouted Castlewood games and recruited competitively for the best players. To succeed in high-school sports, one began by succeeding in Castlewood. Duke Rice and a number of other high school and college stars were all there competing with Hunter. In the early years they were pretty much athletic equals. They all went through the pledge Hell Week of wearing one green and one white sock, and calling the full-fledged members "sir," before they could put on the uniform and play the games. Castlewood played against other local athletes who went on to stardom like Charlie Tyra and Kenny Kuhn. Tyra played for Atherton High, the University of Louisville, and then for five years in the NBA. Many thought that in high school Kenny Kuhn was a better athlete that Paul Hornung. He was consistent in football, basketball, track, and baseball, where he became a "bonus baby," going directly from Male High to the Cleveland Indians. Duke Rice wanted desperately to go to the University of Kentucky; instead he ended up at Virginia Tech and gained a name for himself by shutting down Jerry West, who was playing for the University of West Virginia before his Hall of Fame career with the Los Angeles Lakers.

If Hunter Thompson had signed on to the sweaty camaraderie and aggressive competition with his initiation to the Castlewood Club in 1950, he became bonded to it following the events of July 3, 1952.

After a three-month stay in the Louisville Veterans Administration Hospital, Jack Robert Thompson died. He was fifty-seven; Hunter was fourteen. His death had been agonizingly slow. The sense of fatigue and visual problems must have gotten progressively worse; he had also suffered from thrombophlebitis of his right leg for eight years. While the cause of death officially given by the V.A. physician was chronic viral bronchopneumonia, Virginia Thompson thought otherwise, and requested an autopsy. The results indicated a rare disease, myasthenia gravis. It is a progressive neurological disorder, one form of which is hereditary. The disease affects the immune system in such a way that nerve endings are rendered unable to stimulate the muscles. Visual problems, drooping eyelids, and general loss of energy appear years before the disease progresses to the point when the body's immune system is incapable of fighting off the most harmless virus.

It was a time of wrenching change on Ransdell Avenue. There is no "good" time to grieve the death of a parent; and a long, slow, obvious slide into death can heap agony on the whole family. Hunter did not get slammed to the ground immediately after his father's death, but he was pummeled repeatedly by it over a period of years. The end seemed inevitable, yet when it was so slow in coming, a spark of optimism could appear. The finality of death could extinguish even the most ardent sense of hope. When such a slow death is at last a reality, one can feel a great sense of relief. That emotion can quickly turn to guilt, for one is not supposed to feel relieved because of the death of a parent—certainly not the oldest son on the passing of his father.

The emotional oscillation between relief and guilt forms a deep pit of anger over such a loss at such a time. If these feelings go unvented, they tend to live on with an energy of their own. And they can emerge in the strangest of ways.

T he day was a photo opportunity for the Louisville Chamber of Commerce, all blue sky above and fall leaves below. Around the corner onto the stretch of Ransdell Avenue that goes slightly downhill came someone on a bicycle. He glided silently and effortlessly, carving his way just beyond the piles of yellow and crimson leaves that had been carefully raked into mounds awaiting collection. The bicyclist skimmed one pile to his right side, the next to his left. He appeared to move like a slalom skier. Turning left, he headed up Glenmary Avenue, and within a few minutes he had traversed the entire Cherokee Triangle area, dipping and gliding his course around dozens of monstrous leaf piles, a tight smile on his face. He appeared to be enjoying himself.

Within a half hour, every fire truck in the eastern part of Louisville descended on Cherokee Triangle, now completely blanketed with dense smoke from innumerable piles of smoldering leaves.

"Everything Hunter did, he planned out painstakingly," said Neville Blakemore. "With the leaves, he rigged a spring-loaded clothespin with an old kitchen match. It would take a while before any fire really got going, and by then he'd be gone. He was mobile, unobtrusive, and never got caught." Blakemore described this incident as the beginning of a progression of well-planned "events" that evolved, during high-school years, from mere acts of adolescent excess into "dangerous aggression." As a senior at Male High, Thompson's behavior had deteriorated to the point where, as Blakemore commented, "I would characterize him by saying that when you were with Hunter, you had to be prepared for anything to happen."

Months after his father's death, Hunter started high school at Atherton High, close to home, but he quickly transferred to Male High, on Brook Street in downtown Louisville. He may have transferred to Male High to start with a clean slate, where fewer people knew of his father's death. Others, including Gerald Tyrrell, went to Male because of the academics and the long tradition of the school. Regardless, for those who knew him first in the tenth grade, during the academic year 1952-53, few knew anything about either parent. His father was a void, never mentioned, yet conspicuous in his absence. In those days in Louisville, divorce was rare. Single-parent females were infrequent. And his mother did leave an impression with many: "She was a heavy drinker," said Susan Peabody. The house on Ransdell Avenue was beginning to look less like suburbia, more like disturbia.

It was the summer before the start of high school that both Hunter and his mother found jobs to take up the financial slack. Virginia worked as a secretary at the Granite State Fire Insurance Company. Raising Hunter is a verboten topic for Mrs. Thompson: "I will talk about many things," she said, "but I will not talk about raising Hunter." She did recall some sense of the burden of having to go out into the world to make a living while raising a three-year-old, a twelve-year-old, and Hunter. "I don't know how I got through it. My husband's mother had four boys, and her husband died when they were young." When Virginia Thompson asked her mother-in-law how on earth she had coped, the reply was "It was just a nightmare."

Many recalled Mrs. Thompson as a heavy drinker; none could provide details. She seems to have kept to herself, as few recalled her out about town other than when she was working. During his high-school years, Hunter's friends would not hang out at the Ransdell Avenue house as so many had when both parents were alive. A friend from that time, Norvin Green, described Hunter's typical reaction to his mother's sharp discipline, especially when he knew he was in trouble. Thompson would say, "I gotta get out of her way!" and do his best to avoid the same disciplinarian who had instilled in him the courtliness and manners he could show when required.

When Virginia was working at the Louisville public library, she had a peculiarly hostile style of responding to the multitude of inquiries a reference librarian must field. She loved to read at work, and when she was interrupted by someone with a question, she would shoot that person a killer look, as if to say, "What are you bugging *me* for?" Co-workers remarked that her character was ill-suited for anyone in a service role.

Her mother, Mrs. Ray, moved in to help care for the family. Hunter took a job that some feel ended a promising baseball career and all early dreams of a future in athletics: he worked at

Nopper's Pharmacy, and while he was there, he ate as much ice cream as he could. In his tenth-grade picture he looks chubby. Also, Hunter didn't grow that year, and that was the time to make or break it in high-school sports. The year before, he'd been about the same height as Duke Rice; now when he got to high school, Duke was suddenly six feet seven and Hunter was only five feet nine. "He ate a lot of ice cream at Nopper's" was the observation of Tyrrell, who had competed alongside Thompson in every sport until that year, when Hunter called it quits.

There are other opinions as to why Hunter left behind the dream of becoming an athlete and turned his energies in other, less productive directions. Duke Rice felt that it was directly linked to the death of Hunter's father, seen by Rice as "the stabilizing force in his life that kept Hunter active and encouraged him to play ball. It's like the old saying 'Sports kept us off the streets and out of trouble.'" For other high-school friends, the theories varied. Ralston Steenrod spoke of "Hunter's resistance to any discipline but his own. If he didn't want to do something, he simply would not, and no one was going to change his mind." His mother made the observation "He was just never any good at sports."

Neville Blakemore attributed his dropping out to "a fear of pain and the risk of personal injury bordering on physical cowardice. He avoided actual fights, though he must have had many challenges." This theme of knowing intuitively when to back off, being aware of a point of no return, repeats itself many times in Hunter's life. He would do shockingly outlandish things, yet he always stopped short of physical injury to himself or others. It was as if Thompson had some control over the inner rage, but learning how to fine-tune it, how to harness those engines, was a slow and painful process.

In explaining Thompson's behavior, a one-word explanation was used by Sam Stallings, Jr., himself a fallen athlete by his sophomore year at Male High: "Whiskey."

Stallings feels that alcohol was at the root of every problem Thompson had during those years, and he was in a prime spot to observe: the two were like Siamese devils in high school, joined at the spot in the brain that elicits rage. Both were in league to wreak havoc and mayhem on the world around them. In spite of their synergy, there was a rather significant difference between them. Sam Stallings, Sr., was a past president of the Louisville Bar Association, a man of rough, yet persuasive oratory, and well connected politically. A series of photos of him with President

Harry Truman adorned his law offices. In many ways, Sam Stallings, Sr., represented everything that Hunter did not have: a powerful, wealthy father who would come to his rescue whenever he got in trouble.

4.

Very Male,

Very High

The percentage of freaks among people in general is high, but it is especially high among teachers.—Leon Trotsky

culpted above the Brook Street entrance to Louisville Male High School is an elf. In one hand he holds a scroll of paper, in the other he rests his chin. He ponders the numbers he has added together on the paper. He has added 23 and 146. The result is an erroneous 179. Since 1915, when the building was completed, he has occupied a

small niche above the front steps. By Hunter Thompson's senior year, forty years of Male High students had trooped up and down the stairs under the elf.

Louisville's Male High has since moved; the elf remains and ponders. But the empty wooden halls continue to radiate with tradition, honor, excellence, and career; many of the teaching staff at that time were from Ivy League schools. Many held doctorates in their field. They formed pipelines to their alma maters for the students showing promise.

Thomas Jefferson's "academical village," later the University of Virginia, was the inspiration for Male High. The Ivy League connection is obvious in Male High's motto: "For God, For Country, For Male." The school mimicked Yale right down to its mascot, a bulldog named "Old Sam."

To attend school there in the early 1950s, one had to take either college preparatory courses or ROTC. The principal, W. S. Milburn, was a former Marine sergeant who had spent part of World War I training Signal Corps troops on Parris Island. Despite Milburn's stiff military background, he was considered a fair man, about whom his wife commented, "He never paddled his children in his life—I had to do it all myself."

In the fall of 1952, the same year as the election of Dwight Eisenhower and Richard Nixon, the future class of 1955 walked under the unmathematical elf. In all, there were 533 students in that class; 282 would graduate within the allotted three years. Keeping to the earliest of personal tradition, Hunter would not make it on time.

Across the country, around the world, whenever two people meet and discover they are both from Louisville, they never ask where the other went to college; it is always "What high school did you go to?" There were three big Louisville high schools: Atherton, from which Hunter had transferred, Dupont Manuel, and Central High, among others in the growing community. Atherton and Manuel were rivals in sports, but neither was a purely college preparatory school. Central High was a segregated black high school. If attending Male High carried with it a mantle of prestige and tradition, then membership in the Athenaeum Literary Association was the crown above the mantle. The Athenaeum had been a school-sponsored literary society based at Male since 1862. In the early 1950s it and several other high school literary societies severed their ties with Male. Reflecting the new schools in Louisville's east end, both public and private, they took members from a number of high schools. Consequently, when Hunter Thompson became a member in his sophomore year, many of the members with whom he met, discussed literature, and helped write articles for their handsomely bound yearbook, the *Spectator,* were not in class with him every day, and only saw him once a week under structured circumstances of the Athenaeum meetings.

Some of the Athenaeum members, including Hunter, had been together as an intact social group from the Cherokee Triangle neighborhood, and through membership in the Castlewood Athletic Club. But not all were tapped for Athenaeum. Approximately half of the Castlewood members went into the Athenaeum each year with the balance joining another Literary Society, usually the Delphic Literary Society.

There was a history and tradition to the Athenaeum that dated to its founding in June of 1862—the same week that Robert E. Lee took command of the Confederate Army. The Association's annual, a mix of photos, essays, and a chronicle of the year's events, took its name from Rapin's English literary standard of the day, during the late 1600s and early 1700s. Most of the members came from upper-middle- and upper-class Louisville, from the elegant suburbs of St. Matthews, Glenview, and Anchorage, several miles to the east.

The east end was home to the Louisville Country Club, the gathering places for inner-sanctum society, where in earlier years Hunter and Gerald Tyrrell had attended Cotillion dancing school. Farther to the east was Anchorage, Kentucky, home to the Owl Creek Country Club. Typical of the Athenaeum's and Hunter's social contacts in that neighborhood were Judy Stellings and Louise Reynolds. Stellings's father was known as a "G. E. Yankee"—a high-level executive who moved his family south when General Electric built Appliance Park in nearby Buechel in 1950. The Reynolds family was Reynolds Aluminum.

The deepest of Louisville's pockets—the Bingham family—sent their sons to New England prep schools, but their daughters attended Louisville Collegiate Girls School, quite literally in Hunter's back yard. Hunter and many Athenaeum friends attended parties held at the Bingham estate, Melcombe, on a bluff above the Ohio River. The property had been purchased by Robert Worth Bingham, the former Ambassador to Great Britain, one of whose wives had been heir to the estate of railroad magnate Henry Flagler. David Ethridge, son of the *Courier-Journal*'s editor, was also a peer; his family estate was the

Trigg Mansion, a twelve-room brick structure that dated from the 1850s.

The Athenaeum was loaded with the sons of power and money and influence. Neville Blakemore's father was a bank president. George Logan's father was a judge, and the region's leading neurosurgeon had two sons in the Athenaeum, Lawrence and Richard Jelsma. These young men were no titled idlers, either. They had taken their parents' expectations to heart. They knew what they wanted to be when they grew up, and they knew the intricate choreography of getting there as well as they knew that of the Cotillion. "At Athenaeum meetings," recalled Tyrrell, "you always wore a coat and tie. Whenever you saw someone from the Athenaeum, you always shook hands like proper little gentlemen, which, of course, we were." To do well in school, to become a class officer, to be a good athlete: the Renaissance Teen. "Those were the kinds of values that we shared."

It was heady company for a kid whose father had just died, and whose mother worked as a secretary in a bank where many of the Athenaeum boys' fathers were officers. Membership in the Athenaeum was a tradition in the Thompson family as well. Hunter's uncle Sterling Thompson had been a member at Male High in the class of 1917. For both Hunter and his mother, membership in the Athenaeum gave a sense of status, and of keeping up with the part of the family that was a success both financially and socially, yet had done little to help after the illness of Jack Robert. The Sterling Thompson Insurance Company, in the same Stark Building that had once housed Colonel Wheeler's insurance company, was making money. Further, Sterling Thompson's daughter Cynthia would marry William Cowger, a Louisville mayor and two-term U.S. congressman. At least Hunter was in Athenaeum, and in the opinion of his mother, Virginia, "That was considered a great social asset."

In the first year at Male High, if Hunter Thompson had just lost a father, he had also just found dozens of brothers. The Athenaeum Literary Association welcomed him with open minds, some with slack jaws. "Shock value. That was Hunter's forte," observed Larry Jelsma. "He was a skunk of a different stripe" was Floyd Smith's observation. "He was different. The character was there, the humor was there. His insights were there. He was not a late bloomer, I guarantee you," he concluded.

The progression of Hunter's "different" behavior continued; as time went on, it seemed that he did not want acceptance from the group so much as recognition, attention, and a shot at the limelight. Hunter's "car" at the time was a set of three wheels. To drive it, one sat on top of a wooden crate that covered a refurbished washing-machine motor. People would see him buzz by, and mutter, "There goes Hunter . . ."

Many of his antics involved extensive, detailed planning, and were executed with precise timing and a sense of theater. Norvin Green made the point that "to a great extent, his whole life was playacting." Much of it was amusing, and in the early stages no one thought to question why Hunter was up to his tricks. They were great fun. Hunter would crack his bullwhip, have a boy named Bill Smith run into Nopper's Pharmacy and fall down, just as Neville Blakemore burst in shouting, "There's a maniac running down Glenmary Avenue whipping dogs," as customers buying Preparation H and corn plasters stood around in total disbelief. Again with Bill Smith, at the Bard Theater: he'd buy a ticket and see the movie. Then, as the crowd surged out onto the sidewalk, a long black 1934 Plymouth pulled up, two men in front, two in back, each dressed in black. In the middle of the evening crowd, Smith bellowed "My God! They have come to get me" as he was dragged into the car and whisked away. It made the papers the next day. "Neither episode hurt anyone," Blakemore stated. "They were difficult to do, and required elaborate planning, where all the contingencies were reviewed. But they just got worse—more dangerous, more damaging."

Another time, Hunter's group was angry at the manager of a local theater for bouncing them after disrupting the crowd. They plotted. Someone wanted to let the air out of the tires on the manager's car, and remove the valve stems so they could not be re-inflated. Someone else suggested putting sugar in the fuel tank. The car the manager drove was a late 1940s Dodge, where all the controls—lights, wipers, choke, even the throttle—were in the form of knobs that one pushed or pulled. Hunter's revenge: pull out all the knobs and bend them.

Thompson showed a fascination for guns that began at an early age. One night in his room, he was showing Gerald Tyrrell how to use his .22 rifle when it accidentally went off and fired a shot through the floor. No one else was at home. The two went downstairs and found that the bullet had come out of the ceiling and disappeared behind Mrs. Thompson's china closet. She was never informed.

Alcohol came into the picture in the spring of his first year at high school. Hunter, Gerald Tyrrell, Jimmy Noonan, and David

Bibb had all attended a dance at a girls' high school, and paid one of the black waiters ten dollars for a half-pint bottle of gin. "We had some ginger ale, and we made gin bucks," said Tyrrell. "Sitting at the big rock by Athenaeum Hill in Cherokee Park, we got silly. Hunter would become more noticeable, maybe more erratic or wild. But he wasn't a fierce drunk, and he wasn't a mean drunk."

At times, he used strange ways to procure alcohol. Ralston Steenrod recalled an episode in which he drove with Hunter to Lexington for a high school basketball game. Hunter asked to stop at a liquor store, and returned with a bottle of bourbon. "He held the place up by showing the clerk his ten fingernails, and saying, 'See my ten fingernails?' All this I heard later out in the car. Hunter showed the guy his fingernails, and got him so frightened or intimidated or confused that he handed over the bottle he asked for, just to get him out of there. Hunter could have gotten killed in that incident, but he was not harmful. He might verbally intimidate you, but he would not lay a hand on you for anything. That was not his style."

When each pledge class came through the Athenaeum Hell Week, they feared Thompson. While they might have to steal a bowling pin for George Logan, or have Richard Jelsma pour molasses in their hair and make them eat raw eggs, they needed to be drama majors to satisfy the bizarre demands of Hunter. Some were trained to throw a fake epileptic fit in the middle of a busy restaurant, bouncing on the floor, screaming and flinging about wildly, then running out, only to laugh over it for hours. Bill Smith was commanded to take a rubber frog named "Wretch" to a spot in clear view of the classes at Louisville Collegiate Girls School, and beat it with a stick until the whole school stood with their faces pressed to the glass windows in numbed awe.

For Ralston Steenrod, the key to Hunter's creative way of relating to people, and making things around him happen at a pace different from what anyone expected, was his keen perception and skill "to challenge your conventional ideas—every opportunity he got. He'd put the hook in, test you, see what kind of ideas you were made of. If you were sensitive about one area, the pressure would start on that one."

Burton Shelley's parents owned a prosperous company that manufactured industrial tanks. They lived in a large house with Louisville style. Shelley, however, was about five feet one in high school, and his head was shaped like a light bulb. His diminutive size, in all its adolescent interpretation, was his "pressure point," and when he came through Hell Week, Thompson delivered the ultimate ego blow.

It came in two stages. First was Shelley's assignment: with Thompson hulking a foot taller, and all the others watching, Shelley was ordered to go into Taylor's Drug Store and purchase a package of prophylactics. "And ask for them from the woman clerk" was Thompson's final command. Shelley summoned all his courage. He went into the store. He sweated. He paced. He gnashed his teeth. Finally, he did it. He returned triumphant. "Now," Thompson informed him, in his typical muffled chortle, "go back in. Go up to the same lady. Tell her you want to exchange them . . . because they are too big."

Humor, the anthropologists tell us, is a polite way of showing our fangs. At some point, Hunter Thompson realized that the Athenaeum Literary Association was not his cup of tea. He stopped being polite. He began to resent. Before this, a day of rebellion might have been as bucolic as skipping class and going with Norvin Green to drink chocolate milk, eat cheese (all shoplifted), and read poetry in Cherokee Park. Typical teenage things. Or stealing a garbage can, filling it with ice and beer, stashing a few buddies in the trunk to save money going into the drive-in. Others would join in: bonfires atop Athenaeum Hill in Cherokee Park, with Hunter as the caterer of beverages, putting a cooler in the trunk of someone's car, counting, ". . . forty-seven Budweisers . . . thirty-three Millers . . . just enough bourbon here . . ." precisely as he would later take stock of his mind-altering paraphernalia in the trunk of his red convertible on the way to Las Vegas with his Samoan attorney.

"I do think he was resentful" was Floyd Smith's version of Hunter's developing rage. Stewart Smythe painted a more vivid picture, an entire landscape of hostilities. "Hunter was raised in Louisville's upper class. Not upper-middle class. All the kids had money. Hunter had none. Hunter Thompson, in Athenaeum days, owned two suits. The material things other kids had was mindboggling. The difference in wealth and power created an enormous resentment. Look at some of the houses his friends lived in out in Anchorage. They were not 'houses.' And the biggest factor was that, in so many ways, he had more than they did, but nothing to show for it." Smythe produced a three-by-five card. On it he had sketched stick figures. Hunter was at the center, head and shoulders taller than the others, all standing around, looking toward him. To the side, he had written:

Bright

Handsome

Tall

NO MONEY

RESENTMENT

HUNTER: Insult everybody

Break every rule

People admire him—outrageous behavior

People pay him attention

Smythe went on to describe the surfacing sense of sarcasm, and Thompson's lightning-fast verbal ability to "disparage anything that anyone thought was good. It became more pronounced later on. Also, Hunter had this 'split' within him. He looked just as preppie as everyone else in the way he dressed, but he was infatuated with hoods. The ducktail, greasy hair, cigarettes rolled up in the sleeve of a T-shirt. Hunter would make fun of those kids, or the movie portrayal, but he really wanted to be one. He really wanted to rebel against conformity. Put the two together and that is why he wrote *Hell's Angels*—he identified with them so strongly, yet when he was in Athenaeum, to act and dress like that was definitely not cool."

In his first year at Male High, Hunter set fire to a small eatery where students went for lunch. He had been playing with fire—a cigarette lighter—and decided to test the flammability of the wallpaper. It burned. So, too, the wall. So, too, the sense of hospitality of Joe Anders, the owner, and W. S. Milburn, the principal: the students were no longer allowed off-campus lunches.

"Hunter's idea of a good time in his second year at high school was to drive around town, find a construction site, and just destroy the place," related Larry Jelsma. "Dump over the outhouse, let it roll down the hill, dump out all the nails. Essentially, he would vandalize the place."

Add in the chemistry of Sam Stallings, Jr., mix with bourbon, and the downward spiral began to tighten. "Hunter drank whiskey at an early age," commented Stallings. "Unfortunately, so did I. So we had something in common there. Also, we never liked to go home. Always creatures of the night. A dance would end, and we would always attempt to find a party until the wee hours. I remember one dance where we stayed out for the whole weekend. We came to school Monday morning in our tuxedos."

A social embargo on Hunter was started by parents first; during his last year at Male High, his fellow Athenaeum members reached a point of intolerance, and attempted to do something about it. Hunter always chose his company well. Along with the son of the federal district attorney, and the son of a retired British diplomat, Hunter was caught buying liquor at Abe's, long considered an easy mark for the group. Gerald Tyrrell said, "My father was real unhappy having to go down to police headquarters and get his son. My father told me Hunter was off-limits from that point on. I then made great grades because my social life was severely curtailed."

Within the Athenaeum, Hunter was becoming more and more of a problem, especially when Hell Week came, and the helpless pledges were sitting—or bending—ducks. Hunter could beat up on them, and if they attempted to retaliate, they'd be thrown out of the club. "Paddling. He was brutal with the pledges. Really horrible. Unmerciful. Hunter was really into a lot of physical beating and pounding. He was out of bounds, getting them into trouble, and really giving the Athenaeum a bad name. My major job," said Larry Jelsma, president during Hunter's junior year, "was trying to control Hunter. He was absolutely uncontrollable. Everybody's parents were calling up: 'Hunter did this . . . Hunter did that.' Our big concern was that he was leading the sophomore class astray. We—the entire legacy of the Athenaeum—were going to hell in a handbasket if we didn't do something to counteract Hunter. He was Fagin from *Oliver Twist.*"

Hell Week was the only time Thompson ever lashed out physically at other people—when they were under orders to subject themselves to anything and everything the members might dish out. By this point, the young men from the Athenaeum viewed his shenanigans with amusement tempered with hesitancy, as they might a stage performer occasionally asking for audience participation.

The reports would come in: Hunter pouring sulphur across the top of lockers at the Collegiate Girls School, and lighting it; appearing at the Athenaeum Christmas dance with an entire department store of stolen festive lighting; flooding the first floor of the high school with three inches of water during an assembly;

dumping a truckload of pumpkins at the entrance to the Brown Hotel, or chasing the history teacher, Mr. Gearhart, around the classroom, threatening to hang him out the window by his ankles.

Thompson clearly showed aggression, but with women he was more reserved. "I never remember Hunter as having a girlfriend at all," pointed out Neville Blakemore. A medical suggestion was offered that the classic alcoholic syndrome includes shriveled liver, shriveled brain, and shriveled testicles.

There was one girlfriend—a platonic relationship that was carried on in letters sent from jail, the Air Force, and New York City over a three-year period. Even she had similar observations of Hunter's awkward, shy style of relating to women, as opposed to his brash self-confidence that was the hallmark of his dealings with men. Hunter, the girlfriend felt, was more than a little bit bashful and shy with women. He was the guy at the dance who would just stand around. He was not aggressive with women.

Sam Stallings pointed out that even though they often would end up the night at the aluminum company heiress Louise Reynold's liquor cabinet at six in the morning, knowing that when people came down for breakfast it was time to leave, "for all the crazy stuff we did—and when he and I got it together it was poison, I mean something was going to happen—we never went into whorehouses."

Stallings was a fighter. His father described him as filled with anger, anger against anything. One time he came home with both wrists broken. Another time he came up to David Watkins in the hallway at Highlands Junior High School, slugged him, and broke his jaw. Watkins went around for the rest of the year with it wired shut. But even when Sam got into fights, Hunter would stand back and watch, shouting encouragement for his friend, but not mixing it up. "He was destructive toward material things," Stallings noted. "He wasn't a fighter. He and I differed there. I would get into scrapes where he wouldn't. He wasn't afraid; it just wasn't his bag. He liked chaotic situations. He would tear up things when he was drinking. Sober, he was a nice guy—me, too—but drinking, we were assholes."

5.

Controlling

Chaos

Take, for instance, a twig and a pillar, or the ugly person and the great beauty, and all the strange and monstrous transformations. These are all leveled together by Tao. Division is the same as creation; creation is the same as destruction.
—Chuang Tzu, *On Leveling All Things*

etween the times drinking with Sam, setting fire to Joe's Diner, or taking out his resentful hostilities by paddling Athenaeum pledges, Hunter had enough control to channel some of his energy into being creative. Ralston Steenrod graduated from Princeton as an English Literature major. He recalled high-school editing sessions to meet the publishing deadline for the

Athenaeum's *Spectator*. At three in the morning, he and Hunter would be the only two not passed out. Hunter would still be typing madly. "His lucidity after midnight—he was great. He was still going strong. Getting stronger as the night wore on and the morning came." Steenrod would then drop Hunter off at Ransdell Street, where he observed, "every available wall of Hunter's room had books stacked up two feet high. He would party hard, go home and read voraciously for a few hours, and then go to school." His high-school English teacher, Harrell Teague, a Yale graduate, saw the brilliance in Hunter's writings. Steenrod stated that Teague "would cut Hunter some slack because he recognized what talent there was." Teague would allow Thompson to miss deadlines, marking him down for that, then marking him up for his creative effort. "Brilliant and unpredictable" was how Teague's widow paraphrased her husband's opinion about the future writer. Steenrod was even more impressed: "When I graduated from Princeton as an English major, I realized that in high school Hunter was as well read as most of the people I was graduating with. He was just that far advanced when he was seventeen."

Thompson's early creativity caught many of his peers off base, providing more evidence that he did, in fact, lead separate lives from them, and was not spending all of his time being booked by Probation Officer Gilbert Dotson, down at the Detention Center. By many, he was considered the Athenaeum Association's "token thug" and was expected to destroy things, not put them together. It was with a sense of disbelief that many reacted when, during a meeting in his junior year, he stood in front of them and began reading what most thought might be a few short lines of "How to Firebomb a High School in Three Easy Lessons."

"Nobody could believe it," Larry Jelsma said. "The first time Hunter stood up there reading for thirty to forty-five minutes. Single, narrow lines. All written in ink. Page after page of this. We all just laughed so hard we cried. He was telling stories about people in the club carrying on. He went on and on and entertained the entire club. Nobody could believe that Hunter could have done this, actually written something, let alone something so hilariously entertaining. There was the guy who was truly the token anti-intellectual, who had produced this thing, and entertained the whole group. I have no idea what it was—just descriptions of people and things that had happened. Everyone else's piece was about five minutes. Hunter went on and on, and we loved it. And he loved it. He snickered and chuckled in his own devilish way all through it."

Creativity and destruction—there seemed to be no middle ground, particularly so during his senior year. In the same time period that James Dean was studying in Lee Strasberg's method-acting class and winning the Donaldson and Perry Award for his Broadway role in *The Immoralist,* Hunter Thompson stumbled upon a vehicle, a road map, and an audience for his own fiery, spiked, vitriolic brand of creativity.

Somewhere along the continuum of literature's more shocking creations was Sebastian Dangerfield. He walked with complete impunity right off the pages of J. P. Donleavy's controversial best-seller, *The Ginger Man.* Written by 1954, the book never hit the mainstream American public until later. But Thompson was always a few steps ahead of the game. The main character, a uniquely maladjusted American student in Dublin, was the spiritual lost brother for Thompson.

Dangerfield was smart, but refused to go to class. He was suave. He could put on the most mannered social airs, yet reveled in his "common, spaghetti-eating background." While the name Sebastian means "deserving of honor and respect," he felt he was at the bottom of the social ladder. His values were food, drink, and flesh. He drank others under the table, snarling at the bartender who had told him he'd drunk enough, saying, "Five for the road." He wrote in incomplete sentences, producing great showers of sparks of thoughts, yet his alter ego confided, "One thing I'm sure of, I'm no great writer. I'm nothing but a hungry, sex-starved son of a bitch." He wore sunglasses and refused to go outside without them, asking, "Do you want me to be recognized? Do you?" His motto was: "We Have the Fangs of Animals," and his modus vivendi was spat out as "All I want out of this life . . . is my rightful place and for others to keep theirs." Repeatedly, he stiffed his landlords, sneaked out on his wife, and avoided all forms of responsibility. His power over people, his conniving use of theatrics were honed to an art form, becoming his signature style of interacting with others.

It was Donleavy's first novel. The world seemed confused over how to deal with *The Ginger Man.* These were, after all, the bull's-eye years of the Eisenhower era, the decade of *The Man in the Gray Flannel Suit,* by Sloan Wilson. In the pendulum swing of emerging sensibilities, this was also the decade in which the roots of the '60s tumult were finding considerable nurturance; some reviewers spoke of Donleavy's book's profoundly existential comment on the human condition, compared it with the wry, pointed humor of Henry Miller, and even quoted Judge Woolsey's opinion when he allowed the release of James Joyce's *Ulysses* from the banishment of obscenity. People smuggled early copies of *The Ginger Man* into the country in the same way they had *Tropic of Cancer, Tropic of Capricorn,* and *Naked Lunch.* When it finally appeared in bookstores, the American public made it into an immediate best-seller.

"Hunter read everything," Steenrod pointed out. "Henry Miller, I recall. And Hunter gave me his copy of *The Ginger Man.*"

Floyd Smith knew Hunter well in Louisville, as well as later in New York and on the West Coast. "I remember way back then, Hunter was trying to live out *The Ginger Man.* It had a lot of influence on him. The whole bar scene, the kind of rugged, masculine, macho approach to life."

Thompson needed some way of capturing and moving the ideas, the images, the scenery that ran wild in his mind. If Donleavy could crank out a first novel that paid his rent, brought him international recognition while all the time flogging the backs of every imaginable social standard, why couldn't he?

Hunter's senior year was marked by repeated scrapes with the law; local police officer Gilbert Dotson had made it a personal vendetta to "get" Hunter Thompson. His every move was watched. The year was also punctuated by a public slap in the face by the same group—the Athenaeum—who had taken him to their hearts just two years before. By now, his "separate" life was becoming more obvious and more invasive to the club's sense of social integrity and values.

Larry Jelsma was worried about the basic viability of the Athenaeum, given that the younger members were quite impressionable, and Hunter's impact on them had put the club "in dire straights. We needed to straighten things out. Our big goal was to keep people like Neville, Burton Shelley, and Marshall Eldred from being led astray by Hunter. Hunter was just like the devil— the glint in his eye—run off with him and have some fun. Fun? It was trouble. And it became more and more malignant as he got older."

Hunter, with an able assist from Sam Stallings, Jr., went through the second half of his senior year hounded by the authorities. To this day, the case of "The Wreckers" goes unsolved. Stallings claims not to have been involved: "I knew I didn't do it. I didn't think Hunter did it either, but there was a lot of vandalism in churches at the time. Horrible damage. Probably twenty churches. Thousands of dollars. It was crazy. The culprits kept leaving notes calling themselves 'The Wreckers.' There was one detective downtown—Dotson—he reminded me absolutely of Joe Friday. And he thought Hunter and I did it. I'll bet you they had us down there twenty times, taking our handwriting, grilling us. It was cops-and-robbers, and it went on and on. We got into so much trouble. Whiskey, that's what got us into trouble. He was rebelling against authority. And even though we got into trouble together, Hunter wasn't close with anybody."

The outlaw's separate life was now being seen more clearly by the Athenaeum. "He was in a lot more trouble than any of us really knew at that time," Blakemore offered. "I think it was born out of frustration, economic disadvantage. He was missing the academic boat because of his discipline record. But the family did not have the finances, and that was it. His brother Davidson got a football scholarship to Vanderbilt." Jelsma was more to the point: "He was, by that time, a true psychopath." When some club members heard that The Wreckers had vandalized a church, and cut off all the left sleeves of the choir robes, they thought, because it was so bizarre, "That sounds like Hunter."

Thompson was not the only Athenaeum member to get into trouble. One time about forty of them were tossed in jail overnight after creating a ruckus at the Reynoldses' house. And one night out at Judy Stellings's family's brand-new house, another friend helped Hunter consume an entire bottle of Mr. Stellings's Yellowstone whiskey. It hit Hunter's friend the hardest, and he was forced to make his exit after vomiting on Mr. Stellings's shoes, then falling backward, breaking a glass coffee table. Thompson, always a friend in such situations, dragged his buddy up the muddy hill to where Hunter had parked his mother's black Chevrolet. He hosed the mud off, put the teen in the trunk, and somehow delivered him quietly to his home, without his parents knowing a thing. Another Athenaeum member, Joe Bell, was a reported expert on demolition, wiping out mailboxes and small trees with the greatest of ease. And Bobby Walker was shot dead while playing with a loaded revolver.

So the Athenaeum looked the other way at Hunter's excesses, and as they all headed toward graduation in May, they celebrated their last spring together with an annual spring ball at the Brown Hotel. After the dance, many went back to Burton Shelley's house, continuing the party. Hunter was one of them, but instead of partying, he decided to play around with a new toy purchased by Shelley's parents. It was an expensive little device, somewhat ahead of its time, and something so crude in its technology that no one then really new what to do with it. As the first applications of personal computers were for kids' games, so, too, were the early uses of cumbersome, poor-quality wire tape recorders. However, Hunter's creativity saw potential in the gadget.

After quietly locking himself inside a dark closet with only alcohol, the tape recorder, and his thoughts, Thompson sat for hours while everyone puzzled over his disappearance. Somewhere in that night, Thompson found his vehicle, the tool to snare his thoughts, the instantaneous transfer of his showers of sparks of ideas to a place where they could be kept captive and stored for later use. Like cryogenic bodies, they could be unleashed at some future time. Like Narcissus and the reflecting pool, Thompson used the tape recorder over and over, experimenting with words, thoughts, and inflection. Then it was time for the trial run.

"It was four-thirty or five in the morning, just getting light outside," recounted Blakemore. "Hunter appeared from nowhere, and began playing back stuff he had spoken into this tape recorder. He would play it, rewind it, play it again. We all circled around in the middle of this huge living room. We sat there and laughed until we cried. It was just really funny. 'Play that again,' we'd say, and he'd rewind the tape. God! It was entertaining."

"The only detail of what he recorded that I remember," said Stewart Smythe, "was him saying 'What the hell was that noise outside? It must be a truckload of whores from Camp LeJutte.' Well, of course there was no noise, no whores, not even a Camp LeJutte, but he just let his mind ramble, and roll on into that tape recorder. He saw himself for the first time. We all sat, entranced, and listened. It was absolutely hilarious. Hunter found out how to record what was going on in that mind of his, and he got an incredible audience."

6.

Endgame

n the first Saturday of May 1955, William Faulkner, the Shah of Iran, Lyndon Baines Johnson, and Hunter Thompson saw Willie Shoemaker ride Swaps to a length-and-a-half victory over Nashua. The Kentucky Derby was sensible, stylish, and sober: the winning horse's owner, Rex Ellsworth, was a Mormon, and he

drank ice water, not the traditional victor's mint juleps. It was a year of changing traditions, and ushering in a wave that would become the future. In January, Dwight Eisenhower became the first President to conduct a televised news conference. A month later, the first military advisers were sent to Saigon. A man named Harlan Sanders began selling Kentucky Fried Chicken, Disneyland opened, the Dodgers finally beat the Yankees, and Bill Haley provided a new name for the style of his smash hit "Rock Around the Clock": rock and roll was born.

"Young people of America, awake from your slumber of indolence and harken to the call of the future! Do you realize you are rapidly becoming a doomed generation? Oh ignorant youth, the world is not a joyous place. The time has come for you to dispense with the frivolous pleasures of childhood and get down to honest toil until you are sixty-five. Then and only then can you relax and collect your social security and live happily until the time of your death," went Hunter Thompson's award-winning "Open Letter to the Youth of Our Nation." He went on to speak of man's duty to serve his country, to say that there is no excuse for juvenile delinquency, that he had worked hard, and that he had not run around or stayed out late at night. He also signed the letter, printed in the Athenaeum's *Spectator,* "Fearfully and disgustedly yours, John J. Righteous-Hypocrite."

Down the homestretch toward graduation, Hunter seemed to have solidified his place among Athenaeum members. In the *Spectator*'s photo section is a cartoon showing him preaching from behind a podium: "Dr. Hunto" is the caption. In the annual parody of its members, they had the man pegged:

H. Thompson   WANTED FOR: You name it

ALIAS: Marlon

USUALLY FOUND: Innocent

CHIEF CHARACTERISTIC: Seven-year itch

Given a confidence boost by his discoveries of *The Ginger Man* and the tape recorder, and now fully aware of the audience he could command, Thompson had two pieces published in the *Spectator* at the end of his senior year. While the second, titled "Security," did not win a prize, it seemed to come more from the heart than had the work of "John J. Righteous-Hypocrite."

"Security . . . what does this word mean in relation to life . . . is security a utopian goal or another word for rut?

"Let us visualize the secure man . . . a man who has pushed

ambition and initiative aside . . . and settled in a boring, but safe and comfortable rut for the rest of his life. His ideas and ideals are those of society in general and he is accepted . . . as a respectable man. . . . What does he think when he sees his youthful dreams of adventure, accomplishment, travel, and romance buried under the cloak of conformity?" He ended the essay by asking the reader a rhetorical question: ". . . who is the happier man, he who has braved the storm of life and lived, or he who has stayed securely on shore and merely existed?"

In answer to his own question, Hunter stormed his way right into jail that spring, and as usual he was with Sam Stallings, who cited the incident as one of the craziest ever: "We got into trouble in Danville, six of us. We did so much damage in that town, and when we got in jail we did about two hundred dollars of damage to the jail. To a jail! All six of us in a big cell. Hunter loved it. He led that charge."

Then came three consecutive nights of trashing a filling station, and Officer Dotson closed in, leading Hunter out of high school in the middle of the day in handcuffs. Gerald Tyrrell and others watched the Thompson-Dotson show, Act 73. "To be taken out of Male High in handcuffs? Well, that was bad. That was not acceptable social behavior." It was becoming a tradition, one quite unlike the rest of Male High.

Yale, Princeton, Brown—that year's Athenaeum sent ten students to these Ivy League schools. They had all made their plans. They were all following family traditions, American traditions. Neville Blakemore, then on his way to Princeton the following year, recalls, "In the late spring, when these things were being decided, standing in the hall, somebody asked Hunter, 'Where are you going next year?' and he said, 'I don't know . . . I don't know. But I'm going somewhere.' Well, there was a tinge of desperation in his voice, in that virtually everybody was going on to something else, and he was not. Shortly after that was the incident that got him in serious trouble."

Hunter Thompson stood at military attention, spine straight, chin tucked, eyes straight ahead. He wore a coat, tie, and jacket. He was a head taller than many of the people around him, who circled, all eyes riveted on him. This was a three-dimensional version of the stick figures drawn by Stewart Smythe, with the taller Hunter in the center of the ring of fellow Athenaeum members. "Mr. Thompson," they each barked out sharply as one by one they approached until they were jaw-to-jaw. "I remember Porter Bibb standing inches away from him and *yelling* at him, so angry that he slapped a book on his thigh for emphasis," said Blakemore of the Athenaeum's last-ditch effort to get the train back on its tracks. " 'You will behave,' Bibb had shouted. 'You will do this, you will not do that.' Robert Seiler came up to him—I think he despised Hunter—and he said something very short. But each member of his class braced him publicly in front of all the rest of us, in an attempt to straighten him out. I remember Hunter standing there and taking it."

Thompson was not invited to the next meeting; it was an attempt to excommunicate him. "The Athenaeum had a little inner-sanctum kangaroo court, and they invited me," recalled Floyd Smith. "I didn't know what it was for. They thought they had a big enough group there to bounce Hunter out. I thought it was outside the bounds of the Athenaeum's constitution. I didn't like the fact that it was a secret meeting. But people were saying, 'We've got to look at our careers and reputations here, and we've all got to remove ourselves from this guy. He is really tainted material now. And because he's part of the Athenaeum, we are all being tarred by the same brush.' I didn't think it was going to make a hell of a lot of difference down the road, and it didn't, but these guys were being stampeded by their parents. There were all kinds of speeches, and they voted for impeachment. It was exhausting. The meeting went on and on. And at the end, some bright parliamentarian said, 'O.K.—now that we've voted to impeach him, you guys don't seem to realize what impeachment is. That means we're going to have to have a trial now.' And everybody just sort of groaned and said, 'You mean we have to go through this again? Oh, no!' So we just put it off until next week. But it must have been horrible for Hunter."

Eleven days before graduation came the final straw, the Cherokee Park incident that flung Steenrod, Stallings, and Hunter in three different directions. Steenrod, about to graduate with a 97 average, had been accepted at both Yale and Princeton. After the incident, Yale rejected him, and he had to spend the entire summer living with the dean of admissions before Princeton allowed him to enter. And all Steenrod did was drive the car.

"We were coming back from a party one night and I was driving," Steenrod said. "Hunter was in the middle seat, and Sam was on the right. We were taking Sam home. Sam wanted to stop and get a cigarette. We were driving through Cherokee Park; it's night; there were cars with couples parked. We stopped at one car. Sam got out, came back, said they didn't have any cigarettes. We drove along, passed another car, and Sam said, 'Stop here.' So Sam got out of the car. Hunter and I were just talking to each other, not paying attention to what was going on, but he was there for a long time. He came back, got in the car, and he had some cigarettes. Then after we drove away, Sam said that the guy had gotten so frightened that he had given Sam his wallet. Sam offered to split the proceeds with Hunter and me. I don't know what Hunter thought, but I know what I thought. Anyway, we dropped Sam off, came back, and I dropped Hunter off, and as I was going home, I was arrested driving through St. Matthews."

Neither Steenrod nor Thompson ever knew what actually happened inside the parked car where Sam Stallings found cigarettes and eight dollars. As both Steenrod and Thompson were minors, Stallings's case was separated legally from theirs, and dealt with in a different part of the court, at an earlier date. Sam was represented by his father. Before the case ever came to the Judge, Sam Stallings, Sr., veteran attorney, was in action on his son's behalf. He tried to bribe the young man in the parked car, Joseph Monin, into dropping charges.

For Monin, the whole saga was such that after it was all over, he told Officer Dotson, "Look, if I'd have known it was going to be this way, I'd have took the [bribe] money and run. I would not have gone through all this!"

Parked in his red Pontiac convertible with his date and another couple in the back seat, Monin had heard a car with a bad muffler drive by slowly, then back up. "This guy got out of the car and came up on the passenger side and said, 'Hey, buddy. Do you have a cigarette?' And I said, 'Yeah.' That was Sam Stallings—I didn't know then, but that's who it turned out to be. And then he said, 'I'll take your money, too,' and he had a gun. 'O.K.—no problem,' I told him."

Monin had eight dollars, and Stallings took that and the car keys, throwing them up onto the hillside, where Monin and his friends searched for them with a cigarette lighter. The people in the Pontiac got the license number of Steenrod's car, found their car keys, and called the police from a pay phone, eight blocks from Virginia Thompson's house. When the Louisville police found out from Steenrod that a Stallings and a Thompson had been with him earlier in the night, their eyes must have lit up like Crusaders finding the tracks of the last Infidels.

The police brought Monin along and went directly to the Stallings residence. They knew their way to the house. "Sam's dad came to the door, and you could tell that neither had much love for the other. The words that were exchanged! They went straight upstairs to Sam's bedroom where he was lying in bed like he'd been there all night, except you could tell he'd just got there. And they started checking everything. They went over to this trash can, and started digging around, and pulled out a pistol."

Officer Dotson, victory in sight, coached Monin, and told him what to expect. "Sure enough, Sam, Sr., came by the filling station where I was working," recalled Monin. "Came by a couple of times. And he was wanting me to accept a bribe, and just drop the charges. I probably would have if he'd given me back the eight dollars plus a little extra money. But this Mr. Dotson, he kept working with me, wanting me to push and push, so I kinda went along with him, 'cause that's what he wanted."

During the hearing, the defense put forth by Sam Stallings, Sr., was a piece of theater, one that evidently swayed the audience slightly, as young Stallings was let off with a fifty-dollar fine. "I was damned glad to get out of that place," admitted Monin. "Before Sam, Sr., ever got through, they said I was raping the girl. The guys in the car heard her screams and stopped to save her. He had turned this thing around. I was damned lucky to get out of there. I didn't want to get involved with no more of this kind of stuff. But a little bit later I came out of my house to go to school, and the top of my convertible had been sliced, and the radio stolen."

Hunter's hearing took place on June 15, 1955, before Judge Luis Jull of the Jefferson County juvenile court. Hunter's face was painfully familiar to Jull: a repeat offender, a living reminder that all of the Judge's years of pioneering legal innovations in dealing with juveniles and their families had entirely missed the mark. Today's case of seventeen-year-old Hunter Stockton Thompson was where the buck stopped. Jull had decided that the case, the individual, and his ultimate judicial mandate were each departures from the norm. It was clearly a time to be unconventional, to throw precedent to the wind.

In the larger of the two juvenile court rooms Thompson waited with his mother, Virginia, and two attorneys, Sam Stallings, Sr., and Frank Haddad. As a 47-year-old widow, Mrs. Thompson was doing her best, working as a secretary at Courtenay Ink Company since her husband's death two years before. She was the head of a household that consisted of Hunter, two younger sons, and her mother, Memmo. The three sons were unimaginably different and the strain of raising Hunter as a single parent—let alone the other two—had worn her thin. Juvenile court was not held every day, and consequently the cavernous waiting room was packed, crammed to overflowing with wailing children, screaming mothers, and shouting teens—a bedlam of sweat, noise, and confusion.

When Judge Jull's caseworker, Officer Dotson, called for ". . . all the people in the Thompson case," he needed a strong voice. The four—mother, son, and two attorneys—were herded through the crowd. At six feet three, handsomely athletic, full head of close-cropped hair, dressed in a dark coat and tie, Hunter Thompson looked more like an assistant to one of the attorneys than the defendant in the case.

They waited briefly outside the tiny ten-by-fifteen-foot hearing room for the Judge to finish with a case, then were ushered in to sit in front of Jull in uncomfortable straight-backed wooden chairs. Also in the room were the four plaintiffs in the case, two young men and two young women.

In the stillness of the small room, Hortense Karem, Jull's docket clerk, handed the thick Thompson file to the social worker, who read out to the Judge a summary of the case, and the defendant's pleading.

There had been a pre-hearing conference between Jull, the two attorneys, and the social worker because of some conflicting testimony. The discrepancy in the testimony was significant, and hinged on whether or not Thompson had even been involved in the robbery of Monin and his friends, and if a gun had been used.

Stallings had already been fined for disorderly conduct. That the offender's fine was a paltry fifty dollars, and that his offense had been bargained down from armed robbery, was a clear reflection of local politics: Sam Stallings, Sr., had been president of the Kentucky Bar Association and was an influential man about town.

Regardless of the conflict in the testimony, Jull stated to all that "as a last resort" he was turning Thompson over to the Kentucky State Youth Authority. The attorneys argued vehemently that such a move "would ruin him for life."

The attorneys and Jull argued back and forth; Hunter remained mute and impassive. Dotson and the social worker reminded them that Thompson's previous visits to the courthouse were numerous, involving drinking and destruction of property, that the youth had always promised to mend his ways, and had always ended up right back where they all were now.

Jull spoke directly to Thompson: "I feel I have done you an injustice by waiting so long to take a positive step." Hunter dodged eye contact, as if he were somewhere else.

A man easily given to bombast, as hot-tempered as his son, Stallings fired back at Jull: "If we save this boy now, we'll get our reward in heaven!"

Jull barked out, "And if I do something that is dishonest in my mind today, will I get a reward in heaven?"

Frank Haddad, an associate of Stallings, conferred with him, and asked the Judge for some time "to work things out." He added that Thompson had decided to join the Air Force, "which would make a man out of him."

Jull agreed in concept to the extra time, but differed as to where it should be spent; it was dictated by the Judge that Thompson, even though a minor, should spend the next sixty days in the adult county jail, thus forgoing his impending high-school graduation. Then he was to go immediately into the Air Force.

Further, Jull stated, should anyone attempt to post bail for Thompson before he turned eighteen, on July 18th, his case would be brought immediately before the court for final disposition. He wanted to keep Hunter in jail, and this was his way of assuring it.

No one was expecting this tactic. Pandemonium erupted. Hunter's mother begged Jull, pleading, "Please don't send him to jail!" She was in tears. The attorneys voiced their dismay.

Jull had seen enough. He shouted down the pleas, asking, "What do you want me to do, give him a medal?"

Even one of the female plaintiffs blurted out, "But he tried to help us!" repeating her version of the crime, which had Hunter keeping Sam Stallings from doing even more than stealing eight dollars.

But Jull's mind was made up. He repeated the one-man verdict: sixty days in jail. No bail.

Thompson had sat for the duration like a statue, staring at the Kentucky flag next to Jull's bench.

Years after the case, Frank Haddad recalled the episode clearly. He registered no surprise over Thompson's later involvement with the Hell's Angels. His view of the young Hunter was of "a kind of a guy who had no fear. He didn't give a damn whether Jull would give him sixty days in jail or not. He was not going to open his mouth or beg or plead with Jull for help. He didn't say a word throughout the whole proceeding, didn't give a damn, and was not going to lower himself to beg for anybody to help him." While all the Athenaeum Literary Association donned caps and gowns and signed one another's yearbooks, Hunter languished in jail. Tossed out of school, tossed out of the Athenaeum, he was a majority of one in a society that had rejected him.

Few, if any, in the Athenaeum were surprised or concerned about Hunter's imprisonment. Stewart Smythe said, "We expected him to land in jail. We just wanted to know when he was going to get out. That was nothing for Hunter. I figured he'd ultimately die doing something like running with the bulls at Pamplona. And Hunter would not be gored by one bull—no! He'd be gored by a dozen bulls." Jelsma acknowledged that Hunter had always been a man ahead of his time. "We had a lot of guys who went all the way through college and then dropped out. Hunter dropped out at the beginning!"

Even without his suspension, he would have had difficulty graduating. He never got a mark higher than the 89 he received in freshman French. And the future journalist nearly flunked typing. The highest grade he got all during his senior year was a 72, and that was from Mr. Teague, who, appropriately, "cut Hunter a lot of slack." In a class of 251, his academic ranking was 241. Everyone knew he had made a mockery of the rules for "The Male High Gentleman" that were spelled out in detail in the *Student Handbook.* However, when it came to his performance on national standardized tests, taken in his junior year (for college applications he never made), his true colors came shining through: percentile ranking of 99 in social studies, 92 in math, and 91 in English. There were indeed great, blinding shower storms of sparks inside that head. Thompson just needed a change of environment to unleash them.

His actual graduation was not noted until the next year, the 100th anniversary of Male High, after Thompson had sent in transcripts from courses taken in the Air Force. Beside his name is an asterisk and the statement "No Photo Furnished." But this would prove no problem. Hunter Thompson would make up for lost time and missed photo opportunities, especially now that he was leaving behind all that Louisville had stood for.

7.

Upward

Mobility

If . . . the formula Father= Society should be reversed as Society= Father, the effect on the development of a satisfactory social attitude is unaltered. . . .

The psychopath [is] literally an excommunicant in the matter of socially acceptable goals. . . . Consequently, all his activities . . . are restraint-free, sometimes strikingly bizarre, always unappreciative of consequences.

—ROBERT LINDNER, *Rebel Without a Cause*

 clang of iron cleaved Hunter Thompson's adolescence from his adulthood. The jail cell door slammed shut with a ring of serious business to it; this was the "big people's" jail, not some child-care center for truants. When the key closed the lock, Judge Jull's concept of justice appeared to stretch ahead forever like a human Möbius strip.

To incarcerate the frothing energy and intellect of a seven-teen-year-old Hunter Thompson was like driving a Ferrari in first gear only. He stewed, he thought, he experienced volatile mood swings, and undoubtedly renewed every anti-societal vow ever entertained.

A long-standing sociological axiom holds that rich kids get into trouble, poorer kids get into crime. Hunter was a struggling lower-middle-class kid running with an upper-class crowd; he got into jail. The young Sam Stallings, off the legal hook for a $50 fine, was keenly aware of the discrepancy. "His getting that jail time was probably the best thing for us, 'cause I never did see him after that. He went directly into the Air Force, and that was it. But for four years, we were tight and he was crazy. We didn't care much about consequences. I knew my dad would get me out of jail. I thought he would get Hunter out that last time. Hunter got hurt when my dad left him in there. It broke up our camaraderie."

Thompson never carried a ball and chain around his ankle, but to be sentenced to the Jefferson County jail in 1955 was to carry the heavy baggage of social stigma. Everyone wore the same uniform known as "the jailhouse blues"; the denim shirt was labeled "JAIL." Visitors could be seen on Sundays, and then only through a plate-glass window. Both inmate and visitor sat in a long row of small cubicles facing each other, and spoke through tiny holes in the glass.

Inmates were housed two to a cell, an area about six feet wide and ten feet long with a toilet, a sink, and a table. Each row of cells opened onto a walkway about a hundred feet long. Days started early. Lights came on at 5 A.M.; breakfast was at 5:30; lunch at noon; dinner at 4:30, and the lights went off at 9 P.M. sharp. The only entertainment was a radio. For a nocturnal animal like Thompson, this must have required some adjustment.

One of Thompson's friends during high school years observed the changes Hunter was going through. She was one of the very few who visited him in jail. While everyone in Louisville knew where Hunter was, only one Athenaeum member visited; Hunter's status with them had changed. His friend commented on Hunter's thoughts at the time. He was bored, but he hated the social stigma; he felt ashamed to be there. After his girlfriend visited him in jail, Hunter indicated that he wished she had not come to see him. It embarrassed him to be seen in that situation; he was sure he would be known as a "jailbird" when he got out.

He talked about what a depressing place jail was. He was going to straighten up his act and go on.

Over his first seventeen years, nearly everyone had enjoyed very good times with Hunter, and endured very bad times with Hunter. There seemed no middle ground. His friend recalled the insult of having been stood up by Hunter for one Athenaeum Christmas dance—she thinks he was in jail at the time. And she recalled a typical incident not long before he was imprisoned. Her mother had prepared a serving tray, complete with bottles of bourbon, for a party she was hosting at their home in Anchorage. Hunter had dropped by, breezed through, and the bourbon bottles had all disappeared. Her father, livid, got on the phone to Virginia Thompson. Virginia told him it would be impossible to wake Hunter up. Apparently Virginia was always covering for him.

While in jail, Hunter wrote not only to this friend, but to over a dozen of his other pals. He wrote volumes. He seemed to crave this form of once-removed contact, where he could describe his outrageous behavior without fear of social retaliation. He rejoiced in telling others, through the mail, of the most minute detail of what he was doing. He showered them with what amounted to a daily diary, written with a slightly different slant for each reader.

He thrived on the news of what was going on in the world outside. He got angry when people did not write back, or when he lost track of someone's address.

One of the letters he received was from the Athenaeum, who wrote him a letter denouncing him, his girlfriend said. That was in one of his letters to her, too. Somebody had written to tell him that they had denounced him, excommunicated him.

Ironically, it was through another Athenaeum member, George Logan, that Hunter's deal for an early release was made. Thompson was let out of jail after thirty days, spent a week in Louisville before exchanging one blue uniform for another, then headed out of town and into the Air Force. The deal had been made by George Logan's father, an attorney and former juvenile judge. Logan stated that his father "was able to persuade Judge Jull that if he would probate Hunter, he personally would see to it that Thompson would stay out of trouble. It was understood that Hunter would not harass the Male High staff, and would go right into the Air Force." As part of the deal, Thompson was remanded to the custody of Almond Cooke, a wealthy Louisville Chevrolet dealer.

The entire arrangement must have been the crowning episode in Thompson's ongoing love-hate relation with authority, the upper class, and especially attorneys: first he was abandoned in jail by one powerful lawyer, only to be let out a month ahead of schedule by yet another.

"You are not on probation," Judge Jull intoned the good news to Thompson, just turned eighteen and now back in street clothes, but still making no eye contact with the older man. Then came the bad news, a kind of legal plague that would cling to him like a growth for three more years. "But you will be watched. The court can intervene any time until you are twenty-one. For the time being, I think you have had enough." That was the last the two ever saw of each other. But it was Thompson, of course, who had the last word with the system that had kept him from sunlight for a month.

It was early in the morning—very early, around 4 A.M. The black Chevrolet, lights out, cruised silently to a stop directly across the street from the house of a Male High teacher who had aided and abetted Officer Dotson's pogrom. The tranquillity of a hot August night came to a rude and shattering halt as a salvo of full beer bottles hailed through the front windows. As lights popped on inside the house, the Chevy slunk away, only to return.

"There was a teacher who lived just off Eastern Parkway," Norvin Green recalled. "Hunter trashed the house by throwing bottle after bottle through the windows. Hunter was determined to get his revenge. More than once. On succeeding nights! He thought this was a fairly nice way to get revenge, a sort of terrorist tactic. Hunter was always an anarchist in his philosophy."

For the Louisville police department, the "short list" of potential terrorists was a very short "short list." But by the time they could do anything, Hunter had left for the Air Force.

The experience of jail is an individual thing; what one makes of it is an intensely personal matter. For some, it is intended to be a "house of corrections," like liquid White Out, to atone for human mistakes. For others, there is honor and tradition in serving time for one's deeper convictions, should they run counter to those of society. The famous dialogue of Emerson and Thoreau, "What are you doing in there?" versus "What are you doing out there?" was captured in spirit by Ken Kesey and his Merry Pranksters' anthem of the '60s: "You are either on the bus or off the bus." Kesey later used much of his own jail experiences in the book *Demon Box*. Timothy Leary, drawing on personal experience, has stated that he "never trusts a philosopher who has not spent some time in jail." Brendan Behan, at the impressionable age of sixteen, was caught in a Liverpool shipyard with a suitcase full of explosives. Jailed as an Irish terrorist, he turned the experience into *Borstal Boy*.

The jail experience did not seem to have an impact on Thompson's beliefs—beyond affirming all of his existing sentiments regarding Louisville and its unyielding class structure. The city was an understimulating, unforgiving, narrow-minded dowager of a community, and he was pleased to leave her behind.

In the fall of 1955, just weeks after his eighteenth birthday, armed with no high-school diploma, possessing no skills or training that anyone could see as "job related," with no goal in life except to get out of Louisville, he found himself on a bus headed toward San Antonio, Texas. He carried Air Force orders, a keen interest in electronics—especially tape recorders—a heart laced with anarchy, and a high-RPM mind that had finally gotten out of first gear.

8.

The

Great Blue

Yonder

andolph Air Force Base was Hunter's first stop in the Air Force: three months of pledge-like hazing under a relentless Texas sun. Twenty miles from San Antonio, the base is a city of mazes: buildings, hangars, and runways in the middle of nowhere. It is a dusty, forlorn, and busy way-station to tens of thousands of crew-

cut, uniformed, anonymous eighteen-year-olds.

At first, the adjustment was difficult for Hunter. He wrote to one friend about his painful, persistent homesickness; she had thought he'd be thrilled to be far away. Then again, the first three months of Air Force regimen was no cake-walk. It was more like a sequel to jail, with calisthenics and marching drills added in. Hunter's torrent of letters continued to deluge many of his friends. He would write to them when his eyes were dry from fatigue, when his arms were pincushioned by inoculations. Late at night after lights-out, he would write by the light of a flashlight.

Reveille was at 4:45. The barracks were cleaned until 6 A.M. Breakfast; clean the barracks again; march in the sun; then it was time to stand in line for lunch. During Air Force basic training, the afternoons were often spent taking psychological tests to determine skill sets that would dictate one's vocational future. Each day's program was like the one before and the one to follow. After testing, all would march back to the mess hall, stand in line for dinner, eat, then—for the third time—clean the barracks again. After dinner there was one free hour, then lights out at 9 P.M.

In his previous incarnation, nine o'clock at night would usually have found Hunter just beginning to wake up, stretching his limbs, and perhaps making a phone call to Bobby Butler or Sam Stallings or Norvin Green to locate a party. No longer. The good times were behind him, and he complained bitterly, but went ahead with the show so well that he rose to the position of squad leader, in charge of eighteen men. He complained in letters to George Logan and Gerald Tyrrell that he lived in fear of his own as well as others' mistakes. Some of this fear may have been the echoing of Judge Jull's ". . . you will be watched . . . until you are twenty-one"; the remainder was the reality of tough, no-nonsense Air Force life. If the barracks were dirty or some rule was broken, it was the squad leader who paid the price. He seems to have managed to keep himself and eighteen others in an adequately straight line, and graduated as an airman in early December of 1955.

What he had shown on the lengthy psychological and vocational interest forms was an interest in electronics—the tape-recorder-as-career, perhaps. On the 18th of December, 1955, precisely five months after his eighteenth birthday, he began Air Force electronics school at Scott Air Force Base in southern Illinois, an hour-plus drive from Louisville. At that time, Scott Air

Force Base was where one went for schooling in all forms of electronics and radio communications. Located a half hour's drive from St. Louis, Scott was home to the 375th Air Wing and the Air Force Communications Command. During those years, thousands of airmen went through training at Scott for radio transmission school. However, this was the base for operational radio, not entertainment radio. Being a talk-show host was not on the options menu.

After a few months in the service, Thompson seemed to have lost all traces of homesickness. He later reported to many friends, including Henry Preston, a fellow airman at Eglin Air Force Base, in Florida, that he had envisioned a career in the Air Force. Thompson was swayed by the romance of becoming a pilot. Or perhaps it was the difference in pay, $475 a month versus his $80, that piqued his interests. He attempted to get into the Air Force aviation cadet program, where those selected go from high school to an airplane, becoming commissioned officers upon graduation. The program ceased to exist with the advent of the Air Force Academy, but it was intended to select and train that rare individual capable of making the jump. Thompson never made it. It may have been his height—there was a limit on one's sitting height from the waist up, in order to allow the ejection seat to function, and Thompson has short legs for his overall height. Further, the cadet program had exceptional requirements when it came to things that Hunter had never really excelled in: high-school grades and citizenship. As unique as he was, entrance to the cadet program was an extremely rare exception, not the rule. So it was that Thompson shuffled off to Scott to study electronics and radio communications.

In between basic training and radio school, Hunter found enough time to return to Louisville and "run the road" to Nashville with Norvin Green. "We took off in his car and drove down," Green stated. "We had an interesting time. Drove through the hills at high speeds, listening to "Rock Around the Clock," stopping at various roadside taverns to get beers—weren't served at a couple of them—but got enough beer to keep us going. Hunter had an old Chevy at the time. I don't know if it was his mother's or his. I do remember this car had bullet holes in it. I think he probably put them in it, but he'd talk like they were the scars of some booze-running escapade. He liked to do things like that—to play-act."

In December of 1955, nobody seemed to make much of a deal about Hunter Thompson being back in Louisville. He was not the only future attraction unnoticed in town. On the night of the 8th, the Rialto Theater, where Hunter and Gerald Tyrrell had spent Saturday afternoons with their bean shooters, cancelled its regular showing of the movie *Tarantula* ("100-Foot Spider Spreads Wild Destruction"). In its place, the theater hosted the annual Philip Morris Employees' Night, starring country-music idol Hank Snow. One of the lesser-known acts that opened the show and went virtually overlooked was a country singer just two years older than Hunter: Elvis Presley.

Back at Scott Air Force Base, however, Hunter did not go unnoticed. He was becoming his usual, loud and boisterous self, and he paid the price. Norvin Green remembered visiting him there. "Lots of nights, Hunter had this routine. He'd go to a place called the Pine Top Inn. He was a regular, sometimes about the only person. He had this deal with the barkeeper, who'd give him a pitcher of beer and leave him alone. Hunter and I'd sit there and talk until the place shut down around us. That's where he'd write all his letters. Just sitting there, minding his own business, sipping beer and writing letters until all hours of the night."

On another visit, Green recalled, "We went drinking and everybody was under-aged. We went into East St. Louis to drink. We were broke and the other guys wouldn't loan us any money, but eventually we got back to the base. Some of his group had decided to trash Hunter's room. They had poured white shoe polish all over his bed." Green inspected the damage, then wandered downstairs and fell asleep in the empty bed of an airman out on pass, only to be rousted by a sergeant who had tracked the white shoe polish to Norvin's feet. "He woke me up saying, 'O.K., airman, you're in big trouble. We know all about it.' The sergeant thought I was the airman who'd vandalized the place with the shoe polish, and by the time I explained that I was a civilian just there visiting, it was Hunter who got in a load of trouble."

Revenge was always a motivator for Thompson; he got back at the others for the white-shoe-polish incident, and eventually told Green about his sly tactics. "At the base, they had rooms with two men to a cubicle. Hunter used to come in, pretty loud and crazy. He urinated down the hallway, and in and out of the various two-man rooms. The next weekend, the sergeant in charge ordered all the partitions torn down. The cubicles were gone, and they made it into a big open barracks again." In Green's mind, all this was another example of the Thompson charisma that he had seen in high school. "It is really hard to describe. That was Hunter. He was pretty carefree. He was intelligent. He was multi-faceted. He did provoke certain changes around him."

In the middle of an endless prairie of sand fleas, land crabs, rattlesnakes, scrub oak, and sand dunes stood a series of wooden bleachers. For miles in every direction there was ceaseless, relentless wasteland. Yet the bleachers were packed. The sun appeared as a huge psychedelic beach ball just above the eastern horizon. It radiated torpor, lethargy, perspiration, and war. Four thousand Cold Warriors, each in a three-piece navy business suit, were being broiled communally. The air was as heavy as lead, but the sudden brain-piercing electronic feedback from the P.A. system sent shivers up and down their sweaty backs. The men stirred uncomfortably. Some stuck fingers in their ears, but now only a seagull's screech and the wind were to be heard.

The P.A. system crackled to life again and a voice blared the men into a new reality: "Six burning, four turning: the B-36. Wingspan of two hundred sixty-three feet. Fuselage length of three hundred twelve feet. Crew of nine. Range of five thousand two hundred miles. Payload of twenty-five thousand pounds; that's fourteen times what General Doolittle dumped on Tokyo. Coming in at three o'clock low."

Four thousand necks and eight thousand eyes turned toward the west. A distant droning noise became a moving speck; the speck grew in size until it became the Air Force's number one winged defender against Communism, totalitarianism, Fascism, and "isms" yet to be defined by the reigning Eisenhower-Nixon government.

The din of the approaching squadron of B-36s grew until it became all-encompassing. Sitting in the bleachers felt like riding a giant vibrator in the middle of the Sahara. A wedge of the giant planes approached the bleachers at one thousand feet. An old brick factory building stood in a clearing of pine trees four hundred yards from the bleachers packed with the military-industrial complex representatives. Immediately it was engulfed in a magenta ball of napalm. One plane, errant in its timing, dropped a 500-pound bomb so close to the stands that the men in three-piece suits, after discovering that their deafness was not permanent, found pine needles and twigs decorating their vests. In Air Force parlance, this effect was known as "razor burn."

Great balls of napalm, smoldering craters the size of shopping malls, forests blown to confetti by a modestly off-target 500-pound bomb. Welcome to Eglin Air Proving Ground and its famed Fire Power Demo, a bi-annual Fourth of July blast put on for every aerospace executive worth his weight in Defense Department contracts. These shows were a vast pyrotechnical fun house that combined an area the size of Rhode Island with the spirit of a serial killer.

This sand dune on the rim of infinity, Florida's bleak Panhandle, was the 1950s retort to the dropping of the Iron Curtain and the Soviets' first atomic explosion in 1949. Many battles of the Cold War were fought here, in intense heat. Preparation for doom and dress rehearsals for death were key to the ethos of Eglin. Jimmy Doolittle's squadron had trained here before their thirty seconds over Tokyo. Bombing and strafing techniques used to take out German V-1 buzz-bomb launching sites had been perfected at the expense of the scrub oak and flocks of egret. An entire city of wooden houses had been built on the dunes around Elgin to replicate urban Tokyo; then the Air Force's finest had summarily executed the city in a metal hail of incendiary bombs as practice for the firebombing of Tokyo in 1945.

It was Eglin that had controlled the flight of the first pilotless B-47 drone. Its technological breakthrough was rewarded on its very next flight when it was blasted into smithereens by a Bomarc missile: another first.

Death, destruction, pyromania, and a post-McCarthy paranoia that Armageddon had already been launched, and was whistling through the air and headed directly for Pensacola, comprised the operative mind-set at Eglin Air Proving Ground when Hunter Thompson arrived in July, 1956, after electronics school ended.

The 30th of August, 1956, marked the unveiling of "Airman Second Class Hunter S. Thompson—Staff Writer" for the *Command Courier*. Within a week, the September 6th sports column carried Thompson's name; by January 24, 1956, he appeared as the *Courier* sports editor. There must have been a sense of déjà vu for Thompson when he found himself writing for a paper with the same name as the paper he had been weaned on in Louisville, the *Courier;* and a sports section using the same name as the Athenaeum's yearbook, the *Spectator.* If he felt right at home, it showed in his work; his sportswriting was a logical extension of his letters to his friends. Many amounted to a first-person argument as to why Adolph Rupp, at the University of Kentucky, was capable of building dynasties as well as character; urging readers to bet on Iron Liege in the Kentucky Derby (he won), then General Duke at Belmont (he lost); favoring Floyd Patterson to beat Archie Moore for the heavyweight boxing title (he won); and rooting for Louisville's basketball team over Canisius (he lost). But win or lose, he showed no qualms about stating publicly what he thought.

The intensely first-person "me and my buddies" style went so far that in one column Thompson interviewed former Athenaeum member Porter Bibb, who talked about the University of Louisville's Charlie Tyra's ability to shut down Wilt Chamberlain, then playing for the University of Kansas. Thompson never mentioned that Bibb was a high-school friend. Nor did he mention that he had traded elbows and hook shots with Tyra, on his way to a career with the New York Knicks, when both were fourteen-year-old Castlewood Athletic Club members. It was a piece of insider's humor, and clips of the article were fired out to his friends all over the country. The columns were engaging, all Hunter, and a radical departure from the norm of the Eglin *Courier*'s journalistic style of all fact and stale stuff.

While his formal entry to journalism was netting him just $130 a month, it did give him the chance to inject his own pent-up creative juices into a newspaper whose more exciting bannerlines trumpeted clarion cries such as: NEW PHONE SYSTEM GOES INTO EFFECT AT FIELD NINE, DEPENDENT MEDICARE PAMPHLET SCHEDULED FOR RELEASE SOON, and a line guaranteed to snag the eye of every callow nineteen-year-old who thought he'd escaped the tyranny of Mom and Dad, only to find himself up to his ears with orders from ranking soldiers: TEN TIPS ON WATER SAFETY: NEVER SWIM ALONE.

"V OODOO IN THE ORANGE BOWL"—now *that* was more like it! And when Thompson, aged nineteen, began to unleash his verbal stuff, he strutted the eye-grabbing style and the imagination-twisting content that marked his words for the rest of his career. Thompson was on to something, and he knew it.

The gist of the "Voodoo" article was that a new rule prevented the Orange Bowl Committee from inviting Coach Bud Wilkinson's powerhouse Oklahoma team to play in that year's Orange Bowl game. National Champs the previous year, and in the middle of the longest collegiate win streak ever (47), the team was prevented by the new rule from making back-to-back Orange Bowl appearances; the Sooners had been there a year ago. In their place, a distant second-place Colorado team would appear. The ruling probably did cause consternation among the officials. But Thompson cranked up the torque, created his own vision, and dragged his readers with him inside the committee's conference room.

> We can easily imagine the tearful scene . . . we can see the members of the committee slumped in their chairs, ex-pressions of glazed agony on their chalk-white faces, lis-tening to the chairman announce that Colorado will be invited to play. . . . At this point we can see one of the more high-strung members of the group leaping to his feet and, with a wild cry, jamming a huge pin through the midsection of one of a group of battered voodoo dolls lying in the middle of the table. The thoroughly pierced dolls, representing members of the ruling body of the Big Seven conference, had doubtlessly absorbed brutal torture up to that point. . . . The Orange Bowl howled like a disinherited son; but to no avail. The Big Seven stood firm on its ruling and the deed was done.

In the dorms and fraternities of Yale and Williams and Princeton, in the front room of his mother's house on Ransdell Avenue, VOODOO IN THE ORANGE BOWL was being avidly consumed. Hunter made sure everyone he knew got a copy.

George Logan recalls Hunter's sense of battle while in the Air Force—battle with authority. "I heard from him in the Air Force, about his agreed-upon parting of the ways. Hunter's version was that he talked constantly about his Commander down there. Hunter would wax eloquently in his letters about making that man's life a living Hell. This may or may not have had any truth." The officer Logan referred to was Colonel William S. Evans, Chief, Office of Information Services. The base paper was under his re-sponsibility. Luckily for Thompson, Colonel Evans was kept quite busy organizing for the Fire Power Demos, and could not read every item. Pieces such as "Voodoo" slipped by, as did Thomp-son's column, "Maggot's Folly." In this, a "Rum-dumb schizoid" football player, Maggot, was demonstrated the evils of alcohol by his coach, who placed a glass of water and a glass of alcohol on his desktop and dropped a worm in each. When coach asked Maggot to explain the cosmic significance of the worm in the alcohol shriv-eling and dying, Maggot replied, "All I have to do is drink plenty of alcohol and I'll never get worms." Most of Thompson's published matter was lively, but nothing that begged to be censored.

The first touchdown pass caught in the first Super Bowl was caught by Max McGee. The ball was thrown by Bart Starr; his backup quarterback was Zeke Bratkowski. Before their careers with the Green Bay Packers, both McGee and Bratkowski had played for the Eglin Eagles during the time that Hunter covered all sports. Max McGee and Zeke Bratkowski were not the entire team: it was a super-star, talent-heavy dynamo that crushed opponents like palmetto bugs, and put a half-dozen players into the pros. Ollie Matson, Zeke Bratkowski, Max McGee, Jim Dooley, Pat Patterson, Carroll Dale, Rod Serls, "Big Mo" Modzelewski, and Leo Fleming were on the same team at the same time; coach John Sparks called it "the best Service side ever." It could have competed with many professional sides.

For someone with Thompson's history of idolizing sports figures, he now found himself in their midst, a Valhalla of sweaty jockstraps and the odor of deep-heat balm. And it was not as if these other players were potential future pro-bowlers; McGee and Bratkowski had already been with, respectively, the Packers and the Bears before their Reserve units were called to active status because of the Suez crisis. They represented much more than seasoned professionals: McGee was part of the two-time World Champions of the National Football League.

As the base sports editor, Thompson would fly with the teams to various bases around the country, use his press pass to sit in the best seats, and turn out a column that could have passed for any of the dozens of letters he would also fire off to high-school friends to keep his network alive. In short, it would seem that Thompson had a dream job, where as long as he turned out his column, his responsibilities and obligations to the Air Force tedium were minimal. He streamlined his efforts to such an extent that he had spare time on his hands—a commodity that never fit well with such a high-strung, constitutionally anxious individual.

To add to his earnings, he accepted a job at the Fort Walton Beach *Playground News* in early February of 1957. He turned out a column called "The World of Sports," but could not use his name; the Air Force prohibited moonlighting. Thompson would have to work in anonymity, not an easy task for an ego-driven writer keenly invested in creating his own myth. But he was paid almost twice his monthly Air Force salary at the one-day-a-week job for the newspaper.

In many ways, Thompson appeared to be in hog heaven. He had two jobs doing what came naturally: kibitzing in his own letters-to-my-buddies style about what every red-blooded American youth dreamt—the sports heroes surrounding him. And as if to presage things to come, he had an illustrator—Hartley—whose vivid renderings for Thompson's columns added a synergistic flair. He even got space to talk about the new wave of American cultural idols when he blamed "the ruination of the national pastime"—yet another Dodgers-Yankees World Series pair-up last October—on Elvis Presley.

He had time to go drinking with his friends. He was busy taking on-base courses in speech and psychology that were offered by Florida State College in Tallahassee. He spent his weekends either flying with the teams to Denver, Washington D.C., and New Orleans, or going to fraternity parties at Florida State. He enjoyed a life that few other teenaged airmen could ever envision. He was getting feedback from all around that the writing he was doing was not just good, but different. Still, he fumed on the inside. He had a big vision of himself, and it was not one that involved being under the thumb of anyone's editorial control.

The Seagull Bar is a few miles south and east of Eglin, on Okaloosa Island. It is a tidy wooden structure that clings to the south side of the Intracoastal Waterway like a crab at low tide. This was the unofficial official Air Force watering hole. Decades of servicemen had nicknamed it "The Dirty Bird."

At a few minutes past three in the afternoon on an anonymous sun-soaked day in 1957, a small gaggle of tourists, fishermen, and traveling salesmen sat around the rustic bar inside The Seagull. Over the bartender's head was the place's namesake: an inverted wooden dinghy about fifteen feet long.

The front door opened, sunlight jabbed the darkness, and in walked a newcomer; he passed the wall covered with a collage of old black-and-white "flyboy" photos of Doolittle and Peck and dozens whose names were not so well known. He took a seat near the drinkers, and said in a low mumble, "Earthquake at four o'clock sharp."

The conversation turned lively at this point; "What the hell" was heard all around. No one ever considered the Florida Panhandle an earthquake-prone location. And the tall stranger was putting his money where his prediction was—he was betting them on it, waving ten-dollar bills. As the time closed in on four o'clock, a half-dozen intrigued drinkers coughed up their money. The bartender held the pot. At a few minutes before four, the instigator of this bet-a-disaster scheme seemed to turn chicken. He spun around toward the drinkers, saying, "Wait, for Christ's sake! It might not be at four o'clock sharp. It . . . it could be delayed!" Thinking they "had" him, there was a scramble to retrieve their money from the bartender. After all, who delays an earthquake? The stampede was stopped short when the voice of doom said, "Look, it might be at—uhh, 4:02. Or 4:03. Certainly no later than ten after. And it's gonna be one hell of an earthquake." The bets were back on.

There was considerable silence immediately before and after the hour of 4 P.M. Twelve eyes riveted the interloper, who stared idly at a tuft of eelgrass on the far side of the Intracoastal. Three minutes after. Six minutes after.

At seven minutes after four, The Seagull—the bar, the dinghy, and everyone and everything in and around it—was rocked with a clap of noise and a jolt of shocking, lurching movement underfoot that seemed to have come straight from the Devil's Howitzer. Every drinking glass in the place rattled like wind chimes, and the chained dinghy swayed as if caught in bad surf. Many and various exclamations were uttered, the most controlled of which was "Thank you, gentlemen," as Airman Second Class Thompson pocketed the equivalent of nearly a month's pay and headed out the door. Crossing the parking lot to his battered old Chrysler, its hubcaps and radio sold off to pay bills, he nodded modestly and thankfully at a sharp glint of sunlight bouncing off the wings of a single jet plane disappearing over the horizon. Thompson had friends in high places. The old sonic boom trick had worked again.

If there was an easier way to make money than sportswriting, Hunter had not stumbled onto the secret formula at Eglin. Yet in the summer of 1957, sportswriting had taken a distant second place in his interests and motivations. And his behavior with the teams showed it. On trips to cover games in New Orleans, and at Bolling Air Force Base, the season's "big game," against a team the nearby Pentagon brass staffed with hand-picked collegiate stars, Hunter and Henry Preston "had a real good time. But we didn't even see the damned ball games. Hunter and I were having too good a time in Washington, D.C.," Preston recalled. Thompson had begun to rely on other people's recollections to compose his own writing.

Preston was a natural ally for Thompson; he was related to the Brown-Forman distillery family in Louisville. Further, both were bright and troubled. "We went into the service under similar circumstances," Preston said. "My issues were reckless driving and continuing to drive with no license." The two met taking a psychology class.

They shared another common denominator—drinking—and it usually took place at The Seagull. "It was right on the beach; you could bring your boat up there," Preston observed. "I remember sitting in The Seagull with Hunter, drinking tremendous amounts of alcohol. His capacity was tremendous. Drink, drink, and drink. Enormous amounts of whiskey. We would talk about everything in the world. But he could remember everything after the fact. Hunter has a marvelous capacity to remember things when he is drunk. I mean that is one of the things that made him a great Gonzo writer. You know, I could keep drinking and keep talking, but I couldn't remember a damned thing!" It was what Ralston Steenrod had called Thompson's "lucidity after midnight."

P reston had managed to get an "early out" from the Air Force, and Hunter wanted one, too. He had become enraptured with the television broadcasts of Robert Kennedy in his role as chief counsel to the Senate committee investigating labor rackets. Their exposé of the underworld connection between Teamsters Union officials Jimmy Hoffa and Dave Beck had hit a nerve.

Like many others, Thompson liked the charismatic Robert Kennedy. Certainly the "good guys-bad guys" morality play, a first on nationwide television, was popular across the country. Perhaps he sniffed destiny: in fifteen years, he would be sitting by the pool at Hickory Hill, chatting with Ethel Kennedy and playing with the children.

In high school, Thompson had never talked politics with any of his friends. He had never run for office, and his classmates had clear difficulty figuring just what office he might hold (he had been elected "Censor" in the Athenaeum). It may have been a coming together of his jail experience, where he felt firsthand the power of attorneys, with the Air Force experience of the power—absolute power—of rank. Whatever the reason, he became fascinated with the Bobby Kennedy-Jimmy Hoffa trials.

Preston observed the transformation, and its impact on Hunter. "Hunter was absolutely obsessed with the Senate hearings and Robert Kennedy. It was the only damned thing he would write about in that period. He was fascinated with all that shit. He really liked the job Bobby Kennedy was doing, and he stopped writing about sports altogether. But he was the sports editor! So here he was; he had all these guys on his back from the base paper and the town paper who said, 'Don't write about that stuff, write about sports.' So Hunter was really interested when I got an early release from the Air Force, because he wanted to get out and do things other than just sports.

"I had been in trouble. Got court-martialed and beat it. I was a big hero among people who didn't have many stripes. I told Hunter how to change his job classification to make it look like you were absolutely no use to the Air Force."

Before leaving the Air Force, Hunter managed to break away from the thrall of Bobby Kennedy long enough to write a few more good sports pieces. In Thompson's column about the 1957 Indianapolis 500 race, he railed out against a Vatican newspaper, Billy Graham, and a Mobile, Alabama, columnist. Each had called for the abolition of auto racing. "All racing, which is a race to death, must be abolished," the Vatican paper had pronounced. Graham had portrayed the sport as "legalized mayhem," and its followers as akin to heroin addicts. Thompson's position was that if 200,000 people wanted to risk their lives watching the Indy 500, then a "handful of crusaders" had no right to tell the spectators it was too dangerous, and no right to "take away the livelihood of a legion of courageous and highly skilled drivers." He ended his column stating, "Naturally there are risks. There are risks in everything." Then, in the same spirit as his soon-to-be-famous slogan "When the going gets weird, the weird turn pro," he quoted Jean Behra, a French race-car driver: "Only those who don't move, don't die. But since they do not move, they are already dead."

In the pile of sports columns that Thompson wrote before severing ties and getting his own "early out," in November, 1957, he managed to refer to everything from Supreme Court decisions, a Russian exercise journal, and the boxing promoter

Cus D'Amato. In his Joe Louis piece, which Thompson considered his best (he sent copies to the entire network), he showed his ability as a wordsmith and a painter of pictures:

> Now the thundering ovations are for another champion, and true to the rule, yesterday's hero is but a memory; incompatible with the picture of an aging man, troubled with a bad heart and faced with a future on a financial treadmill . . .
>
> The pages of history are dotted with the stories of "fallen idols" whose exploits lent a little luster and richness to the colorless lives of the millions who cheered them on, paid them homage, and then condemned them to oblivion as a new champion mounted the throne.
>
> The story of Joe Louis is an old one; the story of a star which has outlived its light; the soaring meteor which failed to explode in mid-air at the height of its climb, but plummeted down to the earth with the millions who, moments before, had stared wide-eyed at its beauty.
>
> The world likes to look up at its stars. A meteor which falls out of the sky is not only dead when it hits, but digs its own grave by the force of its fall. Just as the crowd stares curiously at a fallen meteor then wanders off . . . the applause of the worshipping thousands has died into the whispering of the curious few. The end is inevitable.

Using a sheet of Colonel Evans's News Release stationery, Thompson sent out a letter dated November 8, 1957. It was his last installment of the Air Force chapter in his evolving myth; he had the article reprinted in the front of *The Great Shark Hunt,* twenty years later. It held special significance; proof positive that not even Eglin Air Force Base could hammer him into acceptable shape.

Invoking the violent yet playful distortion that would become the classic Thompson style, Hunter wrote to his friends of his fantasized parting gesture to the Air Force. Driving wildly, in a car with neither muffler nor brakes, on the wrong side of the road, he celebrated receiving his separation papers by hurling a wine bottle into the base gatehouse. Thompson described himself as such an out of control iconoclast that his unnatural and uncivilized behavior had sent the base classification officer totally around the bend: he was admitted to the Eglin neuropsychological hospital.

"Shit!" Henry Preston said when he opened the letter recently arrived from Eglin Air Force Base. "That letter blew my mind! I thought it was great! He got out!"

The twenty-year-old Thompson's Air Force discharge was in early November of 1957. At the time, he still sported a full head of hair, he smoked Kaywoodie Briar pipes, and had a penchant for Bing Crosby music. He had gained so much self-confidence that after receiving his high-school diploma in the mail, he actually applied for a prestigious Grantland Rice Scholarship at Vanderbilt. Rejected, his eyes looked north. He made a brief stop in Louisville. He shunned a job at the sports desk of a St. Louis newspaper, and headed to New York City and a two-week stint as sportswriter for the Jersey Shore, Pennsylvania, *Herald.*

When Thompson had received the offer, he saw the word "Shore" and thought of beautiful beaches. Instead, he found a moribund town among coal mines and icy rivers. His first job would be a short one. The newspaper's owner had offered the use of his car and a date with his daughter, and Thompson accepted. Before work the next day, he packed his bags in the trunk of his old black Chevrolet and parked it near the office. It was an afternoon newspaper, and the owner habitually came in near noon. After a while, Thompson heard a noise coming from the street that sounded like a giant dragging his fingernails over a blackboard. Thompson quietly sneaked out into his car, and headed for New York City with no goodbyes. The night before, he had gotten his boss's car stuck in a muddy field, and the bumper had ripped off and a door had crumbled like a gum wrapper when a farmer used a tractor to yank him free.

9.

The Smoldering

Hatred of a Peasant

Manhattan smells like the litter box for the Kitty of the World. . . . The Big Apple, polished with Rockefeller spit and wiped on the tight pants of a multitude of Puerto Ricans, it is ready for the chrome and nibbles of Friday-nighters from everywhere. Junkies are stirring in their warrens, pizzas are primping in their ovens, Wall Street is resting its bloody butt-hole and the Statue of Liberty wears a frown that won't quit. As City College professors, disgruntled over martinis, talk about dropping out and farming rhubarb in Oregon, neon signs all over town rejoice because it's the longest night of the year.—Tom Robbins, *Even Cowgirls Get the Blues*

Vulgar of manner, overfed, overdressed and overbred; Heartless, Godless, Hell's delight, Rude by day and lewd by night.—B. R. Newton, *Owed to New York*

ew York City in late December, 1957, was a strange time for the arrival of a highly ener-gized twenty-year-old with a two-word résumé, "sports writer." It was a quiet time, an in-be-tween time. Kerouac's best writing was behind him. Allen Ginsberg had read *Howl* in San Francisco in 1955; William Burroughs was in the middle of writing *Naked Lunch,* living in Tangiers. Gay Talese, Jimmy Breslin, and Tom Wolfe were working on newspapers. The dissent of the '60s was nowhere near reaching its critical mass. This was a time of conformity, when the books *Power Elite* and *The Organization Man* spoke to the "silent generation" about the dangers of fealty to large corporations. No response was heard.

But all across Greenwich Village, to the trained ear, strange sounds were in the air. They were the the sounds of the new. They varied in theme from place to place. Yet all seemed to come from the hundreds of cold-water garrets, high above the sweat and tedium of the workday bustle on the streets below. The noise of the new seemed to come from look-alike, tiny spartan rooms with one bare light bulb, a wine-stained mattress on the floor, dog-eared copies of Kafka and Camus on the desk. It was the scratch of pen on paper as the future writers of America shivered in the cold, ate peanut butter on stale bread, honed their style, and collected their rejection slips and paid their dues.

Thompson steered clear of the freezing top-floor attic. Instead, he rented a Greenwich Village grotto near the corner of Fourth, on Perry Street, a subterrannean cave below the street level behind a huge furnace that kept the room blazing hot in the coldest of times. One entered Thompson's living space by first going down a few stairs from the street, then opening a huge, heavy fire door. All the windows were painted black, as were the walls and the ceiling. It was impossible to tell the time of day. To get to the main room, one crossed a catwalk. On one side was the heating plant for the entire apartment building. The door to the furnace was broken; orange and crimson flames leaped about wildly, illuminated the black hole by flickering menacingly on the walls. This was the environment in which Thompson lived, slept, read, and wrote: underground writing from Hell.

He also got a job and went to school. He worked as a copyboy for Time-Life on the twenty-ninth Floor of the RCA Building. The company paid half his tuition to attend the General Studies program (open to the public) at Columbia University.

T he city was brand-new in many ways to Thompson, but his social swirl quickly became populated with old friends. Thompson actively solicited every former Athenaeum member he could round up. T. Floyd Smith had left Yale, and was studying at Columbia. Porter Bibb and Paul Semonin graduated from Yale, then moved to New York. They would not only stay in touch with one another over the following years, but would blaze paths for Hunter. In addition to being the Louisville group's leading Fitzgerald expert, Semonin, in the very early '60s, was the one to stumble on the tiny, overlooked mining town in Colorado known as Aspen. Porter Bibb would come full circle, hooking up with Hunter, Jann Wenner, and *Rolling Stone* magazine in 1969 while doing a documentary with the Maysley Brothers on the Rolling Stones' concert at Altamont.

The grotto at 57 Perry Street became a home away from home for displaced Louisvillians. "The car blew up on our way to New York, so we hitchhiked" was Norvin Green's explanation for making an untimed crash landing at Perry Street. "Bobby Butler and I got to New York. We looked up Hunter. He was living in a basement apartment and wasn't home at the time. So Bobby kicked in the window, and we went in." The two went out on the town later; Hunter returned, found twenty dollars missing, and called the police. Norvin returned alone to find a fuming Thompson waiting with the police, who were immediately sent after Butler, but to no avail. "It worked out O.K." Norvin said. "We sat around and drank for a while, and then I hitchhiked home. Hunter wasn't that thrilled."

Thompson went out of his way to look up his old buddies, paying an unexpected but memorable visit to Gerald Tyrrell at Yale. In the spring of 1958, while Tyrrell was playing pool in the St. Elmo fraternity house, Thompson "just came wandering in the front door smoking his pipe. We'd been in touch off and on. He spent the weekend. I had a date with a girl from Grace-New Haven School of Nursing, and Hunter came along. It was the last time I ever saw her; she thought Hunter was acting weird."

Later, when Tyrrell visited Thompson in New York, he found him living in abject poverty with a Chinese girl, a lone jar of peanut butter in the refrigerator. He parked his old Chevy wherever he wanted, putting all the parking tickets into the glove compartment, which was so crammed full that it would not open. "He'd take a ticket, slide it in the glove compartment, and say, 'The car's registered to my mother in Louisville. As long as they don't tow it, so what?' "

Actually, Thompson lived high on the hog at least once a week. Porter Bibb was working for *Newsweek* when Thompson was with Time-Life. Their offices were just across the street from one another. At both places, on Friday night it was a requirement that writers had to stay around their desks until early Saturday morning to proofread material before the galleys went to the printer. At *Newsweek,* one simply had to hang around. At the more established Time-Life, the program was different: Friday nights were catered by the Twelve Caesars Restaurant downstairs in Rockefeller Center.

"They would roll in these gigantic carts of roast beef, ham, salmon," Bibb said. "All the food you could eat. And an open bar on every floor of the editorial offices. Hunter would invite me over, and I would infiltrate and mingle. The theory at *Time* was 'We'll keep you on the floor and near your desk. Even if you're dead drunk, you will be there to check the copy before it goes to the printer.' You never saw Hunter doing any work at *Time.* But we had fantastic Friday night drunks, courtesy of Henry Luce."

T he free food, the Friday nights drunks at *Time,* all ended when Hunter unleashed his anger on a Coke machine. This would become another signature act, to be repeated over and over again: on his next job, he would smash the office candy machine at the Middletown *Daily Record*; at the New York offices of *Rolling Stone* he would detroy a soda machine; a similar scene at the Presidente Hotel on Cozumel while trying to start an interview; and again at the Chicago offices of *Playboy,* where after a fight with a girl friend, he heaved a telephone with a six foot long chord at a picture window that was eight feet away.

It was man versus machine, and the machine inevitably lost the battle; at Time-Life, he used his heavy, steel-toed shit-kicker boots and a baseball bat to demolish the Coke machine. Thompson was always unpredictably moody. He didn't shift emotional gears smoothly. There seemed to be a volcanic force inside, one that he could not always channel appropriately. Luckily for him and those around him, it was usually an inanimate object that caught his wrath. His acts of destruction invariably seemed to catch those around him by total surprise—and that seems to be the key.

Other employment was available. Floyd Smith and Paul Semonin were sharing an apartment with Smith's sister, who worked in advertising and knew of an opening at their office. F. Scott Fitzgerald had done copywriting, and had received praise and a bonus for his jingle for an Iowa dry cleaner: "We Keep You Clean in Muscatine." Thompson decided to interview.

He wore his normal uniform for that time period—coat and tie, Kaywoodie Briar pipe—as he took his résumé to the hiring manager. The advertising executive was impressed. He reconfirmed Thompson's age—"Just turned twenty-one?"—and went on to exude: "A man who has accomplished so much in such a short period of time! I am truly impressed. Truly impressed." Then, looking once again at Thompson's résumé, he made a suggestion. "Mr. Thompson, I want to offer you a job, but with one consideration. What I'd like to do is to get you to steer your creativity into the area of fiction. What do you think of that?"

"Hunter couldn't contain himself anymore," Floyd Smith recounted. "At the man's job offer, Hunter jumped up out of his seat, chortling, 'Goddamn, goddamn, man! Fiction? What the hell do you think you have in your hands?' " Smith added, "With Hunter, a good laugh was always more important than a job."

Most of Thompson's nights—or early mornings—were spent reading. Always the nocturne, while Gonzo journalism evolved, New York slept. "Hunter liked talking about literature," Floyd Smith observed. "He had a less disciplined approach to it, but was probably better read than any of us. Philosophically, I always felt that he was firmly based in the stoicism of Hemingway and the hedonism of Fitzgerald. Also, the romanticism of Fitzgerald to an extent, because as a young man then and in Louisville, he was quite a romantic."

Gene McGarr, a Time-Life co-worker, had an insight into Hunter's literary interests. He said that Thompson had read all of Fitzgerald, and was enthralled with *The Sound and the Fury.* "He was trying his damnedest," McGarr observed, "to perfect his style. Ultimately, he did—it was himself, writing just as he speaks. But at that point, he wanted very much to be a great fiction writer. He felt stuck in journalism."

Floyd Smith talked more about the times in New York: "We'd sit around in black turtlenecks, in his basement with the bed behind the furnace. Have little parties. Drink beer. Go down to the White Horse bar on Hudson Street and look for Dylan Thomas. And Hunter had a social life; he had two or three girlfriends and was obviously sleeping with one or two of them. The ladies have always liked Hunter. He has had no problem with them. He was not your typical 'hanging out with the ladies' kind of guy. I thought he was somewhat indifferent to them in a way, but he liked them back, too. We weren't as sterile and impotent as people think we were back in the '50s."

Porter Bibb introduced Thompson to a whole new group of people, and it started at the wood-paneled Yale Club bar. It was in the same bar that 22-year-old F. Scott Fitzgerald had threatened suicide by attempting to jump from the French windows. "Hunter, Paul Semonin, and I sat there getting very sloshed in the big lounge of the Yale Club," Bibb said. "They were both consumed by this girl. I guess she was Paul's girl, but Hunter was enamored of her as well. For lots of different reasons—mostly competitive reasons—I had to find out who this was. I ultimately married her about three months later.

"Her name was Diti Walker," Bibb continued. "She lived with a bunch of people in an apartment building at Eighty-eighth Street and Columbus that had been the Russian consulate building. She introduced the three of us to things that I had never heard of, and I am pretty sure were new to Hunter. This was the world of pot smoking, bebop jazz, the whole Kerouac kind of world. Diti was into Wilhelm Reich and had an orgone box." Quite faddish at the time, this was a wood-and-metal cubicle to sit in and capture one's orgone energy. The troubled psychiatrist Wilhelm Reich thought the box could serve as a cure for many ailments.

The group would stay up all night, smoke dope, drink all day, and discuss the undiscussible. "Until that time, I had never had a serious discussion about an orgone box," Bibb said. "This was a revelation. I think Hunter and Paul were too cool to be as shocked as I was, but underneath we were all both shocked and enamored of it all."

The times they were a-changing. For the first time ever, Floyd Smith saw someone smoke marijuana. He reacted sharply: "At that time, I considered anything to do with marijuana a hanging crime." There was a hint of subversion in the air, too, as one of the group, Smith recalled, "went off to Cuba to fight a revolution. Wait ... I don't know. ... I think he just went down there to score some dope." Little did any of Thompson's group realize that in just a few more years "to score some dope" *meant* fighting a revolution.

For Thompson, a view of the future came when a friend, John Clancey, invited him to a Columbia Law School speech in early 1958. The speaker was Thurgood Marshall, then head of the NAACP legal staff. The audience was lily-white. The speech was filled with warnings that change was in process and the audience should get ready. After his address, Marshall, a naturally imposing man, draped himself across the podium and waved a beckoning hand to the audience. "Now ask me some questions," he said. "Ask me some really tough questions."

Thompson did not ask any questions, but was thoroughly impressed. Here was a true underdog of society speaking to the best and the brightest—on his own terms.

Even before being fired from Time-Life, Thompson complained of having too much time off. Now that he had loads of free time, he read constantly. F. Scott Fitzgerald and, to a lesser degree, William Faulkner, became his guiding lights.

When Hunter was in New York, William Faulkner went to the University of Virginia, where Henry Preston attended classes. But Hunter never made the road trip to Charlottesville to see his literary idol for himself.

"I remember we always used to talk about 'Barn Burning,' and about 'Winter Dreams.' Paul Semonin introduced him to that," said Floyd Smith.

Faulkner wrote "Barn Burning" in the year after Hunter was born, and it won the O. Henry Award as the year's best short story. In part, it is about caste-like class differences in the post–Civil War South. A main character is a white sharecropper with a premeditated mission to vent his great volcanoes of enmity against Southern gentility. It tells of a family's futile attempts to control a man driven to avenge his sense of injustice against Southern aristocracy by burning down their barns.

The hero glows with hatred. At the opening, a justice of the peace orders him to leave town. In one vivid scene, Ab Snopes, the sharecropper, and his son "Colonel" visit their employer's mansion: "Big as a courthouse. Safe from him. People . . . a part of this peace and dignity . . . beyond his touch . . . barns and stable and cribs . . . impervious to the puny flames he might contrive." Uninvited, Snopes stomps past the butler and into the house. On the way, he has purposely stepped in a pile of horse manure. He proceeds to tread across an expensive French rug, his foot "leaving a final and fading smear."

The Southern aristocrat—Major de Spain—demands the carpet be thoroughly cleaned. It is not, and the feud cranks up. Ab Snopes's pay is docked. The Major's barn is torched. Snopes is shot and killed. The story ends at dawn; it exudes a sense of social and personal alienation, and the need to go on alone. It speaks volumes on human loss, as the story is told from the point of view of Colonel who is entering manhood.

Fitzgerald's "Winter Dreams" also describes a loss, but a different kind. It is a story that Fitzgerald wrote for money after Zelda refused to marry him because he was broke. "Winter Dreams" tells of a young man, Dexter Green, who falls into a confused love with a wealthy Southern girl, then goes into the military "welcoming the liberation from webs of tangled emotions." After the service, Green moves East to New York, "where he had done so well that there were no barriers too high for him." The hero's sense of self mirrors Thompson's when he is described as "completely indifferent to popular opinion." As in many of Fitzgerald's works, the hero finds himself surrounded by the usual swirl of Yale graduates, where he tries—unsuccessfully—to make more money than they are making.

In the end, Dexter Green is emotionally crushed when he discovers his former love has opted for domesticity, and lost her beauty and spunk in the process. "Winter Dreams" leaves in its wake a sobered man with a sense of permanent psychological change. "The mysterious denials and prohibitions which life indulges" was Fitzgerald's own synopsis of the meaning of the piece. But for Thompson, the meaning was probably the loss of Louisville rather than of a woman; the loss of an irretrievable time he had wasted as an out-of-control adolescent, and a place that had changed forever.

A fascination with the 1920s seems tough to figure for someone living a few doors away from Norman Mailer, eating Henry Luce's rare roast beef, and smoking dope while discussing orgone boxes. But the perpetual Louisville attitude—its sense of celebration, the air of wealth, and the silent but deadly class system that Thompson was raised in—was a vestige of Fitzgerald's generation.

"A lot of us grew up in Louisville with a strong identity with Fitzgerald, the Lost Generation, and the '20s mentality," said Porter Bibb. "Louisville *was* a museum piece. It *was* caught in amber. A lot of us who had time to think about it really thought we were somewhere else, in another time. Or we certainly wanted to be." Many of the Athenaeum members—including Bibb—were quite serious about becoming writers, and looked to their Literary Association's more serious side.

"I thought that Hunter screwed up his early life to the point that becoming a writer was the only avenue for him. You don't have to have a college education to be a writer. You just have to write and be reasonably good. If the Athenaeum had had an invisible applause meter, Hunter's frequent expositions would have been the greatest crowd pleasers of his era. I always thought that Hunter had a genuine native streak of genius inside him as well as the dark side of the American culture that is in perfect sync with Fitzgerald."

Romancing the dollar, infatuation with extravagant automobiles, intensely ambivalent and thoroughly enraptured by the very rich, cutting alcohol consumption to only thirty beers a day to go on the wagon to write—this was Fitzgerald in the '20s. It was Thompson all his life. So, too, was Fitzgerald's sense of fantasy mixed with burlesque, his constant groping for that permeable membrane separating the real from the dream, and in his writings a synesthesia of the senses that predated the drug-induced hallucinations of the '60s.

Thompson would sit for hours reading and outlining *The Great Gatsby*. He typed long passages from the book, just to capture the feel. He wanted to understand intimately how *The Great Gatsby* ticked with such American precision. He made a three-page-long outline, and kept it folded carefully in his pocket. It would stay there for years. He would hang on to his carefully prepared document until the right time—*just* the right time—came along, and he would use the outline to help him update his version of the American Dream. That time would come, and he would be prepared. But first he needed a Zelda.

Sandra Dawn Conklin had come to New York City after graduating in 1959 from Goucher College in Towson, Maryland. Her parents had divorced before she left for college; her mother ran a travel agency in DeLand, Florida, her father remarried and was a successful businessman in Port Jefferson, New York. At college, Sandy was known as intelligent, articulate, and an independent thinker. She had a distinct reputation for keeping a tidy room, punctuality in changing from winter to spring clothing, being planful and organized in her coursework, and singing with the school's a capella group, The Reverend's Rebels. (Goucher College is just below the Mason-Dixon line, and was founded by a Methodist Minister.) Her degree from Goucher landed her a job in New York City as a secretary-receptionist at Nuclear Research Associates, a company that monitored underground explosions. Later, she worked for United Airlines.

Her roommate in New York, with whom Sandy had shared a suite at Goucher College, was the wife of Gene McGarr, who was working with Hunter at *Time*. Soon Sandra felt as if all the men she met in New York were from Louisville. Paul Semonin was the first, then Hunter. They all seemed to get along quite well, in a carefree, unattached sort of way. A mutual friend fixed her up with a blind date—someone studying English at Princeton. Sandy and her date had barely gotten past introductions when she found he was from Louisville, Kentucky. "Oh! Do you know Hunter Thompson?" she asked of Ralston Steenrod.

Hunter and Sandy began to date, but not before her friends first met and described Hunter to her, and warned Sandy against emotional involvement. He was a fascinating guy, they told her, one of a kind, energetic and outrageously entertaining in an un-housebroken sort of way. He was physically attractive, too, they concurred; but for God's sake, do not get involved. "To be in love with him," one close friend told Sandy, "would be sheer hell."

One hallmark of Sandy's character was her singleminded sense of determination; it bordered on stubbornness. Disregarding advance warnings, when Sandy first met Hunter, she fell in love with him. It was unrequited love, as Hunter kept her at an arm's length, emotionally, not wanting the responsibilities and dedication necessary for a long term relationship. Over time, Sandy's persistence maintained its power.

In the eyes of Hunter's crowd, she was no Zelda. First, she came across as quite sane. Everyone liked her. They found her good company, and an anchor of sorts, a steadying influence on Hunter. But given his larger-than-life presence, she was always simply with Hunter and was difficult to assess on her own. Porter Bibb's recollection of Sandy from that time was "What a really sweet girl. But what the hell is she doing with Hunter Thompson?" He, like others, perceived her as "sweet," "bland," "nurturing," "supporting," even, in the words of post-AA vocabulary, "enabling." "I haven't met that many of Hunter's women," Bibb went on, "but I have learned that he likes them that way—nesters."

Sandy was from a Southern family, having spent considerable time with her mother, a travel-agency owner from Deland, Florida. During college, she became reacquainted with her father. "There was some sort of bad blood between Sandy and her father," Gene McGarr said. "Hunter hated the very notion of her father, even though the two never met." Bad blood aside, Thompson and his friends would often find themselves in his future father-in-law's baronial Upper East Side apartment, drinking the man's 30-year-old Scotch.

Often after one of these parties, Thompson would go off and

commit crazy pranks. As Fitzgerald had done, one evening he jumped into the fountain at the Plaza Hotel, only to be tossed out by a foot patrolman who chided him that the water was filthy. The cop broke Thompson's bottle of Jack Daniel's, and told him to do whatever he wanted south of 57th Street, " 'cause that's where my beat stops."

McGarr was Thompson's favorite to play gags with. The two copyboys lived seven blocks apart; while Hunter was subterranean, McGarr lived at the top of a six-story apartment building with stairs like a ladder, so tough to climb he used to pitch quarters out the window and ask kids below to buy him cigarettes. They had an easygoing relationship, and when McGarr returned late one night and found a few Ballantine ales gone from the refrigerator, he figured Hunter had dropped over. The next morning he knew it for sure: his entire apartment building, from the old Chinese man down below to the little girl playing in the hallway on the fifth floor, had been traumatized.

"I got home after midnight," McGarr related. "Other than the missing beer, I knew nothing. The next morning, as I walked up the stairs, the Chinese man took one look at me and threw himself against the wall, shouting things I could not understand, and giving me the evil eye. When I said 'hello' to the girl playing on the fifth floor, her mother pounced on her and dragged her inside, locking the door with a bang." McGarr was being treated like a leper with open sores, and had not the slightest idea why.

Hunter had gone to call on McGarr and, finding an open door but no one home, proceeded to provide his own entertainment. Taking off his belt, he slapped the walls and floor repeatedly, the belt making a sound like pistol fire. After the mock whipping, Thompson began a terrible wailing that slowly tapered off in volume, then suddenly became a shout: "Oh God! Please, please, PLEASE! DO IT AGAIN!" And, of course, he would oblige. The one-man sadomasochism show went on until lights from every floor, including the next building, came on, heads popping out, yelling, "Stop that, you beast!" Finally the police stormed the narrow stairs; Thompson opened the door like a courtly Southerner, a magazine in his hand, asking what all the commotion was about. They searched the apartment. "No bodies, no marks," McGarr was told. But for the rest of his stay in the building, McGarr was treated badly by his neighbors.

"There was no way I could get revenge," McGarr expressed with dismay. "That is, until the night at Dirty Julius's Bar, when I started talking to the gay guy from Switzerland." The two went back to Hunter's grotto, where McGarr played an upright piano that Thompson had, and sang several rousing Irish drinking songs, aiming his baritone voice directly up the heating vent to the rest of the building till sounds of angry protest were heard. Then he left. While he never found out what happened to the Swiss, McGarr did appear at a court hearing and presented himself as a character witness for Hunter, disputing the vocal majority—all from Thompson's apartment building—who were present trying to lynch him. "There were dozens of people there, saying things like 'Your Honor, the man never sleeps . . . constant noise . . . shrieking sounds at 4 A.M. . . . parties constantly . . . We have wives and children and jobs,'" recalled McGarr, who told the Irish judge they both worked at Time-Life and led quite proper lives themselves; it must be someone else in the building causing all that commotion. "An extraordinarily entertaining guy" was McGarr's declaration of Thompson from the late '50s.

There were endless nights and early mornings when the two would roam New York, often with a gin bottle to fuel their adventures. McGarr spoke about one particular night when they were followed by a bum "who smelled so bad you could not stand to be downwind of him." The bum tracked them relentlessly, asking for a drink; the two refused, but finally rewarded his perseverance by making him lie down on the sidewalk, and pouring the gin into his mouth. "We just couldn't figure any way to give him a drink without touching him" was McGarr's explanation for this. Thompson poured some liquor into the bum's mouth while he lay on his back on a mat in front of the Savannah Club, a swank night spot. Then Thompson lost his accuracy, and added a dash of gin to the eyes. The man stormed to his feet, blinded, and proceeded to thrash his way into customers coming out the door of the club. Spewing gin and reeking of foulness, he scattered the partygoers like a blinded Frankenstein.

That particular night ended with the two of them, a few ounces of gin left, sitting on a bench in Washington Square in a gray dawn, watching people in full business uniform going to work. An old black man carrying overstuffed bags materialized from the crowd. He walked directly toward them, singing, "The shit rain's a-comin', the shit rain's gonna fall." "We looked at each other," McGarr said, "and we both whispered conspiratorially, 'He knows! He knows!'"

T he city pools were closed at night. But Thompson, McGarr, and their dates climbed the cyclone fence of the Leroy Street pool, a few blocks south of Sheridan Square, and proceeded to disrobe and dive in to cool off. Out of the dark, a few teens appeared and kicked their clothes into the water; Thompson chased them off. Within five minutes, reinforcements appeared. This was the turf of an Italian gang, and when ten returned, the four picked up their belongings and started to leave. "We looked at the fence, and it was suddenly filled with faces," McGarr said. They took their dates and catapulted them over another part of the fence, telling them to run to Seventh Avenue and find a cop. "Then the fight began." The last McGarr could recall was "a guy in front of me, my ears ringing terribly. . . . I could not raise my arms, I was so weak from fighting. The guy had a stick, and broke it over my head."

When he regained consciousness, the police had run off the locals; McGarr found Thompson in a fetal position, covered with blood. The two were taken to St. Luke's-in-the-Fields Hospital. They were such bloody pulps that the staff placed them in a tiled room with a drain at the center and hosed them off; only then could their injuries be located. Concerned about possible brain damage, the staff wanted to keep Thompson overnight. He refused. The police asked if they wanted to press charges. After realizing that if they did, there could be more ugly retaliation, they declined. Both McGarr and Thompson were soon on their way out of the urban jungle, and McGarr clearly recalled that "after that gang fight, Hunter took to carrying a lead pipe."

Thompson left Time-Life and took a position where he could actually write—as a reporter for the Middletown, New York, *Daily Record.* Before he left, he had some friends over to the black grotto and, during the event, unleashed a series of creative gestures the likes of which his friends had never previously experienced.

"It was not unusual to be sitting around with Hunter," McGarr said, "and for him suddenly to let out a whoop or an Indian shriek, and take whatever was in his hands and throw it at the ceiling. He got into a tiff with Clancey once, when he broke John's favorite coffee mug."

On a cold February night of 1959, Thompson's apartment was baking, and after a few drinks, so was Hunter. He went into the kitchen area and came out with a large bag of flour. He began an unusual dance. It started with a little hop-step—a Kentucky jig, perhaps—while he held the sack of flour in front of him like a precious icon, muttering something and tapping it rhythmically: a flour-drum song. As his hops turned into leaps, his sack of flour became an active volcano.

The more he danced, the more the flour spilled out, over drinks, people, and the walls, until the once-black room looked as if a snowstorm had swept through. "I think he was anointing the place, or cleansing it of his sins" was McGarr's assessment.

The party was just beginning. Going out to the street, past the flames from the huge furnace doing their own macabre dance against the coal-black walls, Hunter stumbled over a large sack of lye. He announced to the group in his typical declarative monotone, "I *must* have this bag. It may be important." His friends knew when to leave well enough alone. The four of them stumbled out into the freezing night air. Thompson led the small group, wearing a dark, flour-dusted trench coat with epaulets, an eighty-pound sack over his shoulder.

Across the street from the Riviera Bar, a tiny, popular, packed watering hole for navy-blue-suited professionals, Thompson abruptly stopped. With his free hand, he pointed to the front door of the little place, and said, "Stamps. I need stamps." No amount of logic would keep him from his assigned mission, but at least McGarr had the presence of mind to remove all valuable objects, and leave them in the safeguard of their dates.

Somehow the two did manage to get from the tiny front door to the bar at the back, where the room widened out. The bartender looked angrily at the small white cloud rising from the lump of lye that had just been flopped on his tabletop, and said, "You can't do that." "What do you mean, 'I can't do that'—give us some beer," Thompson said.

At that time, McGarr saw two men he described as "middleweights—maybe bigger" coming toward them. Thirst was forgotten, but the bag of lye was not. Still complaining about poor service, McGarr dragged Thompson and his bag away. They struggled through an increasingly angry crowd, who suddenly came alive as the bag split wider and wider, spewing plumes of noxious white powder. Voices boiled, tables toppled, and navy-blue suits turned sky-blue; the cramped bar looked like a bad day in a bakery. The two were pushed and shoved toward the narrow opening onto the street amidst yells of "Get out of here, you idiots!" As the sanctuary of the cold outside seemed nearly within their grasp, a bouncer appeared, saying to the crowd, "Now just form a circle for us," and began punching it out with Thompson. The entire bar was filled with a cloud of white, the powder beginning to form residue on people's Scotch-and-waters. McGarr wrestled Thompson away from the monstrous bouncer, and launched the two of them against the front door. From across the street, when the door blew open, it looked as if a huge cannon had gone off: a sudden vomiting of great billows of white powder, a shaft of light, and then flailing arms and legs.

They managed to escape relatively intact. Later that night, when they were licking their wounds at a place called The Kettle of Fish, an old black man came up to Thompson. He handed him one of the epaulets that had been ripped off his overcoat in the fight in the Riviera, and said, "That was the greatest show I've ever seen." McGarr wasn't sure whether it was the same black man the two encountered in the gray dawn of Washington Square; regardless, the man's prophecy seemed to have come true.

The Middletown *Daily Record* was the first daily in the world to have offset printing, and around *Time* magazine many spoke frequently of "the experiment in Middletown." Thompson was hired as a general reporter and carried a camera for possible newsworthy shots. He lasted long enough to make a couple of lasting impressions, then took the fatherly advice of his boss, editor Al Romm, and headed out into the world for more experience.

In Middletown, Thompson shared lodgings with other young reporters, including photographer Bob Bone, who remembers being pulled out of a deep sleep one night by noises Thompson was making. Many people snore loudly while asleep. Some even talk. Hunter Thompson was the only person Bob Bone ever heard laugh heartily while sleeping. "He woke me up, then I woke him up. It was quite peculiar, but it was Hunter. He told me he was laughing at a dream he was having: several cretins dressed in black leather were coming out of the New York subway at rush hour. They all had bullwhips, and were lashing the commuters into a panic. He thought it was the greatest scene imaginable."

Another of Thompson's nocturnal escapades involved the syndicated *New York Times* columnist, James Reston. Thompson was fascinated by the man who turned out a 700-word-a-day column and often went where no other columnists had ever gone. Reston's scoops included the Dumbarton Oaks and Yalta Conference papers, and Stalin's last public statement—a letter to Reston. He was not so much a cut above, but a cut to the side—different, unpredictable, and always enjoyable. He ate Chou En-lai's lotus leaves, reported on his own acupuncture appendectomy while on tour in China, and created a talking computer, Uniquak, as a gimmick to dissect Eisenhower's long-winded speeches. Other reporters were envious of his ability to get the insider's insider report, the "bar talk," and have it put in print. Reston worked his staff like a baseball manager, picking the best: David Halberstam, Russell Baker, Tom Wicker, and Tony Lukas. And, indirectly, Hunter Thompson.

"Hunter was always going on about how he could get in contact with people in power if he was just tenacious enough," Bone recalled. Near midnight, with a handful of other reporters challenging him, goading him on, Thompson began working the phone lines. After an hour of calls, Hunter found himself ear-to-ear with his journalistic muse; he had James Reston on the phone. "We were all amazed," Bone said, "but Hunter was the most amazed of all. He didn't know what to say. He just hung up."

Bone left the *Record* to work on a financial magazine in Rio de Janeiro; Hunter would hook up with him later. Before Bone left, Hunter was asked to leave. The *Record* had a candy machine, and when Hunter put in his nickel for a Three Musketeers, he got nothing. Management had always criticized him for wearing tennis shoes to work, then removing them and walking around barefooted. The day of the candy machine episode, he still had his shoes on, and proceeded to kick the daylights out of the metal dispenser. Suddenly there was a cascade of sweets as all the candy bars let go at once. Hunter took only one, but Al Romm came in later to find the rest of the office helping themselves.

"You have got more than your share of idiosyncrasies," Romm said to Hunter after the candy machine incident. "Other writers have earned their right to be idiosyncratic—you are being idiosyncratic without any backup. Go earn the right to be flaky!" Romm felt he was seriously giving good advice. His description of Hunter was that "for a tyro, he was pretty good."

Out of a job, Thompson rented a small cabin in the woods near Middletown, and grew a beard. Many who knew him thought this a Hemingway-like affectation. Bone defended him, saying that if he claimed he was going to be a great writer, it really didn't matter if he started with the life-style, then worked his way into the material.

In the late fall of 1959, Thompson and Paul Semonin responded to an ad for writers on a start-up newspaper. It was called *El Esportivo*. It focused on bowling, and it offered positions in Puerto Rico. The weather was turning cold in New York. Thompson and Semonin ended up in a bungalow near beautiful Luquillo Beach, a four-mile-long stretch of palm-studded tranquillity just east of San Juan. The neighborhood was called Loiza Aldea; Thompson liked it because of the animistic practices of the locals.

The relationship between Hunter and Sandy had continued, and Hunter had continued to keep the determined Sandy at bay. Only rarely did he allow his softer emotions to show through to even those who knew him well. On one occasion, in discussing with friends John Donne's *Devotions XVII* (from which Hemingway took the title *For Whom the Bell Tolls*), Hunter expressed a deep sense of human connectedness while reading the passage that contains the phrases "no man is an island." Many of his friends who were surprised at this were even more taken aback when he showed them his own poetry. Written as an ode to Sandy, he described her as "my little flower of love."

Both Hunter and Paul Semonin thought that Sandy was coming from New York to be with him. She ended up with Hunter, and Semonin described the two as "very much in love." Semonin ultimately left them, to spend time in London with Porter Bibb, then took a Master's degree in Political Science from the University of Ghana.

El Esportivo was intended to be a weekly supplement to the San Juan *Star,* an English language paper, the brainchild of William Dorvillier. As editor of the *Star,* Dorvillier had been involved with the Puerto Rican publishing world since 1940. Thompson's immediate boss was a thirty-one-year-old writer, William Kennedy, who had gone to Puerto Rico in 1956 to work for Dorvillier on another project. Kennedy and Thompson would both become contributors to the *National Observer.* Dorvillier would go on to win the Pulitzer Prize in 1961 for his editorial writing on the separation of church and state; Kennedy would win the 1984 Pulitzer Prize for fiction.

It seems that Thompson made some impression on Kennedy; his characters Legs Diamond and Bailey have much in common with Thompson. In 1992, Kennedy recalled of that time, "I remember seeing a few issues of *El Sportivo,* but I am not even sure if it was in English, Spanish, or both."

Thompson liked the location of his bungalow because Caribbean voodoo was performed here. In fact, Hunter tried a little magic of his own. After a game of touch football on the beach, he, Paul Semonin, and another *Star* employee, Ted Klemens, went to eat at a place Hunter frequented. At the end of the meal, Thompson bellowed out to the waiter, "Put this on my tab," and they all walked out, only to be confronted by the owner, who stated there was no such tab. After a fruitless search through the bungalow for a ten-dollar bill, Thompson decided to deal with the matter by simply avoiding the restaurant. The owner called the police, and all three were tossed into the San Juan jail overnight.

The newspaper job never materialized, and after spending his last dollar for food and drink while writing sections of what was to become *Rum Diary,* he, Sandy, and Paul Semonin got free passage by crewing on a sailboat, but got only as far as Bermuda. While the venture had begun aboard a boat named "Fat City" it was the shipwrecked character of the trio that attracted a front page article in the Bermuda *Royal Gazette Weekly,* in July 1960. Their plight in paradise was summed up by Semonin, who told the newspaper that this free-form mode of traveling was educational. "Why settle down so early in life? . . . There is meaning somehow in all this, but right now it's a little hard to find."

Gene McGarr was studying in Germany on a Rhodes scholarship when a telegram arrived. "Hunter said he and Sandy were literally living in a cave, and eating cabbages they'd steal from people's gardens," McGarr said. "I wired them a hundred and fifty dollars; they got to New York, but when I tried to get my money back, Hunter was off to the West Coast. He still owes me."

Sandy stayed with Hunter long past the brief stint in Puerto Rico and the circuitous return to the States. A new decade required a change of scenery for Thompson, and Sandy would join him once he figured out where the next font of inspiration was. Back in New York, the direction signs were in place; one could see them right down from Perry Street, at the White Horse, and at the Cedar bar. All signs pointed west.

In 1960, Dennis Murphy's book *The Sergeant* had become a best-seller. However, Murphy had lost most of his book earnings at the blackjack tables in Reno, and was now spending time in New York awaiting the sale of the film rights for which he had written the screenplay; Rod Steiger would play the leading role. "My editor at Viking was Malcolm Cowley—Kerouac's editor. Jack and I were introduced and hit it off well," said Murphy. "We would go from the White Horse to the Cedar to Googie's to the San

Remo. We would roll into the bar, have a few drinks, then Kerouac would pull out my latest reviews. He kept them stuffed inside the pocket of his coat. He'd begin to read them to the entire bar. Real loud!" Kerouac was contagiously gregarious when he drank mildly, and for a brief time he and Murphy were the best of buddies.

Murphy lived in Big Sur. Henry Miller lived in Big Sur. In the March, 1960, *Life* magazine, there was a feature on the area, with a photo of Miller and Murphy sitting together, looking out at a distant fog bank. The place beckoned to any artist, let alone a young writer with a personal sense of manifest destiny.

John Steinbeck was reaching his peak of popularity. Steinbeck was from Salinas, just inland from Monterey and north of Big Sur. He had been delivered by Dennis Murphy's grandfather. Dennis and his older brother, Michael, were used by Steinbeck as Cal and Aron Trask, the models for the Cain and Abel–like brothers in *East of Eden.* Thompson had read Steinbeck and Miller. After he read Dennis Murphy's *Sergeant,* he loaned it to Gene McGarr, saying they must seek out the author in California. McGarr was headed back to school; Thompson would have to go without him.

The area around Big Sur had long held a place in the minds of writers, poets, artists, and seekers. Robert Louis Stevenson marooned himself in Monterey in 1879. In 1910, Carmel had an international reputation as a "vortex of erotic erudition," and as a dynamo of creativity. It powered Jack London, "the progenitor of the red corpuscle in literature"; he would write, then search for abalone, and eat underdone duck while drinking martinis. At the same time, Upton Sinclair wrote there while living on nuts, zweiback, and fruit. The list of names of those who merely passed through forms a memorial to the arts in the twentieth century: Lincoln Steffens, Gertrude Stein, Alice B. Toklas, Carl Sandburg, Ansel Adams, Imogen Cunningham, Sinclair Lewis, and John Steinbeck.

An article on Big Sur had appeared in *Harper's.* The title alone guaranteed instant celebrity status: "The New Cult of Sex and Anarchy." It caught the spirit of Henry Miller, Dennis Murphy, John Steinbeck, anarchy, cheap wine, sex, fog, and the future, all packed on one tiny crumpled piece of forest sticking defiantly out into the Pacific. This dot on the map was the place to be. Thompson split the gas and the driving with Paul Semonin. The two took a "drive-away" red Pontiac across the country to Seattle, stopping at the Mormon Tabernacle in Salt Lake City to hear a campaign speech delivered by John F. Kennedy. The owner of the car was in Seattle; Semonin stayed there; Thompson hitchhiked south to Big Sur. When the two men headed west, Thompson left the directions to Big Sur with Sandy.

10.

New Cult,

Old Stuff

ver since some convicts blasted through the final curve in U.S. 1 in 1937, Big Sur has been known as *the* place to go to launder one's karma. Those who blazed the tortured, twisting asphalt trail that snakes its way through the fog were men with serious prison records, wearing horizontally striped uniforms with numbers on their

pockets. Their labor was supervised by mean-spirited wardens with itchy trigger fingers on big-bore guns. Many workers died in the effort. It comes, then, as no great surprise that there is a dark side to the legends of Big Sur, that in the years since it became accessible to the public there have been times when the laundry detergent ran short.

This fifty-mile stretch of crumpled rock, pine, and otter-studded primal drama is a long four-hour drive north from Los Angeles, and three hours south from San Francisco. It is isolated to the point of being insular; it is scenic to the point of incredulity. Its isolation has preserved its beauty.

It is a long-standing joke among people who live in the Big Sur area that while the rest of the world thinks of these fog-flocked mountains as an artist's colony or some form of community, there never really has been any gathering of truly great artists living here. But in the words of Dick Price—the late co-founder of Esalen Institute, the place that institutionalized the Human Potential Movement—"This place should be used as a buffet, a smorgasbord; experiment with what you eat. Select from the range of offerings. Out of that, get something tasty for yourself that you can take out of the place, something that only happens in this special place."

Thompson made his selections from the curious buffet of humanity that lived near him on the property of Slate's Hot Springs. The area then consisted of the natural hot sulphur springs and baths close to the ocean, and a jumble of old wooden convicts' shacks, log cabins, a house with an annex, and the lodge. They lay scattered among tall pines and fields of blazing yellow mustard and daisies, on a plateau two hundred feet above the booming surf. Thompson had been hired as a "caretaker" and guard of the "big house" by the owner, Murphy's grandmother, Bunny Murphy, in the winter of 1960–1961. Beginning in April 1961, Richard Price and Michael Murphy were breaking ground for new construction on the place. They planned to change the name—and the spirit—of Slate's Hot Springs to the Esalen Institute. The idea for the change was in a very embryonic stage—"just an idea," Murphy said. Hunter's job as caretaker was to guard the "big house," look over the grounds, and maintain law and order. Thompson's interpretation of the job involved cleaning up the reputation of the fabled hot sulphur springs; to bring them out of the age of West Coast bohemia, and into the Age of Aquarius. It was no easy task to scrub a legend off the map.

Good karma and bad karma: Big Sur is a land of contrast. The dark side of Big Sur during Thompson's two years there began with the tragic death of the wives of Dennis Murphy and Clifford Irving, who were then living on the Murphy family property at Slate's. While driving north to buy groceries, their car went off a cliff, killing both women and leaving Dennis with two daughters to raise.

In a cabin owned by San Francisco poet and City Lights Bookshop owner, Lawrence Ferlinghetti, Jack Kerouac suffered terribly from the delirium tremens. In his book *Big Sur* he wrote about the experience of the D.T.s as "a twisted feeling of no-more never-again, agh," and of being on the beach, seeing his "friend" the garter snake turn into "the evil serpent of Big Sur." His visit to Slate's was traumatic. He saw another evil omen, a dead otter, floating beyond the surf. Of the hot sulphur baths that Thompson had been hired to clean up, Kerouac was not impressed: ". . . the combination of the strange silent-watching fairy men, and the dead otter out there, and the spermatozoa in the pool makes me sick."

On a perfectly clear day, a psychology professor from the University of California at Santa Barbara was killed when a rock tore through the convertible top of his car while he was driving through Big Sur.

Dennis Murphy, no stranger to violence, was attacked by Jay Kipp, a local artist, and stabbed with a knife in the lodge. He was stabbed nine times, one wound barely missing his jugular vein.

Richard Farina, married to Joan Baez's sister Mimi, was killed in a motorcycle crash heading out of Big Sur to a book-signing party in Carmel: his book, *Been Down So Long It Looks Like Up To Me* had just been released.

Many years later, in 1985, after one of the periodic forest fires that have ravaged the area, Esalen co-founder Dick Price was killed by a huge rock unleashed by the burned-off undergrowth. Dennis Murphy, who knew the area intimately, said, "A huge boulder hit Price. Eleven tons. It crashed down when he was walking out in *my* canyon! They charted its path. It hit a grove of redwoods and one piece crucified him. That country is *cursed.* I knew it. Kerouac knew it. Hunter knew it."

The good karma: Big Sur bears no resemblance to anyplace else in the world. It has a climate all its own, a character of its own, and has always been populated by characters of its own. The ocean, the surf, the rocks, mountains, trees, fog, and sun all speak in unison. They communicate in primal tones of a grandeur of space, and of an articulate silence that implies immense knowledge.

> This place is a real menagerie, flavored with everything from bestiality to touch football. . . . The list of tenants reads something like this: one photographer, one bartender, one publisher, one carpenter, one writer, one fugitive, one metal sculptor, one Zen Buddhist, one physical culturist, one lawyer, and three people who simply defy description—sexually, socially, or any other way. There are two legitimate wives on the property; the other females are either mistresses, "companions," or hopeless losers. Until recently, the shining light of this community was Dennis Murphy, the novelist, whose grandmother owns the whole shebang. But when his book, *The Sergeant,* became a bestseller, he was hounded by people who would drive hundreds of miles to jabber at him and drink his liquor. After a few months of this, he moved up the coast to Monterey.   —*Rogue for Men,* JULY, 1961

This was Thompson's literary rendering of Big Sur; *he* was "the writer," John Clancey was "the lawyer," one of the "mistresses" was Sandy, and Joan Baez was one of the "companions." Thompson was also one of the people who had driven hundreds of miles to hound Dennis Murphy and drink his liquor: Michael Murphy's understanding was that Hunter came to Big Sur in search of Dennis, after being overwhelmed when reading *The Sergeant.* "Hunter definitely came out here in search of Denny," Michael Murphy said.

But Thompson and Dennis Murphy became good friends, so all the jabbering and liquor was forgotten. The *Rogue* article was Hunter's first piece published in a nationwide magazine, and its title told the story of what really intrigued him: "Big Sur: The Tropic of Henry Miller."

> When I hear the word CULTURE I reach for my revolver.
> —NOTICE WRITTEN IN COLORED CHALK OVER HENRY MILLER'S KITCHEN DOOR.

Before the time of Henry Miller, there never had been a colony at Big Sur, just people passing through. The bulk of the characters formed an endless line of unpublished poets, dropped-out English teachers, graduate students from Berkeley and Stanford, and some of what Aldous Huxley referred to as "fringe lunatic."

It was life in free-form, even when Miller lived here; nothing was ever adequately organized to be labeled a "cult." Before Esalen opened, the most complicated attempt at organization was during Hunter's stay; Jo Hudson (the "one metal sculptor"), Jenny and her brother Michael New, and Joan Baez built a trimaran that Jo Hudson launched and sailed to the South Pacific. Any sense of colony or cult left the area a few months before Thompson arrived: Henry Miller went to Europe, and never returned.

Instead of meeting Miller, Thompson met Miller's close friend and personal secretary, Emile White, who lived in one of the old convict's shacks just a stone's throw from Thompson and Sandy in the Big House annex. The two never got along, and Thompson described him in *Rogue* this way:

> People are always taking Emile White, publisher of the *Big Sur Guide,* for a hermit or a sex fiend; and Helmuth Dietjen, owner of the Big Sur Inn, looks more like a junkie than a lot of real hopheads. If you saw Nicholas Roosevelt, of the Oyster Bay Roosevelts, walking down the highway you might expect him to flag you down, wipe your windshield with an old handkerchief, and ask for a quarter. . . .

As Jeremy Wilson (the "one physical culturist") put it, the general reaction to the article was consistent with the sense that "Thompson's actions created an image some did not like." Even in his absence, Miller's name was enough to sell Thompson's article. Thompson was always keen-eyed to the commercial value of things, and he was not alone. When the *Rogue* article appeared, it carried a photo of Thompson, seated, feet up on a table, above the surf at Slate's. A coffee cup was in his grasp. If one looked closely, the word NEPENTHE could be read. In Greek, this means "banishing pain and sorrow." In Big Sur, it meant roughly the same. It was the name of the area's most popular bar, where if the effects of the liquor failed to banish pain and sorrow, the breathtaking view would. The owner, Bill Fassett, was at first angered that Hunter had stolen a mug. But after some deliberation, he decided it was good publicity. Eventually, he too jumped on the commercial bandwagon. He put up a high-powered telescope, trained it on Henry Miller's house across the canyon, and charged the public twenty-five cents a peep.

Miller's legacy loomed large when Thompson got to Big Sur; he was the lionized repatriated expatriot, the ultimate iconoclast, the champion of free love. In the decade of conformity and suburban torpor, his books *Tropic of Cancer* and *Tropic of Capricorn* were banned by the U.S. Post Office and Customs Departments. Consequently, everyone had read them. Miller's life-style during his sixteen years at Big Sur was another attention grabber, and was repeatedly making *Life* and *Time* magazines when Hunter worked for that organization as a copyboy. Miller had written about the life-style in his 1957 book, *Big Sur and the Oranges of Hieronymus Bosch.* Miller's books sold well in Europe, but he could not figure out a way to get his royalties into the United States, and consequently lived in near poverty. He composed and sent to many of his friends an "Open letter to all and sundry," which was reprinted in part in the *New Republic,* offering to barter his watercolors for food and clothing. He included his measurements, and added, "Love corduroys." The donations streamed in. So, too, the people.

When Allen Ginsberg wrote Miller asking if he could visit, Miller wrote back, "Dear Friend—Please do not drop in." Ginsberg did not, nor did Kerouac. Ferlinghetti did use a line from one of Miller's books for the title, *A Coney Island of the Mind.* But these three may have been the only ones to "not drop in." Droves of seekers—early groupies—would appear at Miller's shack's doorstep, bring their offerings, and often state that they came "to join the cult of sex and anarchy." When Miller told them that no such cult existed, they would pull out the aging *Harper's* article and unfold it as proof.

Even before Thompson arrived, the list of characters populating the area did, as Hunter put it, "simply defy description—sexually, socially, or any other way." An amateur anthropologist was constantly running naked in the canyons. A physicist from Berkeley would dance to the music from Miller's hand-cranked Victrola clad in just his blue-and-gold University of California jockstrap. A Henry James scholar lived in a tent with his wife and children, and played the violin while cooking penguin for dinner (". . . a delicious meal," Miller noted). A former actor burst into Miller's shack at 2 A.M., grabbed the author by the throat demanding to know where the music from Beethoven's Fifth Symphony was coming from. "God," Miller explained, and the man away into the night convulsed in laughter. Flying saucers were reported. A European concert pianist would perform in a convict's shack so close to the road that drivers would stop to listen.

Thompson may have written about people going out of their way to badger Dennis Murphy, and he certainly was aware of all the people streaming through Big Sur in search of Henry Miller. But he was fascinated with how this "celebrity thing" was played out; he wanted some of what they had, and he wanted it badly. He craved their kind of status.

"Hunter never actually met Henry Miller," said Floyd Smith, who visited Big Sur in the early '60s. "But Sandy had a good friend who was house sitting [convict-shack sitting] for Miller when he went to Europe. Hunter would go over, just to soak up the 'essence.' " Smith also stated that Hunter "admired very much the style with which Henry Miller kept himself clothed and fed. All these people from all over the world would show up on his doorstep. With gifts! Thompson thought that was really the way to go, the way it should be."

Thompson once stopped Emile White returning from the mailbox, heavily loaded with Miller's correspondence. He asked White if Miller had much trouble with uninvited guests. The point that Thompson conveyed clearly to White was that "when he became famous, he didn't want to put up with a lot of disturbance of that sort." White was too shocked to answer; it was the end of June, 1961, and in the first week after the U.S. Post Office Department allowed Grove Press to publish *Tropic of Cancer*, it had sold 68,000 copies. Thompson's article in *Rogue* had yet to appear.

"Sandy was always saying to me that Hunter was going to be a great writer" was the amazed recollection of Dennis Murphy, who knew Hunter from touch football matches on the lawn, and good Irish social drinking at night. He didn't know if Hunter could spell; it was just not part of the relationship, and that made Sandy's comments seem all the more off-the-wall to him. One day when most of the group was working on the trimaran, Dennis sneaked into Thompson's room in the annex of the Big House. What he found stunned him: a thoroughly annotated copy of *The Sergeant* and the beginnings of *Rum Diary*. "Hunter had studied my book like a Bible, and I didn't even know he had a copy," Murphy recalled with lingering amazement. "He had taken it apart sentence by sentence, underlining, marking in the margins with questions and comments like 'notice how this character is introduced,' 'this is a good idea to fit these pieces together.' He had studied it and never said anything to me! And as for *Rum Diary*, when I saw some of the vivid scenery from his times in Puerto Rico, I knew he had the makings of a writer."

To those who were around Slate's more often than Dennis, Thompson was seen clearly as a struggling writer. "He was totally determined to make it as a writer," said Jo Hudson. "Was there any question about it? No! And when he got an article rejected, it pissed him off. He would come back hard again." Hudson recalled Hunter's concerns about having his article published in *Rogue,* which was then a competitor to *Playboy.* "He hated *Rogue* and *Playboy.* He hated what they stood for. But they were number one paying magazines." The romance of the dollar won out over old Louisville sensibilities.

Hunter had different styles of interacting with people at Big Sur. He seemed to seethe with resentment toward Emile White, while getting along famously with Jo Hudson. The two men would pile into Jo's car at night, stick a couple of beers between their legs, and load up the back with their dogs and go deer hunting. "The Senseless Killers Club" was what some called it—running down deer blinded by Hudson's headlights on Route 1, or shooting wild boar that roamed the Santa Lucia Mountains. As Hudson told it, "Hunter was very impressed by macho animals. I don't know about people; I don't think he cared for macho people. But I had a whippet with nuts the size of cannonballs, a serious hunting dog. I also had a Doberman, and Hunter had a scraggly shepherd. He loved the Doberman breed—he raised them later, he loved their image so much. We'd go deer hunting at night quite often. Only got a few, but it was hilarious."

The two men and their dogs would cruise along the curves of Route 1 until a group of idly standing deer was spotted; the dogs would all fall out the car door on top of one another, in a howling furry jumble. Then the men drove after the pack as the whippet raced at forty miles an hour, nipping at the deers' legs. This was high sport to Thompson, who would tell his friends in Louisville of the life of the gentleman gamesman among the bohemian woods where, when hunger struck, he dispatched one of his many well-trained pedigrees to drag down a deer: venison for everyone! Thompson always had a way of embellishing. "I think out of fifty chases we only killed two deer; one of the two got spooked by the headlights, the dogs, and all, so that it ran right into the car and dropped dead in front of us" was the more accurate version given by Hudson. "And another thing," he added, "Hunter's dog was a mutt."

Joan Baez's kittens were also "mutts." But when Hunter, amidst a room crowded with poets, sculptors, and the ultimate singing pacifist, commanded the whippet to "get the cat," the results were shocking. The kitten's neck was snapped instantly—the dog was a trained killer. Hudson recalled the incident as analogous to shooting off a gun inside: "Joan would have a problem with *any* kind of aggression. With that, she was horrified. But she made no scene about it. It was a very, very awkward thing." Hunter's reaction was to shuffle off. He did not apologize. His impassive mask-like face showed no emotion at all. "He never did it again," Hudson said, "but it was like him to push people's buttons just to see what would happen."

Thompson's relationship with Baez, Hudson said, "was a little bit of a stature problem." Joan Baez was born into pacifism in the same degree that Thompson was born into a legacy of Kentucky feudal violence. Her father was an engineer who had left the Los Alamos atomic bomb project because of his deep Quaker beliefs. She had lived just blocks from Thompson in Greenwich Village, on Macdougal Street, but the two never met until after her arrival in the area around Christmas of 1960. Her move to the West Coast was simultaneous with the release of her first album, simply titled *Joan Baez.* It quickly became the number three album on the American charts.

At Slate's she lived with her boyfriend, a Harvard dropout, Michael New. Thompson's job gave him free room; Baez and New paid $35 a month rent for a one-room convict's cabin whose sewer system was constantly overflowing. Squishy wooden planks covered the walkway to the entrance. She stated she was so naïve at that time that when one of her concerts was said to be SRO, she had to ask someone what the initials meant.

If Thompson thought that Joan Baez was a barefooted poor flower child, the thought was banished during the summer of 1961. Needing a flashlight, Baez and New had driven into Monterey to a hardware store. It was closed for lunch. Instead, she went around the corner to a British Motors Distributor, wrote a check for $6,000, and drove back to the little wooden shack with the bad plumbing in a silver XK-E. None of this was lost on Thompson; nor were the sales of *Tropic of Cancer,* which he observed with care. While Emile White would return from the mailbox lugging bags of Miller's fan mail and royalty checks, Hunter found rejection slips. He was so broke that Sandy was frequently sent to San Francisco to work at a job for a while.

Hunter's duties as caretaker at Slate's were minimal, and the rent was free. Hunter would write all night, sleep late, then get up and walk out to greet the day on the covered porch connecting the Big House with the annex where he and Sandy lived. Hudson lived just opposite the Big House. He saw Sandy as "a delightful-looking gal," who would pass by every day walking barefooted through a field of flowers on her way down the hill to the baths. Hunter, on the other hand, had a different morning ritual. He would come outside, bang his head accidentally on the low roof, and shout "Son of a bitch!" Hudson observed that "the next day, and the next day—he would do it again. I never could understand how he could drive a motorcycle without killing himself."

Hunter was struggling to write, but enjoyed the place and the pace. In the late mornings, he could always be found basking in the sun on a magnificent rocky point that juts out over the Pacific. There he would drink his coffee in the NEPENTHE mug, and read *The New York Times.* Sandy would bring him a breakfast of bacon and eggs. He would read, eat, and drink. Then he would hoist his trusty .357 Magnum and blast an unsuspecting kelp bed. He did it on days with good news; he did it on days with bad. "He was a good shot," Hudson said. "He'd get those little seaweed balls that float, hit them three hundred yards out to sea."

There were the typical Thompson practical jokes, the stunts that no one could predict, some that only a few might think humorous. Thompson and Hudson had poached and killed a wild boar. They were nearly caught by the groundskeeper, but managed to escape by hiding up a tree, Thompson with a dead pig in one arm, a rifle in the other. The boar was eaten, but its inedible parts made a number of appearances of their own, some quite theatrical. Early in the morning, going to use the bathroom in the annex, Sandy lifted the cover of the toilet and, while turning to sit, saw something rather out of the ordinary. In the toilet bowl was the bloody, severed head of the wild pig. A while later, just a short time before the regular weekend invasion of the baths by dozens of gays from as far away as Los Angeles, the pig's head came again, floating across one of the regal old lion's-paw tubs that had originally been in the San Francisco Palace Hotel.

The last part of the boar was presented to Alzie Webb, a woman who rented a part of the property from the Murphy brothers' grandmother. She ran a motel that catered to people using the baths, yet turned a blind eye to the specifics of what went on down the hill by the sulphur springs; she kept busy running Saturday night services of a branch of The Church of God of Prophecy, a branch of Jimmy Swaggart's Assemblies of God, with Fundamentalist hymn-singing and speaking in tongues. A devoutly religious woman, she got into her car one Sunday morning, looked in the rearview mirror, and found it adorned with pig testicles.

But not to think that Thompson was merely spending all of his time playing with the sex organs of a wild swine, or killing kittens, or wracked by the moral dilemma of having his first piece of serious literature published in a t-and-a magazine—he had a job as caretaker, and that meant responsibility.

"The very first night I went down to break ground and start the whole Esalen thing, it was quite late. I just went into the main bedroom in the Big House, and went to sleep," recalled Michael Murphy. "So there I was in bed—in *my* bed—and I looked up to find this very tall man, armed with a pistol, shining a flashlight in my face. This monstrous guy was standing over me and saying, 'Who are you? Who the hell are you?' And of course I was saying, 'Who are *you?* My grandmother owns this place!' 'How can I be sure?' he said back to me. And of course this was my first meeting with Hunter Thompson."

Murphy was there with Dick Price during June and July of that summer. Both were psychology graduates from Stanford, with a shared vision of how to make the world a slightly better place. Price had done graduate work in clinical psychology under Talcott Parsons at Harvard, while Murphy had spent a year and a half at the Sri Aurobindo ashram in India, studying spiritual transformation. Price had had personal experiences with psychosis and hospitalizations; his vision of the "new world" stressed a more therapeutic and clinical perspective, while Murphy's included the blending of Eastern and Western thought. Slate's Hot Springs was getting ready to bring heady solutions to a troubled world; Aldous Huxley, Alan Watts, Abraham Maslow, and Fritz Perls had received invitations and were headed toward Big Sur.

Neither Price nor Murphy had any place in their vision for the parking lot full of pink Cadillac convertibles that were beginning to converge on the baths every weekend. As Price had looked back on this strange collision course where weekend-long homosexual romps were smashing headfirst into their attempts to bring the world an expanded consciousness, he remembered, "We were not trying to pass judgment on anyone, but we couldn't have that going on and do what we were planning to do. So we would try and close down the baths at ten in the evening. You would go down there in the mornings and there would be broken beer bottles, chaos. We had to clear that out, gays or non-gays, if Michael and I were going to do anything about Esalen Institute. We put up a barbed-wire gate at the entrance. And Hunter, who had a lot of aggression and a lot of homophobia, would first try and explain in a very polite way that we had the lease now. We wanted to do something different."

The gathering of gays had gone from a couple of occasional

well-mannered visitors to a virtual turf battle. Hudson's view was that "Hunter thought they were invading his scene." Thompson would get theatrical about his nightly patrols, putting on his "shit-kicking boots" and wrapping a blackjack around his wrist with a lanyard and letting fly in a loud boom, "Let's go stomp those faggots!" Most often, his thunderous voice could be heard long before he ever descended to the area where the tubs and sunning tables were; anyone hearing him would grab his belongings and flee.

Thompson's first attempts, Hudson recalled, were quite diplomatic. "Hunter had this wonderful deal living here with Sandy. Living this kind of life, doing his writing, having the baths more or less to himself. He and John Clancey would go down there, sit up all night, and talk politics. Lionel Olay and Hunter would talk endlessly about literature. It was like an outdoor study. Now these guys started coming down. Hunter felt they were ruining his scene." The first tactic was for Hunter to go down to the baths with his little billy club, sit by the edge, and talk civilly to these people. "He wasn't too interested in what they had to say, though," Hudson went on. "He was playing these guys along. He would get just a little bit more obstinate with them. Then he would take his billy club and just start tapping them on the shoulder to emphasize his words." Thompson's words were that he did not appreciate the gays being down there. "It was not like 'I'm going to beat you motherfuckers up.' It was just this funny little intellectual game. And suddenly, they would realize: Who *is* this guy and what does he want with *me?* That was the strategy for several nights."

As time went on, the number of pink Cadillacs kept increasing, and Thompson did his part to enable the Human Potential Movement with even more violent tactics. Now the theatrics were something out of a cross between *Gunga Din* and a John Ford Western; at the top of the walkway leading down to the baths, he would fire his Magnum into the air a couple of times, bellow "Let's go stomp those fucking faggots," and descend on the baths with three or four madly snarling Doberman pinschers. "The Night of the Dobermans" is how locals recall it: a mad romp around the baths, maybe thirty or forty naked men doing whatever naked men who are willing to drive pink Cadillacs all the way from L.A. or San Francisco to Big Sur are prone to do. Suddenly, above the boom of the surf, above the riot of their own partying, came the sound of pistol shots, the voice of Hunter Thompson, and enough canine snarling to ice their blood.

As Thompson approached the baths, there was a mass exodus of frightened, partly clad partiers. The parking lot became a *son et lumière,* with flashing headlights and the squeal of tires. Thompson thought it a particularly effective night on the job.

The following night, Dick Price and Michael Murphy were having dinner with Alzie Webb in her end of the Big House. "An enormous stew, with beans and a salad," Murphy recalled. "It was beautiful. We had the house all to ourselves. Some friends were down. The night was gorgeous, even though this madness would reign outside by the baths." In the middle of dinner, Mrs. Webb burst in, hysterically upset, saying that there was a terrible fight going on between Hunter and the boys in the bath. Price volunteered to see what was going on. Through the window, Price caught view of Thompson dragging himself up the trail from the baths, shaking his fist wildly, shouting something that they could not quite hear. He was clearly in distress. Price decided to defer to the sensitivities of his guests, and pretended to look the other way. After all, this was Thompson's job.

"Hunter had come back here with Maxine, this huge lesbian friend of his from San Francisco. She used to let him drive an old Ford convertible she had. They had picked up a soldier hitchhiking from Fort Ord, and the three were going to soak," Hudson recounted, adding that there was a reason for calling the baths "the alligator pit." "They were laying for him. Heavy-duty guys. Hunter told me, 'It looked like the Olympic swim team.'" The soldier turned and disappeared. Maxine stood her ground, flailing into the men as they grabbed Thompson's billy club. They could not get it off his wrist; if they had, they would have beaten him to a pulp. Instead, they gang-tackled Thompson, picked him up off the ground, and were wrestling with him. They were trying to maneuver around and throw him off the cliff and onto the rocks, about eighty feet below. "A bone-crushing distance," Hudson confirmed.

Maxine was a large woman. She carried a large purse; were it not for a naked two-hundred-pound lesbian with a mean handbag, Hunter Thompson would have become shark bait at age twenty-four, with a Puerto Rican bowling magazine and one article in *Rogue* his only legacy.

Finding himself on the receiving end of a nasty mob by the edge of a swimming pool for the second time in as many years, Thompson stomped past the "big house," while Price, Murphy and their guests munched on their stew, and locked himself in his room. For the rest of the night he punctuated the silence of Big Sur with rifle shot fired through his unopened window. In the morning, Murphy looked out to find a horizontal line of bullet holes, and Thompson's clothes hung on the line. "They were stiff as a board with blood," Murphy said.

Big Sur was in a state of flux, and whether Thompson wanted to move on or not became a moot point. Someone sent a copy of the *Rogue* article to Murphy's grandmother in Salinas. She didn't like it at all. Bunny Murphy had hired Hunter; she might as well fire him. She was a force to reckon with. Aged eighty-six, she had a nose like a parrot, was one-eyed like a pirate, and rode in a long black Cadillac chauffeured by a mahogany-skinned Filipino. "She would not take shit off anybody" was her grandson's description. She rolled into Slate's one afternoon, buzzed down the electric window in the back of the limousine, and called for the caretaker. Thompson approached.

"Young man," she said, holding up the copy of *Rogue* with one hand, pointing a crooked finger at it with the other. "You have twenty-four hours to get out of here."

"What if I won't go?" Thompson inquired, not out of anger but from a state of disbelief.

"If you don't, then I will call the sheriff."

Thompson would not forget Big Sur. He would return over and over, but he would not stay. And neither would Big Sur forget Thompson. "He had a soft center that he never showed people," Jahn de Groot observed. "He blackened Sandy's eye a few times, and stole all my Revere ware," countered Shively Erway, bartender at the Nepenthe, who evidently forgot to inventory the famous missing coffee cup. "I always thought he was just silly" was Jo Hudson's take on Hunter in those years. "When he entered a room, all the men turned toward him; by the time he left the room, all the men tried to act just like him" was de Groot's assessment of the impact of Thompson's charismatic presence. But it was a trait that people could not take in large doses. "People were quite fond of Hunter, enjoyed him tremendously, thought he was a breath of fresh air and a stimulating guy to be around," said Floyd Smith, "but people really did not want him as a houseguest."

Mike Murphy missed Sandy and Hunter; after they left, it was different. He had seen Sandy as "very attractive, and very natural. Intelligent, but not an intellectual. A perfect figure, with lightly freckled face, and sandy-blond hair. I thought most clearly, 'My life is different from Hunter's, but to be taken care of by Sandy—that must be wonderful.' I missed them for that. And Hunter was enormous fun; making beer that exploded, always doing something different and unpredictable. I missed the both of them.''

In his expulsion from Big Sur, Thompson was cast out of a community of castaways; even with an international reputation as a pornographer, Henry Miller had been welcomed here with open arms. Thompson seemed to be taking iconoclasm to new heights.

In 1962, San Francisco was clearly where it was all going to happen, because it was beginning to happen. The philosophical and social ferment there was not a case of intellectual measles that every generation must go through. It was a genuine revolution, still in the vat, but brewing quickly.

San Francisco is an easy drive from Big Sur. You come out of the woods and fog just a few miles north of the Nepenthe. The road straightens out, cuts up the valley of produce farms past Gilroy and Morgan Hill, then passes by San Jose heading due north. In three hours you are in the City by the Bay. Thompson took longer; he took two years. He left behind his Nepenthe coffee cup, his Dobermans, and Sandy. He became the first person to go from Big Sur to San Francisco via Rio de Janeiro.

11.

The

Monkey Who

Couldn't

Say No

 n the midday sun of summer 1962, Copacabana Beach was a circus of Carioca hedonism as large throngs of people clad in tiny strips of cloth flew kites, kicked soccer balls, juggled fruit, drank beer, danced in the surf, and tanned their hides in preparation for Carnival. Regardless of the time of year, Rio is always getting ready for Carnival. Loping along in the sand, weav-

ing his way past groups of effervescent beachgoers, was a strange sight: a tall dark-haired man sporting several days' growth of beard, wearing the tattered rags of a shipwrecked sailor. He looked gaunt and bone-weary; instead of tanned, he was jaundiced. He wore oversized black pants, and his right pocket seemed stuffed to the brim.

Avenida Atlantica borders the beach. It is a long, wide, gently curving raceway with no traffic lights, where cars rocket by, making it exceedingly challenging for pedestrians to cross. Out of the speeding locomotive of traffic, an M.G. convertible suddenly jerked across all lanes and screeched to a halt in front of the tall scruffy figure with the baggy pocket. Bob Bone leaped from the M.G. and greeted Hunter Thompson fondly. Hunter promptly introduced Bone to the resident in his right pocket, an alcoholic monkey who had just thrown up.

Thompson apologized for the odor, then explained that he had picked up the little monkey as a traveling partner. When the two found themselves in a bar in Bolivia and low on cash, a man offered to buy Thompson a drink if he could buy the monkey a drink every time as well. Thompson got to drink as long as the monkey did. Monkeys' livers are the size of a lima bean, and he soon became dependent on alcohol, and would go through the D.T.s, thrashing wildly with clonic muscle jerks and a rolling of the eyes and foaming at the mouth when Hunter was broke and unable to drink. At times the scene was so pitiful that Thompson would buy the monkey a drink, and forgo his own.

Luckily, Hunter had adopted the monkey toward the end of his alcohol moratorium, a mandated on-the-wagon period that a physician in Ecuador had imposed after diagnosing Thompson's hepatitis. It had been a perilous and penniless four months getting to Rio, and it was accomplished only with unique skills and extraordinary traveling partners.

Bone had arrived months ahead of Thompson, and was working a full-time job as an editor for the magazine *Brazilian Business.* Hunter had reached Rio after months of traveling a rugged, dangerous off-track route from the Caribbean, through Colombia, Ecuador, Peru, and Bolivia. He was free-lancing, supporting himself entirely on payment for articles accepted. Hence his wardrobe, his beard, and his jaundice. Thompson did have a semi-official connection with one newspaper, and produced several articles that painted vivid pictures of the social and political conditions in South America. Just four years before, Vice-President Richard Nixon had been stoned by a snarling mob in Caracas, Venezuela; and just months before Thompson's arrival, *Life* magazine's cover article on Rio read SHOCKING POVERTY SPAWNS REDS. It was a time of social and political polarization when Latin governments, each in its own way, used the tall menace of Castro's power in Cuba to serve their own means. Communism became a one-size-fits-all tool for social pogroms and extracting monies from foreign governments—especially the U.S.—that were fearful of the spread of Communism to developing nations. It seemed the entire continent was vibrating with political ferment and instability—a perfect time to capture some sketches for another chapter in *Rum Diary,* and a fascinating period for a young, unfettered journalist with a rapidly growing interest in political maneuvering.

Latin America was incredibly inexpensive. Modest hotel rooms could be had for fifty cents in places like Quito and Guayaquil, Ecuador; in smaller towns, prices plummeted. In Rio on Copacabana Beach, the top-flight Hotel California's single-room rate was $5.50 a night. In large cities, meals might cost a dollar; beers were five cents. Thompson covered seaports, mountaintops, and Inca ruins before finally stumbling into Valhalla—the half-nude gaiety that is Rio. If he had pulled out all the stops, ordering French cheeses, Peking duck, and aged Scotch from midnight room service, and taken first-class trains, he could possibly have spent twenty dollars a day.

Before leaving the States, he had sent a letter to Clifford Ridley, the editor in charge of free-lance writers for the *Wall Street Journal's* newspaper, the *National Observer.* He stated he was a journalist with experience on the Middletown *Daily Record* and was headed to South America, and he included some clips of his writing. His letter was forgotten until he sent Ridley a piece on elections in Aruba. Before he could respond, Ridley received another piece, on hanging out among "reportedly savage Indians" whose business was to smuggle Scotch to Colombia's Guajira Peninsula. Thompson claimed that his drinking capacity and his "lifelong acquaintance" with Jacqueline Kennedy got him through the smuggler's initiation rites that involved consuming as much of the contraband as possible. "In the mornings, it was Scotch and arm wrestling; in the afternoons, Scotch and dominoes."

Ridley saw something interesting in these vivid, first-person glimpses into a life the average American could barely imagine.

He began paying $150 an article, but paid for no expenses: as a free-lancer, it was assumed that Thompson might be selling the same material, or variations on the theme, to others. He was. After visiting Barranquilla, Colombia, he told Ridley he would soon have "seen most of Colombia at close range. If nothing else, I will have a lot of photos and, hopefully, an immunity to dysentery, which is now on me in full force."

His home-town paper had last carried the name of Hunter Thompson when Judge Jull warned him ". . . you will be watched . . . until you are twenty-one. . . ." When the *Courier-Journal* bought Hunter's article about his days on a barge going up the Magdalena River toward Bogotá, he was twenty-five, and out of the reach of American justice. Thompson had parlayed his photography skills, sharpened while he was in the Air Force, into a letter from the barge owner to the captain. It stated Thompson was to ride first class, and free of charge. In return, Thompson would send pictures of the man's boat in action. In between photo sessions, Thompson dodged the heat and the rain, making a tent out of the tarpaulin covering the cargo. At the bow of the barge, Thompson set up shop, writing notes and watching as it chugged past towns steeped in history, filled with Spanish colonial architecture, with names like Zambrono, Pinto, and Mompós.

Taking a break from his writing, he would lean back and sample the cargo. It was a beer barge. He was clearly at ease, writing, "free ride, free beer, nice tan, plenty of rest." After fearing for his life among the Venezuelan Indians, he sat back and sucked up "a moment of peace in a life of madness." The only noise Thompson could hear above the screech of parrots and the bass-drum boom of the diesel was the hooting and banging of the deckhands: they had locked themselves belowdecks in the cargo hold with five thousand cases of Cerveza Aquila. Thompson drank alone.

Thompson had a way of burning his bridges just before he got to them; his relationship with the *National Observer* was nothing different. He became angered at the paper for not understanding his plight. "Poverty, dysentery, boredom" was Ridley's recollection of the mantra that Thompson would write to him. The image Thompson sent back, in a long series of letters to Ridley, was of a naked man living in a hollow tree with six porcupines, all foraging on unripe berries and heligomites found squirming under rocks.

True to form, Thompson complained in such exquisite and

lively prose that Ridley actually edited several of Thompson letters ("after removing material not suited for the average American family, and all the totally incoherent stuff") and printed it as an article that showed the other side of the formal dispatches. In the *National Observer,* Ridley recalled from the letters the central theme to Thompson's lifelong relationship with editors and publishers: He was perpetually broke and brazenly vocal. Everything Thompson had to say centered on money—or the lack of it. He told Ridley there seemed to be some universal assumption that he was on a "Divine Dole," thus rendering payment unnecessary. Sarcastically, he informed Ridley of his trust that the editor had an adequate background in personal economics to grasp the reality of his situation.

Despite indigence and a bad cold picked up in Bogotá, where his hotel had no hot water, Thompson reached Quito. He took the train to the port town of Guayaquil, a seventeen-hour, four-dollar expedition that scrapes its way over the Andes at an altitude of 11,841 feet, then cascades to the sea. Thompson called Ridley—it was the first time the two had ever spoken, and the air was cleared for a while. But not for long.

His hotels were never quiet, possibly because he was nocturnal and the rest of the world diurnal. Bells kept him awake; people kept him irritated; sickness and bugs kept him bilious.

In Guayaquil, Thompson told Ridley, he nearly went nuts. He was suffering the pains of dysentery while holed up in a cheap hotel next to a church, whose clanging bells repeatedly bounced him around the room like a Ping-Pong ball: a madman in the belfry, a growth in his gut. Still, he pressed on toward Rio.

In Bogotá, Thompson tried to find the former dictator Rojas Pinilla; he had received his share of publicity in 1957, when he had summarily executed all in attendance at a bullfight who would not rise and salute him. To Ridley, Thompson made the observation that Pinilla "is without a doubt the only dictator whose name is in the phone book in the capital city over which he once held sway. He lives in the best section of Bogotá."

More train trips, more dysentery and an eighteen-pound weight loss, bleak comments that "optimism is a rare commodity here," and "democracy is about as popular here as eating a live goldfish . . ." Thompson let loose with more pleas of poverty, yet added some vaulted self-praise. There seemed no other source.

Again he blasted Ridley, his sole source of funds, for not having received payment. Thompson spoke of himself as a fount of intelligence and vision, of bravery and diplomacy; he was also suffering his fourth bout of dysentery and described his stomach as feeling as if a tree were growing in it. There was more dire news: He had contacted hepatitis, and was ordered not to drink. On the wagon, on the dole, and immobilized by Montezuma's revenge, he wrote Ridley he could hear the jingle of the hotel's cash register ringing up another day's charge to "Señor Thompson, the gringo with the messy room."

In stumbling down to Rio, Thompson saw some eye-opening scenery, and not all of it was palatable to his sense of social justice. In Cali, Colombia, he had spent some time with an Englishman who amused himself by driving golf balls off the roof of his apartment in the general direction of the city's slum district. This hung tight in Thompson's mind, as did a scene at the Hotel Cuzco in Cuzco, Peru, where the waiters pulled down the blinds so that wealthy tourists eating dinner would not be offended by the impoverished Indians who came each evening to squat and watch them eat.

It was while in Cuzco, near the Incan ruins of Machu Picchu, that Thompson was stung by a poisonous insect. It paralyzed his leg. Undaunted, he used whatever money he had to take cortisone and antibiotics. Through the use of infrared lamps, he healed enough to use his camera tripod as a makeshift cane, and he caught the train to Rio.

No Orient Express, the narrow-gauge trains were made in Romania. The seats were straight-backed, and made of a spine-cracking wood. Each car had one room with two metal footpads over a hole in the floor for a toilet; the kitchen was right next to the rolling, clattering latrine, and skinned chickens and raw meat would lie for hours on the floor under a cloud of flies.

Thompson crossed the Bolivia-Brazil border at the tiny town of Puerto Suárez, Bolivia. This was true Butch and Sundance country, where the travel books of the time spoke of the town as "the ipecac center of the world" (a powerful medicinal emetic), a commodity that found a far greater need in other places. The train ride was prohibitively long and desperately slow, and Puerto Suárez itself was noted as "a place best avoided: it offers nothing to man but mosquitoes. There is a primitive hotel for the hapless traveller trapped there."

It was with relief that Hunter Thompson and his alcoholic monkey crossed the border and chugged full throttle toward São Paulo, then Rio. One can imagine him sprawled across a slivered wooden bench seat, his luggage propped for cushions, chaparral and bony cattle flying past the window, the fever of hepatitis now behind him. He would fumble for some change in the right country's currency, or perhaps just steal a beer when the bartender was looking the other way. One long draw for himself, one cupful for the monkey: a few more thousand trestles, and all this will be just another reason for night sweats and an occasional shriek. As he commented to Ridley he looked at the time spent traveling to Rio as an investment. He had struggled through the Third World countries, leaving so much of himself along the way that he'd decided to settle down once in Rio. He longed to live like a human being for a change, and to continue investigating his new world. He felt he'd be cheating himself if he were merely to breeze through.

Thompson lived in Rio first in the YMCA, a centrally located brick building filled with vagrants and worldly dropouts. It cost $6 a week. After receiving checks from the *National Observer,* and hooking up with Bob Bone, he moved into his own ninth-story apartment. He even had a maid—it cost about $50 a month for a three-room apartment two blocks off the beach. The maid service ran $12 a month; now Hunter could afford to be "Senhor Thompson with the messy room."

Thompson would screw up all his self-discipline, go visit an oil camp or get an introduction to a fourth-tier bureaucrat, and try to squeeze something newsworthy out of it. Especially in Brazil, it is more than who you know: it is who you are related to, and how much money you can give to the cause. A broke, unconnected gringo occupies the lowest tier of priorities for politicians in Brazil. Hunter was numb with boredom.

S oon after moving to the ninth-floor apartment, he and a Dutch stained-glass artist, Bob Goehrling, would go at dusk to a garbage dump inland from the beach, and shoot at rats. In Rio, the rats can weigh as much as a beagle, and carry diseases unknown to the medical community. It is a sight to see small children and old women wearing long leather boots, kicking the toothy rodents out of their way as they scramble over a mound of refuse the size of a small shopping mall in search of something edible or useful. And there would be Goehrling and Hunter, his .357 Magnum in hand, blasting away at the rats, shouting at the kids and women to stay clear of their fire.

This was no Big Sur; in a flash, the Rio police were on him, but not before he could hide his weapon. The police, perhaps bored themselves, wanted to interrogate Thompson. He was trundled into their tiny Volkswagen Beetle and hurried to headquarters. During the drive, and then while being questioned, the Rat Killer suddenly became the Southern Diplomat, cajoling, turning on the Thompson charm. Under the paternal gaze of framed photos of President Goulart and Pope John XXIII, Hunter thought he had these dime-store cops in the palm of his hand. He leaned back in his chair and put his feet on the desk. Everyone was having a fine time until a handful of .357 bullets poured out of his pocket and clattered across the floor. It then took real diplomatic intervention to extract him from jail.

It is doubtful that many Brazilians read Thompson's piece on their President in the *National Observer,* but if they did, few would have been pleased. He panned President Goulart, who, the year before, had unsuspectingly ascended from the Vice-Presidency when a military coup deposed President Quadros while Goulart was visiting Red China. Thompson referred to Goulart as "weak and hapless . . . a small-time politician who rode the greased rails of circumstance to the country's highest political office." While Thompson was showing himself to be no shrinking violet in speaking out on foreign officials, he predicted the future course of Brazilian politics by using an American-made crystal ball. He expected that a legitimate voting process would replace Goulart; instead, it was a massive, anti-Communist military coup, led by General Branco, an official not even mentioned by Thompson in a series of a half-dozen mini-portraits of potential successors.

Less than two weeks before the Kennedy assassination, Thompson reviewed a book written by one of his muses. J. P. Donleavy had followed up *The Ginger Man* with *A Singular Man,* and it spoke to Thompson directly. Perhaps both Donleavy and Thompson had changed over the years. Thompson referred to the impact of *The Ginger Man* as analogous to "being dragged into a beer-brawl in some violent Irish pub." But the new book hit him at a more surreal and cerebral level, "like sitting down to an evening of good whiskey and mad laughter in a rare conversation somewhere on the edge of reality."

In Donleavy's new book, he sketched a scene so bizarre that even Thompson appreciated it, and drew creative inspiration—of a perverse nature—from it. Thompson was fascinated that the hero of the book was, upon his death, to have all his money in small-denomination bills put in a steel receptacle a foot in diameter and six feet high. After considerable publicity, at midnight the public would be allowed to rush for the money, using only fishing poles and croquet mallets. The mad scene would be filmed for posterity. Thompson wrote that one might think only a madman would create a mob scene in downtown New York with his life's earnings, but that the man is perfectly sane, because "he simply is pathetically lonely, and what makes Mr. Donleavy a first-rate author is that he can write about loneliness with a deep and tough-minded compassion." He went on to discuss the promiscuous mistress and the hero with "weird, orgiastic habits," and sums it all up by saying, "That is what the book is about: Innocence and love and loneliness and dreams, and the madness of trying to preserve such fragile baggage in the great hustle of today's reality."

He ends with a description of his own sense of humor as living on the highest plateau, "where humor is forever at war with despair." Here lives fear, and here lives its neighbor, loathing. The two speak to each other through words of laughter.

Thompson moved out of his ninth-floor apartment, with the maid and the balcony view, and shared a place with Bob Bone before going back to the U.S. in the fall of 1963. One reason for the move was that Bone's apartment had a phone. This was a rare and wonderful commodity, as it often took months and stiff bribes to get one installed. Having a direct link with the outside world was a clear advantage for a free-lance writer.

Another factor played heavily in Thompson's move. Bone and Thompson returned to his apartment one afternoon to find the maid in a Portuguese frenzy, making the sign of the cross and pointing with clear desperation to the open-air balcony high above the busy street. The monkey was nowhere to be found. The bilingual explanation they pieced together from the distraught maid was that, wracked with an attack of delirium tremens, the monkey had taken things into his own furry little hands: he had leaped to his death off the balcony. The place was cursed; it was time to move.

Bone recalled the days in Rio with Hunter as a roommate, when he was sporadically pecking away at the mythical *Rum Diary* ("He'd tell me, 'You're in here somewhere, Bone, you're definitely in here somewhere . . .'"), and always trying to get something more than his link with the *National Observer,* even though Bone felt the $150 an article allowance was "very favorable." In February of 1963, Thompson was both enthralled and aghast when reporting on the Brazilian Army's shoot-up of a local club after its owner had killed a soldier for not paying his bill. While this kind of retrograde patriotism would seem to intrigue Thompson, in his piece "Brazilshooting" he deplored the whole of Latin America where when civil authority is weak and corrupt, the Army is King by default. He paraphrased George Orwell's saying "In the kingdom of the blind, the one-eyed man is king."

For Bone, this emotional amalgam of intrigue and outrage was at Thompson's core. "That was kind of a favorite theme of his, where powerful people had no regard for those without power. He was always semi-serious on these things. He wrote about things at one level, about how awful such things were. But I am sure he enjoyed it on a different level, because his whole idea of surprising people by violent events was always a big thing for him. That was a really amusing picture for him. It was one of the things that defined Hunter's character—the fact that he enjoyed that kind of thing. He was always principally amused with the idea of shaking people up. In fact, one of the things about having Hunter around your house was 'How long can the neighbors take it?' He had a way of baying at the moon and doing embarrassing things that might cause people to call the cops."

Bone went on to emphasize the gap between the man in the *National Observer,* and his roommate in the apartment overlooking the beach. "At that time, during the Rio days, Hunter talked a wild game, but he was writing pretty straight copy. He had to get published by the *National Observer* to pay the rent. But he discovered his success later when he began to write just like he talked."

Thompson said that the reasons for going back to the U.S. were that "Basically, Rio was the end of the foreign correspondent tour. I found myself at the point where I was twenty-five years old and wearing a white suit and rolling dice at the Domino Club—the foreign correspondents' club—and here I thought, 'Jesus Christ, what am I going to do now?' Then I would roll the dice more and more. And I wrote less and less, and worried about it until I'd have a nervous breakdown, or just the kind of thing I would have two or three times a month, and then go for years without its surfacing. It [the nervous breakdown] kinda makes you change whatever you are doing. So, I came back to the U.S. in a sort of frenzy of patriotism, Kennedy, Peace Corps. I was happy to get back here."

Other pressures worked to get Hunter back to civilization. Always marked by zealous singlemindedness, Sandy took the easy way south. With no warning, she flew down to Rio to sit on Hunter's doorstep. He was overwhelmed by the gutsy move. He was touched that she had adequate faith in him that he would take her in, and he did. But the two were cut off from friends, family, and the new decade. Further, Hunter could sell just so many articles on Brazilian topics. It was time to leave Rio.

"He appeared at the *National Observer* offices in Maryland, just outside Washington, D.C.," recalled Bob Semple. It was spring of 1963. It was the first time anyone there had ever laid eyes on him, and he looked just the way they expected: sunglasses, tropical shirt, and shorts. "He had this marvelous blonde with him. She was holding back a beautiful Doberman pinscher," Semple said.

It was Agar von Estobar on the leash, and Sandy Dawn Conklin Thompson holding him back. They had been married quietly across the river from Louisville, in a "marriage parlor" in Jeffersonville, Indiana. The quiet ceremony took place on Monday, May 20, 1963. Gerald Tyrrell and Jimmy Noonan, old Athenaeum friends, had visited with them the night before. They all met at Noonan's apartment, and Tyrrell recalled that Hunter was mumbling, often incoherently, and it was not due just to the effects of alcohol. His interpretation was that Hunter had brought back something organic from his trek across South America, and this was causing his thought and speech to become indecipherable. "He got married down here," Tyrrell said, "as a concession to his mother. I recall Sandy as a little blond-headed girl without much to say. But Hunter was really spaced out. He kept saying, 'Oh, yeah, yeah, you know, man. . . .' Everyone would nod sagely, but we did not know what the hell he was talking about. I was nodding, and going along with him, but I could not understand him."

With a head filled with strange chemicals, a beautiful blonde by his side, and Agar von Estobar as the best canine, Hunter Thompson glided over the threshold into matrimony that would last, in one form or another, until he filed for divorce in March, 1979. The *National Observer* began to pay his expenses for authorized articles, and he and Sandy roamed the country with abandon, sending in stories on a folk-music festival in Covington, Kentucky; visiting with the racehorse Kelso at Belmont Park; hitchhiking and getting paid for it (what would Kerouac have said?); a logging championship in Quincy, California; and setting up camp in Woody Creek, Colorado, where Thompson bought some property near Aspen, the town that Paul Semonin had stumbled upon in 1961. He did an article on the Aspen Institute for Humanistic Studies, a sort of Esalen in the Rockies, which was in his back yard. As Thompson said of journalism, "I have always looked at it as a way to get somebody else to pay for my continuing education."

Kennedy's assassination occurred just months after Thompson's return to the United States. American culture was never the same, and American students were waking up with a bang. A new word was beginning to be whispered; the term was "counterculture," and it came from the general direction of Berkeley.

Thompson and Sandy headed farther west to inspect the increasingly vocal next generation. Thompson was fast closing in on his twenty-seventh birthday, and on March 23, 1964, he fathered a child. When Sandy and Hunter and Agar went west, they took with them their own addition to the baby boom. The youngest Thompson's first name was Juan. His middle name was Fitzgerald.

12.

Never
Danced on
the Head of
a Pin

The Menace is loose again, the Hell's Angels, the hundred-carat headline, running fast and loud on the early morning freeway, low in the saddle, nobody smiles, jamming crazy through traffic and ninety miles an hour down the center stripe, missing by inches . . . like Genghis Khan on an iron horse, a monster steed with a fiery anus, flat out through the eye of a beer can and up your daughter's leg with no quarter asked and none given. . . .
—HUNTER S. THOMPSON, *Hell's Angels*

hompson had come to the San Francisco Bay area in search of the "counterculture," and he had stumbled upon it. He began by writing about the poetry scene in San Francisco. He was nostalgic for the old days when he would ride up from Big Sur to drink wine with Richard Brautigan, Jack Thibeau, and Gary Snyder. He missed the old times, and

lashed out about how it was being ruined by the influx of topless joints and tourist attractions.

The assassination of John Kennedy was the shot from the starter's gun for a yet undefined future. The Berkeley campus was a rumbling volcano whose eruption had been getting closer as each year passed. Nearly a year before the Free Speech Movement popped the cork on campus revolution, Thompson wrote about the "scene" in the San Francisco Bay area in his article "When the Beatniks Were Social Lions." He documented some of the sources of the magma that would soon erupt across the Bay at the University of California in Berkeley, saying that the time was ripe "for breaking loose from the old codes . . . and for doing everything possible to unnerve the Establishment."

Many of the more vocal and motivated students in the protests were not University of California students. This was an important fact to Thompson, never a full-time college student himself, yet always politically sensitive. He wrote about this phenomenon in *The Nation,* in the article "The Nonstudent Left." Its focus was recent legislation in California that precluded nonstudents from participating in political protests originating on the Berkeley campus. These political activities had quite recently shifted focus from free speech to the Vietnam War. The law was analogous to saying you can't watch the circus unless you already lived under the big top. The mentality behind the law, Thompson argued, was primitive and tragic, and a shining example of what the crisis at Cal was all about.

Thompson pointed to the mid-'60s level of paranoia, a state of mind that he was always attuned to like a dog to a whistle. He portrayed the establishment's view of the non-student left as "loping along midnight streets with bags of seditious leaflets . . . red banners of protest . . . cablegrams from Moscow, Peking, Havana."

Always a step ahead of the times, Thompson used a chapter from his own past as a "non-student" at Columbia University to explain *why* the majority of Berkeley protesters were not full-time students. The status of the non-student was the natural choice, he said from experience, for any bright kid who has the "wild feeling . . . that the major he's after is not on the [University's] list. Any list." Thus, the non-student becomes his own guidance counselor, and steps outside the system. There were thousands of them, Thompson wrote, drifting around looking for the right place to learn. They were like "an Army of Holden Caulfields looking for a home and beginning to suspect they may never find one." Thompson said of his personal adventures with this form of autodidactism, "I kinda played around with college and then I figured any more of this would be a negative. There is only so much to get out of it. There is only so much to learn—and that is *how* to learn."

Always driven by a sense of anger looking for an unsuspecting target, Thompson lashed out unmercifully at the hippie mentality and life-style in a *New York Times* Magazine article, "The Hashbury Is the Capital of the Hippies" in May 1967. Then, near the article's end, he waved his ambivalences at the readers, demonstrating his self-spoken psychological makeup as "partly hillbilly, partly Kentucky Gentleman." He vigorously scoffed at the hippies for moving from Berkeley to the Haight-Ashbury section of San Francisco ("from pragmatics to mysticism, from politics to dope, from the hang-ups of protest to the peaceful disengagement of love, nature and spontaneity"). He laid blame for this tidal change on two factors. First, the hippies were, by nature, lazy, apolitical, unmotivated by money, and totally lacking aggressiveness. The second reason for the change away from political activism was the reverence of the hippies for Dr. Timothy Leary and his role in the use of LSD. Thompson wandered the scene of the Haight-Ashbury, acting as an underworld *Fielding's Guide,* providing vicarious kicks and useful travel tips to the timid yet curious *New York Times* reader. At the top of his list was the scene in front of the "Drog Store," a gathering place not dissimilar during those times to the Jmma el Fina, the main marketplace and entertainment center in Marrakesh, Morocco. Anything could be purchased, everything could be seen; Thompson found a long-haired bongo player wearing "a spangled jacket that originally belonged to a drum major in the 1949 Rose Bowl parade . . . an all-star cast of freaks . . . twitching and babbling in time to the music . . ." and "a thin man with wild eyes who took an overdose of acid nine days ago and changed himself into a raven." Thompson went into great detail in his discussion of the effects of LSD as killing any spirit of activity, and replacing it with a dead zone of the mind. He wrote one line about the effects of the chemical that would, in twelve years, return to haunt him. At the time, it seemed an accurate take on the Haight-Ashbury form of "internal entertainment," where a $5 cap of LSD provided the user with his own hallucinatory command performance of "the Universal Symphony, with God singing solo and the Holy Ghost on drums."

Thompson stated, upon his return to the U.S. from Rio, that

he was filled with patriotism. Yet his sense of the future as being a better place did not coincide with the blind optimism of the hippie movement. He was too paranoid himself to allow the indulgence of letting go of the rudder of his ship of life; someone might take away his control. Thompson despised this goal-less group of hedonists who lived in a chemically induced state, and he spoke to *The New York Times* audience of the hazard of the widespread tendency "to mix two or three drugs at a time. Acid and alcohol can be a lethal combination. . . . The only way to write honestly about the scene," he explained, "is to be a part of it. If there is one quick truism about psychedelic drugs, it is that anyone who tries to write about them without firsthand experience is a fool and a fraud."

He went on to write that the orgies, drugs, and craziness were not confined to this colorful, demotivated ragtag band of latter-day bohemia; "the current Haight-Ashbury scene is only the orgiastic tip of a great psychedelic iceberg that is already drifting in the sea lanes of the Great Society." Thompson hinted that he had spent a great deal of time among the upwardly mobile professionals in the Bay area, and they consumed marijuana like beer, while maintaining bank accounts and spotless reputations. Thompson was riding this upscale iceberg, and it was the unenlightened part of society, those who had no firsthand experience with uppers, downers, sideways, screamers, and twisters, that looked more and more like the *Titanic.* He predicted that culture was on a collision course with chemicals.

Thompson had thus publicly positioned himself as a gourmand of psychedelics, as allied with "upwardly mobile professionals," as an aggressive, competitive player in the game of changing society's rules through radical means, and as an outlaw who refused actually to be a part of anything, even an outlaw motorcycle gang. Only through his creative blending of a motorcycle gang, his friendship with a best-selling novelist, and the lust for learning about "life on the edge" that he shared with many intellectuals did Thompson manage to pull together these divergent forces into a career coup.

Hunter Thompson's personal path to the summer of 1967 had been no easy voyage, and his initial motivation for writing the book *Hell's Angels* was not out of a curiosity over just how badly the motorcycle gang had been represented by the press, nor was it motivated by any theory-based inquiry into the sociology of an American subculture. Thompson was broke. Juan needed new shoes.

Thompson, Sandy, and Juan lived for a while near Glen Ellen, a small town in Sonoma County where Jack London had lived. He, Floyd Smith, and Paul Semonin would poach deer after dark in the woods behind the small house. Agar flushed one animal that ran, startled, between Smith and Semonin. Hunter brought it down with his .357 Magnum, firing into the dark. "It was not," Smith pointed out, "the hairy-chested, in-the-woods-macho thing for us. We liked the sport, and enjoyed eating what we shot." For Hunter and his family, it was free food in tough times. Sandy was taking care of the baby, and Hunter was doing his nocturnal writing. Perpetually in search of a great piece of fiction, Thompson was still trapped in journalism. In the calendar year 1964, he had sixteen pieces published in the *National Observer,* where he was unofficially dubbed "our West Coast free spirit." But even at $150 a piece, and expenses for travel, raising a family of three on $2,400 a year was below the poverty belt, free venison or not.

The family relationship at the time, Smith recalled, was for Sandy one of pure "hero-worship. She would get mad at me, though, thinking I was a bad influence on Hunter, taking him away from his writing. She was quite disciplined, and my visits did not fit her style." Another good friend of the time, Jack Thibeau, recalled Sandy as "a great woman; wonderful, sweet, sensible. She had to live with a very difficult man. And she admired him. When Sandy said his name—'Hunter'—it was different from how anyone else pronounced it. There was a special meaning in his name for her."

During the summer of 1964, Smith and Thompson visited the Republican National Convention held in the Cow Palace. Smith had gotten a job working at the convention, and had the requisite press credentials to get in anywhere. Thompson went along with him, and saw some of the behind-the-scenes action as the Republicans nominated Barry Goldwater, and William Miller as his Vice-Presidential running mate.

What made the most lasting impact on Thompson came from visits to the respective broadcasting booths of Chet Huntley and David Brinkley, and Walter Cronkite. Huntley and Brinkley had a well-oiled team, with dozens of assistants helping gather news and regulate the chaos of the mob scene in such a way that the news could be reported cogently. It was clearly a team effort. In stark opposition to this style was Walter Cronkite, who seemed to be running a one-man show. Alone, Cronkite was watching a number of television monitors suspended in his little box above the convention floor, and making all the decisions on his own. "Hunter sat there observing carefully," Smith recalled. "He was very impressed by Cronkite's one-man show." If Cronkite could do all this with little help from others, why not Thompson?

Genetically gifted with the energy level of three people, Thompson roamed far and wide in his free-lancing, yet always managed to drop *in* to the one place where everyone else was a dropout. Thompson was always showering his friends with clips of his writing, and renewing old friendships whenever possible. At this point in his career, his friends were his only audience. Big Sur still tugged at him. He traveled to Montana and Idaho to do a piece for the *Nation* on Hemingway's Ketchum, stealing the huge elk antlers from over the front door of the Hemingway family house, then returning them shyly the next morning.

Thompson would make his arrival in Big Sur known in his typical way. In the middle of the night, trying to locate a friend staying in one of the small log cabins behind the Redwood Lodge, he wandered about shouting the person's name, yet got no response. His next effort at communications was a little more primitive: he began firing his .357 Magnum pistol in the air. "There was a couple in the cabin next to where Hunter was firing his gun. They were from Iowa," Jahn de Groot said, "and they packed in thirty seconds and left in a minute. They never came back."

The entire Thompson family would occasionally come to Big Sur. At that time, Hunter had a pickup truck; he and Sandy would leave it parked, with Juan inside and Agar outside, guarding with canine ferocity. Anyone coming close to the truck would be snarled into submission. On the times when Sandy and Juan stayed home, Hunter would come down to the baths with Lionel Olay, talk literature, and drink and pop pills all night. "They would just be starting to crash when I got up," recalled Jo Hudson. "That was a scene that Sandy was excluded from, not that she'd want to be part of it."

At one point, Thompson timed his consumption poorly. He was to write an article on a concert Joan Baez was giving at Esalen, but instead began an early binge on amyl-nitrate inhalers, pills, and whiskey. He passed out, missed the entire concert, if not the day, and had to use the more lucid memory of friends to reconstruct the event. Hunter had found another labor-saving device in addition to the tape recorder—confabulation. He could glean a few facts from his friends, splice it with his inimitable style, and phone in an article, all the while recovering from a terminal hangover.

Hunter did keep a straight head about him when necessary. In 1965, during the filming of the movie *The Sandpiper,* Richard Burton and Elizabeth Taylor stayed at the Esalen Lodge. Hunter, Mike Murphy, and Fritz Perls all elbowed one another in their attempts to man the tiny bar and serve Taylor. Thompson wandered around the movie actress in his awkward, shuffling style, saying nothing, but intensely curious, and trying to catch a glimpse of her famous cleavage, and her violet eyes.

In the fall of 1964, near Big Sur, an event took place that the national news media swooped down upon like hungry birds of prey. Over the Labor Day weekend, at the annual gathering of Hell's Angels and related motorcycle gangs, two teenaged girls wandered into a midnight beach party with wide eyes, and left with bruised thighs. They went to the local police, already hair-triggered by the presence of dozens of bikers, and reported that they had been raped. The ensuing publicity included a *Newsweek* article ("The Wild Ones"), a *Time* article ("The Wilder Ones"), *New York Times* coverage, and the issuance of a 24-page report by the California Attorney General that detailed the life-style of this new public menace.

> The emblem of the Hell's Angels, termed "colors," consists of an embroidered patch of a winged skull wearing a motorcycle helmet. . . . Many [Hell's Angels] affect beards and their hair is usually long and unkempt. Some wear a single earring in a pierced ear lobe. Frequently they have been observed to wear belts made of a length of polished motorcycle chain which can be unhooked and used as a flexible bludgeon . . . Probably the most universal common denominator in identification of Hell's Angels is their generally filthy condition. Investigating officers consistently report these people, both club members and their associates, seem badly in need of a bath.
> —Excerpt: *California Attorney General's Report*

None of the lurid publicity was lost on *The Nation* magazine, based in New York. Entering the one-hundredth year of publication, it had been founded in 1865 largely to guard the rights of recently emancipated slaves. For a century, it had done its weekly best to focus critical attention on social issues. It was in the forefront in questioning assumptions of society, governments, and leaders.

In Thompson's time, the editor was a man who had repeatedly announced the avalanche before the snowball had begun to roll. Carey McWilliams had written best-selling books about the plight of migrant workers, prejudice against the Japanese, and anti-Semitism when such issues were mere whispers among polite society. McWilliams had begun his career by writing the biography of Ambrose Bierce, the second man to enlist after Fort Sumter was shelled, and a lifelong critic of society. Acerbic and bitter, Bierce had written a book, *The Devil's Dictionary,* as well as the world's most concise book review: "The covers of this book are too far apart."

H. L. Mencken had been a muse and a colleague of McWilliams's. His approach to society involved his stance of "shaking up the animals" of culture; his best-known quotation would endear him to Thompson's heart while writing about the Hell's Angels: "Nobody ever went broke underestimating the taste of the American public."

After having read Hunter's previous piece in *The Nation,* McWilliams sent Hunter newspaper clips on the Hell's Angels, a copy of the Attorney General's report, and a request for Thompson to do the definitive article on separating fact from fantasy. The average reader was drawn to this gang like a rubbernecking motorist passing a bad wreck. What did this say about the future, McWilliams wondered. What does the snowball really look like, and when would the avalanche hit?

In the Hell's Angels, McWilliams saw "the edge," a new life-form squeezed out from underneath a rock by the pressures of a society in flux. Thompson also saw "the edge," but more because of his profound attraction—a bent social tropism—that had always drawn him toward that shadowy territory where predictability and logic start to flicker and fade. In high school, Thompson had a fascination with gangs and hoods; now was his chance to act on those fantasies, and to buy Juan new shoes in the process.

By any analysis, the Hell's Angels were a group of overgrown adolescents, stuck in their rebellious mind-set as a way of life. They defined themselves by their opposition to any and everything. The strength of their antagonism was the source of their faith, and, like all holy wars, their greatest enemies, their most violent bloodbaths came from within: battles against rival splinter factions, other motorcycle gangs competing for their bottom-of-the-barrel status.

It was inverse Darwinism, where The Great Society's least fit tribe survived in a jungle of grease, gears, and chains, fighting turf battles with broken beer bottles, performing initiation rites that included baptism with a bucket of human excrement. Their sexual mores mandated random gang-banging and frequent woman-swapping, all rewarded by the demented Cub Scout icons of merit badges for buggery (black wings to be proudly sewn onto the sacramental vestments) or red wings for cunnilingus during menstruation. When it came to homosexuality, they were brutally honest, saying, "Man, when you got a head full of uppers, and your pants around your ankles, anything warm, round with hair around it is fair game. It don't matter who it is; it's how it feels. If it feels good, then do it."

The Hell's Angels looked at violence as an exercise; the more you did, the better you were at it. Some considered the Hell's Angels cultural deviates. In fact, they were a culture all their own. They had not played around with "normal society" and then sold out; they had simply never been offered membership, and never expected to be.

When Hunter Thompson received the offer and the packet of news clippings from Carey McWilliams, it included a financial offer to do an article; brief, factual, investigative, and honest. Thompson, no stranger to the ins and outs of the greater Bay Area after covering the San Francisco and Berkeley scene for a couple of years, knew just where to go to find the group. Throughout the years, when people met Thompson for the first time, they were always struck by how straight he appeared: short hair, no earring, no facial hair, no publicly visible tattoos. The most outlandish feature was the gaudy aloha shirts, as common in many parts of the West Coast as a three-piece suit on Wall Street. In first meeting the Angels, at the bar of the dilapidated DePau Hotel in San Francisco, Thompson wore a Palm Beach madras plaid sports jacket, and looked like an aluminum-siding salesman from Terre Haute. The Angels were impressed by his brazenness, his interest in them as a group who had gotten a bad publicity rap, and by Thompson's prodigious capacity for alcohol. The first night he showed up to play pool at the DePau, they all ended up back at Hunter and Sandy's apartment at 318 Parnassus Avenue, with the last Angel jump-starting his Harley, much to the neighbors' distaste, at 6:30 A.M., and roaring with a deafening blast up the hill and into the fog. It was a scene to be repeated innumerable times for the next year.

Thompson was near the bottom of the barrel when McWilliams's packet of articles arrived, and he jumped into the project in the same spirit as when he was covering the drug scene in

Haight-Ashbury. Thompson also had an inside source; he had stumbled upon a reporter for the San Francisco *Examiner,* Birney Jarvis, who was a "recovered" Hell's Angel, and who provided Thompson with valuable insights and a verbal road map of where to go, who to approach, and what not to do in order to mine the dark ore of Hell's Angels reality.

The research for the article also consisted of compiling considerable factual data to test the hypotheses of the Attorney General's report, and of the coverage by *Newsweek, Time,* and *The New York Times.* Hunter stated that before the media onslaught, the Hell's Angels San Francisco chapter had been reduced to a mere wisp of its former self, with a grand total of eleven members, one of whom was facing expulsion. What with police harassment and wars between gangs, the greasy menace was in its death throes.

"The difference between the Hell's Angels in the papers and the Hell's Angels for real is enough to make a man wonder what newsprint is for," Thompson stated in *The Nation.* "It also raises the question of who are the real Hell's Angels." He described responses from the law-enforcement world to an Attorney General's questionnaire as reading like "the plot synopsis of Mickey Spillane's worst dreams." In Thompson's eyes, any group who could shoot a good game of pool, engage in serious drinking until dawn, have the strength and coordination left to jump-start and drive a Harley-Davidson 74, and still somehow find a way to exist outside the chalk circle of normal, acceptable society is a group worthy of investigation. As Thompson put it, "The Hell's Angels and I had a lot in common, but I had a gimmick. I could write."

In Thompson's magazine article, he took offense at the publicity howl as obscuring the real issue, where the establishment press was portraying the evil Hell's Angels as "a conspiracy of bogeymen" and the public was being duped into thinking that everything will return to normal "once the fearless snake is scotched . . . by . . . minions of the establishment." He showed, case by case, that the allegations of the Attorney General and other police reports were erroneous and misleading; the hype was so distorted that the *Time* article had omitted the first page of the Attorney General's report stating that the rape charges in Monterey—the fuel that started the conflagration—had been dropped. He found crime statistics that showed a phenomenal increase in teenage V.D. rates to be a far more troubling social issue. The Hell's Angels were a mere drop in the bucket of more serious crime in the state of California; Thompson felt that the press were so seriously invested in maintaining the status quo that they were reticent to do the investigative footwork required to probe the roots of the problem. They might be frightened of what was uncovered: spots of decay in the society of which they were all a part—where no journalist is an island, either.

Thompson concluded the article with a quote obtained while shooting pool with one of the Angels. The man said, of the recent and unexpected crush of publicity, "Since we got famous we've had more rich fags and sex-hungry women than we ever had before. Hell, these days we have more action than we can handle."

By the time the article appeared, in the May 17, 1965 issue of *The Nation,* the money Thompson had been paid for it was long gone. His phone was disconnected, the rent overdue. It looked as if the time was ripe for another downhill slide into "one of those nervous breakdowns, or whatever you call them." The sum total of commotion the article had kicked up was a Letter to the Editor from a woman who had taken deep offense at Thompson's comparison of the ferocity of the Angels with that of wild boar. She demanded that Thompson inform her just where such wild boar existed, as those she had found in France and Germany were "shy as wood pigeons." Hunter was busily looking for another freelance assignment, his involvement with the motorcycle gang behind him.

Soon afterward, however, Thompson's mailbox was jammed with offers to do an entire book on the Hell's Angels. One publishing company offered him fifteen hundred dollars if he would simply sign a statement of intent. "Christ!" he recalled. "For fifteen hundred dollars I'd have done the definitive text on hammerhead sharks and stayed in the water with them for three months!"

While Joan Baez was singing "We Shall Overcome" to a Sproul Hall gathering of ten thousand students trying their collective best to bust the system, Hunter Thompson was in Oakland trading straight shots of whiskey with Mouldy Marvin, Mother Miles, and Charger Charley the Child Molester. If Joan Baez could use her voice to lead the world toward more peaceful pastures, Hunter Thompson could use his pen to seek truth among the bearded, benighted, unwashed, and unwanted cultural rejects who hung out in places like Charley's Geneva Club or the Bridgeview Bar.

Thompson encountered difficulties with the Angels from the start; their vehicle of choice was the American-built Harley-Davidson 74, stripped of all excess weight for optimal performance. Thompson recalled the initial transportation issue clearly: "They kept on offering me these Harleys to buy. I rejected the ones they offered me. They were pissed off about it, but every one they offered me was hot." He also recalled the ease with which he slid into their embrace, oiled by his own personality makeup. "I didn't have to do anything at all. That is one reason I decided to do the book, thinking back on it. Some part of me—whatever you want to call it—so much was a gut feel that it was easier than anyone would think it could be. For me it was a natural thing."

That was "Part One"—buying a bike to ride with the Hell's Angels. Thompson finally bought his own BSA 650 Lightning, a British bike that was tolerated as marginally acceptable; one other Angel, Frank Reynolds (Freewheeling Frank), also rode a BSA and he was a full-fledged, dung-initiated, red- and black-winged satyr. "Part Two" of Thompson's book writing was a tougher challenge. He had more difficulty with the publishing world than with the Hell's Angels. "I had an agent and I fired him," Thompson said. "He would not send the publisher my outline for the book. It was sold as a quick paperback. Then when I sent a few chapters in, they decided it was a serious book. They decided they had better sell it as a hardcover, so they put it up for auction. And I had Grove, Viking, and Random House to choose from. The agent I had then, some punk, would not send the outline. Ballantine, the publisher, asked for some writing. I had written only one chapter. It was almost nothing, so I had to write an outline. Probably more for administrative purposes. All I had to do was give the outline to him. When I wrote the outline for what I thought at that time was going to be the rest of the book, the agent thought it was so childish and silly that he would not even send it."

There was Thompson, his advance money spent for rent on the Parnassus Avenue apartment and a BSA 650, and he could not consummate the deal of his life because of an agent in New York who thought his outline was more folly than fact. Thompson was infuriated. Jack Thibeau, a good friend of Hunter's in San Francisco during that time, recalled that Thompson "saw the book as a good shot. In his own expression, he'd always say, 'You've got to have a good eye for the opening.' He saw that this was his shot. I was hanging around with him when he was writing it, and he would say, 'I can take one day off. Maybe two. But never three.' He would always go home and go to work on the book. He worked very, very hard on that."

No agent would stand in Thompson's way. "The publisher

kept calling," said Thompson, who had evidently used part of the advance to get the phone reconnected. " 'Where in the hell is the outline?' I said, 'I sent it to the fucking agent.' I called him, and he said he hadn't sent it . . . because he didn't want to embarrass me! I said 'Fuck you. You're fired!' And I sent in my carbon copy to the publisher. It was a ten-page piece of craziness. I don't think I ever went back to it at all. I don't think I did anything like what I said I was going to do. Outlines are only political documents. Things that people give to their bosses and say, 'This is what I just bought.' You can't give them something scratched on the back of a paper bag. An outline is something like a résumé. It means nothing. All lies.

"In a sense, an agent could have changed my life," Thompson continued. "Most writers wouldn't say 'fuck you'; it is hard enough to get an agent, without firing him right away on your first book, and then sending the publisher something he says is going to ruin your future in publishing. But that is the tendency to take risks that I have—that was also a characteristic of the '60s, the propensity to take risks like that, or to go out on the streets and probably get busted or beaten."

Getting a contract for one's first book is a time of celebration. For Thompson, it was a time to replace his Saab, a rickety old car with a two-cycle engine and a broken frame that actually bent when going up the steep hills of San Francisco. "Hunter used to curse and swear at the thing," Jo Hudson observed. "He always had in mind that he was going to get some sort of revenge, so he brought the Saab down to Big Sur to have a funeral for it." Thompson took the car to Hurricane Point, where the ground slopes gently toward the edge, then plummets straight down for two hundred feet. He soaked the inside of the car with gasoline, pushed it until it was rolling, and, just as it fell off the edge, assassinated it with his .44 pistol. "It went down into the ocean," Hudson affirmed, "and as far as I know, it is still there. But it never exploded or did anything fancy. I was embarrassed because it was contrived. Call it poetic license or whatever. It was so much theater, but what the hell; he wanted to do it. It was a good gesture, and we got away with it. I imagine he did it just to write about it later."

Thompson's celebration was complete. It was time to get on with the work. He had his foot in the door, and even if this was not the door to the great room of fiction, he would take what he was offered: a bona fide license to *shock*. If the tabloid mentality wanted sex, aggression, and strange creatures—watch out, because the Hell's Angels offered them in large quantities:

> Smackey Jack stories still circulate whenever the clans get together. I first heard about him from an easygoing Sacramento Angel named Norbert:
>
> "Man, that Jack was outta sight. Sometimes he'd run wild for three or four days on pills and wine. He carried a pair of rusty pliers around with him and we'd sic him on strange broads. Man, he'd jerk em down on the ground and start pullin their teeth out with those goddamn pliers. I was with him in a place one time when the waitress wouldn't give us a cup of coffee. Jack climbed right over the counter and took out three of her front teeth with his pliers. Some of the things he did would turn your stomach. Once he pulled out one of his own teeth in a bar. People couldn't believe it. A lot of em ran out when they saw he was serious. When he finally got the thing out, he laid it on the bar and asked if he could trade it for a drink. He was spittin blood on the floor, but the bartender was too shook up to say anything."

Thompson spent a lot of time exploring the origins of the Hell's Angels, as a part of the larger culture, as well as looking closely at what went on within their own territory. One of his favorite authors at the time was Nelson Algren. Thompson mentions Algren's *Walk on the Wild Side* and his old favorite Faulkner's "Barn Burning" as the best examples of literature depicting "white trash." His point was that the origins of the Hell's Angels was in the post-World War II Okies and Arkies, displaced by the Depression to the West Coast, in search of the promised land. Thompson wanted permission from Algren to quote from his book. "I admired Algren, and still do. I thought at the time that no living American writer had written any two books better than *The Man with the Golden Arm* and *A Walk on the Wild Side.*" Thompson asked for permission to quote. "He refused to give me permission to use it." I wrote and asked for permission to use that stuff he wrote about the Okies, the white trash that moved West. The prick said 'no.' So I said, 'All right, you bastards, if that's the way you feel about it, I'll just write it better; my own version.' That's where the [characters] the Linkhorns come from. I had to make that up." Thompson turned sociologist, and drew on Algren's characters, the Linkhorn family, as examples of post-W.W. II social alienation, and the growing popularity of the outlaw-as-social-hero. "It is a sense of being cut off, or left out of whatever society one was presumably meant to be a part of," Thompson wrote. It reflected a greater illness in American society. The Angels, Thompson said, were simply "rejects looking for a way to get even."

The Hell's Angels' own version of New Year's Eve is the fabled Labor Day Run; in 1964 it had been to Monterey, where the alleged rape took place that started the whole star-burst of publicity. In 1965, Thompson went with them to Bass Lake, at the foothills of the central California Sierras, and expected the unexpected. He described this Angel holiday as "a time for sharing the wine jug, pummeling old friends, random fornication, and general full-dress madness." Freewheeling Frank had been there in the years before the Monterey episode, and had come back alive with descriptions of the three-day *carnaval noir* that would make one's hair turn white. His surreal depictions were reminiscent of scenes from William Burroughs's *Naked Lunch,* but were actually the reality of Bass Lake's Labor Day Run in the days before the publicity brought out hundreds of policemen:

> His broad meanwhile was yanked and thrown upon the ground, one Angel saying to her, "You better get yourself a real old man!" Pulling her pants off her he poured wine all over her pussy. And then he got down and scarfed her box out licking the wine up. After he'd finished, he'd called out, "LET'S TURN HER OUT!" Many who liked the broad immediately got in line waiting their turn. In the background motorcycles roared like thunder as they raced down dusty trails around and around the encampment. Occasionally one would hit a bare stump throwing rider and motorcycle up in the air. . . .
>
> What looked like a barbarian sale of women began as the evening shadows closed in. Upon an orange crate women were being stood with their hands tied behind them and auctioned off. The sign read: CHICKS FOR SALE. WE ACCEPT ANYTHING. A tall lanky Angel by the name of Buzzard was the auctioneer. He would stand and describe the tall or shortlike broad, describing how she sucked and fucked. Quoting, "Here is a broad I have before me, who is not only a nympho, she is also a bisexual. She can take care of your old lady as well as you. What is my offer?" The beautiful broad with the long brown hair and a large bust with slim hips was quickly

yanked from the orange crate as the long black whip cracked around her neck and jerked her from it. . . .

On the way to Bass Lake, the president of the Hell's Angels, Sonny Barger, asked Thompson who he was. "A writer," Thompson told him. Barger said, "Just as long as you write the truth." For a long time, Thompson thought that was all they wanted from him. And in their own style, they would come by Thompson's to see what "the truth" looked like. At Hunter and Sandy's apartment, late at night, a few would appear unannounced, to read out loud to each other passages of the embryonic book. Their reaction was orthogonally different from Thompson's expectations. The Angels found highly insulting the parts that Thompson thought of as gentle and funny; the most lurid, brutal scenes were responded to with great belly laughs. "It was almost like reading your book in a bad translation in another language," Thompson said.

As time progressed, more and more of the Angels would appear for the "readings." When the crowd got to be a dozen or so, late at night, drinking and popping pills while reviewing the writing like Cro-Magnon scholars, Thompson said, "I'd have to leave the room. I wasn't sure which one of them would flip out, pick up a huge instrument, and wail on me with it."

At times, he even tried to use the Angels for his own purposes. Consistently overdue on his rent, Thompson used to send either Terry the Tramp or Tiny, a 6′5″, 270-pound Angel, to the door when the Chinese landlord came collecting. On one particular rainy San Francisco day, Terry the Tramp appeared at Hunter's place after stopping at a Goodwill store to buy a coat. It was an aged, decrepit ankle-length fur coat, which he wore with his native garb: black leather motorcycle boots, his sleeveless Levi's "colors" over the fur shag, a full beard, and tiny round sunglasses. He looked like an abominable snowman masquerading as John Lennon, and smelled like a garbage heap (after initiation, one's "colors" cannot be washed). The landlord began to pound at the door, and Hunter told Terry to just go and "hulk." It didn't work. To the Chinese landlord, all Caucasians looked alike; he showed no sense of intimidation. Thompson finally managed to keep him at bay temporarily by sending his Dobermans to meet the doorbell; they spoke an international language.

Hunter Thompson's real contribution to cultural advancement in the '60s was not only his investigations of the scruffy societal anomaly best described as "mutants" who pointed a finger toward a "wave of the future that nothing in our history has prepared us to cope with." There was more to his role than being the Margaret Mead of scum; single-handedly, he hooked together three groups of the more disparate factors of the '60s—or *any* decade. He became the Impresario of the Weird. Then, after tossing these different people together, he watched what unfolded.

The groups he brought together were: the Hell's Angels; the reigning king (and his court) of Bay area counterculture forces, Ken Kesey and the Merry Pranksters; and the more straight-laced Bay area intelligentsia. For a touch of bi-coastal brio, he added the poet Allen Ginsberg and the writer Tom Wolfe to the list, telephoning Wolfe and sending long tape recordings he made when all of this stew came to a boil at Kesey's log cabin in the woods in La Honda, in the hills above Stanford.

Public television, before it gave us "Sesame Street," gave us Hunter Thompson and Ken Kesey. Thompson knew of Kesey before their coincidental meeting in the studios of KQED. Hunter was in awe of Kesey: "I was impressed with Kesey as a writer at that time. After *Cuckoo's Nest* and *Sometimes a Great Notion,* no other writer around had written two books like that. A real achievement. I liked him a lot. Still do. Maybe he is crazy as four goats. Maybe I am too. When I read his books, I was impressed with the 'shock of recognition.' I recognized that high white stone. I was in an odd position of not being a follower, not a Merry Prankster, but of being a skeptic. I could probably get in a lot of trouble with Kesey if I dealt with him more often. Kesey was very kind to me. He helped me sort through my thoughts on the Hell's Angels."

The introduction of Kesey to the Angels came immediately after the two counterculture writers met. Thompson had to return a borrowed Brazilian drum record from an Angel, and took Kesey with him to the Box Shop, a transmission-repair garage and hangout for the Angels. Thompson described the meeting: "It came together at the TV studio, then I took Kesey out to the Angels' garage. We got ripped-up, torn apart, crazed. Kesey ended up bringing the whole thing down to his house in La Honda." Thompson saw a chance to continue "pushing other people's buttons" to see what would happen; now he was advancing to masses of people, masses of buttons. He was ecstatic. "I said, 'Christ! I can't miss this one!' "

Up to that point, Thompson had prided himself on his split social personality. As Jack Thibeau observed, "Hunter was a guy who had three or four levels of social activity at all times. He was all over the place. He doesn't like to be bored. He always wants to have something to do, something fun to do. He keeps weird hours; between two and six in the morning, when everyone else is asleep, he's got to find someone who is up at that time. He knew everybody in San Francisco, which is a city of easy fame. He knew the extremely rich, the regular rich, and guys like me. I was managing a rock band then."

Thompson's approach to his diverse persona was stated a little differently. "I was involved in that whole San Francisco scene at the time of the non-student left—lawyers, professors, students—and I was keeping my 'left-hippy acid-laced life' separate from my 'Hell's Angels, Oakland violence-laced life.' But it was inevitable that one day I would pass through the gates at Kesey's, and it was during the time I was doing the Hell's Angels book. It was just inevitable that I gravitate there, through the people I knew."

The confluence of Kesey and Thompson was an interesting one; both possessed great charisma. Upon their arrival, their presence was felt in a way that changed the room temperature and speeded the tempo of the music. Thibeau, who spent considerable time at the fluid-family commune among the ancient sequoias in La Honda, saw Thompson as "having considerable shamanistic qualities to him. He really is imbued with great, powerful insight and vision. He sees the world—it is very painful for him—he sees the world as a fatality all the time." Kesey, who had his own following of Merry Pranksters, was referred to as "a tarnished Galahad" by a judge who sentenced him for a marijuana possession charge. To thousands of Bay Area people who attended his "acid tests" in Los Angeles and San Francisco, there was no tarnish. He shined, and he loved it, saying, "It is like Janis Joplin said: 'Once you've had a taste of the limelight, you always want more.' " To parents in the area, it seemed that he held their children in a state of temporary custody.

Herb Caen's column in the San Francisco *Chronicle* would provide the public with periodic updates on the meanderings and sneak attacks of Further, the Merry Pranksters' psychedelically painted old school bus, and its Day-Glo passengers. Around San Francisco, where the standards for normal behavior are slightly skewed from the national average, they were seen as harmless entertainers, an extension of the mimes, musicians, jugglers, and magicians that appeared every night on Union Street or by Fisherman's Wharf. This bunch just had their own transportation.

Kesey's true intention was to physically invade the mind of

America on a cross-country crusade with his crack infantry, the Merry Pranksters, aboard the rolling Trojan horse, Further. Its driver was Neal Cassady, the manic, speed-talking, pill-popping hero of Kerouac's *On the Road.* With an assist from Thompson, this became the focus of Tom Wolfe's *Electric Kool-Aid Acid Test.*

Thompson tended to stay in the background of publicity. He was undoubtedly envious and curious of someone only two years older who had written two best-selling, consciousness changing pieces of fiction, then left it all behind to exist in "Edge City."

From July, 1963, through early summer of 1967, when Kesey began serving jail time for two marijuana busts, life at La Honda homestead was lived in the ultimate "here and now." Kesey had bought the property with proceeds from the *Cuckoo's Nest.* Populated by intellectuals from Berkeley and Stanford, as well as street people; idealistic, yet without any blueprint for the future; peace worshipping, yet constantly harangued by the San Mateo County sheriffs—they were the beat from which the West Coast's syncopated rhythms emanated.

Thompson's inherent suspiciousness (his self-described role as "a skeptic"), coupled with his rancid attitude toward the un-motivated hippies, didn't allow him to fit naturally with the peace-loving pranksters for more than a few long drug-sodden weekend blasts. Thompson never really fit comfortably into the mind-set of the '60s, other than being emotionally consistent with the bright red anger and outrage of the times. He was a carnivore among vegetarians, an armed warrior in a crowd of Gandhi disciples, and he was ten years older than the bulk of the baby-boom generation. But he did successfully use that time period to further his own education. When you bring along three-dozen Hell's Angels to Kesey's as your party guests, that can be enough to *make* some sort of history.

Before the Hell's Angels arrived, in August 1966, the collection of people around La Honda included Richard Alpert, the colleague of Tim Leary's at Harvard during their experimentation with psilocybin; Allen Ginsberg; the novelists Robert Stone and Larry McMurtry; Freewheeling Frank, Black Maria, the Hermit, and Gretchen Fetchin the Slime Queen. Other integral parts of the group were Neal Cassady and Jerry Garcia. As the leader of Kesey's in-house band, the Grateful Dead ("the loudest, longest band in the world"), Garcia took his inspiration from Cassady, saying, "Until I met Neal Cassady, I was headed toward being a graphic artist. . . . He helped make the Dead become the band we are. He presented a model for how far you could take yourself with the most minimal resources. Neal had no tools. He didn't even have work. He had no focus, really. His focus was just himself and time."

Jack Thibeau compared Thompson and Neal Cassady. "Hunter was a stronger person than Neal," he said. "Hunter was always totally grounded. As crazy as things got around there—and I don't think they could have gotten any crazier—Hunter would remain grounded. If three helicopters filled with state troopers landed and everything went nuts, Hunter would go off and negotiate with them. Neal would do something to get them all arrested."

When Thompson and the Hell's Angels arrived at La Honda, the forest setting seemed to have been designed by an LSD-laced mind. Christmas lights flashed like fireflies, burning day and night, hanging from the lower branches of the trees. The huge ponderosas are as old as the Magna Carta, twenty-five feet in girth, and over a hundred feet tall. All of these lumbering giants were painted Day-Glo colors, as were people's faces. When seen in the long rays of sunset or caught by the headlights through the fog, the impact was otherworldly. Strangers stumbling upon this either bolted away into the dark or stayed for months. As Kesey would say, "You are either on the bus or off the bus." Yet, curiously, at this point, the man whose best-selling book would open with the sentence "We were somewhere around Barstow on the edge of the desert when the drugs began to take hold" had never dared to try LSD. He was afraid of himself.

Between two of the trees, close to the shack where Kesey wrote the final part of *Sometimes a Great Notion,* was a mechanical "thunderbird," strung up by wires. One could sit in it and flap its wings and make strange noises over a carefully rigged speaker system.

Off to the side of the front yard was a metal construction of a Kama Sutra love position, to which a garden hose had been tied and left turned on, so that it appeared that the man was in a perpetual state of orgasm. The electronic system installed on the grounds and aboard the bus truly brought the woods alive with the sound of music. It was more than huge loudspeakers blaring Bob Dylan, accompanied by Neal Cassady's jabbering commentary over the imaginary radio station KLSD. Every person, place, and thing was wired to send and receive; it wasn't so much a log homestead as an electronic force field. Microphones hidden in the woods across the road captured and replayed, with a one-second delay, every word spoken by the staked-out sheriffs, who found it all very disconcerting disconcerting but could do absolutely nothing nothing nothing about it. Microphones were stuffed down Further's carburetors; they were nailed up next to squirrel's nests, dangled over burbling waters, hidden in the bathroom and in the "screw shack," or taped to Pranksters' stomachs at dinner hour. Musical, mechanical, natural, and biological, it was all just joyful noise on man's march to the Great Wherever.

This was the wondrous scene that greeted the Hell's Angels, and LSD was the drug (legal at that time) that was offered as they clomped across the tiny footbridge from Route 84, where they parked their bikes. Few of them had ever been on anyone's guest list, and certainly never forty all at once. Their approach had been the ungodly dirty thunder of eighty cylinders of unmuffled American motorcycle, and the noise rolled around the steep canyon until it sounded like theme music for the end of life on earth. Many, including Thompson, thought that might be the net result. The Angels and the Pranksters were mutual cults of anarchy, and beyond that seemed to have very little in common. And yet there were some similarities, such as the way each group found new members: neither group *picked* members; they *recognized* them.

The party itself consisted of seventy-two hours of drinking, drugging, dancing, and sex acts of every imaginable sort. The energy seemed to come in waves, where for hours everyone would be dancing inside the log house, on the lawn, and in the woods. Then a peaceful calm would wash over; the electronics would amplify sounds of erotic grunts and moans. Frisbees, soap bubbles, dogs, and children seemed everywhere, under a gauze of marijuana smoke. The tempo of human movement was dictated by whatever music was playing; Dylan, Jefferson Airplane, or the Rolling Stones. After one crest of energy, some would nap, then rally to make a beer run, while others would begin the next wave of dancing and drugging. The time of day was irrelevant; it all kept flowing as long as the chemical and spiritual supplies were in stock. Allen Ginsberg and Hunter tape-recorded the entire party for Tom Wolfe, while Kesey filmed the Pranksters for an eventual movie.

At the end of the fest, the Angels' industrial-lathe philosophy of "when in doubt, bore it out" had melded peacefully with the Pranksters' dictum of "go with the flow." As one Angel, who had arrived expecting blood and left with a flower in his beard, put it, "It was all ha-ha. No thump-thump." And the key to ha-ha was the Angels'—and Thompson's—first experimentation with LSD.

Philosophically, Kesey and Thompson differed over the use of the drug that galvanized a generation. LSD was symbolic of the death of the old way, and the possibilities of the new. Kesey had one way of looking at it: "All of the people that were hanging around together were already talking 'revolution' in kind of vague terms. We were educated enough to know that the beatnik kind of revolution just wouldn't work. It was going to take a revolution of the consciousness. I don't think anybody invented this; I just think a bunch of people just realized it at the same time and joined forces without ever knowing that there was an army.

"When we got into acid as a group of people, we felt like we were dealing with the end of time. I felt that writing was done for the future, and that we were cut off from the future. I did not feel that *Cuckoo's Nest* was going to be read in three or four hundred years. It was a different consciousness that we were writing. I could not do the same kind of writing I had been doing. We got into what I would call Rorschachian art. Tim Leary, Bob Dylan, John Lennon, Bill Burroughs—we were all reaching in to wrench the language apart. If was as if the syntax were anchoring us to something older—something ancient, something staid—and we were trying to tear it out. The slate was ours. We wrote on it what we wanted. We felt that the consciousness revolution was going to take us off physically—like *Childhood's End.*"

Kesey had been introduced to psychedelic drugs as a paid participant in research being done at the Palo Alto Veterans Administration Hospital; he had returned to work on projects of the psychiatrist Leo Hollister, a professor at Stanford. The outcome was the book *One Flew Over the Cuckoo's Nest,* where Kesey saw the American Dream through the eyes of inmates at a psychiatric facility; the Dream was distorted and perverted, and not allowed to develop fully. The book was about the sickness in America being in the consciousness of the people.

Two of Hollister's colleagues also doing legitimate research with LSD were Benjamin DeRopp, a neighbor of Hunter's in San Francisco, and Joe Adams, a psychiatrist from Stanford who was closely involved with the evolution of Esalen. Thompson had been aware of LSD from his first days in Big Sur, but had been warned by Adams against taking the chemical. "I had known about acid for about five years and they counseled me that I was far too violent to take it," Thompson recounted. "I had heard all the acid stories years before Leary or Kesey. I was around people who were doing it, and they decided I was too violent. I was locked up—just too many horrible tales. I had good reason to believe I was a violent person—still am in some ways—the potential is there. It just seemed like a bad drug."

Thompson balanced the violence he felt within, weighed it

carefully with his propensity for taking risks, and came up with a decision: "I am a little more comfortable with violence than some people. I have been beat up so often that it doesn't worry me to get beat up. That is an attitude that allows you to take risks."

Having an approach to life somewhere between that of a barely guided missile and a leather punching bag, Thompson weighed the potential for human explosiveness at Kesey's, with LSD flowing like wine and with the estimable company of several-dozen men who knew no societal rules and could, potentially, regress in an instant into knife-wielding, barbaric animals. "I just measured it," Thompson said. "I took it for the first time in the company of a hundred Hell's Angels, and all that madness down there at La Honda. There was a maximum possibility for a violent breakout. Whatever violence was in me would probably come out. Once you get totally out of control, I thought, the odds are that not too much worse can happen to me than this. So I'll eat the acid, which I did." The results were puzzling—perhaps disappointing—to him, but the Hell's Angels were not dangerous, and not destructive. That behavior seemed relegated to their levelheaded mind.

"These people who had been telling me I was a violent person were crazy. I'm not violent at all, 'cause you know with acid you have been to the bottom of the well. When weird things happened to me at Kesey's like a tree turning into a snake, I was not afraid. It was a relief to me to realize that after being told by experts that I had to watch myself—'one of these days you are going to kill somebody'—that whatever there was down there, I brought it up. And I did it in the company of violent people, the Hell's Angels."

The issue of creativity, a basic rationale for controlled as well as personal experimentation with LSD in the late '50s and early '60s, was only an afterthought to Thompson's experimentation at the La Honda party. He did it as a macho kind of ultimate personal dare.

Thompson had found a new form of chemical kick. "In a sense, LSD allowed me to trust my instincts," he commented. "So I had a good time! It was wonderful! I never had any trouble with acid. What I like about it is that it cleans out the pipes. I still take it twice a year . . . three times . . . whenever I can get my hands on it! But it's no fun alone. It's too much work. But it is nice to blow out the steam. Like a cleaning factory. All the tubes rattling. You find out what is in there when you clean it out."

The most "violent" incident during the party at Kesey's was when Neal Cassady stood naked on one side of the road, shook his fist, and showered obscenities onto the sheriffs watching through binoculars on the other side ("while his wife was being gang-raped by the Hell's Angels," Thompson noted). Later, when Thompson tried to use Cassady's name in describing this scene in the book *Hell's Angels,* the lawyers at Ballantine would not let him. He was infuriated. "See what the fucking lawyers do?" Thompson declared. "They made me take Neal Cassady's name out of that book." Thompson was relegated to referring to Cassady as "the worldly inspiration for the protagonist of several recent novels." He had to use a footnote to add that the real name was dropped "at the insistence of the publisher's lawyers."

In his analysis of just what made the Angels tick, Thompson expressed considerable surprise that once acid had removed the tops of their brains, they didn't turn the party into a massive bloodbath. He seemed disappointed, perhaps looking forward to some large-scale destruction and flaying of the aimless, drifting Pranksters. It *was* all "ha-ha," and Freewheeling Frank had Sandy Thompson and LSD to thank for a sudden agnostic conversion. He came away from the three-day carnival ride with these impressions: "At the time, I was a perfect symbol of the newspaper image of a Hell's Angel. I trusted no one. I felt no love and did not understand love other than sex. Love meant sex to me. . . ." Freewheeling went with the flow; like any kid at his favorite amusement park, he began his evening out with friends by standing in line for his favorite ride—a gang-bang—then stopped at the refreshment stand before seeing the leader of the Big Parade. "I took the acid and was still going up. . . . Everybody was stoned out of their mind on weed and wine. Ken Kesey had on a white robe and a hood. . . . Bob Dylan wailed 'Subterranean Homesick Blues.' . . . I was attracted to Hunter Thompson's wife . . . but it makes a difference how I was attracted to her. I was attracted to the beauty of a woman for the first time. I don't think one time during the high of my acid did I think of my wife. If I had of, it would have been a mark of evil. I no longer think dirty or filthy of women since I took LSD."

A few months after the La Honda meeting, Kesey and Ginsberg asked Thompson for help. The Hell's Angels had crashed into a throng of Vietnam protesters heading to picket the Army Induction Center in Oakland. Hunter was requested to bring them all together with Sonny Barger, the Angels' "Maximum Leader," and negotiate some peaceful resolution before another planned Vietnam Day Committee protest march of some ten thousand. The tensions were different from those at Kesey's; there was blood on the Angels' lips and zeal in the protesters' eyes. Ginsberg, then teaching at Berkeley on a Guggenheim Poetry Fellowship, had written a poem, "To the Hell's Angels," which was published in the widely read counterculture newspaper, the *Berkeley Barb*. The opening line read: BUT NOBODY WANTS TO REJECT THE SOULS OF THE HELL'S ANGELS (or make them change)—WE JUST DON'T WANT TO GET BEAT UP. Hell's Angels put pacifism in the same category as Japanese motorcycles. A new strategy was clearly called for. The night before the huge, nationally publicized march, a meeting in Barger's Oakland home gave the protesters a chance to march in peace. Ginsberg, Kesey, Neal Cassady, and Hunter Thompson, along with several Angels, talked philosophy, played Bob Dylan and Joan Baez records, smoked dope, chanted mantras, and dropped acid.

Ginsberg, like Thompson, had always been fearful of LSD. He had had bad experiences on it, and was afraid of revealing his inner ignorance under the drug's influence. Recalling the night at Barger's, he said, "Again, being a coward, I didn't take any acid and everybody else did. So I was the goodly saint. Kesey, Cassady, and a couple of others all got zonked on acid. We got into some political arguments with the Angels, and Kesey very wisely got me off my high horse. Then I started singing the Prajnaparamitra Sutra and that was very soothing and pleasant."

The high point of the evening came when Ginsberg expressed his feelings for Barger. "That goddamned Ginsberg is gonna fuck us all up," Terry the Tramp said later. "For a guy that ain't straight at all, he's about the straightest son of a bitch I ever met. Man, you shoulda been there when he told Sonny he loved him. . . . Sonny didn't know what the hell to say."

Thompson commented, "Allen is a good-hearted fucker, but here is Ginsberg setting up all these rendezvous with the Angels, and I was the organizer, the point man. For Allen it was a weird time, and people asked me to do all kinds of weird things. But Allen had a good time, because Barger was in a good mood and he humored Ginsberg with his 'We're all in this together.' Barger never believed a fucking word! That is what I tried to tell Ginsberg. *They are mean fuckers!*"

Soon after the meeting, Barger sent his classic telegram to President Johnson (". . . We feel that a crack group of trained gorrillas [*sic*] would demoralize the Viet Cong . . ."), and the issues with the peace marchers seemed forgotten. However, trouble for Thompson was brewing. When the Angels found out that he was not going to share any of the millions they thought his book would make, they confronted him in their own style. He was "stomped" so suddenly that he didn't know who hit him. Out of a bloody haze, on his back, at night on a lonely beach, he saw one Angel pick up a huge stone and hold it over his head. Tiny, his onetime roommate, stopped the other Angels just short of killing Thompson.

He got in his car and drove away, weaving down the road, trying to straighten his pulverized nose and keep blood from obscuring his view. He heard a rustling and turned to find Magoo, an Angel, who had passed out in the back seat. He stared at Thompson in utter disbelief. Thompson stopped the car and said, "You'd better get out. I'm leaving." Thompson headed to the emergency room of the Santa Rosa Hospital, where doctors put his scalp back on his forehead and arranged his nose somewhere to its original place. In summarizing his experiences with the Angels, Thompson quoted Joseph Conrad's Kurtz, from *Heart of Darkness:* "The horror . . . the horror." Thompson never visited the Angels after that; they really *were* mean fuckers.

Thompson had begun his journey into the "Strange and Terrible Saga" with a short magazine article that blasted both barrels at the press for breathing life into a dying, decayed bunch of hoods. His book ended up having the same effect, only exponentially. There was money to be made in this counterculture thing, and a lot of it came Thompson's way when *Hell's Angels* hit the best-seller list in 1967, the Summer of Love, and hung there like a glob of 50-weight motorcycle oil. Fashion magazines did not overlook leather motorcycle jackets and heavy chain belts; the Angels hired a P.R. man, and began to charge for photos and interviews. The American fascination with the group seemed to have no end; books, articles, coffee-table photo collections were snatched off the presses by an eager public.

When Thompson's book came out, the first printing was sold out before publication. He went on a publicity tour, got to New York, and found no copies. "Every biker in the country must have bought it," Thompson said, speaking of the kind of riders who rode the bikes immortalized by the Beach Boys in their song "My Little Honda." "The kind of people who read my book are the kind of people more likely to steal them." In Chicago, on WFMT, he was interviewed by Studs Terkel, who recalled doing the taping while "sitting in a little bar, below the radio station. Hunter was drinking Wild Turkey, *and* he had a six pack of beer. Both!" In the process of the interview, Thompson managed to state that the Hell's Angels' type of violence was everywhere in the country, and it was a reflection of President Johnson's policies. "Lyndon Johnson would make a good Hell's Angel," he said. "Mentally," the President would qualify, "where violence is taken in a much more sophisticated and respectable form." In Denver he met Norman Mailer in a TV studio. Each was promoting a new book; it was Mailer's eighth. "He was a guy on the make," Mailer said. "He said things like, 'I am here to promote on this goddamned show. This book has got to sell. I wanna get a little back.' Hunter comes out of something that has not yet been measured. Of all the writers I know, I probably understand Hunter the least."

If there was money in selling headbands and bell-bottoms to mainstream America, Thompson saw another opening with the overwhelming success of his writing style. Write the books . . . and they will buy. He needed time and quiet to plan his next assault on the American public. Hunter retreated with Sandy, Juan, and the Dobermans from the fog of Parnassus Avenue to the Rocky Mountain splendor of his cabin, Owl Farm, at Woody Creek, Colorado.

13.

Tricks

of the

Trade

he scene would ice the blood of any Secret Service
agent. Fifty yards from the crowd, two men leaned
toward one another in heated debate, across the
wing of a fully fueled Lear jet. One, with a heavy
five o'clock shadow and dressed in a three-piece
suit, occasionally nodded or shook his head. The
other was tall, starting to bald, and appeared to

punctuate his comments like a fencer, jabbing holes in the air with a lit cigarette extending from a holder. So engrossed in discussion were they that neither saw the wing-tip tank, a cigarette jab away. So stunned were the observers that none moved.

This was Hunter Thompson's first and only personal rendezvous with Richard Milhous Nixon, over the fumes of aviation gas on the apron of a runway in Manchester, New Hampshire, early in the 1968 Presidential race. There was potential in that meeting: Hunter could have taken a shortcut to becoming a cult hero, rather than the slow, bruising route he did take. Newspapers the next day could have trumpeted the momentous news around the world: JOURNALIST EXPLODES SELF: KILLS PRESIDENTIAL SHOO-IN; SAVES COUNTRY FROM DECADE OF DOOM, DECEIT, AND DESTRUCTION. There was precedent for this form of self-immolation; Buddhist monks in Vietnam were doing it left and right. Madame Nhu had publicly referred to them as "barbecues."

In Richard Nixon, Thompson found a walking, talking bull's-eye. In his mind, Nixon was a living memorial to the "rancid genes and broken chromosomes that corrupt the possibilities of the American Dream."

Thompson had shed his own post–Hell's Angels hibernation, coming at national politics like a hungry animal. After spending half a year in Woody Creek, he went to New Hampshire early in 1968 to see for himself if there was a "new" Nixon, one whose tactics and attitudes had changed since his narrow loss to Kennedy in 1960, and his loss in the 1962 race for his own's state's governorship.

Pageant magazine picked up Thompson's expenses for this excursion, and the journalist came away with some shattered expectations. He went to find a "braying ass" and came back with the assessment that the man had "one of the best minds in politics." Thompson watched during numerous press conferences across the state as Nixon listened to questions, and provided the answer that was "always right for the situation."

Nixon could have been an Honorary Mormon; he never smoked, and the bar scene, Thompson noted, made him nervous. Nixon was secretive to the point of paranoia, as Thompson discovered when he was tossed out by a guard while trying to take notes during a local telecast. After observing Nixon's mediocre rapport with a live TV camera, Thompson offered his services to the candidate as a speechwriter, guaranteeing to change Nixon's public image in a day. The offer was met with a blank stare. Humor was in short supply in the Republican camp.

Thompson wanted an interview with Nixon to be the center-piece for his article, but it was not forthcoming. Robert Semple, who had known Thompson from *National Observer* days, was also covering Nixon. He recalled Thompson's perseverance, following the candidate everywhere he went, racing at high speeds over narrow icy New England roads, drinking straight out of a bottle of Jack Daniel's as he drove. Ray Price, then a Nixon speechwriter, finally caved in, and arranged for Thompson to ride a short distance with Nixon in his limo to the Manchester airport. Price had come up to Thompson and said, "the boss wants to talk football." Hunter was commanded to do only that, and warned not to discuss anything remotely political. For an hour they drove in sub-zero weather; Thompson and Nixon in the back seat, Pat Buchanan, Price, and a Secret Service man in the front. Thompson expected that if he hinted at any other topic, the limo would screech to a halt and he would find himself abandoned on the freeway median strip, so he obeyed Price's directives. If it was a journalistic coup for Thompson, it was Nixon who won the battle.

The two men rode along through the grim winter night. Instead of talking politics, they talked football. That had been the "handle" that allowed Nixon's aides to stick the two together in the first place; their boss was tired of campaigning, and wanted a diversion from the tedium. He put politics behind him and instead, much to Thompson's surprise, spoke of having learned some inside tips from legendary Green Bay Packers' coach Vince Lombardi that had caused Nixon to bet on the underdog Oakland Raiders in the Super Bowl of a month before. (The Raiders lost.) Thompson was stunned to discover that Nixon recalled not only the name of the wide receiver who caught Oakland's last touchdown pass (Bill Miller), but spontaneously shouted out the player's alma mater: "That's right, yes, the Miami boy!" Nixon, who shared with Thompson a reverence for the great sportswriter Grantland Rice (the Vanderbilt scholarship that Hunter had applied for), continued to render Thompson slack-jawed, telling the journalist that campaigning messed up his football season.

It was not Nixon's detailed knowledge of the facts of the game that startled Thompson, but the colorful zeal that suddenly erupted in a politician previously perceived by Thompson as robotic. During their conversation, Nixon told Thompson that if he had it to do all over again, he would like to be a professional sportswriter. Thompson felt that this was the ultimate con, a fantastic whopper from a man starved for power. Nothing Nixon said could be believed, not even after-hours small talk.

When the limo stopped on the runway, Nick Ruwe, a Nixon advance man for New Hampshire, watched as Nixon and Thompson talked near the Lear jet's fuel tank, an arm's length from destruction. After Nixon left, Ruwe told Hunter he'd almost had a heart attack watching it. That night, Hunter set his cross-hairs on the man who would provide him both target and ammunition for his ballistic writing over the next several years. Even as the 1968 election was beginning, Thompson summed up his sentiments for the "new Richard Nixon," saying the only way he would touch the man would be "with a long cattle prod." For Thompson, the combination of evil and success that he saw so transparently in Nixon was a source of endless fascination. This was the man to whom he would dedicate *The Great Shark Hunt:* "To Richard Milhous Nixon, who never let me down." As for Nick Ruwe, his future after Nixon's election was a backhanded slap from the spoils system, where successful politicians remember those who helped get them to the top. Ruwe was given an ambassadorial appointment—to Iceland. Who says Nixon had no sense of humor?

Back in Woody Creek, Thompson continued free-lance writing. He had attended the Democratic Convention in Chicago in 1968. After having been manhandled by the riot-control police, he felt even more strongly about the changing scene in America, and in its politics. He wrote a few articles on this subject, but it was not a productive period for his creativity. One night in early 1970, at a long dinner in Aspen with Jim Salter, screenwriter of *Downhill Racer,* Slater suggested that Hunter cover the upcoming 1970 Kentucky Derby for *Scanlon's* magazine, whose editor, Warren Hinckle, had known Thompson in the Bay area. Great idea, and no time to lose; Hunter called Hinckle at 3:30 A.M., and the response was positive. They tried to get political cartoonist Pat Oliphant to illustrate the piece, but ended up settling on Ralph Steadman, a Welshman.

Thompson arrived a few days before the Derby, two years after the assassinations of Robert Kennedy and Martin Luther King, in the midst of Black Panther protests at Yale, and just as Nixon ordered troops into Cambodia. Thompson's first act was to spread a rumor that the horse race would be shut down by black protesters; the Kentucky Derby had yet to be integrated. Thompson was angry about the segregation, and had come home to plant the bomb.

His Derby reporting was a classic piece of muckraking. He

and Ralph Steadman, there on his first trip to the U.S., roamed the city and the Derby, in search of "the mask of the whiskey gentry." They were an odd couple. Steadman is slight and short, and speaks with an elite British clip. Conservative, retiring, with a dry sense of humor, Steadman does not stand out in a crowd. With Thompson as his guide, that was not necessary. What the two shared was a skewed insight into the more primitive, unvarnished corners of human nature; Thompson used words for his descriptions, while Steadman sketched and painted. Further, the two discovered they each enjoyed an occasional drink.

How, Thompson asked, could an entire city, swollen like a balloon with like-minded outsiders, spend three straight days in total alcohol-fueled debauchery, many missing a horse race that lasted but two minutes yet that united them all in a sodden bond of revelry, while the entire world around them was blowing itself up? In Hell's Angels lingo, Louisville was all "ha-ha"; the rest of the world was all "thump-thump."

Steadman sketched while Thompson wheedled press passes, tried to Mace the Governor, got thrown out of the Pendennis Club, and wrote a nosology of inebriation: strutting drunk; staggering drunk; and stumbling drunk. The two searched high and low for the symbolic face in the crowd that represented the incest, ignorance, and xenophobia of Thompson's Louisville.

He was merciless with his home-town people. He slung mud at their racism: "Smitty's daughter . . . went crazy in Boston last week and married a nigger!" Their traditional academic ties, including those of many of his then still-close friends, were crushed: ". . . the kid wrecked the new car. . . . Send him off to Yale, they can cure anything up there." Thompson helped the newcomer Steadman with the more sophisticated details of Kentucky cultural anthropology: the true Kentucky Colonels are easy to spot if you know how—when they vomit, they are careful to miss their clothing, but always get some on their shoes.

Thompson finally found the face in the crowd that he had searched for. When he woke up the morning after, he saw that face, destroyed by drink and disease, bloated out of all proportion, as if a caricature in a "once-proud mother's family photo album." He was looking in the mirror.

The race was over, the mud was slung. It was time to get down to the dirty business of writing the article, piecing together something linear and coherent, using handwritten notes scribbled during the days of daze. Steadman picked up quickly on what had really happened, saying that the two had come to Louisville to observe the terrible scene of drunken frenzy only to discover "You know what? It's us . . ."

A sudden turn of events simultaneously gave Thompson a bout of writer's block, and his entrance to the Journalist's Hall of Fame. On Monday, May 4th, as Thompson was driving Steadman to his plane, the car radio bellowed forth that four students protesting Nixon's orders to invade Cambodia had been shot by National Guard troops at Kont State, just 250 miles away. Thompson was stunned, and could think of little else. He holed up in a New York City hotel room and found that he could not complete the article. Instead, he spent hours each day in the bathtub drinking White Horse Scotch straight from the bottle. The Kentucky Derby article was to be *Scanlon's* cover story, and the bulk of it was still inside his whiskey-drenched mind. Copyboys were sent over to Thompson's room; out of futility, he gave them handwritten notes from his notepad. An hour later a copyboy was back, asking for more. Thompson was disbelieving. He called Hinckle in San Francisco, who said the stuff was wonderful. Thompson sent the entire notepad over the Telecopier, then slunk back to Aspen, feeling tawdry for his butchered effort at investigative journalism.

Within a few days of publication, the phone rang off the hook and mail poured in. The jagged realism of the raw, elemental thought-bursts—where the story was the scene, not the main event, and where anger was the vehicle—hit a nerve that was in direct synch with the increasingly fragmented and indignant American culture. Entitled, "The Kentucky Derby Is Decadent and Depraved," Thompson described the Derby as "an atavistic freakout with nothing to recommend it except a very saleable tradition."

Thompson quickly learned that after this episode no one would question his work ethics. If the message that came with the success of the Hell's Angels book had been "Write the books, and they will buy," the message now was "Scribble the notes, and they will applaud."

A letter came to Thompson from Bill Cardoza, then with the Boston *Sunday Globe,* and a drinking companion of Hunter's during the cold New Hampshire primary in 1968. He lavishly praised Thompson's style of journalism, and referred to it with a term the South Boston Irish used to describe the guts and stamina of the last man left standing at the end of a marathon drinking bout. The term was "Gonzo."

The spring of 1970 was a heady time for Hunter Thompson; he had become deeply involved in local Aspen politics, first organizing the mayoral race of attorney Joe Edwards, then his own campaign for sheriff of Pitkin County. He based his approach on a unique anti-development platform that stressed tearing up all the pavement and replacing it with sod; changing the name of Aspen to Fat City; putting public stocks on the lawn in front of the courthouse in which to punish anyone profiting from drug deals (he stated that no drug worth taking should be sold for a profit; this would preserve the drug culture that was an integral part of the city's ambience). He seemed to have turned a corner with his anger, getting into the thick of the fray, becoming an active participant in the process of change. He was quite serious about his political venture; it also made great press, especially when he shaved his hair to form a forward-looking arrow.

In the midst of all this came a job offer. It came from a San Francisco-based magazine. It was a newly minted attempt to cash in on the burgeoning addiction to rock and roll. It was started by a Berkeley dropout with brilliant ideas and a mercurial management style, who ran through money like a sailor on shore leave, and who ran through personnel like Attila the Hun. The magazine was *Rolling Stone,* and the publisher was Jann Wenner.

Wenner had heard of Thompson through one of his editors, John Lombardi. During the summer of 1967, Hunter's old friend from Big Sur days, the free-lance journalist Lionel Olay, had died. Thompson had connected with Olay as he had with few other people, and his death at the age of forty-one was hard to take. Thompson wrote about Olay's death, as a symbol for the end of the '60s, in a biting, caustic article that center-punched the Summer of Love. The article, titled "The Ultimate Freelancer," was first published in the Los Angeles *Free Press,* and it immediately caught the eye of Lombardi, then the editor of a Philadelphia underground newspaper. Lombardi read the article, thought it was riveting, "like reading Céline." He put his discovery to the ultimate test: he read it to his mother, who did not like it. That was ample confirmation for Lombardi to call the L.A. *Free Press* requesting the right to print it. Thompson called back, asked a few questions about the East Coast paper, and told Lombardi, "Sure, print the fucker." The piece read like exploding hand grenades, launched at every imaginable target including the ultimate psychedelic drug proponent and anti-establishment figure, Timothy Leary.

> . . . cheap, mean grinning-hippy Capitalism . . . pervades the whole new scene. . . . While the new wave flowered,

Lenny Bruce was hounded to death by the cops. For "obscenity." . . . and the world we have to live in is controlled by a stupid thug from Texas. A vicious liar, with the ugliest family in Christiandom. . . . mean Okies, feeling honored by the indulgence of a George Hamilton, a stinking animal ridiculed even in Hollywood. And California . . . elects a Governor straight from a George Grosz painting   Ronnie Reagan, the White Hope of the West. . . . And there's the chill of it. Leary's would be "drop-out generation" of the 1960's. The Head Generation . . . a loud, cannibalistic gig where the best are fucked for the worst reasons, and the worst make a pile by feeding off the best. . . . Promoters, hustlers, narcs, conmen . . . The handlers get rich while the animals either get busted or screwed to the floor with bad contracts.

Three years later, Lombardi went West to work for *Rolling Stone,* a magazine whose state of intellectual development embarrassed him. He wanted to do something to improve it, to get the magazine beyond just reporting and into good writing. "Hunter used to talk about the sound of wind in the writing," said Lombardi. He was one of the first writers Lombardi invited to come to San Francisco and interview. Jann Wenner and Lombardi came in to the magazine's Third Street offices on a Saturday specifically to meet Hunter. Wenner had a huge, round antique table, and a "Huey Newton"-type wicker chair that appeared to dwarf the short owner-publisher even further. Neither had laid eyes on the journalist flying in from Colorado, and in their wildest imagination were not prepared for what ambled through the doorway around noon.

"He was a bizarre sight," Lombardi said. "We were waiting and waiting for Thompson. He finally shuffled in. He was wearing his famous 'gook' Hawaiian shirt, and carrying a six-pack of beer, which he didn't offer to anyone. He had a little case under his arm, a straw bag or something with all kinds of things coming out of it: papers, string, very strange-looking. And he wore a Dynell wig; a cheap gray lady's wig that he kept taking off, straightening, putting back on. And his sunglasses, which he did not remove. And, of course, the cigarette holder."

Lombardi and Wenner listened to a one-sided monologue about Thompson's approach to the sheriff's candidacy, and immediately heard—and saw—the markings of a new chapter in the life of their magazine. Lombardi heard the notes of a unique writing style in the way Thompson spoke; using terms such as "fun hogs" in reference to the hard-core Aspenites, and "greed-heads" for the moneygrubbing land and ski-area developers who were trying to steal away their Rocky Mountain Camelot. "He was inventing vocabulary," Lombardi noted.

As the afternoon rolled along, neither Lombardi nor Wenner, who had called the meeting, were allowed to insert a word edgewise. Thompson unleashed a filibuster of what the magazine people immediately saw as a sign of things to come: the voting and buying power of the fifty percent of the adult population who had never before voted. Again, Thompson was looking at politics, the possibilities that could come from enfranchising the dropped-out hippie youth, millions strong yet politically mute.

There was no give-and-take that afternoon; it was all Hunter. The only hiatus from his verbal tirade was when he periodically got up to make room for more beer. Each time he trekked down the hall to the men's room, Wenner sank lower and lower in the wicker throne until Lombardi saw him looking like a cartoon character, just his head above the table. Thompson knew the impact he was having. "He is a great actor," Lombardi confirmed, but it was Wenner who had difficulty processing what was going on.

Wenner had dropped out of Berkeley during his freshman year, but kept his ties to the school newspaper, the *Daily Cal.* He was always in the thick of things, standing next to Mario Savio when he defied a restraining order and leaped on the stage at a faculty meeting in the Greek Theater to exhort the crowd to protest. Wenner was beside Savio, microphone in hand, as the free-speech leader was dragged off the stage by police. And in 1967, Wenner had reviewed the galley proofs of *Hell's Angels* in a column he wrote for the *Daily Cal;* he dismissed Thompson's work as that of "another hippie journalist."

In founding the first magazine to target baby-boom music fanatics, using a $7,500 loan, Wenner had stated his main purpose was to provide him a vehicle "to meet John Lennon." For now, he had to settle for Hunter Thompson, and he was clearly perplexed. During one of Thompson's trips to the men's room, Wenner turned to Lombardi and pleaded, "I know I am supposed to be the youth representative in this culture . . . but *what the fuck is that?*"

The first piece of Thompson's writing published in *Rolling Stone* was, essentially, the transcription of his monologue in Jann Wenner's office. "Freak Power in the Rockies" was about his attempts to become sheriff of Pitkin County. Its denizens had moved there as a bucolic, affordable, intelligent alternative to the plight that had wracked Haight-Ashbury and other urban centers of the counterculture, especially after the riots in L.A. and Newark in 1965 and 1967.

Many people observing the "Thompson for Sheriff" campaign from a distance might well have thought it the effort of a writer with money to burn from the royalties of a best-selling book, and a lust for getting his name in the news for unusual behavior. Thompson did have precedents; Norman Mailer and Jimmy Breslin had run on a ticket for the mayoralty of New York, and a Chicano attorney, Oscar Zeta Acosta, had organized the Latino vote in East L.A. and given incumbent Pete Pritchess a run for sheriff. Acosta, who would soon become immortalized as the 300-pound Samoan attorney in *Fear and Loathing in Las Vegas,* had come to Aspen during the summer of 1970. He met Thompson in the Daisy Duck saloon; the meeting was arranged by Mike Solheim, who had known them from his days running a bar and coffeehouse in Ketchum, Idaho. Bill Kennedy from the San Juan *Star* was also there.

Thompson's campaign poster, executed by a local artist and close friend, Tom Benton, was a departure from the usual tasteful Aspen posters. It showed a bold, yard-high, neon-blue clenched fist. Close inspection of the poster shows that the fist has six fingers, and is squeezing a peyote button in the very center. When Henry Preston, Thompson's old Air Force buddy, visited the campaign headquarters on the second floor of the Jerome Hotel, "Hunter was so whacked out he didn't even recognize me," said Preston. Regardless, the campaign drew serious attention from the most unlikely source: the Hell's Angels, never known for political sophistication.

In the third week of October, 1970, as voter organization was building steam, a man with long hair, beard, and mustache parked his chopped Harley-Davidson in front of Aspen's Public House Bar and removed his polished metal Kaiser Bismark helmet. He walked inside, ordered a double bourbon on the rocks, and asked the barmaid where he could find the house of his friend Hunter Thompson. Even then, local Aspenites were mildly protective of the journalist, but when the Harley rider snapped open a switchblade and stirred his bourbon with it, directions to Woody Creek were quickly provided.

The biker appeared at Hunter's, telling him he was a friend of the Oakland Angels' president, Sonny Barger, and that if Thompson was elected sheriff, he would be killed and his house blown up. The Angels, evidently, were still in a stomping mood, and this threat was not to be taken lightly. Months before, Thompson had holed up in the house of his friend David Pierson, then the Mayor of Richmond, California. Pierson had refused a zoning variance to some blacks in his community; they had protested by circling Pierson's house. As Mayor, Pierson requested police protection and got a second cordon of big angry men in the form of police. The Angels caught wind of Thompson's whereabouts and tried to come after him for a sequel to the stomp; they had to wait their turn as they formed the third ring around Hunter inside Pierson's house. It looked like a cheap production of Dante's Inferno.

Now, for the next three days, the biker hung around the campaign headquarters, and came on with such violent suggestions for political strategy that even Thompson was taken aback. Bromley, as the biker was known, offered Hunter's campaign people guns and explosives to blow up bridges, and suggested that he act as Thompson's bodyguard and beat up several people. Some of his specific quotes included: "Tell me who's doing it and I will wipe them out . . . we'll kill them . . . there will be blood in the streets up to our ankles." Thompson and his campaign manager, Mike Solheim, went to the incumbent sheriff, Carrol Whitmire, on a tip that the biker was actually an infiltrator. He was. He had been hired sight unseen by the sheriff to investigate, among other things, the theft of dynamite from the Aspen Skiing Corporation, which ran the ski slopes. But no one had an explanation for why he had been urging the use of violence among Thompson's campaigners, or why he suddenly disappeared.

The Colorado Bureau of Investigation was asked in; they made a quick call to Solheim, telling him to take Hunter and everyone else out of the Jerome Hotel, retreat to the house in Woody Creek, six miles north of town, and arm themselves. Sandy and Juan were hidden with a friend of Solheim's in Aspen. Along with Acosta, Bill Kennedy, and Solheim, Thompson armed himself to the teeth and hunkered down in the single-story log house alongside Woody Creek Road at the foot of the broad Woody Creek valley. Nothing happened. It was all very anticlimactic. There they were, all armed-up and no place to shoot; they were prepared like no other political campaign in memory. Had anything actually happened, there was Acosta ready to sue, Kennedy ready to render the action into fiction, Solheim ready to pour drinks, and Thompson with his typewriter ready to write it up for the readers of *Rolling Stone* magazine.

Curiously, his actual intention in running for sheriff was to play the role of smoke and mirrors, to deflect interest away from Ned Vair, a friend of Hunter's running for a seat on the county commission. However, when Thompson founded the Freak Power Party as a clowning diversion to allow Vair to sneak aboard the body that dictated land-use policy, it all backfired. Suddenly there were newspaper reporters showing up from every major paper in the country to investigate just what "Freak Power" was all about. When the incumbent, Carroll Whitmore, stood in front of a sheriff candidate's meeting of three hundred, he stumbled badly over his words, and said, "If I seem nervous, it's because this many people scare me. I want the job real bad." Thompson, on the other hand, sucked up the limelight like any rock star; there was no missing of photo opportunities this time. Even *Time* magazine, which Thompson felt had stiffed its former employee by not reviewing *Hell's Angels,* put a photo of him, his head shaved, into its "People" section.

"Sheriff Thompson" was perfect Rocky Mountain hype, but it never came to be; Thompson lost to the incumbent by a 1523-to-1068 vote, actually closer than anyone had expected. "If we can't win in Aspen, we can't win anywhere," Thompson said, yet his intrigue with the political process had been triggered, and would continue to roll. "Politics is an art of survival. I don't see politics as one thing over here, and life over here. I see them together. Politics has to do with controlling your environment, which is one of the main reasons we are here," he said later. "It is like watching big weights move around. If you measure success or failure in life, having control of your environment would be one of the criteria. Politics is one way to do that. Besides, I didn't really want to be sheriff. I just wanted to own him. We did pretty well in those elections, scared the piss out of people. We had a say. We had a voice. And did I feel like I could really move around those big weights? You bet I did!"

The coverage and experience, like that of any opportunistic writer, went into "Freak Power in the Rockies." His zest for the political process continued in 1972, when Thompson began to cover the George McGovern Presidential campaign for the magazine. Thompson brought new targets and new readership to a magazine previously focused on the music world, but now broadening its horizons.

As an attempt to take the magazine into new, more profitable areas, Jann Wenner had used great promises of the future to lure away Alan Rinzler, a Harvard-educated senior editor at Macmillan in New York, to start Straight Arrow Press in San Francisco. While still at Macmillan, Rinzler had been working on a book of photographs of a Chicago motorcycle gang, one of the myriad motorcycle books of that day. An *Esquire* editor had asked if they could use some of the photos in an article they were doing. The author of the piece was Hunter Thompson; Rinzler read it and said to himself, "Who is this guy Hunter Thompson? . . . He seems really interesting."

14.

High-Bouncing,

Gold-Hatted

Drugger

ireworks marked the first serious editorial meeting between Hunter Thompson and Alan Rinzler, shortly before *Rolling Stone*'s serialization of *Fear and Loathing in Las Vegas*. In the black of a Palm Springs evening, after having consumed LSD, Thompson approached Rinzler carrying a box full of Roman candles. He lit one. He handed

it to Rinzler. In his typical monotonic, challenging way, he said, "Hold this."

"It was a real metaphor," Rinzler noted. "I had worked with a lot of different writers—Tom Robbins, Toni Morrison, Shirley MacLaine,—but I soon realized that this was going to be different. Really different." The relationship lasted from the Las Vegas book through *The Great Shark Hunt* and *The Curse of Lono,* over a decade during which Rinzler helped shape a vast amount of creative material, and observed pernicious changes in the man and his abilities.

Rinzler's first impressions of Thompson were that the writer was a "big, scary, athletic, red-necked guy, very animated, always holding a glass, smoking a cigarette, and jumping all over the place." Further, this editor had never met any writer with Thompson's drug-driven, drug-dependent style. "Hunter would juggle alcohol and speed. The speed would get him up and get the adrenaline flowing. It would make him even more manic than he usually was, and give him racing thoughts. Then the alcohol would give him a sense of euphoria. That was the balance he was trying to achieve. Later, unfortunately, he switched from amphetamines to cocaine—around '74 or '75. Cocaine is a nastier drug, a more debilitating drug. You have to do more and more of it."

Rinzler found Thompson very intimidating and was instinctively wary of him, never letting his guard down. Adding to that circumspect relationship was Thompson's repeated use of dark humor in referring to Rinzler's ethnicity. "Hey, you Jews are really smart and rich, and you are always going to get in there and be the boss over guys like me," he would rail. Thompson had never worked with an editor with such an intense style before; Rinzler would literally sit up all night, elbow-to-elbow with him, working to get inside his world, and then come back out with the semblance of a finished product. Thompson, given his hubris, perceived Rinzler as an authoritarian threat. To edit Thompson meant to impose control, to exert judgment, perhaps to take away some of the essence of his freedom of expression. And Thompson's ability to express himself was his only ticket to ride. He knew no other trade. If Rinzler felt threatened by Thompson's hypomanic bluster, Hunter undoubtedly felt vulnerable to his editor taking a scalpel to his creative efforts.

Years before Thompson began his new work, he had sat at his writing area on Perry Street. Underneath a banner emblazoned with Fitzgerald's dictum, "Action Makes Character," Thompson typed long passages from *The Great Gatsby,* in an attempt, he told Alan Rinzler, to "know in his own neurological system how it felt to write that kind of prose."

"I want you to know that we're on our way to Las Vegas to find the American Dream," yells the narrator of *Fear and Loathing* to a mute, terror-struck hippie hitchhiker caught in the back of the red Chevy convertible, screaming east across the desert near Barstow at 110 miles an hour, shortly after "the drugs began to take hold."

If ever Thompson was in need of some form of American Dream, it was at this point in his life. On a personal level, he had passed the symbolic, end-of-youth age of thirty. In his family life, there were problems brewing; after the birth of Juan, Sandy had experienced a series of miscarriages, and some felt she blamed Hunter. Professionally, after the Kentucky Derby article, Thompson had made little progress. His leap into politics had been educational but not successful. To top it all, Nixon was now *President.* Yet, in unfolding the yellowed outline of *Gatsby,* he showed that even he had hope.

When Thompson first read *The Great Gatsby,* as a high-school student, he must have felt that "shock of recognition" hit heavily. Daisy Buchanan and her friend the golfer Jordan Baker had together spent their "white girlhood" in Louisville, where Daisy had met and fallen in love with Gatsby, an officer at Camp Zachary Taylor. Further, Nick Carraway, like so many of Thompson's close friends, had gone to Yale; Carraway introduces himself in the book as a member of a "clan" and also descended from "the Dukes of Buccleuch." However, at present, his father ran a hardware store. Perhaps the most brilliantly waving red flag for Hunter was on the first page of *Gatsby,* where Carraway passes on his father's most basic mental posture toward the rest of the world: that "a sense of the fundamental decencies is parcelled out unequally at birth."

The story was in Thompson's neurological system before he had ever started to type its passages. And while he was enthralled with the writing of Fitzgerald, Thompson felt that new times dictated an update to this whole West Egg-East Egg American Dream, with its overtones of class difference that had rankled Thompson for years.

For Thompson, all arrows seemed pointed at Las Vegas, that sordid little oasis in the middle of the desert. It was a land unto

THE LOUISVILLE COURIER-JOURNAL

Jack Robert Thompson and Virginia Ray Thompson on their
wedding day, 1935, in Louisville, Kentucky. He was an insurance
adjuster; Virginia had attended the University of Michigan.

At age five, Hunter's last sign of obedience to authority: wearing a scout uniform, giving the proper salute.

Seventeen-year-old Thompson wears penny loafers, Bermuda shorts, and a full head of hair.

Wigged out. The American flag was a constant article of clothing for Hunter during his active political days.

Running for sheriff, Thompson shaved half of his head accidentally, then completed the act.

Wearing a sheriff's star, Hunter looks more like a
Vulcan than an Aspenite.

Glory days in Aspen when Hunter appeared surgically attached to a telephone, his cigarette and Sandy. This would end with his 1979 divorce trial.

Hunter loading up.

Roxanne Pulitzer and Hunter Thompson during a break in her "I Slept with a Trumpet" divorce case, in West Palm Beach, November 1983. While the two had met only once, at a dinner party the night before, Thompson would produce such a scathing piece of journalism for *Rolling Stone* that Roxanne was warned by a close friend never to read the article. She never has.

Seattle, 1987: History is made as Abbie Hoffman hugs old friend Tim Leary; Hunter stands by.

Hunter Thompson applies lipstick before addressing a student
gathering at the University of Washington.

Hunter Thompson is caught doing his best Richard Nixon imitation
after the 1990 "Life Style Bust" trial in Aspen.

itself, where values seemed pure and untouched by the '60s revolution. In Nevada, the punishment for sale of marijuana was life in prison. Yet prostitution was a regulated business, as perfunctory as stock and bond sales. This is where blue-haired grandmothers cash Social Security checks, fill plastic buckets with quarters, then spend days defending their slot machines, trying to hit the big one. Some did hit it. Las Vegas was a carnal, venal, legal fantasy for anyone who could afford the gas to get there. It was West Egg, East Egg, and the Golden Egg, all rolled into one.

In writing *Fear and Loathing in Las Vegas,* Thompson was true to his *Gatsby* outline, right down to the length: discounting blank pages and Ralph Steadman's lurid caricatures, both books are 182 pages long. It is in the opening scenes, where the drug-filled convertible zooms east across the wasteland desert, and Thompson babbles manically at the terrified hitchhiker, that the reader is smacked across the face with just how little has changed since Fitzgerald expressed his opinions in 1925.

The issue of race was important in *Gatsby,* where the Buchanans talked of Daisy and Jordan's "white girlhood" and the importance of being Nordic. Race—and civil rights—were at the root of Berkeley's Free Speech Movement, and a core of the ethos of the '60s. Thompson's update? His 300-pound attorney, he tells the hitchhiker, is a foreigner. "I think he's probably Samoan. But it doesn't matter, does it. *Are you prejudiced?"* he demands, knowing not even a fool would answer "yes" to a wild man screaming, waving a can of foaming hot beer with one hand, swatting away imaginary bats with the other, while straddling the front seat of a top-down convertible going 110 miles an hour. For the duration of *Las Vegas,* the attorney, who alternates between counseling Thompson and doing "the big spit"—the perpetually nauseous superego—never has a name. He is always just "my attorney." On one hand, this is a brilliant piece of symbolism: in this new day, anyone, even an anonymous, dark, overweight foreigner, can become part of that previously super-elite group of society's genetically correct rule makers. Take that, you Nordic Louisvillians!

On the other hand, the real-life inspiration for this nameless, vomiting barrister was a man of profound personal importance to Hunter, a close friend for a brief time, until he disappeared from a boat sailing out of Mazatlán, in 1974. Oscar Zeta Acosta was the legendary "Brown Buffalo." In real life, he was a near full-blooded Aztec Indian, who prided himself on his heritage. There was a strong synergy between the two: an appreciation for bizarre humor, a fondness for drugs and drink, and a disregard for personal safety that flowed together like a high-octane fuel. Many of the scenes in *Las Vegas* are less fabrications of Thompson's creativity than re-creations of actual drug-induced weirdness.

As if rehearsing for their roles in *Las Vegas,* Oscar Acosta rented an apartment in Aspen the winter of 1967-68, and spent considerable time with Hunter. While his employment washing dishes and an odd construction job was a divergent career path for someone who had practiced law in an Oakland storefront legal clinic, there was another important dimension to Acosta that magnetized Hunter's attention. While Juan, and Marco, Oscar's son, would watch in awe, the Brown Buffalo would put on a robe, stand in front of the huge stone fireplace in Thompson's main room at Owl Farm, and preach. Raised by Mexican parents as a strict Catholic, Acosta had received some formal religious training when stationed in Panama in the Air Force. He loved an audience, and he had spellbinding oratorical powers. As he read from the Old Testament, ad-libbing interpretations, Hunter, Juan, and Marco would gather to listen. "Basically, he was performing," Marco said. "Hunter would be mesmerized by his preaching and quoting from the Bible. Juan just sat there, with his eyes open wide. No one could believe how he could go on and on."

F itzgerald used music to add edge to his scenes; Jay Gatsby commanded a houseguest to play on the piano

"In the morning,
In the evening,
Ain't we got fun"

at a moment when things were turning catatonic. Later, when Gatsby goaded Daisy into telling her husband that she had never loved him, Mendelssohn's Wedding March floated through their Plaza Hotel room. Thompson got a similar effect, and even snared nostalgia of earlier times, when he opened the book with the attorney listening to the little religious ditty about sitting in a railway station, waiting to go home, while Hunter played, over and over again, the Rolling Stones' "Sympathy for the Devil.

Of course there is the car, the ultimate in rolling American status. The bigger the boat, the better. Gatsby's car was "a rich cream color, bright with nickel, swollen here and there in its monstrous length . . . with a labyrinth of wind-shields that mirrored a dozen suns. . . ." It was West Egg on wheels. For Thompson it begins with "The Shark," a red Chevy convertible; then after refusing a Mercedes ("Do I look like a goddamn Nazi? . . . I'll have a natural *American* car or nothing at all!"), he zips around Vegas in "The White Whale," a Cadillac convertible that gets badly stained from the attorney's drooling vomit. But it "was a wonderful machine: Ten grand worth of gimmicks and high-priced special effects. Rear windows that leaped up at a touch, like frogs in a dynamite pond."

Jay Gatsby had two grand parties at his house, and if Las Vegas is West Egg, then Circus-Circus is Gatsby's mansion. Thompson finds the American Dream twice in that casino. The first time, while masquerading as a sportswriter to cover a motor-cycle race for *Sports Illustrated,* he feels he has found "the main nerve" of the American Dream. This sudden realization comes while drinking Wild Turkey at a revolving bar, and watching the action. If what Thompson sees are in fact the "fantastic *possibilities* of life in this country," then he has stumbled, in an ether-fueled stupor, into a nocturnal madness rather than a dream. And that is his point. What does our culture have to offer in this hedonic mecca? Let him list the menu items: "Shoot the pasties off the nipples of a ten-foot bull dyke" . . . have your image appear on a neon screen, two hundred feet tall; for an extra 99 cents, say whatever you want . . . watch a high-wire trapeze act with "four muzzled Wolverines and the Six Nymphet Sisters" . . . "a half-naked fourteen year-old girl being chased through the air by a snarling wolverine, which is suddenly locked in a death battle with two silver-painted Polacks" . . . and while staring out his hotel window he suddenly envisions a "vicious Nazi drunkard . . . two hundred feet tall . . . screaming . . . 'Woodstock Über Alles.' "

If Louisville and the Kentucky Derby could run decadent and depraved for one long weekend a year, Las Vegas was doing it non-stop, year round, and people from every class and every state flocked there like pilgrims to Lourdes. As Thompson had done at the Derby, he read newspaper bannerlines about bombings in Vietnam, or watched Nixon on TV while whacked out on the drug adrenachrome, taken from a live human adrenal gland. Las Vegas, he decided, was no place for psychedelic drugs: "Reality itself is too twisted."

Drugs, rock and roll—they are all there, especially the drugs. Even if one has a clear head, the city of Las Vegas is as exhilarating and fantastic as it is petty. With Thompson's turbo-consumption, one feels hung over just reading the pages. He made drug and alcohol ingestion into an aerobic exercise. His only comment on the aftereffects of ingestion was to quote a conversation overheard between two truck drivers: "It's tough to wallow with the hogs at night, and then soar with the eagles in the morning." But where was the sex? The Devil's triumvirate is left incomplete; there's very little sex in his books. Thompson responded to this later by saying, "It is tough to stay married for fifteen years and write about orgies."

Instead, he and the 300-pound Samoan had met Savage Lucy, a religious freak with huge shoulders, a chin like Oscar Bonavena's, and a penchant for drawing charcoal sketches of Barbra Streisand from her television. She had come to Las Vegas to present fifty sketches to the performer in person. The attorney tossed purple caps of acid at her. It seemed to work, but Thompson had other plans for his attorney's woman, who "had the look of a beast that had just been tossed into a sawdust pit to fight for its life." At this point, they were covering the National District Attorneys Conference on Dangerous and Narcotic Drugs. The D.A.s were the revenue agents of the '70s, but to Thompson they were little different from his motorcycle gang of seven years before. He wanted to take Lucy and "turn her out." "We can keep her loaded and peddle her ass at the convention. . . . She's perfect for the gig . . . these cops will go fifty bucks a head to beat her into submission and then gang-fuck her."

The D.A.s, Thompson implied, were brainless thugs. And if they were in charge of preserving moral values in Nixon's land, imagine who was running the show in Vietnam. Thompson and "the attorney" went far beyond the in-your-face ridicule and scorn of the law enforcers as people and moral guardians. In rich dark humor, he demonstrated that the greater joke was not about the district attorneys; it was about the American Dream itself.

Thompson established the fact that the law-enforcement officers knew nothing about the drug world. He thought of educating them by offering his hotel room as a "life-slice exhibit." He described the room's ambience as that of a failed zoological experiment involving whiskey and gorillas, where the bed was a charred tangle of springs, and the lights around the shattered mirror had been replaced with Christmas bulbs. The carpet was green with marijuana seeds. The floor of the bathroom was so thick with vomit, soap bars, grapefruit rinds, and broken glass that Thompson commented, "I had to put my boots on every time I went in there to take a piss."

The problem in America, Thompson insisted, was more profoundly sad than the ignorance of the D.A.s; his own people had missed the boat. In a moment of reflection, he discussed "the fatal flaw in Tim Leary's trip." The Woodstock generation had been maimed, lost forever, because the LSD-induced optimism, the visions of a better world were erroneous. The '60s generation fell for the basic acid fallacy that "someone—or at least some *force*— is tending the Light at the end of the tunnel."

The American Dream, Thompson joked, was right there in Circus-Circus, underneath the Forty Flying Carazito Brothers and the trapezing three Korean Kittens. The owner had always wanted to run away and join a circus when he was little. "Now the bastard has his own circus," Thompson pointed out, "and a license to steal, too. It's pure Horatio Alger, all the way down to the attitude." He tried to contact the owner of Circus-Circus, and was stonewalled by his secretary, who told him "to fuck off. She said she hates the press worse than anything else in America. Journalism is not a profession or a trade," Thompson continued. "It is a cheap catch-all for fuck-off's and misfits—a false doorway to the backside of life, a filthy pus-ridden little hole nailed off by the building inspector, but just deep enough for a wino to curl up from the sidewalk and masturbate like a chimp in a zoo-cage."

Certainly the dream of "the attorney" ended up somewhat on the ragged side. When the real-life 300-pound Samoan attorney read the Las Vegas manuscript, he said to editor Alan Rinzler, "My God! Hunter has stolen my soul! He has taken my best lines and has used me. He has wrung me dry for material." Acosta had a clear dimension of macho black humor in him as well, and a druggie style that was transparent in the book. Regardless, his emotional take on it, he said to Rinzler, was that he felt "ripped off again."

Acosta's concerns were so strong that the publisher's libel attorneys asked him to sign a waiver stating he would not sue. The book almost never made it to press as Acosta stewed and deliberated over what to do. His son, a law-school graduate, stated that without the waiver, the book would never have been published. Not only was the story and the portrayal of Oscar Acosta cut neatly from real life, his photograph was to appear on the back of the original hardback book. In Thompson's portrayal of the "300-pound Samoan attorney," only his ethnic origins had been changed. The action in Las Vegas was such a true extension of Oscar Acosta's style of life, that when his son read the book, he stated that "it was hard for me to put the real 'crazy' personality of my father in context. I did not see how it was any different from reality. He really was like that. People should not make any mistake; he lived his life with drinking, drugs, music; almost like one constant party. Then he could get up at five in the morning and do a full day's work. So the *Las Vegas* thing was no different than his real life."

Further, much of the dialogue was transcribed from taped conversations. "Hunter still has them," Marco Acosta said. "They basically just had an open tape recorder going all the time. The verbal give-and-take in the book was based on those tapes." The libel issue was finally settled. A deal allowed Straight Arrow Press to publish the book without a libel waiver, in trade for giving Acosta a publishing contract for two of his own books, which he managed to complete before disappearing.

T he ending of *Fear and Loathing* leaves the reader facing the failed American Dream, as did the conclusion of *Gatsby*. The book ends with a scene in the Denver Airport, where Thompson rustles up some fake Doctor of Divinity identification to purchase amyl-nitrate poppers. "Another fucked-up cleric with a bad heart" is how he puts the state of his health, mirroring that of the nation. "A monster reincarnation of Horatio Alger . . . just sick enough to be totally confident." If you can't buy happiness in this day and age, you can still get some pharmaceutical whoop and giggle to help make it through the night. And it can be hard to tell, but that green light at the end of the dock might be just another acid flashback.

N ot only did Thompson do his own editing of the manuscript for *Fear and Loathing in Las Vegas;* he rewrote it five times. He intended this short piece to be a quality effort, a tightly drawn American classic, fueled by the central spirits of the times and then worked over in detail. It worked. At the *Rolling Stone* offices, he dropped the first dozen pages on the desk of editor Paul Scanlon, and walked away chortling. When Scanlon read the manuscript, he buckled with laughter. Pulitzer Prize-winner Tony Lukas called it "the definitive piece on that time period." George Plimpton said of it, "Amazingly true." Norman Mailer observed, "When I saw *Las Vegas,* I just knew he had the mark of excellence." *The New York Times* provided the book with an epigram: "The Best Book of the Dope Decade."

15.

Rock

and

Roll

ver dinner at one of Aspen's fine dining places, Arthur Rock and Jann Wenner were joined by Hunter Thompson, who had just come from the sheriff's campaign headquarters. He carried a large clear plastic bag. It was filled with bloody animal entrails. He dropped it on the restaurant floor next to Rock's seat, saying nothing. Rock

did not react; he had expected something weird, having heard about Thompson. Throughout the dinner, not a word was said about the colorful, squishy pile on the floor. Near the end of dinner, Thompson had had it. Turning to Rock, shaking his bizarre doggy bag, he said, "Don't you know what this is? These are dead animal guts." Arthur Rock simply smiled.

Arthur Rock had begun life as the son of a Rochester, New York, candy-store owner. After Syracuse University and Harvard Business School, he had begun his West Coast ventures in 1957 as a thirty-year-old investment banker with the brokerage firm Hayden Stone. Fortuitously, a memo crossed his desk from some disgruntled employees of William Shockley, who had shared the Nobel Prize the previous year for inventing the transistor. They were looking for financial backing to start a company of their own. He responded. In a brief span of years, Rock helped start several companies, including Fairchild Semiconductor, SDS (or Scientific Data Systems), Teledyne, Intel, Advanced Micro Devices, and Apple Computer. In 1984, when *Time* magazine put him on the cover, he was valued at $200 million, saying, "Never has so much been made so quickly." His initial companies were the start of what is now known as Silicon Valley.

One of his deals involved Max Palevsky, the founder and former president of SDS, who became a venture capitalist himself after a 1968 stock swap with Xerox relieved Palevsky of running the company and rewarded him with a large part of the $930,000 valuation of the deal. In mid-1970, Jann Wenner had approached Arthur Rock for an infusion of money to keep the magazine rolling. In turn, Rock called on Max Palevsky, in Los Angeles, who met with Wenner in December and agreed to put in about $200,000; a small part was Rock's money. In turn, Palevsky, who, like Wenner, had attended Berkeley and dropped out (of a Ph.D. program, after graduating from the University of Chicago), thought that he was getting near complete power of the *Rolling Stone* checkbook. The deal did not work out as it had been explained to Palevsky. After about a year, Palevsky became very close friends with Wenner's wife, Jane, who lived at his Bel Air home for a while. ("We were never lovers" Palevsky was careful to point out.) Palevsky felt that it was inappropriate for him to have any further role in the company, although his investment and his business acumen were sorely needed, if not appreciated.

In Palevsky's eyes, doing business with Wenner was tricky business; Palevsky didn't trust him. And in his dealings with Thompson, Palevsky wondered about the sources of his creativity, saying, "He has one of the deepest dark sides of anyone I have ever met. I really wonder where all that anxiety and anger comes from."

Wenner had flown Palevsky to San Francisco, taken him to dinner, and tried to talk the businessman into staying on but playing a lesser role; Palevsky turned it down, and got entirely out of the magazine business after making no money for himself or Arthur Rock. However, he played a significant role in a political sense. He was the connective tissue between the motley, iconoclastic hippie crew at *Rolling Stone* and the 1972 Democratic Presidential candidate, South Dakota Senator George McGovern.

At the end of the 1968 Democratic Convention in Chicago, while Hunter Thompson was recovering from tear gas and from police ramming his gut with a nightstick, three men plotted an assault on Richard Nixon, four years down the road. Max Palevsky helped with raising money; George McGovern was the candidate; and Frank Mankiewicz, who had been Robert Kennedy's press secretary until his assassination in June, would help coordinate the charge. They faced an uphill battle.

In December, 1971, with Palevsky and Rock as part owners of *Rolling Stone,* the magazine staff retreated to Esalen and discussed the possibility of covering the entire Presidential campaign, from start to finish. The timing was crucial; in July of that year, the 26th Amendment had been ratified. Millions of baby boomers at least eighteen years old would be able to vote for the first time. With a folk hero like George McGovern battling a warmonger like Richard Nixon, how could the spirit of protest, part of the founding ethos of *Rolling Stone,* go wrong? The champion of the drive to cover the campaign was Hunter Thompson. Many on the staff disagreed with his concept, arguing that the average *Rolling Stone* reader was interested in rock and roll and in dope news, not national politics. Besides, they felt it would be costly— Thompson had developed a nasty habit of running up expenses for short jaunts; they could just imagine what a solid year of travel would do to the magazine's unpredictable finances. For days, the staff met, drank, drugged, argued, soaked in the hot tubs, and were photographed by a young artist who had paid her own way to come to the meeting, Annie Leibowitz. In the end, Hunter's logic won out, and Wenner agreed to bankroll his yearlong immersion in the daily fisticuffs of American politics. But Wenner was crafty about it; he and Alan Rinzler wrote an agreement into Hunter's contract that all campaign coverage expenses were to be repaid from whatever book advance he received through his agent, Lynn Nesbit, at International Creative Management in New York. "Spend whatever you like, Hunter," he was told. "It is your money."

Thompson spoke of the mentality he carried into his initial foray in politics on a national level. He said that in the early '60s, "Jack Kennedy gave people a sense that if you could get over the fence and across the White House lawn without being caught, the President would talk to you. He'd be amused," Thompson said, "at least civil. He wouldn't chop your hands off. The rebellion of the '60s [after Kennedy] carried with it a kind of naïve sense that since we were right, then the 'right' thing would prevail. Eventually we would stop the war, and find better ways to live. Some of those life-styles were just seeds at that time, but they would evolve into something."

The concept of covering a Presidential campaign was relatively virgin territory, even for newspapers, and Thompson's vision of doing it in his full-participatory style was something of a groundbreaker. Only a year before the *Rolling Stone* conference at Big Sur, the Los Angeles *Times* had just hired its first national political correspondent.

This particular campaign was, McGovern agreed later, "a '60s campaign run in the '70s." It blended parts of the spirit of both decades, and in doing so became something that will never again be replicated. The '60s naïve sense of the "right" thing prevailing was present in the missionary-like zeal and human understanding of McGovern, son of a Methodist minister. Robert Kennedy had said of McGovern, "He is the most decent man in the Senate." McGovern was kind and humanistic, characteristics more avuncular than political. Even Thompson said of him that he could use a little more of "the dark kinky streak of Mick Jagger in his soul." On the other side of the battle line was the high-tech, win-at-all-costs incumbent, Richard Nixon.

In framing the politics of the time as a drug metaphor—the best way to understand the era as well as Thompson's writings—it was the time of turning the corner from the popularity of marijuana and LSD to the new popularity of amphetamines and cocaine. The former gave beautiful visions; the latter produced nonstop efforts. Jann Wenner's favorite paraphrasing of Timothy Leary caught the spirit of the times, when former hippies were all emerging from business school: "Turn-on, tune-in, drop-out, make money."

Politics, especially on a national level, is an ultimate high. Cravings, obsessions, and fantasies dominate the motivation of men with even the most remote chance at the White House. Thompson used the analogy of a beast in heat: "the bull elk in the rut . . . his loins . . . heavy with blood." Bull elks, like politicians with a scent of the White House, rush through the forest with the single-mindedness of a giant cannonball. They attack one another "with all the violence of human drug dealers gone mad on their own wares."

"Political junkies" is a commonly used term, and it refers to the atavistic allure of power that drew Thompson's attention as well as the candidates'. The drug metaphor that runs through Thompson's writing on the campaign was more than apt. Experimenting with drugs can provide feelings of power, self-confidence, illusions of limitlessness, feeling alive and in the moment. So, too, with political experimentation.

It seemed perfectly fitting that Hunter Thompson's investigation of the 1972 Presidential campaign would give readers vivid insights into the chemistry of politics. Who else was there on the American scene more perfectly constructed to communicate to this particular coming-of-age generation just what the high adrenaline rush of the Presidential race really felt like?

Thompson was equipped, and *Rolling Stone* provided the vehicle. No other publication before or since could have provided the platform, tolerance, and readership for Gonzo political journalism. Porter Bibb, the former Athenaeum from Louisville, had coincidentally been brought into *Rolling Stone* to shore up their financial management. His view is consistent with Rinzler's, that few other editors would have had as much patience and appreciation as Wenner. "Once *Rolling Stone* established its credentials as 'the source' on rock music, it could feed the kids anything. Hunter was absolutely born to *Rolling Stone*." Bibb went on to describe the way Wenner opened the creative gates for Thompson. "The two had a tremendous love-hate relationship. But the thing I admire most about Jann is the rightness of his gut instincts as an editor. He understands what works better than any editor I've ever met. Hunter and Jann could not have had a more symbiotic relationship, but with Hunter, Jann did not edit. And that was Hunter's saving grace."

Wenner let the presses roll. Who else would have printed articles titled "The Million Pound Shithammer," "Crank Time on the Low Road," or "Stoned on the Zoo Plane"?

The alliance of Wenner and Thompson was like Peter Pan meeting Peter Pan. Both were spoiled little kids who refused to grow up, who, in reaching for everything they could possibly grasp, built reputations of terror and irresponsibility and amazing creativity. Each had a "damn the body count" approach to life, and if Wenner sneaked in the expense-account clause without Thompson's full awareness, Hunter would get back at Jann, terrorizing him by spitting fireballs of lighter fluid at him (immortalized in an Annie Leibowitz photograph) or hosing down his and Jane's favorite poodle with a fire extinguisher. As head of *Rolling Stone,* Wenner made it clear that it was *his* magazine, and he played an integral role in turning out each new issue. Both Wenner and Thompson were driven men; each seemed umbilically attached to a typewriter, and drawn like a moth to a flame to figures of greater status and fame.

Wenner's errors of enthusiasm—and self-publicity—are as legendary as they are laden with black humor. When Janis Joplin died, he immediately ordered her subscription canceled. When Elvis Presley died, he was heard to react by saying, "It . . . it . . . it is a COVER!" and immediately removing an Andy Warhol cover at the last possible minute. When he fired his personnel, he would play appropriate music. When John Lombardi resigned, Wenner tried to keep the writer from leaving by playing the Beatles' "Get Back." To a notoriously slow writer, he would hand amphetamines and say, "Time to take your medicine." When *Rolling Stone* won the National Magazine Award for coverage of the Altamont concert killings, three of the four writers had already left. Those working at the magazine, where the '60s spirit persisted, where drugs were prevalent and creativity reigned, called it "the endless boogie." But Wenner's quixotic, "love you today, burn you at the stake tomorrow" management style led many employees to coin the corporate slogan "Jann is the Wenner of our discontents."

T hompson called on his old friend from *National Observer* days Robert Semple to assist in getting press credentials to cover the Democratic race. Even though Semple was covering Nixon, Thompson was successful. For the first part of the 1972 campaign, Thompson was teamed with a Boston-based *Rolling Stone* writer, Timothy Crouse, who had been assigned to follow McGovern, while Thompson had been following Edmund Muskie, the senator from Maine. Thompson got along well with Crouse, who, like Mankiewicz, had been abroad in the Peace Corps; the two lent an international altruistic flair that was very much a part of the campaign and its coverage. But Thompson overlooked Crouse's own proximity to literary greatness that would have seriously intrigued him. Crouse's father had worked as a sportswriter on the Kansas City *Star* with Ernest Hemingway. Also, Joe Mankiewicz, Frank's uncle, had been a Hollywood producer who F. Scott Fitzgerald claimed ruined one of his best scripts.

Timothy Crouse spoke with a stutter when Thompson first knew him. During the April, 1972, Wisconsin primary, when Crouse ended up with the winner's story as McGovern beat all contenders, Wenner told him not to write the winner's story. He was there to carry Hunter Thompson's Wild Turkey. Crouse hung up, wrote the story, stopped stuttering, and went on to write his own best-selling book about that campaign, *The Boys on the Bus.*

"What I thought about Hunter all the time," Frank Mankiewicz observed, "was how little he fit the popular notion of him. I thought he was dignified, conservative, well dressed, clean shaven, short hair. I always thought he was very straight and took good care of his body. He drank Wild Turkey, but not a lot. I never saw him unbalanced or spaced out. I always thought that he was quite straight ahead—much more so than some of the other reporters. I was well aware that he wrote for *Rolling Stone,* that he was a Gonzo journalist and sort of a different kind of guy, but not that much."

George McGovern had come across Hunter late one night before the primaries, when Thompson was heavily into drink at a Washington, D.C., gathering at staffer Tom Brady's house, regaling people with stories of his recently lost sheriff's campaign in Aspen. Thompson's term "Freak Power" stuck in McGovern's memory, even though the two did not really interact that night. "I remember him coming up to New Hampshire. I think the first time we visited was in the men's room someplace. I recognized him, shook hands with him, and we talked briefly."

The issue of the "untouched constituency" was of obvious significance to the McGovern campaign, and his staff had a keen awareness of the readership of *Rolling Stone.* There was a mutual respect and appreciation between the reporter and the candidate. McGovern said, "I thought it was important that he be treated with respect. He was entitled to it, in view of the wide audience he was addressing." McGovern, who holds a Ph.D. in history, continued. "I never introduce myself as 'Dr.' McGovern, but I always wondered about the origins of 'Dr.' Hunter Thompson. I did catch him off guard one time. He was sitting with his back to me in a restaurant, and I heard his voice. I said 'Hey, Sheriff,' and he wasn't quite sure who it was calling him that. He was somewhat startled to see that it was the candidate using that title; I don't think he was aware I knew of that sheriff's race."

If Hunter Thompson could meet a Presidential candidate standing in the next urinal, it must have seemed that this was his kind of job. Other aspects of the work suited him as well. *Rolling Stone* never had any female staff members until after the campaign was over; female political reporters were virtually unheard of. It was a fraternity, although many of the journalists were openly jealous of Thompson's unfettered ability to "say it as he felt it." Alcohol was abundant; the hours were weird. While others had daily deadlines, Thompson's was once every two weeks. "I don't think he missed a single one," said editor Paul Scanlon. Alan Rinzler would often find Thompson asleep on his floor in the morning, just a step ahead of the deadline, and broke. "He was always in a state of high anxiety during the campaign. He would arrive at 5 A.M., then sleep on my floor. I would arrive the next morning, and there he would be. He was perpetually short of money and in a state of crisis. I think he craved the constant state of crisis," Rinzler said.

T hompson's writing proved to be exceptional. No one outside of *Rolling Stone* knew what to make of him. Stewart Alsop quoted him, then took him to task for irresponsibility. Even the august *Columbia Journalism Review* came out with a comparative analysis, where, point by point, Theodore H. White's *The Making of the President, 1972* and Dr. Hunter S. Thompson's *Fear and Loathing: On the Campaign Trail '72* were each graded like high-school term papers on key issues such as thesis, audience, and style. The only time they gave Thompson the better grade was on the question "How *was* it on the campaign trail in 1972?" *Loathing:* "B"; *Making:* "C." The true kudo was accorded in their statement "Sponteneity is perhaps the hardest of all stylistic effects to maintain." Thompson, the journal allowed, could cover a lot of ground, be visceral, vivid, and funny. He could keep the reader's attention with his alternative use of facts, personalized fictions, hilarious descriptions, and actual transcriptions of taped events. As in life, the reader never knew what to expect next, and was constantly off balance, entertained, and looking forward to the next surprise. It just might be Frank Mankiewicz trying to walk after Thompson had cut off both big toes ("... very hard to walk with the Big Toe gone ... like taking the keel off a sailboat ... wallowing crazily in the swells ... the only way to walk ... is to use a complex tripod mechanism . . . moving around like a spider instead of a person").

Some thought that he carried things too far at times. In reality, Thompson's writing was to political coverage what Stravinsky's *Rite of Spring* was to classical music, and what cubism was to turn-of-the-century contemporary art. He took it apart, talked about how it looked to him, then went on to the next canvas with total disregard for anything he left behind. In other words, Thompson treated the 1972 campaign just as he had the rest of his life: on his own terms. He was just careful to look and act straight around McGovern and Mankiewicz.

Many readers felt a refreshing touch of reality when Thompson referred to Edmund Muskie as talking with the desperation of "a farmer with terminal cancer trying to borrow money on next year's crop," or Hubert Humphrey as either campaigning "like a rat in heat" or prattling on "like an eighty-year-old woman who has just discovered speed." Most readers loved Thompson's assigning Muskie's piques of hot temper to the occult drug Ibogaine. They laughed outrageously when he suggested that John Chancellor had taken LSD, that Walter Cronkite was dabbling in white slavery, or that Humphrey should be castrated. (In another year, after learning that one of Humphrey's grandchildren had been born developmentally disabled, Craig Vetter, who did a *Playboy* interview with Thompson, gave Hunter a chance to recant. He scoffed at the opportunity.) The *Columbia Journalism Review* responded to this sort of fantastic reportage by giving Dr. Thompson an "F" in the category of "How does he know what he says?" Clearly, such barbs from the pen of Thompson could have hurt the candidate to whom Thompson was attached.

"Hunter sensed that McGovern was the only nontraditional politician in the race," Mankiewicz said. "He liked the purity of the campaign. McGovern was never a leading or prominent candidate until we suddenly found ourselves as front-runners. We were always running a guerrilla campaign, living off the land. So we never worried about Hunter disgracing us. And when we read about Muskie addicted to Ibogaine, or that I threatened him with a tire iron in New Hampshire, well, we all really looked forward to those articles. I think we all laughed. I have always said that Hunter's writing was the most accurate and least factual account of the campaign."

McGovern concurred with Mankiewicz, saying of Hunter's unguided missives, "They didn't disturb me; I figured people would understand it was a 'Hunter technique' for making a point.

He suggested at one point that I'd pull in a couple of million votes if I posed for a picture before the California primary wearing a Grateful Dead T-shirt, holding a can of beer, and leaning against a motorcycle. I suspect he was right." He then concluded with solemnity, "But I did not go through with it."

McGovern went further, crediting Thompson's prescience, saying, "I have always thought of him as the first national press person covering that campaign who thought I was going to win the nomination, and maybe win the White House. I was told that he was an eccentric, brilliant, perceptive reporter, that he reached a wide and young audience, and that he was not to be taken lightly. I always treated him as a serious journalist. I never treated him as a joke."

Especially in the early going, McGovern was more than appreciative of Hunter's presence. Few others took their campaign with what McGovern felt was due respect. "Hunter was a cult figure," McGovern went on. "A campaign like ours was looking for help wherever we could find it. It was natural that we would be drawn to him. And we knew he brought some status to the campaign because he was recognizable. Personally, I thought he would be good at getting under the skin of other journalists. An added stimulus to the whole press corps operation. Get them to pay more attention to us: 'Why is Hunter Thompson traveling with McGovern? What does he see that we have missed?' I thought there would be a certain amount of that."

McGovern won the party nomination in Miami in June, while Hunter and Lucian Truscott, reporting for the *Village Voice,* tried with futility to get John Wayne to speak to Ron Kovic as a representative of the Vietnam Veterans. (Thompson kept a tape recording of Kovic's speech, often playing it over the Press plane's P.A. system, as no major media covered the Disabled Vets' protest of the convention.) Ted Kennedy, behind closed doors, turned down the Vice-Presidential nomination, and six minutes after the deadline, the senator from Missouri, Tom Eagleton, became McGovern's running mate.

When Thompson had signed on in December of 1971, he asked his readers "Is This Trip Necessary?" and noted that his arrival in Washington was *not* noted by any of the society columnists. McGovern, at that time, was seen by Thompson as "hung in a frustrated limbo created mainly by the gross cynicism of the Washington press corps." But here Thompson was, six months later, thick as thieves, fighting in the same ring as his archnemesis, Richard Nixon. There was a headiness in this incredible twist of events. And even if the celebratory atmosphere was quickly shot down to earth when it was revealed that Eagleton had undergone electroshock treatment for depression (and was replaced in the Vice President's slot by Sargent Shriver), the spoils system, should the White House be reached, was discussed. Apparently, Hunter made no requests, but Mankiewicz recalled that, ironically, Gary Hart had made a request to "run the boat that goes between the Virgin Islands."

> I always wanted to get into politics but I was
> never light enough to make the team.
> —Open letter from Art Buchwald to Richard Nixon

As late as the Republican Convention, Thompson—for all his anger and insight and built-in sense of paranoia—made little noise about the break-in at the Democratic Party Headquarters in the Watergate apartment complex on June 17th. Thompson merely hinted that Nixon would have trouble if it ever got as far as the courts. On the other hand, McGovern was publicly outraged at the issue. Looking back, he feels that his voicing his thoughts actually lost him votes. McGovern refers to Watergate as "one of the political mysteries of my life." He does not know why the public reacted so slowly and anemically to Nixon's criminal behavior. The majority leader of the Senate, Mike Mansfield, held an impromptu press briefing each day; on the day of the break-in (when the news appeared on page 50 of *The New York Times*), McGovern recalls him as saying of it, "Oh, it's one of those political pranks. President Nixon has no knowledge of it." McGovern said, "I tried to get various congressional committees to conduct an investigation. Nobody would touch it except Wright Patman, Chairman of the Banking Committee, as some of the moneys were thought to have been laundered through Mexican banks. He was blocked by Jerry Ford. They created a mood where it was impossible to talk about it without appearing like a crank who was exaggerating the issue, and engaging in desperation tactics to try to get attention. I think in retrospect, every time I closed one of my speeches with 'This is the most corrupt administration in American history,' it cost me another hundred thousand votes."

Thompson and McGovern and Mankiewicz spoke a lot about Watergate and about Nixon. "Hunter despised Nixon," McGovern said. "We would talk about the inability to get the country to focus on Watergate," but even Thompson did not come up with any specific suggestions of how to deal with it: if he had, McGovern would have been receptive. Mankiewicz felt that Hunter "always took things much more strongly. Besides, Watergate was criminality, not politics. Also, no journalist likes to begin a story with the words '*The Washington Post* said today . . .' " Further, he felt Americans did not want to believe that the President of the United States was sitting at the center of a criminal conspiracy "and that the charge is being made by the guy who wants his job!" Had Thompson gone head-to-head with Nixon, it seems likely that much of his journalistic impact would have been blunted by the outrageous statements he had made about Nixon in 1968, as well as his coverage of the other candidates in 1972.

Hunter made every deadline; he was careful to swim laps as often as he could, and he was courtly in his interactions with McGovern's staff. Timothy Crouse stated that he was straight for the duration. But he still remained a nocturnal bird. Crouse spoke of his early morning writing binges, with Thompson perched above his typewriter like a prehistoric bird of prey, "arms like wings out to his side, fingers poised over the keys. Very erect, very excited. He'd rip out a burst. Stop. Wait for it again. Then rip off some more." But he stayed away from the weird stuff. "He always had a beer in his hand," McGovern observed, then added, "but what press guy didn't?"

It must have been difficult for him, keeping all that stuff bottled up, just as it was during the first months in the Air Force. Thompson needed an occasional "vent," and he was careful how he did it. On one occasion, Thompson used "bad judgment" and gave his press pass, with his photo and name, to someone else who ran amok on the "Sunshine Express" train used by candidate Muskie. The man drank like a fish, and swore like a sailor; Muskie's staff simply assumed him to be Thompson. At a whistle-stop speech in a small Florida town, Muskie was disturbed and the crowd entertained when Thompson's friend fell down while clinging to Muskie's leg, shouting, "Get your lying ass back inside and make me another drink, you worthless old fart!"

With *Rolling Stone* people, Thompson could ease up on the self-control a bit. These were, after all, friends of a feather. In two scenes, one with John Lombardi, one with Wenner and Rinzler at Max Palevsky's house in Palm Springs, he kicked out the jams with reckless abandon before heading back into the serious business of political reporting. Each was a memorable event, and neither involved his own consumption of drugs.

When Thompson, Sandy, and Juan first moved from Aspen to Washington, driving their new blue Volvo 174 with a "Keep Big Sur Beautiful" bumper sticker and Colorado plates, they briefly rented a house in Silver Spring, Maryland. John Lombardi showed up nearby, trying to do an interview for *Rolling Stone* with James Brown. Brown stiffed the writer, who called Hunter for solace, and ended up going to his house at 3:30 in the morning—middle of the Thompson workday. Hunter and Sandy were both up, and after trying to calm down Lombardi, Thompson repeatedly offered him what appeared to be a joint. "I couldn't understand what he was talking about, and he kept on giving me this thing to smoke, and pretty soon I was out of it. Really out of it. It was not a nice high." Lombardi started to get sick, and Sandy gave him a place to rest in the guest bedroom, where Lombardi finally fell asleep.

"I woke up and there was Hunter dressed in some outer-space-looking thing. He was wearing something on his head that looked like a little flying saucer. He had a fire extinguisher over his shoulder, shooting it all over the room, yelling in jibberish, and jumping up and down on the bed. Then a friend of his came over and both of them were doing this. It was as if I had been invaded by two Martians. He thought it was hilariously funny, and I was vomiting."

Lombardi finally talked Thompson into driving him back to his hotel, through the early dawn streets. When Lombardi complained of more nausea, and asked Thompson to stop the car so he could throw up, Thompson refused, saying, "Just hold it in, man, just hold it in." Lombardi finally got to the sane tranquillity of his hotel, and never understood why Thompson had not stopped the car. "Maybe he had some stuff in the car; maybe he didn't want to get embarrassed in the neighborhood. Later he told me that he had not touched what he gave me—that it was a joint soaked in psilocybin. The point is that he was in complete control the whole time."

Max Palevsky's house, a twenty-minute ride from the Palm Springs airport, was too fine a setting to shoot off fire extinguishers and jump on beds; regardless, Thompson's mischief was again iconic and sadistic. So many of the *Rolling Stone* staff had been invited that Palevsky had to rent rooms in a nearby hotel for his guests. Dinner that night was duck with cherry sauce, done by Palevsky's cook. As an appetizer, Palevsky recalls that Hunter and Sandy bounded in with "some strange chemical. Hunter said, 'I don't know exactly what it is, but it is great stuff!' " In the peer pressure and spirit of the times, everyone took it, then lined up at the serving table in the dining room to put the carefully cooked and carved duck on their plates. "The initial effects of whatever it was that Hunter and Sandy had given everyone then became obvious," Palevsky observed with increasing distortion and discomfort. "The duck, instead of going on everyone's plates, was piling up on the floor."

Palevsky immediately had second thoughts; he had a chronic heart problem. Who knew what this mystery trip could do to him? Would Hunter Thompson or Jann Wenner know what to do with a dead multimillionaire? "Thinking back, I never should have touched it at all," he said. Things got worse as the night went on—people bumping into people, falling all over themselves, totally disoriented and feeling nauseous. "It was a terrible trip."

In the midst of all of this drug-induced mass hysteria were Hunter and Sandy. They leaped around the periphery of the human mess they had created. They slapped their thighs and cackled with glee, like Macbeth's witches: they had not taken anything. They were perfectly straight. Palevsky finally brought himself back to earth with some minor tranquilizers. By the next day all seemed forgiven. "I still have a signed, framed piece of paper on my wall," said Palevsky. "It is testimony that we all made it through that night. I call it The Proclamation of Survival."

The relation between Palevsky and Thompson was more one of observation than interaction. Thompson was fascinated by what he called Max's "MoJo Line." It was nothing more than an early-day FAX machine, and as a Board member of Xerox, Palevsky had several installed, including one to the San Francisco offices of *Rolling Stone.* Thompson found it a godsend. Now he could submit his writing actually after the deadline; it would come jerking out of the machine on the other end of the wire too late to be edited, yet still in time for the printer.

Palevsky spent some time in Aspen, and looked at property to buy. When he settled on a piece of mountaintop land, Thompson threatened him—jokingly—by attempting to buy up land over which the access roads ran; he intended to erect tollhouses and charge Palevsky each time he entered and left.

Other incidents at Woody Creek were less humorous. When the two played handball, Hunter, whom Palevsky described as very good at the game, did a self-styled pre-game warm-up that included ingesting huge quantities of speed. "Then he would stand on his side of the court in the middle of a massive puddle of sweat." Palevsky silently worried about the psychological future of Juan, then eight years old. "Hunter would shoot his guns toward where Juan was playing in the yard. Not right at him.

Mainly over him. But close enough and loud enough that the child went rigid with fear." As if the guns were not enough, Thompson occasionally livened up his son's sense of survival by sending the Dobermans after him. "Again, they would not actually attack, but would terrorize the boy," Palevsky observed.

Palevsky looked back at those strange times, and referred to Thompson as "a talker, not a writer." He then made a summary statement about his impressions of Thompson from that era. "Hunter Thompson is one of the most thoroughly contradictory people I have ever met. Nothing he does makes sense with anything else that he does. There is a great dark side to Hunter Thompson. That is what you see almost all the time. He must have some hurt, some pain deep down inside that causes all of this. I am not sure what it is, but it is obvious that he operates from a source of pain and anger and anxiety. I am not being Dr. Freud in saying this. I am just telling what I have seen."

T hompson seemed to have an incredible nose for the American underdog, and the election results of that year showed McGovern to be a profound loser. But before the final landslide, Thompson again went to Robert Semple to get White House permission to fly on the Nixon press plane. "I personally assured Ehrlichman and Ziegler that Hunter was O.K." said Semple, who footnoted his intercession by adding, "For that, Hunter repaid me by accusing me of kissing Ziegler's ass." Regardless, Thompson found the lone trip—to Oakland—to be a bore; the difference between the two candidates' press tours "was like the difference between a Grateful Dead concert and an audience with the Pope." As Nixon emerged from Air Force One, Thompson was an anonymous face in the crowd, mumbling, "Throw the bomb . . . a thousand years' Reich."

McGovern's loss to Nixon in the Electoral College vote was 520 to 17; the Super Bowl, with which Thompson symbolically ended his book (Miami vs. Washington), was closer but just as boring. The campaign road was over, and the press had disbanded in a bleak ceremony at the airport near McGovern's South Dakota home in an aura like the closing of an orphanage. In the book version, Thompson wraps it up with a phone call to Frank Mankiewicz, tells him about the virtues of persistence, and, around midnight, dons his aloha shirt and walks to the Losers' Club to drench his sorrows in drink.

In real life, the book was ended after a non-stop two-week

editing marathon. Alan Rinzler had given up trying to get Hunter to work in the *Rolling Stone* offices—too many distractions—and put him up in the relative isolation of the Cliff House, where Geary Boulevard meets the Pacific Ocean. "It took about two weeks," Rinzler said of the urgent push to get the book out and beat Teddy White to the stores. "It was intense. We worked with a tape recorder, and my secretary would come out to the Cliff House and take the tapes and transcribe them. Then we would be editing the transcriptions." Rinzler acted as nursemaid, editor, and drill sergeant. "I would have to get him out of bed, get food into him, and coffee." That was just the priming of the pump.

Rinzler's style in working with all authors is to enter their world, be supportive, and get out of them what is required to get the job done. "With Hunter, it was a tricky thing to enter that world. Setting off fireworks was one thing. Staying up all night, doing drugs and trying to keep your mind straight so that you can put the work out? To edit Hunter Thompson was debilitating."

Off the campaign trail, Thompson was also off the wagon. Working with the writer in such an intense mode, Rinzler was in a position to observe a more clearheaded sense of purpose in editing *Campaign Trail* than he did in 1983 when working on *The Curse of Lono*. "In those days," Rinzler said of the early '70s, "he was very serious about his work. After the coffee would come great quantities of Wild Turkey, just to stoke himself. Then he would do more cocaine and alcohol; those were becoming his favorite drugs in that time period. But he was not a babbling idiot in those days."

With his perspective across time, the editor noted that *Fear and Loathing in Las Vegas* was a piece of crafted prose. "After that he was getting lazy; he didn't want to work that hard on each sentence, so he thought, Hell! I've got an hour to write this story. Whatever happens, I can't edit it." But in response to repeated inquiry as to the actual amounts of consumption once the election was over, and beginning with the endless editing sessions at the Cliff House, Rinzler held his ground. "Always. A bottle of Wild Turkey. Smoking grass. Taking speed. Cocaine. All of this, constantly; in the office, out of the office, in the car. The idea was to get something into his body that would anesthetize the pain, the anxiety, the deep sense of depression and loss that is underneath all that anger. I see him as a serious alcoholic and drug addict in a state of total denial. No exaggeration."

16.

God

and Gonzo

at Yale

n September, 1972, in Washington, the McGovern campaign was slogging toward its inevitable doomsday ending, after the candidate had "gone mainstream" and embraced Chicago's Mayor Daley and the AFL-CIO's George Meany in a last-ditch attempt at pulling out votes. McGovern's alliance with Daley was especially galling to Hunter, as the Mayor of Chicago was the

person who allowed the riot-control police, who had roughed up Thompson, to run rampant in August of 1968.

Journalist Tony Lukas was then writing for *MORE* magazine, a competitor of the *Columbia Journalism Review.* His coverage of Thompson was an open door for Gonzo journalism to gain visibility beyond *Rolling Stone* readership. It was also an opportunity for enhancing Thompson's professional credibility, something he had always viewed with considerable ambivalence. The staff of *MORE* was heavy with Pulitzer Prize-winners such as Lukas, who won his in 1968 for covering the double life of Linda Fitzpatrick, daughter of a wealthy Connecticut family, who, in the spirit of the times, wandered through Haight-Ashbury, Berkeley, and Greenwich Village, where she lived for a while in an apartment adorned with posters of Bob Dylan, Timothy Leary, and Allen Ginsberg. She was found murdered in the boiler room of a seedy apartment building. Lukas's piece was front-page news, and when it appeared in October of 1967, his text included translations of hippie slang terms such as "speed" and "acid": the general *Times* reading public was beginning their education on these matters.

By 1972, to write an article where one had to define "grass" as marijuana or "speed" as amphetamine was anachronistic; just go read some Hunter Thompson if you needed to learn.

"When I did the piece on Hunter," Lukas recalled, "the idea was for me was to spend a day in D.C. I was going to encounter a deranged Hunter S. Thompson who would do strange things. In reality, the only bizarre events were his consumption of enormous amounts of alcohol, and taking a machete to chop up a grapefruit." But not to worry; Lukas had his own creative sources, and he could provide whatever bizarreness was required. Lukas had read each bi-weekly piece on the campaign as it had appeared in *Rolling Stone,* and was intrigued by what kind of creature could squeeze such lively juice from such a dead stone as the political race of an outsider against an entrenched President. He found out.

Phoning at half past noon from National Airport, Lukas woke Thompson, who tossed off his less than gentle greeting as the by-product of a "depraved and degenerate" night. After a swim in the Hilton pool, Thompson spoke about the arduous campaign coverage, of the bad hotels and worse food, the non-stop travel, saying that the only thing worse than being on the campaign trail "and getting hauled around in a booze-frenzy from one speech to another is having to come back to Washington and write about it."

He reviewed all this while consuming three Bloody Marys, a tropical-fruit plate, and a cheeseburger before heading back to his room to start his workday—around 4:30. Two agenda items took precedent: an ongoing search for the villain Thompson figured had caused McGovern to flip from a wild-card, free-agent candidate to "just another Democrat," ("I'll track the bastard down, though, until my feet start dripping blood"), and another ongoing saga, trying to get aboard President Nixon's press plane.

Around the mirror in Thompson's room at the Hilton was a fringe of handwritten notes, scotch-taped so as to be unavoidable. He explained: "After one of my debauched nights, I'm totally wiped out. Unless I have that stuff right in front of me, I don't know what I'm doing." The notes included everything from the perfunctory to the profound: "cash check," "swim?" "Booze—case W.T.," "Volvo tires," "Call Semple (Ziegler)," "Stearns—Buchanan." The initials "W.T." meant, of course, Wild Turkey, and the phone call references were his own style of getting to Richard Nixon's press secretary, Ron Ziegler, and his speechwriter, Pat Buchanan. Also taped to the mirror was a rejection note from *Harper's;* they nixed Hunter's idea of coverage of the Alabama-Auburn football game—Zelda Fitzgerald's favorite.

"I would understand by this time if [the White House] didn't think I'd make the best company for the President," Thompson said to Lukas, "but all I want them to do is say so. Refuse me. Ban me from the plane. Then I can blast them. But that's just what they won't do, the canny bastards. All I've gotten for seven days is the silent treatment. Hell, the plane leaves tomorrow." Fortified by the Rolling Stones playing "Jumpin' Jack Flash" on his stereo, Hunter Thompson had arrived for a night's work sometime after five in the afternoon.

Thompson began his night shift like a professional juggler, tossing into the air and retrieving parts of his life; a can of Ballantine's, a lit cigarette in its holder, and a telephone conversation that ultimately granted his wish to fly on Nixon's press plane, all the time spewing commentary to Lukas: "Nobody ever tells me the truth in their office. I have to get them on neutral ground at the very least, which usually means a bar. And I never start writing before midnight. By that time I'm pretty spaced out on booze and speed—I've eaten enough speed this year my brain should be fried to a cinder, like a piece of bacon."

On the way to watch Monday Night Football—Thompson's version of High Mass—the two stopped at the McGovern Headquarters long enough for Hunter to grill "wizard" pollster Pat

Caddell on that day's statistics ("grim," Lukas noted), to chat with bone-weary Gary Hart, and to get an explanation of Thompson's shamanistic mystique within the McGovern tribe. "Hunter pays more attention to the McGovern people than anybody else," explained *Boston Globe* correspondent Marty Nolan to Lukas. "He tells anecdotes about them, makes personalities of them, quotes them at great length. And since so many of the McGovern staff are in politics as an ego trip, they love all that and go on talking to him—at their peril."

Lukas's and Hunter's evening progressed through Wurzburger beers (seven), and bad reception of the Saints-Chiefs game, and then to Thompson's favorite Italian restaurant known for its margaritas (three doubles), Anna Maria's.

"It was getting real late," Lukas recalled, "and Hunter ordered a bottle of wine. The restaurant soon closed and the maître d' requested the unfinished bottle returned." (Washington, D.C., had strange, senseless liquor laws for years; until recently, it was illegal to carry your drink from the cocktail lounge to the dining table.) "The headwaiter made an announcement that all alcohol must be removed, and Hunter simply slid the bottle of wine down on the floor, out of sight. But his foot hit it and made a loud *clang;* that brought the waiter over. He was extremely demanding of Hunter, shouting, 'We *must* remove that' and pointed to the bottle on the floor." At that point, Lukas sensed the imminent apocalypse that is the hallmark of Gonzo journalism, the life on the edge, where the unexpected and dangerous are always within arm's reach. He waited to see what he had come to see. It was late, it had been a long night, but here was the main event.

"Thompson surrendered the wine bottle meekly," Lukas went on, clearly disappointed. "And at that point, I felt compelled to do my own Gonzo." Lukas, in his article, constructed the following:

> Leaping up from his chair, he brings the bottle down with incredible force on the unsuspecting head. It pops like a percussion cap, driving splinters of glass deep into the bartender's bald skull and spewing an eerie mixture of blood and wine all over the surrounding tables and flabbergasted patrons. Calmly, Hunter leans down, picks up a long, pointed shard of glass, rips the bartender's starched shirtfront off, and with cool precision carves "THE AMERICAN DREAM" in bloody strokes on his chest.

Lukas admitted that he was indeed under the influence of Gonzo; some greater force within him took over for a fleeting moment and produced the description of what he felt *should* have happened. Further, in editorial meetings before the article was published, it was consensus opinion "that no one would ever believe that."

Wrong! Mythology works in mysterious ways. It defies logic and carries on in its own land of separate reality. A while after Lukas's article was published, he received a note from Hunter. "Thompson was responding to the article in *MORE,*" said Lukas. "He said something along the lines of 'nice piece, Lukas, but amateurs should beware of Gonzo.' "

It seems that Thompson had gotten on the Presidential press plane just after the article had come out, and sat in front of a couple of English writers also covering the campaign. They began to mutter, saying, "Good Lord, isn't that the man that smashed the waiter on the head with the wine bottle and carved 'AMERICAN DREAM' on his chest?" They changed their seats and cowered for the rest of the flight. Thompson was sure they felt he might suddenly go nuts on booze and speed and somehow blow a huge hole in the fuselage.

In the long run, Tony Lukas was not let down by Thompson. "He *would* get wild," he asserted, and then related the tale of Thompson's invitational semi-appearance at Yale, a year later, the first week of December, 1972. Lukas had been teaching a course at Yale on "The Reporting Tradition," and was asked to recommend participants for a retrospective on the journalistic coverage of the 1972 campaign. "I suggested Hunter and Bob Semple," Lukas said. "Semple was a Yale grad himself, very pleasant, straight-laced guy, and I thought his coverage of Nixon that year had been almost too respectful. I suggested Hunter for balance."

Like many universities, Yale in the mid-'70s was in the throes of change, trying to figure out what it should be when it—and the '60s generation—grew up. It was a bastion of Protestant tradition that found itself in the middle of a sea of racial and social unrest during the time of an unpopular war. The school was rife with odd little contradictions. The staunch anti-Vietnam Reverend Sloane Coffin had, twenty years before, been head of the Yale Corporation committee to investigate charges made by a young graduate, William F. Buckley, Jr., that the relation between students, faculty, and alumni was in dire need of revamping. Coffin had said of Buckley, a Roman Catholic who felt the faculty was thoroughly agnostic, allowing no room for man's spiritual side to develop, "He should have attended Fordham or some similar institution." And in one of the more curious attempts to shrink racial anger, Yale sponsored a lengthy group-therapy session between Black Panthers and Erik Erikson, the only man in the world to have been trained by both Sigmund and Anna Freud.

Thompson had been asked to participate in a daylong program. Beginning with an 8:30 A.M. breakfast with the students of Calhoun College, he would attend one of their classes, then have lunch, followed by a panel discussion of the journalistic challenge of the recent Presidential campaign. He was to arrive the day before, to allow him to "warm up" and get to know some of the students on a less-than-formal basis.

Eustace Theodore, a close colleague of Calhoun College's acting Master, Bob Wilhem, had been trained as a sociologist, and perhaps should have been sensitive to the strange rituals and occult behaviors of the Thompson clan. "The students were terribly excited," he said. "It was essentially the tail end of the '60s, and to get Hunter Thompson to come to Yale was a major coup. There were two or three students who were to drive from New Haven to LaGuardia and pick him up from the shuttle at noon the day before. They were up for it. They would have driven to Texas."

They felt as if they had: empty wastelands filled with no Hunter Thompson. They arrived at the airport at noon and camped out. A series of phone calls between the students and their contact at Yale repeatedly carried the message "Hunter is late . . . Hunter is late. . . ." The last shuttle arrived at 11 P.M. and no Hunter Thompson got off. The students stormed the airplane. Looking down the long, narrow aisle, they saw the figure of a tall man at the back of the plane bending down, picking up a bag. "Hunter Thompson?" they asked. As Hunter stood up, the face of a young woman appeared from behind a seat. "Yes," he replied. "Let me introduce you to my niece." Hunter and the woman exchanged puzzled glances. "Err . . . uh . . . my *cousin!* Yes, let me introduce you to my cousin." She remained silent and nameless as the students made a valiant attempt to drive quickly back to New Haven.

It was an impossibility. After two stops at bars in the Bronx, places Thompson seemed to know, they arrived at Yale at 4 A.M., four and a half hours before the beginning of the breakfast meeting. As always, Hunter was not about to call it a night. His (and his niece-cousin's) room was a guest suite in Calhoun College: a grand, wood-paneled series of rooms, filled with antique furniture and Oriental carpets. Original landscapes and portraits hung on the walls. A large fireplace stood at one end. "Fabulous, fabulous!" Hunter exclaimed as he wandered through his new digs. After a year of cheap hotels while tailing McGovern (he had panned the Milwaukee Sheraton-Shroeder as a "Nazi pigsty" where the management would respond only "if your breath smelled heavily of sauerbraten"), this was paradise.

Almost paradise. "We must rearrange the furniture," he proclaimed to the curious but dead-tired students. He proceeded to yank the mattress off the bed, and drag it to a spot in front of the empty fireplace. "Firewood! Where do you keep the firewood?" he bellowed. "We have got to have a good roaring fire!" It was explained to Thompson that firewood was kept in a locked space, in the Master's quarters, and it would be either impossible or simply in gross taste to wake him at 4:30 in the morning to demand kindling and logs. Thompson would have none of this propriety, and somehow firewood appeared. The most sturdy student left Thompson and his niece-cousin sitting on the mattress in front of a blazing fire at 5 A.M.

Early the same morning, Bob Wilhelm showed up at Calhoun, eager to meet Thompson and start the day's schedule. The students arrived and were equally eager to meet the mythological journalist. At 8:00, 8:15, and finally at 8:30, Wilhelm ascended the stairs to Thompson's suite, knocked on his door, and informed him of the time until breakfast. Finally there came a groggy answer from inside: "No, I can't make it."

So it went for the class Hunter was to attend, and lunch. By early afternoon, Wilhelm had had enough; he pounded on Thompson's door, shouting, "You've already missed the first three events! This is ridiculous."

The door to the guest suite flew open. Thompson stood there in his underwear blinking at Wilhelm like a bear flushed from hibernation. He extended one arm, palm up, and slapped it repeatedly with the other hand. "Bob," he asked, "you want me to come down and shoot up in front of the students? Is that what you want?" He continued to smack his arm as Wilhelm said, "Forget it. Just make the four o'clock panel."

Once again, at 3:30, then at 3:45, like any dutiful servant, Wilhelm went up to the guest suite and banged on Hunter's door, saying, "We have *got* to go." Hunter muttered something from the inside about "my shades" and finally appeared, wandering across campus to the adulation of accompanying students. He was extremely energized and interactive. He seemed to enjoy himself.

His participation in the panel discussion was quite limited— one or two comments of little note. At the end of the open discussion, Thompson went to Wilhelm and said, "I am simply exhausted. Drained. I've gotta go upstairs," and so he did. Theodore felt that they all had enjoyed a "full Hunter Thompson experience. He lived up to advanced billing. It was classic Old Yale with its stuffy traditionalism, superimposed on an individual who was . . . well . . . Hunter S. Thompson."

The story of Thompson's Ivy League encounter reached Tony Lukas months later, when Wilhelm phoned him and said, "Remember when you suggested Hunter Thompson for the panel discussion? Well, do you want to know what happened?" But there were others with more firsthand knowledge; graduating from the Yale Graduate School of Arts that spring was a Davenport College student, Garry Trudeau.

In his freshman year, 1966, Garry Trudeau began to parody the awkwardness of life in those times. The product, a comic strip in the *Yale Daily News* called "Bull Tales," was initially about a gawky Yale freshman who stumbled badly through every social event. For the shy Trudeau, it was autobiographical, but the strip was short-lived. In his junior year, he started anew, and took his humor to a higher level. He began to lash out at campus social issues that mirrored American culture in general: rules and regulations, asserting one's political voice, and protest against the Vietnam War.

His strip was an antidote for depression, with a satirical bite—the essential anodyne for the times. In 1970, when Trudeau graduated, he was given a twelve-year contract by the newly formed Universal Press Syndication, and his work, renamed "Doonesbury" (an amalgam of the name of his college roommate, a Pillsbury heir, and "Doone," a term for a social misfit), first appeared that fall. Soon afterward, Trudeau started graduate school at Yale, and stated that he nearly killed himself being a student by day, a cartoonist by night.

Hunter Thompson was not the first to be lampooned by Trudeau. Brian Dowling, who quarterbacked the Yale football team before becoming B.D. in the strip, said, "I never knew Trudeau [at Yale], but I thought the strip was funny." Millicent Fenwick, as a pipe-smoking congresswoman from New Jersey, and a grandmother, became the character Lacey Davenport. On learning this, she said, "My God! We are all comic."

In the first half of the 1970s, many newspaper editors did not know what to do with "Doonesbury"—put it with the comic strips or put it on the editorial page. With unprecedented style, Trudeau was making vital statements about the social, political, and personal issues of that era. Often, his strip would be jerked out of papers, as during the Watergate hearings when, long before a verdict had been handed down, one of his characters referred to Attorney General John Mitchell as "guilty, guilty, guilty!" Trudeau was insightful, revealing, encapsulated, vitriolic, and hilarious, all at once. It was very much like Thompson's writing; there was a thematic synchronism to the two men's works that captured the unreal texture of the times, and many people's reactions to the events that were hammering an entire generation into a shape never before seen.

Thompson went for over a year without full awareness of his own comic role as "Uncle Duke," who made his inaugural appearance in December, 1974. Flying to the west coast with Joanie Caucus, where she was to start law school at Berkeley's Boalt Hall, Zonker mentioned plans to contact his Uncle Duke. Joanie expressed surprise; she did not know of such a family member. "Well, he's not really my uncle," said Zonker, "he's an old family friend. He writes for *Rolling Stone* magazine." Zonker continued to describe the person, telling Joanie that he is really "quite nice, but a little strange—he's incredibly reckless with drugs. Periodically, mom has to call the police and have him busted. You know, to cool him off." Joanie was dismayed, and asked if Uncle Duke didn't mind such treatment. "Heck no!" explains Zonker. "In California, that's what friends are for!"

The actual appearance of the character Uncle Duke comes soon thereafter; he is in an office at *Rolling Stone,* on all fours, under a desk swatting at bats with a ruler. Duke explains his actions to Zonker: "Yeah—whenever I have too much tequila and coke, I start to see huge, hairy bats." He completes his reunion with Zonker by describing the article he is working on as composed of "just whatever pops into my pill-crazed head. I scribble down part of it, dictate some, and send the rest in by cable." He concludes the introduction to his world by blasting away with his .44 magnum at some beer cans set up in the *Rolling Stone* copyroom.

When Thompson began covering the McGovern campaign trail, he primarily read *The New York Times.* It has no funny papers. In the summer after Nixon's re-election, Thompson was coming down the steps of the Supreme Court building, and encountered a crowd of total strangers who saw him, pointed, laughed, and began chanting, "Duke . . . Duke . . . Duke." He was nonplussed. "What in the fuck madness is going on?" he said to himself. "Why am I being mocked by a gang of strangers on the steps of the Supreme Court?" He then asked someone; it was the first day "Doonesbury" appeared in the *Washington Post,* thus adding one more city of readers to the existing sixty million a day.

Thompson and Trudeau have never met. Trudeau had detailed knowledge of Hunter's work ethics and behavioral quirks, and was thus assisted in bridging—and confusing—the gap between art and life. In the comic strip, after Duke had been appointed Ambassador to China (Thompson claims to have been offered the position of Governor of American Samoa by Larry O'Brien when he was Chairman of the Democratic Party), Duke is lured out of his snowbound Rocky Mountain cabin for a college lecture. Upon reaching the campus, he demands to be paid immediately, and in cash. He uses a sycophantic undergraduate assigned to him to order several grapefruit, cases of Wild Turkey, two albinos, a trampoline, and a long list of prescription drugs from a pharmacy. Late for the lecture, after hallucinating that he has been captured inside a Swiss girls' boarding school, Trudeau finally has him stumbling on stage, saying, "Good evening. Few of nature's wonders have been more widely misunderstood than the playful peyote button."

When asked about the source of inspiration, and the obvious insider view, Trudeau said, "I'd rather not [talk about this], either on or off the record." The connective tissue between the two was more than a similarity of theme. During the Presidency of Gerald Ford, his son Jack had met Trudeau when the cartoonist donated some of his works to the National Women's Political Caucus, a ceremony attended by the young Ford. Trudeau traveled with the Presidential entourage to China in 1975; Trudeau got along so well with the press correspondents, many of whom knew Hunter, that he and Tom Brokaw tossed a Frisbee on top of the Great Wall.

Jack Ford had gone public with the fact that he was a dope smoker; he had also brought George Harrison and Bianca Jagger to the White House. For this, he was put on the cover of *Rolling Stone,* and later made assistant to the editor of *Outside,* a new joint venture between Wenner and San Francisco's Will Hearst III. The Wenner-Trudeau relationship followed; Trudeau wrote for the magazine, and was recruited to cover the 1976 election, even though in "Doonesbury" he satirized Jann Wenner's reaction to dinner at baronial San Simeon, the Hearst family castle.

Trudeau won the Pulitzer Prize in May, 1975. His characters, including Uncle Duke, made the cover of *Time* in February, 1976. Thompson told the magazine that he was not insulted by his characterization; he did confide privately that "if I ever catch that little bastard, I'll rip his lungs out."

17.

To Duke

or Not to

Duke

 have never believed in that Guru trip about drugs," Thompson told *Playboy* interviewer Craig Vetter in the spring of 1974. "You know—God, Nirvana, all that bullshit. I just like to gobble the stuff right out in the street and see what happens, just stomp on my own accelera-

tor." The times had produced a sort of dead zone for the American spirit, where it seemed obvious that both Saigon and Richard Nixon were going to fall, and the only point that all agreed on was that these events would occur to a disco beat. At *Playboy,* it seemed safer to look behind, rather than ahead. With the surge of popularity of *Fear and Loathing: On the Campaign Trail '72,* Thompson's limelight was a spot of brightness that no one could deny.

Thompson had been annoyed at *Playboy* after they had assigned, then rejected, a piece on Olympic-skier turned walking billboard, Jean-Claude Killy. Vetter had known Hunter socially for a year or so, and was asked to approach him for a feature interview. Many were skeptical that he would allow it. It was February; Thompson was icebound in Aspen, and cabin fever had taken hold. His response to the query for the interview, which paid nothing but did include expenses, was "Well, shit! Absolutely! But we can't do it with our goddamn ankles in the snow up here in Aspen. Tell *Playboy* we'll do it if they send us—Sandy and Juan as well—to Cozumel."

"Those were the fat days at *Playboy,*"Vetter said. He told his superiors in Chicago, "Now look, I am going into the wilderness here with Thompson. I don't want any bullshit about the expenses if I come back with the interview. If I come back with it, it will be cheap at any price. If I don't come back with it, that's another story. Because this is not going to be entirely in my control if it gets rolling."

How true. The interview was a Herculean effort for Vetter, and in some sense as well for the vulnerable Thompson, who by now was letting his comic-strip persona, Raoul Duke, do most of the talking. From the first meeting, at the Presidente Hotel on Cozumel, to the final editorial modifications at *Playboy* offices in Chicago, it took seven months, and traversed Mexico, Washington, D.C., San Clemente, and Aspen.

In 1974, the Watergate hearings were being broadcast on TV, and outdrew soap operas by a 4-to-1 margin. Patty Hearst was kidnapped from the University of California campus by the Symbionese Liberation Army, then appeared to turn revolutionary and join forces with them. When the Los Angeles police SWAT team surrounded, rifled, and torched the SLA "safehouse" in Los Angeles, it was put live on television from start to finish. It was surreal anger, and it played in everyone's living room.

Death was all around, wearing establishment suits and ties. Thompson's writing had offered an answer to that kind of authority, and part of the answer had to do with drugs; his intention had been to scare the daylights out of the policy-making people who had absolutely no experience with drugs, no concept of the "fantastic possibilities of life in America."

"Hunter represented what we think of as a '60s consciousness," Vetter explained. "For me and for a lot of people, he stood as a definition for a generation that wanted to say 'We are *not* you. And here is one of the ways you can tell *we are not you.*' Drugs were symbolic of that kind of identity."

One of the many truisms of the '60s and early '70s was that Mexico was always the place to go "to get your head together." It was cheap, scenic, warm, accessible, and drugs were around every corner. It was the West Coast college students' Fort Lauderdale, at half price. Still, just under the surface, there was a totalitarian regime marked by strong-arm tactics, bribes, and corruption, where recreational drug users were often left to rot in fetid prisons. It helped to be "someone," and that was what Thompson was when he hit the powder-white shores of Cozumel. Vetter observed that Thompson "really liked that tightly controlled island culture where everybody knew him five minutes after he was on the island."

Days and nights slid by effortlessly on Cozumel. Whenever Vetter would raise the topic of the interview, Thompson would shirk it off, buy a drink, go exploring in his rental jeep, or head out into deep water in a charter fishing boat—the beginning of *The Great Shark Hunt.* Vetter was dismayed, yet knew that sooner or later something would break. The two went shark fishing and didn't see a fish. To Vetter, it was days of balogna sandwiches mixed with the odor of dead bait and diesel fumes. Thompson reacted more strongly, screaming at the locals piloting the boat, "You fuckers! You take the gringos out and drive 'em around for a while, then just bring them back in. I fucking want to see blood in the water, goddamn it . . . who do you think you're dealing with here?"

Vetter concluded that he was at a dead end. They had spent four days together with lots of alcohol, drugs, and conversation, but his reels of audiotape were as empty as the fishhooks. After a week, Sandy and Juan left to visit her relatives in Florida.

One late night, drinking and arguing at the Presidente ("There is no one who drinks and smokes like Hunter does," Vetter confirmed), the *Playboy* writer had reached an end to both his tolerance and the magazine's expenses. He said, "Look, Hunter. This is it. If we don't get going tomorrow, I am going to have to call *Playboy* and tell them I am on my way back, that this whole thing is a bust.''

Vetter, a writer himself, knows of ''writer's block.'' He described Thompson's as more of an ''entry barrier,'' an unusual difficulty in getting the pump primed, the engines harnessed, and making forward progress. He had worked with Thompson on other writing projects, and was aware of how tough it could be for him to get rolling on a project, even an interview. Perhaps Thompson did not want to reveal his darker underside, the sources of his anger. It could have been that he was incredibly ambivalent about ''going public'' with an actual interview—rather than the thinly disguised autobiographical journalism he had been doing for fifteen years—and allowing someone else to make money at his expense. Perhaps he was just having too much fun in the sand and surf at *Playboy*'s expense.

''For Hunter,'' Vetter said, ''it is always difficult, that moment of breaking through to the work. Just breaking the seal that stands between doing the work and not doing the work. Once you get rolling, you are likely to get rolling for a long, long time with great energy.''

With great spectacle, Thompson broke the seal between play and work. He did so by smashing a huge glass table on the patio of the hotel. The two of them shouted at each other, then Thompson jumped into his jeep, and disappeared into the dark of night. Vetter went to bed. Thompson ended up getting his jeep so thoroughly bogged in the sand that even a local fisherman could not push it lose. Near dawn he appeared, wandering down the beach toward the hotel, stark naked, clothes over his shoulder, like a hobo in search of a nudist camp. He had not slept all night, but went straight to Vetter's room. He woke Vetter up and said, simply, ''Let's go. Let's start.''

Hunter saw every transcription, approved of all modifications, and even helped rewrite the final copy. It was a thorough and readable encapsulation of his days as a journalist, starting with his curious tale of putting on a madras sports coat and wing tips to approach the Hell's Angels in their bar to see if the *Time, Newsweek,* and *Times* articles about them were accurate. ''I think they sensed I was a little strange,'' he acknowledged, adding that ''after fifty or sixty beers we found a common ground, as it were. Crazies always recognize each other.'' Until *Playboy*'s wide audience read that interview, and saw the photos of him, many still believed him to be a figment of their collective unconscious, where his exaggerations were merely some conspiratorial hype job done by the media for their entertainment. Others had started to put together the Raoul Duke character in Thompson's writings with the brand-new Raoul Duke character in Trudeau's "Doonesbury." Only a cartoon, they reasoned, could live a life like that, consume that much stuff, and still be around the next day. But when Vetter commented that Thompson spent as much a year on drugs as the average American does on an auto, Thompson verified "Yeah, at least that much," and then itemized the amount he had paid for cocaine for a 17-day writing stretch.

The previous time *Playboy* had centerfolded a spokesman for the "drug culture" had been seven years before. Sitting cross-legged, garbed all in white, and looking like a shipwrecked sailor, Timothy Leary was interviewed on the grounds of the Millbrook, New York, estate of Gulf Oil magnate-turned-LSD disciple, Billy Hitchcock. At the time, Leary had turned the grounds into a scientific experiment that lasted briefly. With the help of the media, its proximity to New York City, and Tom Wolfe's chronicling Ken Kesey and the Merry Pranksters' journey there, the experiment was about to devolve into a carnival of psychedelia; so, too, the country. The two interviews form bookends to the central guiding themes of the times. Leary had waxed rhapsodical about the "fantastic possibilities" that one could find within one's self. Further, he extolled the virtues of LSD in giving a higher orbit to the slogan of the times "Make love, not war."

By 1974, Timothy Leary was having his passport confiscated in Kabul, Afghanistan, and being flown (first class) back to the United States and maximum-security prison in Minnesota. Hunter Thompson was sitting on a seawall in Cozumel, downing two Bloody Marys, four beers, four spoons of "white substance," and proceeding to produce a lexicon of pharmaceuticals. Marijuana made you stupid. Generic psychedelics produced a "very clear high, an interior high." Speed was merely a motor high, but LSD was, he termed it, "the King Drug." He liked to "take 72 hours and just really run amok, break it all down." He did comment that he never dealt drugs; he was merely another consumer. The key issues of Leary's message had been spirituality, sensuality, and sexuality; the search for a successful culture was the outcome of a successful individual, and the vehicle for the search was psychedelic. That was 1967. This was 1974, and the message seemed to be a self-centered, hedonistic "just do it." Sex of any sort was, once again, nowhere to be found.

Vetter had known Hunter for a few years, since Thompson had shown up four hours late at a Mexican dinner party in Laguna Beach thrown by Lawrence Gonzales. By the time Thompson showed, all that was left was a pile of brown guacamole, and the ruins of taco chips. So through the years as well as through the interview, Vetter had a thorough view of Thompson, and felt that the relation of drugs and power was not a direct equation. "The thing that has always been the absolute hot center of Hunter's interest is power of any kind." It can be football power, political power, the ability to take a lot of drugs and still stay in control ("Booze," Vetter observed, "is of course Thompson's baseline drug"); these form the magma of his psychic volcano. "It is a wild power. A frightening Hell's Angels sort of power, an Arctic wolfman sort of power."

In working with Thompson over a seven-month span, Vetter also came to appreciate his writerly characteristics, referring to him as having the ability to write the funniest violence ever done, and often getting into a fantasy world that even without the influence of drugs took on the characteristics of a drug trip. He would spontaneously pop off with scenes of people engaged in political battles where they were gnawing at each other's skulls. At one point, he wanted to borrow Ron Ziegler's motorcycle. He would then pull a wheelie in second gear at high speed and drive it off the end of the Laguna Beach municipal fishing pier, then swim back to shore and say "Thanks, Ron," and hand him the keys to his drowned bike. Jane Fonda was another fantasy; in long phone conversations, he would entertain Vetter with his visions of creatures from Venus snatching her away, then leaving her to be found washed ashore "with orange duct tape wrapped around her tits." It is this kind of mock violence that Hunter "loves so much in his talking and in his writing."

The professional in Thompson was clearly apparent as he and Vetter worked and reworked the interview. Vetter tried to open the *Playboy* article with a description of Thompson "sitting in a salty bathing suit on a seawall on Cozumel, reading a newspaper for $1.25 that would have cost a straighter, more sober man 25 cents," is what I had written. Hunter saw that and said, 'No. No . . . It is better if we make it 24 cents.' That's close-in craftsmanship," Vetter went on, "not something you could ever teach. Hunter, when he is 'on' as a writer, line by line, letter by letter, is as good as you can get."

Months before the interview was pulled into final form, Thompson and Vetter travelled to Washington to cover what turned out to be Richard Nixon's resignation. Thompson exerted his pull as *Rolling Stone's* National Affairs Editor, and convinced Jann Wenner to assign Vetter, who had a Jesuit education, a story on a Nixon speechwriter, John McLaughlin, who was then a Jesuit priest. Thompson was fascinated by Vetter's Jesuit stories, and loved images like the Lake of Fire, and Garden of Agony. "Thompson would quote the Book of Revelation every now and then in his writings. He saw spiritual power as the ultimate power," Vetter interpreted.

Vetter wrote the McLaughlin story, but it was never published, in part because he was unable to talk to the priest. Vetter and Thompson were staying at the Hilton, and when Nixon's farewell address was to be aired, they symbolically went to the bar in the Watergate complex, Thompson setting up his little portable TV on a cocktail table and finally screaming at the piano player to "shut the fuck up with that damned Barry Manilow crap." Vetter recalls that it began as "a hot damn" kind of moment, but after it was over the light seemed to fade from Thompson's eyes, like a fatally wounded animal. He seemed not to know what to do, where to go. He needed a target for his anger, and it was gone. Moby Dick had been killed, and Ahab lived on. The story was not supposed to end like this; it should be a mortal struggle to the end.

"After Nixon's resignation," Vetter remembers, "Hunter would say, 'I've gotta get out of journalism. I've gotta get out of politics. I've gotta change.'" For a while, he stuck with politics; he heard Jimmy Carter quote Bob Dylan at a University of Georgia commencement speech, and followed him to the governor's mansion, spending time with him and his children. This irked George McGovern, who said, "That's what puzzles me most about Hunter. Why he went towards Carter so quickly. Heck, Carter never started to speak out against the Vietnam war until after our Saigon Embassy fell." Thompson's own explanation for why he did not follow through on a planned "Campaign Trail: '76" was that when he went out onto the hustings, he found himself, not the politicians the main attraction. "I was giving more autographs than any of the candidates," he said as he quit politics for good, even putting behind him the skeletal idea of running for U.S. Senator from Colorado (a position won that September by Gary Hart).

Knowing Thompson's fascination with power, and his ordination as a Doctor of Divinity from a California mailorder Church, Vetter encouraged him to "focus on his ministry. I was only half kidding when I suggested that his career change should get him where he could focus on that ultimate power—spiritual power."

On the West Coast, the opinion differed. While visiting the *Rolling Stone* offices in San Francisco, Thompson previewed his future with *Rolling Stone* editor Paul Scanlon. Over a beer at Jerry's, the staff watering hole, Scanlon was understanding and supportive. "It was my suggestion that Hunter drop completely the Raoul Duke persona." By then, Thompson told Alan Rinzler, it felt "really weird to wake up every day and see yourself in the funny papers." Scanlon suggested several serious writing topics guaranteed to get Hunter's angry, humorous creative juices flowing. He emphasized Thompson's unique ability to get the kind of story that few—perhaps no one else—could. "Try a new approach, and be totally serious, Hunter," Scanlon counseled. "If you want to move forward and be productive, then put Raoul Duke behind you. Forget about trying to act that way."

Scanlon had been the first person to see the initial dozen pages of *Las Vegas;* Hunter had simply dropped them on his desk, and lumbered off wearing a big smirk. Scanlon knew what a disciplined, focused Hunter S. Thompson could do; he also knew how thoroughly Raoul Duke could run amok. In response to Scanlon's impassioned plea, Thompson responded non-verbally. He reached back, pulled out his wallet, and removed a large tab of blotter acid. Looking Scanlon in the eye, he tore it in half, put one away, and ate the other and washed it down with beer.

T he issue of change and of spirituality was in the air that same summer in Newport, Rhode Island, as Thompson and Ralph Steadman went to cover the trials for the America's Cup yacht race. The sense of change was in the construction of the 12-meter craft: America's *Intrepid* was a salty old witch of a boat, and made entirely of wood. The Australian challenger, *Southern Cross,* was aluminum, and among the rank and file of traditionalism this caused a stink of major proportions. "If God wanted us to sail aluminum boats," intoned the skipper of the *Intrepid,* "He would have given us aluminum trees."

Deep-water sailing, where a genikker sail can cost $20,000 and a Barrient winch the same, has been described as similar to standing fully clothed under a spigot of cold water while tearing up hundred-dollar bills. Yacht racing differs from most any sport; few six-year-olds are equipped by their parents to go out and practice yacht racing, encouraged with "It will build strong character." If aristocracy floats, it does so in places like Newport, with all of the charm, decorum, and upper-class pomposity that draws out Thompson's ambivalences like a strong magnet.

Thompson and Steadman spent many hours in the bars of Newport; then the two commandeered a rowboat in the pre-dawn hours before the nationally televised Trial race, and headed toward the great blank white hull of the *Southern Cross*. Thompson rowed; Steadman checked the provisions: one aerosol can of black spray paint, and a flare gun in the event that they needed a diversion of sorts. Across the bay, Thompson managed to catch a crab with an oar that made a sharp whacking sound when it hit the hull. This had been preceded by a haunted-house-like noise from rusty oarlocks, and was followed by a loud, startled "WHOOP!" from Steadman. All of these noises skipped across the water like a flat rock.

The two finally pulled up next to the *Southern Cross*'s hull; here was the canvas for all the world to see, to render something eye-catching. They envisioned the next day as the great blade of a boat cut its way through the water, past a flotilla of smaller onlookers. Faces of people dressed in navy blazers, with yacht-club insignia on the breast pocket, would turn red, and the smaller-boat captains would begin shouting at the crew on board, but it would be shouting into the wind. "The great thing," Thompson had said, "was that, being up on the deck, no one on board the *Southern Cross* would know what the hell the matter was. They would look at each other, knowing that something was wrong, and they'd check the rigging, and someone would say, 'Do you suppose it's the spinnaker pole lift, or something else they're trying to tell us about?' "

Steadman approached his canvas, shaking up the aerosol can with the little BB agitator balls inside. In the quiet of the night, it sounded like a snare drum. Then came the hiss of the paint as he tried to get out the first letter. On the beach, car headlights came on, pointed at them, and the crew on deck began moving around with flashlights. "Time for a diversion," Thompson announced. "I set off a parachute flare. It went right up past the nose of the guy who'd just happened to peek over the rail and look down at us . . . whoosh, within a foot of him before going up, and then it popped open above and the *Southern Cross* began swaying. It lit up the whole scene. There was enough illumination, what with the flare and the jeep headlights and the rest of it, to read the instructions on the damn aersol can."

The rowboat skimmed its way to shore and the two decided to hightail it out of town without even getting their gear from their motel. One pair of shoes remained between the two of them, and both had appointments in New York the next day. Thompson told Steadman to buy a pair in the morning; Steadman told Thompson the next morning was Sunday. Thompson told Steadman that it was quite common for people to wander around New York barefoot—even go to the theater or the Empire Room at the Plaza Hotel. "How would he know?" Thompson asked later. "He was English. I told him the fastidious ones wore black socks. Perhaps he didn't believe me, but by that time I had the shoes on my feet. He couldn't dispute that. He didn't even ask for one. He gave up."

The artwork the two had planned, and begun, would have indeed caused more of a stir than the issue of proper construction material for America's Cup boats. The message was to have been, in six-foot-high letters, FUCK THE POPE.

18.

. . . . .

As in

Magic

black man holds a dead brown monkey over the
exhaust pipe on top of a Zaire River boat, singe-
ing off the hair before cooking. On shore, in the
center of the teeming capital city of Kinshasa,
the marketplace sells live crocodiles, mouths
strapped shut, trussed to a bamboo pole for easy
carrying. A favorite meal here consists of roast

baboon, white-nosed monkey stew, a side of mixed caterpillars and woodgrubs, washed down by a tug on a bottle of palm wine. The city of over two million people spills into a river that was not on the Western traveler's map until a hundred years before, after Henry Morton Stanley finally found Dr. Livingstone. It is a chaotic jumble of bad architecture, potholed streets, pickpockets, and pimps.

Joseph Conrad said of the area, "Going up that river was like travelling back to the earliest beginnings of the world, when the vegetation rioted and trees were king." "The rumble in the jungle," was how George Foreman and Muhammad Ali dubbed it in late September, 1974, when it became the site of the World Heavyweight Boxing Championship, a $10 million fight in a country with a per capita income of $29.

"Bad Genet" was Hunter Thompson's synopsis of his weeks spent covering the fight for *Rolling Stone.* It was his way of implying that life in equatorial Africa took on a meaning so alien it eluded even his powers of understanding. Thompson, Ralph Steadman, George Plimpton, and Norman Mailer, as well as Bill Cardoza, the man who first called Thompson's writing style "Gonzo," were housed there, most of them at the InterContinental Hotel. It seemed like an eternity. The fight was originally scheduled for the 24th of September, but when George Foreman cut his forehead sparring, it was delayed until sometime later in the year. For many sportswriters in Kinshasa, it seemed they might not have a white Christmas.

On the flight from Frankfurt to Kinshasa, Thompson met up with George Plimpton; the two had first met in the late '60s in San Francisco as Hunter was tying up *Hell's Angels.* During the following weeks, Plimpton would come to describe Thompson as "the most idiosyncratic journalist on hand in Kinshasa." Dressed in his uniform of mirrored aviator sunglasses, purple-and-strawberry aloha shirt, Levi's, and oversized tennis shoes, Thompson proved entertaining even during the flight into Africa, when he demonstrated his recently purchased electronic gadgetry. This included an expensive tape recorder and a portable German radio capable of picking up twenty-seven stations. WBSP, of Spokane, Washington, was one of them; "I can tell you a white sale is going on in Liberty's or some such shop down on Green Street—big news in Spokane. It came through clear as a bell," he said to Plimpton. "It's going on Tuesday, if you want to do anything about it."

It was a once-in-a-lifetime thing for Mailer, Plimpton, and Thompson to be in the same place at the same time. All three had been lumped into the recently defined school of "New Journalism." Yet boxing was the real glue between them. Thompson had done some of his best sportswriting at Eglin Air Force Base, when he chronicled the rise and fall of Joe Louis. Muhammad Ali was from Louisville, just three years younger than the journalist. For a 1959 *Sports Illustrated* article, George Plimpton had his nose bloodied fighting Archie Moore. Norman Mailer sparred on "The Dick Cavett Show" with Jose Torres. Mailer, Plimpton, and Jimmy Breslin had formed a committee in 1967 to protest Ali's being stripped of his championship, and prevented from boxing, because of his conscientious-objector military status. However, the curious dynamics between Mailer and Plimpton, the two Harvard men-turned-pugilists, circled around another issue.

Ernest Hemingway had been the world's best-known author-boxer, and he had been a friend of Plimpton's; Mailer had never met him. The relationship between Plimpton and Hemingway had its origins in 1953 in the Ritz Hotel bar in Paris. Plimpton was there for a wedding, and saw a stocky, bearded man—Hemingway—in the hallway outside the bar buying a copy of the *Paris Review,* a magazine that Plimpton had helped found. He followed the author into the bar, told him that he was the editor of the magazine he'd just bought, and asked if he could do an interview. Hemingway said yes. "I wanted to start it the next day," Plimpton said. "I wanted to wander through his old haunts in Paris and ask, 'What happened here, Papa? Let's go to where so-and-so used to live.' He looked at me as if I were daft, and said, 'There couldn't be anything sillier than walking around Paris.' " Over the years, the two met in Pamplona for the running of the bulls ("I didn't want to run, but when Ernest Hemingway is standing behind you and says 'run'—well, I ran"), and in Madrid and Cuba.

Passing through New York, Hemingway called Plimpton and invited him to dinner at the Colony restaurant. Plimpton was supposed to meet Mailer later that evening; he asked Hemingway if it would be all right to invite Mailer, who had always wanted to meet the older writer. It never came about, although Hemingway was curious about Mailer, especially his "contests," for which he was renowned. Plimpton explained a few of them, events Mailer would stage at parties. One involved standing about ten feet apart from another man, bending at the waist, and charging each other until they rammed heads with the sound of a dropped coconut. Another involved a staring confrontation with women; Plimpton referred to them as "ocular showdowns." A third of Mailer's trademark contests involved thumb wrestling, and Hemingway asked for a demonstration. Over a crowded dinner table, Hemingway and Plimpton gripped hands and each began to maneuver to press down the opponent's thumb. The same sense of competition that Plimpton saw in Mailer while covering the press events during the fight delay in Africa had been there in Hemingway, who proceeded to try and crush Plimpton's hand. Luckily, Plimpton's date was sitting next to Hemingway, saw Plimpton's distress, and asked what they were doing. Hemingway eased his grip and responded, "We're pretending to be a pair of Norman Mailers."

In covering the fight, Plimpton wrote about Mailer ("His competitiveness!"), and Mailer wrote about Plimpton ("his fine voice, so reminiscent of the restrained taste for zany leaps and happy improprieties that we used to hear in the voice of Cary Grant"). Both wrote about Thompson. Plimpton caught many different sides of Thompson: the writer who was never seen writing, the paranoid prankster, and the bundle of energy that endeared him to homesick, bored writers stuck in the middle of nowhere with a communications service so thoroughly messed up that when one UPI writer filed a story it surfaced on the teletype machine of a private company in Forest Hills, New York. Plimpton described Thompson's way of moving—the Thompson Shuffle, African Version. His tennis shoes seemed oversized, and his style of walking was a barely coordinated series of lurches. It was as if Thompson were a six foot-three-inch marionette controlled by a palsied hand. In the lobby of the InterContinental, Plimpton would see him approach "in a jack-rabbity, somewhat zig-zag clip. . . . He seemed incapable of taking a small step, so that if he happened to come up to say hello, he would take one last big sideways step to keep from crashing into you."

Mailer saw the same boundless energy, describing him as "a set of nerves balanced on another set of nerves traveling on squeaky roller skates." He was so strung out from chemicals taking him up and down, that "he squeaked if you poked a finger near his belly." It seemed clear that Thompson was enjoying himself, perhaps because during the long delay there was nothing to cover. He was living the Gonzo life, and in the process became a focus of attention of some of the best writers America had produced, and had his myth perpetuated in the works of each.

But Hunter wrote about nothing at all, which Plimpton felt was an integral part of his charm and aura. "Hunter's idea," Plimpton said, "was to watch somebody else watch boxing. He wanted to see [Zaire's President] Mobutu watch Ali and Foreman." In Africa there was no press room, but there was the lobby of the InterContinental where all the writers hung out in little wicker sedan chairs where you would have to peek out to see anyone else, like a collection of spies. Hunter was never among them. Hunter was never at the press conferences. He was never even seen with a notebook.

Plimpton noted that "Hunter and Bill Cardozo would wander off into different parts of the town, doing their conspiratorial thing, always entertaining when they returned to the hotel. And that was what I always thought a part of this Gonzo journalism was. Norman Mailer got sort of upset about this. He used to repeat the phrase of Robert Frost that free verse is like playing tennis with the net down; Thompson's readers were interested in what happened to Hunter. Forget about whatever it was that he was allegedly covering." Mailer, an intense craftsman who sees his writing as a physical extension of his self, felt Hunter could have gotten the same readership had he been covering a grandmother having a flat tire in a shopping mall in Iowa. As a writer, if you were to cover the fight for *Rolling Stone,* you couldn't spend the night lying naked in the swimming pool. However, for Plimpton, "that style *is* Hunter, and yet I always thought that was one of his great appeals."

When Tom Wolfe published his book *The New Journalism,* just months before the Zaire fight, he had included, among others, Gay Talese, Norman Mailer, George Plimpton, and two pieces of Thompson's. Wolfe awarded him The Brass Stud Award for his staying the duration with the Hell's Angels. For getting him the tapes to the Angels' party at Kesey's, Wolfe had thanked Thompson by taking him to lunch at New York's Brasilian Coffee Restaurant; in the middle of dining Thompson had "set off a marine distress alarm. It stopped the place in its tracks," Wolfe noted. Later, Thompson went on record as rejecting membership into anything that Tom Wolfe created. He said, "The people Tom Wolfe finds fascinating, I find dull as stale dog shit."

Plimpton said of his inclusion in Wolfe's book, "I was always a bit puzzled by that. I think of Hunter Thompson as a New Journalist. I don't think I am one." He discussed the difficulty he had being accepted by the Detroit Lions in 1963 when he subbed as a quarterback to write *Paper Lion.* "I didn't get in there very often [he lost 25 yards on five plays]. I loved being looped with them, but most of it was observing, and catching what and how they spoke." On the other hand, Thompson's style is to simply dive in, talk about how it feels, with total disregard for what others might think, constantly alarming and surprising his readers with the bizarrely unexpected. "My work was participatory; Hunter's is Gonzo," Plimpton said, noting that in *Fear and Loathing in Las Vegas,* all mention of the Mint 400 motorcycle race that supposedly got Thompson to Law Vegas to begin with is quickly forgotten. "That is new journalism to me; idiosyncratic, personalized, stylized." And that was just how Thompson behaved for the duration in Kinshasa.

Muhammad Ali invoked the wrath of the Mobutu government with his classic taunts at George Foreman. When he announced that Foreman would have a safer time "shaving a wild lion with a dull razor," and that if all else failed, Ali would "have his friends cook George in a pot," the government protested, saying that such commentary was not good public relations for a developing country. Hunter tried to stir things up by telling the single-minded sportswriters that he had found a real news story. He had sneaked across the river into the Republic of Congo, where he had discovered the construction of a huge torpedo. It was half the length of a football field, and aimed so that it would blow a huge hole in the waterfront area of Kinshasa. The sportswriters were underawed. "They turned away, mumbling," Thompson said.

Thompson and Cardoza killed a lot of the delay time rummaging through the riverside bars. Cardoza was short, but as hyper as Thompson, and would introduce Hunter by saying he was "Big Doctore"—the Chief N'Doke from the Foreman camp. When he wanted a response, Cardoza would take two miniature hands Thompson wore around his neck on a gold chain and shake them at the people. Cardoza would sign his tab with "Pottstown Batal Bogas," after an imaginary football team. Thompson, sure the Nazi criminal was hiding out across the river in Brazzaville, would sign his "Martin Bormann."

Cardoza and Thompson heard about, and tried to locate a house in town that was filled with pygmies. "I don't want to go in there," Cardoza said. "I just want to lie in front of the house and watch them go in and out." Another attraction for the Gonzo tourists came when they learned of a sewer in which a cobra lived; from time to time, he would just pop his head up to have a look around. They decided to put the spot on an Easter-egg scavenger hunt they were planning to kill the boredom.

One episode involved a pair of elephant tusks. "I bought them off a street person," Thompson told Plimpton, adding that they attracted a lot of attention because of the raw state they were in. "I mean, the elephant wasn't attached to them, but he might just as well have been." He had also bought a small car with serious electrical wiring problems; the steering was broken in such a way that it would only turn to the left. He loaded the "raw" tusks into the car and began to guide the strange vehicle toward the Inter-Continental. Hunter explained that driving a car capable of only left-hand turns, laden with raw elephant tusks, through the crazy maze of Kinshasa streets was analogous to running through an airport with a bazooka under each arm. He was flagged down and boarded by a soldier bearing a machine gun. Thompson thought the man was telling him to drive to the city jail, but there was adequate distraction, what with the tiny car going at a good clip over terrible pavement and Thompson shouting at the soldier in Spanish, so that even though the machine gun was at his ear, he managed to get to the front of the hotel. He slammed to a stop, told the concierge to explain to the soldier that Bill Cardoza was in full charge of the operation. Then Thompson ambled through the lobby and up to his room, a tusk under each arm.

In the fifth round of the World's Greatest Fight, Muhammad Ali found himself on the ropes, being pummeled by George Foreman. Ali saw what he called "the Near Room." The door was only half open. Inside, the room was neon orange with green blinking lights. There were bats blowing trumpets and alligators playing trombones. He could hear the screaming of snakes. On the wall were weird masks and actors' clothes. He would always visualize this when he was in the ring and in trouble; to go inside "the Near Room" was to commit self-destruction. He pulled away from his vision, and from the ropes. In eight rounds he knocked out George Foreman. Around the world, 112 million people watched—more than the population of Mexico. Four rows above ringside, within spraying distance of the boxers' sweat, were the $200 seats for Plimpton, Mailer, and Thompson. Only two were filled.

T he next day, Plimpton went to visit Thompson in his room, but his talk was not about the fight. "This is a bad town for the drug scene," Thompson explained after peeping through a crack in the door to make sure it was Plimpton. "In Nevada, you can shoot anything you want into your body. You can get stark naked and lie in the back seat of a Pontiac with the accelerator wired down, and touch the steering wheel from time to time with the toe, and if you lose control at a hundred twenty m.p.h. going along Route 95, all that happens is that you spin out into the desert and kill a lizard. But Kinshasa . . . it's a bad scene."

Plimpton had come to get Thompson's assessment of the fight.

"What fight? Oh, I didn't go to the fight."

Plimpton asked him if he had tried to watch it on TV with President Mobutu, as Hunter had announced.

"Who?"

"The President," Plimpton explained.

"On TV? Frankly, I've had my mind on something else."

Hunter explained that he had sort of taken the night off. He had stayed at the hotel, emptied of guests, and floated naked in the pool. "I lay on my back looking at the moon coming up," he told Plimpton, "and the only person in the hotel came and stared at me a long time before he went away. Maybe he thought I was a corpse." Thompson then reverted to his initial topic of conversation, adding that he had taken a pound and a half of local marijuana ("I am not trying to smuggle it out of *this* country!") and tossed it into the pool water. He then floated in a diaphanous green stain, enjoying the solitude. What a sight: he appeared to be leaking bile. He did comment, "It's not the best way to obtain a high."

Plimpton had been collecting a series of death wishes of artistic people he knew: Truman Capote, Kenneth Tynan, and Norman Mailer, who wanted to be devoured by a lion. Death wishes often tell more about the living person than anything they can articulate in an autobiographical way.

Thompson responded to Plimpton's death-wish query with a startling change in his behavior. The moment before the question, he had been pacing like a caged feral animal, bumping into things, mixing cocktails, complaining about the price of bottled water. Suddenly, he sat down on the edge of the bed and became quite calm. It seemed that what he had to say was well thought out, and as thoroughly rehearsed as a death wish can get and still remain a wish.

Thompson did in fact have a well-developed premonition of an early death, thinking that if he could just make it through to a certain age, he could get away with a lot of things. But after a point, he figured, there would be "a lot of electricity, a lot of negative charges" that would make his sudden death inevitable. "I had a premonition. I had a pretty firm conviction that I was not going to live past the age of twenty-seven. I picked out the number very arbitrarily; there was no real logic to it. I picked out the number before I was twenty years old." Thompson found it puzzling to live past the date of his expected death, referring to the experience as similar to budgeting a million dollars, all to be spent by Christmas, then suddenly finding yourself after the holiday with money to burn. "Then you're still around, and the budget is all fucked up. You are going to have to reschedule." Sitting in the Kinshasa InterContinential, at age thirty-seven, Thompson's style of "rescheduling" was uniquely artful.

"Well, vehicular, of course—something in a very fine car. Back in the U.S., there was a mountain I used to drive over on the way down from Louisville past Birmingham to Eglin Air Force Base—Iron Mountain, I guess they call it: a lot of big houses up on it and rich people from Birmingham and the road is sort of scenic, with big entranceways and fine views, and there's one place where you come around a sharp curve to the left, and straight ahead, down beyond the cliff, is the city, acres of steel mills and Bessemer furnaces and smelting yards below—and my concept of death for a long time was to come down that mountain road at a hundred twenty and just keep going straight through there, burst out through the barrier and hang out above all that in . . . well, it was important that it was the right kind of car, the Jaguar XK 120, though later on I began to connect the XK 140 with the fantasy, painted white, though sometimes I vacillated between white and British racing green, which is very nice too, and it had to be a convertible, of course, because you'd want to feel the air against you . . . and there I'd be, sitting in the front seat, stark naked, with a case of whiskey next to me, and a case of dynamite in the trunk—or boot, it would be in the Jaguar—honking the horn, and the lights on, and just sit out there in space for an instant, a human bomb, and then fall down into that mess of steel mills. It'd be a tremendous goddamn explosion. No pain. No one would get hurt. I'm pretty sure, unless they've changed the highway, that launching place is still there. As soon as I get home, I ought to take the drive and just check it out."

One of Thompson's last comments before taking leave of the site of the fight he never watched, only read about the next morning when someone slid a newspaper under his hotel door, was that he would like to rent a small plane. He would have it fly over Kinshasa towing a sign, like advertising above a summer beach crowd. The sign would read BLACK IS WEIRD.

Plimpton described Thompson, his awkward, entertaining energies and his uniqueness, in his book *Shadow Box.* He sent a copy to Hunter. Thompson responded, but without a word or a single sentence. On a wall in George Plimpton's New York apartment is a framed piece of Woody Creek Rod and Gun Club stationery, sent to Plimpton. On it is the imprint of Hunter Thompson's left hand, in blue ink.

19.

Dinner at the Existential Café

achine-gun bullets passing a foot from the human ear make two noises. The first sounds like the crack of a hard-hit baseball. Next comes a whistling, sucking sound that defies imitation as the vacuum left by the speeding bullet is filled with air. Lying on his stomach wearing camou-

flage, flak vest, and helmet, shielded only by tall elephant grass and other jungle growth, Philip Caputo looked up to see Hunter Thompson approaching him. Wearing his sunglasses, aloha shirt, and shorts, he stooped over slightly from his six-foot-three-inch height, and asked quietly, while waving a finger in loops around his head, "What's that noise? What *is* all that shit?" It was as if he were hearing a tune on a distant radio, but could not remember the words. "That 'shit' is machine-gun fire, Hunter!" Caputo shouted up at him. "And it is *not ours.*"

Hunter scrunched somewhat lower in the grass, between Caputo and Nick Proffitt, *Newsweek*'s war correspondent. It was late April, 1975, and with each day the noose tightened around Saigon. The end was near, but no one knew just when. Proffitt had returned to Vietnam to cover the fall; he had been here before as the youngest Saigon bureau chief in *Newsweek*'s history. Further, he'd been a Marine, and was as war-savvy—and war-weary —as Caputo, who had been a member of the first wave of Marines to land at Danang in March, 1965. For him, this was a psychic journey to suture personal wounds, while covering the war for the Chicago *Tribune.*

Thompson flew to Saigon for *Rolling Stone.* On his way to Southeast Asia, Thompson called Bob Bone from the Honolulu Airport. Bone, living in Hawaii as a travel writer, knew that the journalist had never been closer to the war than *The New York Times;* he had told Thompson that he was crazy, that he'd never been in Vietnam, he knew nothing about it, and was likely to get killed. Hunter agreed. He said to Bone, "Yeah, yeah. I know. I know. But I've got the assignment, so I've got to go." Bone recalls that over the phone Thompson was "really nervous. God! He was nervous about going. But there he was, zipping through Honolulu on his way to Vietnam, hoping to get there in time to get thrown out."

The fall of Saigon was the story of the decade, and the saga of a generation and its mentality. In all previous wars, the brand of internal fortitude required to stay the duration was called "whiskey courage." For the readers of *Rolling Stone,* and for Thompson, this was their first war, and the new generation had different guts: for soldiers and journalists alike, this war took "dope courage."

There were curious similarities between Kinshasa and Saigon. Just as in Africa, every newsman in the world had descended on the rambling decay of a jungle city with the clear intent of witnessing a terrifying beating. Like vultures to carrion, they wanted to smell and hear and feel and taste the spectacle of blood and brutality, to report it into every American living room. It was the main event, never to be repeated; an epic struggle to the end with a clear winner and a historic loser, whose names would forever be remembered.

In the last weeks of April, 1975, the Caravelle and the Continental Hotels in central Saigon were filled with journalists; commerce as it had been known was dead, normal occupants had fled, and the city awaited its own execution. The first floor of the Continental Hotel, known as the Continental Shelf, was one of two gathering points for journalists; the other was the rooftop terrace bar across the square at the Caravelle, which offered spectacular night views of rocket fire. At that time, both were collecting areas for strange types of people, those whose business it was to feed on the death of a country—mercenaries, double-triple-quadruple agents, black marketeers, Air America pilots, spooks, and Hunter S. Thompson.

In a corner of the Continental Shelf, Philip Caputo and Nick Proffitt were trying to squeeze a story out of three North Vietnamese field agents turned informers. They had been "referred" by Frank Snepp, the CIA's military analyst in Saigon. The area of the hotel bordered the Courtyard Restaurant, a scattering of palm-thatched dining areas in the open-air center of the hotel; it was ringed by a series of connected stalls covered with corrugated fiberglass roofs, stuck up on flimsy bamboo poles. Underneath, the waiters would prepare food and seek shelter from the monsoon rains of spring. Caputo finished his interviewing, and saw, seated at a table with *Newsweek* correspondent Loren Jenkins, a familiar face. "I recognized Hunter from the photo on one of his books. I said to Nick, 'Isn't that Hunter Thompson? What the fuck is he doing here?' I mean, it was the last place on earth. Proffitt, who has a wonderful quick wit, said, 'Well, if he wants fear and loathing, he sure as hell has come to the right place.' "

The real-life Thompson did not meet the expectations of either of the veterans. Caputo had expected either someone "looking more outrageous, or maybe with long and gnarly hair." Instead, his impression was of "a big strapping guy; he looked like a defensive end." Proffitt was "surprised how big he was. He looked like a cop. A big ol' beefy detective." Loren Jenkins made the introductions. Neither Proffitt nor Caputo could ever decipher the persona of the chemically induced, zane-master Raoul Duke from the actual Hunter Thompson. "He was half playing Hunter Thompson,"

Proffitt said, "half trying to ingratiate himself to a bunch of veteran war foreign correspondents who themselves were very much of a military mentality."

Loren Jenkins had moved to Aspen as a teenager, and had known Hunter since the early '60s, when they would meet in the living room of Peggy Clifford, an intellectual magnet of sorts for that area. When Jenkins first considered a career in journalism, he had got in touch with Thompson for advice. Hunter's summation of the profession was that all editors are assholes, and to never type out an error with "x"s, but with "m"s and "n"s; it looks more professional. Thompson asked Proffitt and Caputo if he could come along the next day on their regular assignment of covering the ongoing battle at the town of Xuan Loc, about thirty miles northeast of Saigon. It was the last log in the dam, where ARVN troops pitched daily battles with the North Vietnamese troops. The journalists went there frequently; it was always a strange journey, and Thompson's presence added a touch of the bizarre such as neither had ever encountered.

"The morning routine," Caputo said, "involved starting with a couple of good strong French coffees in the Courtyard Restaurant. Then you hook up with your driver, head as close to the action as you dare, and spend the day dodging bullets and mortar and napalm, trying to get a story, trying to find out just how close the enemy—and the end—really is." Proffitt's version was similar. "You just drive until you get shot at, and try to stay alive long enough to write about it."

When Thompson had approached the journalists asking for a ticket into the action, both were chary; someone working with a loose hinge could put them in trouble, "as in killed," Caputo affirmed. It was pretty well known that Thompson came to Saigon with his usual pharmaceuticals, and it was common knowledge who was getting high; one could order opium from room service. Caputo felt that "a lot of times, it was Hunter playing Hunter. I have this feeling that he was almost like a celebrity or a movie actor, who was so identified with the role he played that he couldn't get out of it." Proffitt and Caputo relented, under one big condition. Proffitt told him, "You are not in Las Vegas now. This is a war zone. We leave at 6 A.M., and if you are not there, we are gone. Come along with us, but I don't want any of your shit. *No Gonzo bullshit!*"

The journalists' regular driver, Huong, was a Vietcong double agent, and he drove a gray jeep, with Caputo and Hunter in the back seat, and Nick riding shotgun. As "combat bang-bang guys" for their respective news journals, Nick and Caputo wore helmets, flak vests, and fatigues. Hunter wore a baseball cap, shades, aloha shirt, and shorts. And when they rendezvoused at the jeep early in the morning, Proffitt was nonplused when he saw Hunter, accompanied by "two sixty-year-old room boys in white pajamas, carrying down this huge cooler of beer. Hunter S. Thompson was going to war."

On the first leg of the trek to Xuan Loc, Thompson held to his promise of "no Gonzo bullshit," but he was popping pills and washing them down with beer. They could have been anti-malarial pills; they may have been aspirin. But when Proffitt tried to make a constructive comment to Hunter, who was busily dictating into his ever-present tape recorder, Thompson snapped at him, "Shut up! I'm on a roll."

The French called Route 1, the main north-south road in Vietnam, "the Street with No Joy," and that day was no exception: refugees streamed toward Saigon like frightened animals one step ahead of the dogs. People carried all their worldly belongings wrapped in bundles; children wandered around looking for parents; the wounded and crippled moved with primitive crutches. Tank traps, fifty-five-gallon oil drums filled with concrete, formed an obstacle course, and the jeep weaved between them and through the sea of refugees, who parted their long human line like ants around a tree. Farther on Route 1, the human chaos suddenly disappeared; this was known as No Man's Land, a ten-mile stretch eerily devoid of people or other vehicles. In the distance, the thunder rumble of battle was a backdrop that added to the tension; one knew that the lush tropical growth to either side of the jeep could be filled with snipers from—at this point in the war—the North or the South Vietnamese. "There was always that point where you got really tense," Caputo noted, "because you didn't know what the situation was. You drove along waiting for a mine to go off. Or a sudden burst of gunfire. Instead, there was always the silence. It gave us the fucking willies."

The scenery along Route 1 is classic tropical beauty; for Hunter, it could have been Puerto Rico, Cozumel, or Hawaii: shades of green punctuated with palms, rising on the left to the hills. In a split second, four F-5 fighter jets screamed directly over the jeep at a few hundred feet, deafening them for a moment. Caputo remembers ducking out of pure instinct, as there was nothing else one could do. Then the jets were gone; the silence folded back in on them.

Suddenly, the silence cracked wide open as Hunter emitted a

high-pitched, prolonged nightmare of a scream—"more like a howl" was Caputo's description. The driver, perhaps thinking that someone had been shot, got spooked, lost control of the jeep, careened off the road, and slammed nose-down in a culvert. The engine went dead. An immediate assessment showed that no one, miraculously, was even injured. Caputo didn't know if Hunter was pretending to be drugged up or really was, and had hallucinated. He turned to him and said, "You fucking idiot, what's the matter with you?" Thompson replied, "There were four giant fucker pterodactyls that just went overhead."

They could have rolled the jeep, been killed, or injured someone badly. At best they could have been stranded on foot in the middle of sniper land, twenty miles from Saigon in 117-degree heat. Caputo encapsulated the situation: "It was just not fun."

Proffitt took the matter into his own hands—literally. He spun around stretched himself over the back of his seat, and grabbed Hunter by the throat. "Nick is generally a good-humored guy," Caputo said. "He's a funny guy. He doesn't have a hot temper. Normally he responds with wisecracks." Instead, while throttling Hunter, he shouted at him, "I don't know whether you are straight or fucked up, but you had better get straight right here, or so help me Christ I am going to kill you!" Thompson turned docile, saying nothing beyond a few comments into his tape recorder as they started the jeep and headed to Xuan Loc.

There was a lot of fire, napalming, and bombing in Xuan Loc. Injured soldiers were being airlifted out of the battle zone; smoke towered out of the jungle in black columns. The reporters crawled, hiked, and cowered, finally getting interviews with some of the returning soldiers near the end of the day. Proffitt and Caputo wrapped things up—another day at the office—and started back to the jeep. Hunter was nowhere to be found. They asked their driver, "Where is the tall American?" After a brief search, they saw him in the distance—the unmistakable figure of a tall thin man in shorts, flowered shirt, sunglasses, and cigarette holder— wandering down the road that went straight into enemy territory, as close as the distance of a few football fields.

As he walked, Proffitt and Caputo could see him speaking into his tape recorder while looking around at all the sights, like a man documenting his stroll through The World's Biggest Theme Park of the Terminally Deranged. The war correspondents conferred briefly. They reviewed the five journalistic "W"'s and agreed that although there was minor confusion as to "Who" Hunter Thompson really was, that was his problem; he clearly did not know

"Where" he was headed, nor did he know "What" he was doing: he went on and on jabbering into his hand-held machine. (The comment that Proffitt had tried to make to him earlier in the day in the jeep, when Hunter had snapped at him, was that his recorder held no tape cartridge.) Proffitt and Caputo ushered the wandering Thompson back to the jeep and toward the relative safety of Saigon. Caputo felt that even the real-life version of that day's experience "sounded like some kind of war movie; a wild, crazy kid [38-year-old kid] gets initiated into battle. But it was that sort of tradition."

Thompson was fascinated by the machinery of war, always inspecting various pistols, rifles, and hand grenades, but he never wrote about it. He was constantly bugging Proffitt with questions. "We'd see a contrail," Proffitt said, "and Hunter would say "Do you think it's a B-52? Or is it Russian-made?' I'd say, 'Hunter, how the fuck do I know? It's at thirty-three thousand feet!'"

At one juncture, Proffitt flew for the day to cover a battle at a distant site and could not find room on that night's returning helicopter. Thompson was at a party thrown by *Newsweek*'s Tony and Clair Clifton, who misinterpreted the journalist's absence and announced, "Nick Proffitt is dead."

The journalist caught the next morning's flight back to Saigon. "I was having breakfast in the Courtyard," Proffitt recalled, "and Thompson strutted up to my table. He took off his sunglasses and really looked angry. 'You cocksucker!' he shouted at me. 'You are *alive!* I haven't been able to write for two days because I thought you were dead.'" It seemed Hunter Thompson's inverted anger was more over the fact that he no longer had an excuse *not* to write.

For all its dangers, Saigon held curiosities as well. Regardless of the close calls, Caputo allowed Hunter Thompson to accompany him on a visit to an American Legion post right in the city, a sign of just how Americanized the war had become. "Hunter approached me and said, 'I'd really like to see this, I'd really like to come along.' And I could tell it would be right up his alley; the kind of eccentric, off-the-wall sort of thing that he would be attracted to." Caputo and Thompson could not fathom why there would be such a bastion of Americana stuck in that part of the world. They pictured fat, middle-aged guys with funny hats handing out sauerkraut and bratwurst on Memorial Day. Before they left, Caputo gave Thompson "what I call the uptight establishment press flight instructions. I said, 'Don't fuck around.' He said, 'I won't say a word, how about that?' Great, I told him. I'll do the interview; you just listen. No Gonzo shit. Afterwards, if you want to write the most wild-assed piece for *Rolling Stone,* go ahead. Just don't fuck up my interview."

They found the American Legion Post Number 34 on a street that later seemed to disappear from Caputo's maps of the city. Walking in, they found a dozen bar girls, out of work because of the evacuation. They swarmed the two men like locusts to the harvest, squeezing Hunter's biceps, saying, "Beeg mahn, beeg mahn." Other than the horde of bar girls, the menu on the wall of HAM'N CHEESE . . . HOT DOG . . . BLT, a jukebox filled with country-and-western songs, and a paperback library of Westerns, "you could say you were in a coffee shop or pool hall of Bay City, Kansas," Caputo said. The two proprietors, grizzled, lean, hard-living, hard-drinking veterans of years in the Far East, told their tale of past perfect and future perfect. Living had been great there, everything taken care of, always a "honeywa" to pop you a beer or make life sweet. What were they going to do when Saigon fell? They were going to stay, and sell their know-how to the next regime. They would be needed, they felt, yet after another beer the Legionnaires began edging up to what Caputo thought was a volatile scene. They began bad-mouthing the Congress, the hippies, the press for selling Vietnam down the river.

Caputo had told them they were press, but he deliberately said nothing about *Rolling Stone.* He felt they might respond with a "Fucking dopers; it's O.K. to drink until you are blind, but no dope" mentality, and that Thompson, in turn, might take a poke at one of them; Caputo had been witness to his unpredictability, and his apparent blind eye toward real danger. "I got the general feeling that the interview was over," Caputo said. On the way out, two paintings on the wall caught the stark essence of Saigon, Vietnam, on the 28th of April, 1975. Hung on the wall was a series of battle paintings that documented the legacy of victory and success of the American Army, stretching from Ticonderoga through Antietam to The Bulge. A painting of the Alamo stood out: "It was appropriate for Saigon at the time," he noted. Another, a painting of a trumpet call used at Resaca de la Palma by the Mexican Army in the War of 1846–48 came back to haunt him. He researched it later, and found that the painting was of Santa Ana playing the Degüello. "I found out later that whenever an enemy refused to surrender, the Mexican Army would play a chilling, haunting bugle call. It was a signal that no quarter is to be given. Everybody is to be killed—the wounded, the sick, the women and children. I regarded it as emblematic, one of the single meanings of Vietnam. Really the end of something in American history."

The evening routine for correspondents those last days consisted of returning to the Continental, having a *citron prese avec l'eau,* cleaning off the day's sweat and smell of cordite, and either going to the Caravelle's terrace bar to watch the fireworks, or having gin with tonic, "to ward off malaria," then dining, swapping stories, expressing gallows humor, under one of the palm-thatched oases in the Courtyard Restaurant. It was a bizarre scene; forty or so educated, intelligent, wordly men dining on fine china, beckoning to a waiter for more French wine with the raise of a finger, while the thumps and thuds of bombs and mortar fire formed the audible proscenium to this act of denial in death's jaws. "You could measure the distance of the war by the volume of the booming from the big guns," Caputo recollected. That night was particularly tense; the night before, a rocket barrage had blown up the Metropole, just four blocks away, and at 6 P.M. Saigon had been strafed, and the airport at Tan Son Nhut bombed. All the journalists had watched this beautifully morbid scene from the terrace of the Caravelle. Then they headed to the Courtyard for dinner. At that time, the secret code phrase for final evacuation had been given; when the local radio station broadcast "The temperature in Saigon is one-zero-five and rising," followed by Bing Crosby singing "White Christmas," it was the green flag for each person to go to a pre-assigned location, then to be air-evacuated to ships offshore. A radio was always playing.

Everyone except Thompson was eating under the thatch: coq au vin with a good Beaujolais. Hunter was pursuing other appetites. Proffitt assumed his absence was because "he had set himself up in his room with an old whore; she was about fifty. Everyone knew her from the old days in Saigon. She had been beautiful." Hunter had spent the early evening with Mr. Loong. An ageless Chinese man, Loong was the unofficial procurer for the Continental's residents. There was an extra room that was taken collectively at the Continental and used as an opium den. It was stark, with no furniture, just a stack of cushions and a cassette player. The idea was to order beer or tea, listen to the music, pass around the pipe that Mr. Loong would pack, and talk about the war. "I do not know what Hunter's experience was with opium," Proffitt added. "But I do know that five pipes is a lot." Just before they went down to dinner, someone lit up some Buddha grass, and

Hunter sucked on that while Mr. Loong was packing his gear. There was some opium left over, but not quite enough to make a pipe. As Mr. Loong rolled it into a ball, Hunter went over to him, took the tarry blob, "and chewed it like bubble gum."

With rats curling around their feet and booms of 150-mm. guns for background music, Caputo described the dinner party as after a while, having "a wired-up feeling, with everyone eating with one ear cocked for the sound of *that* rocket"—the one aimed for the Continental.

A sudden crash came from a corner of the open Courtyard, and men with a lifetime's experience interpreting loud noises shouted "incoming" and flung themselves on the ground. But the ground didn't shake, and no one felt the percussion of explosion. It was silent. They all got up, and went over to where the line of fiberglass-roofed stalls was now collapsed atop someone easily identified by two large white tennis shoes sticking out from beneath the rubble. It looked like the male version of the Wicked Witch of the West. A thoroughly ripped Hunter Thompson had lost his balance and lurched into the skinny bamboo supports, knocking the entire kitchen down upon him. People began to grab the fiberglass awning. Caputo said, "Christ, maybe he's dead." Proffitt said, "I hope the fuck so." When Hunter's loud cursing was heard from under the mess, Proffitt commented, "There goes his reputation as the Drug Czar."

The next night, Thompson and Caputo went to investigate another of Saigon's anomalies; the Green Dragon Restaurant, near the Saigon River. There one could dine on lobster and converse with the most beautiful women in Southeast Asia—tall, sleek, sophisticated, multilingual Chinese from Szechwan Province, imported to service the needs of Air America and RMK Construction employees. The women, some as tall as five feet ten, were in strapless evening dresses, spangled with rhinestones. "It was just like we had entered Valhalla," Caputo said. He and Hunter roamed around trying to find two who were unattached. They got the message that you did not just barge in and try and pick up the women; most were "dedicated," regulars for the few foreigners remaining. They headed for the restaurant in the back, through the vale of black beads, complete with a majordomo in tuxedo, serving lobster thermador and Montrachet wines. After dinner, they sat in a booth and were approached by two of the women. "We were actually carrying on an intelligent conversation," Caputo related. "I will never forget their beauty. Hunter and I felt like we were nineteen years old and double-dating." Punctuating the conversation, one of the girls asked for a cigarette; in her low-cut dress she leaned over for it to be lit. She had breasts like varnished beach balls that seemed ready to roll onto the table. They made "war" a difficult concept. "I have never seen tits like that on a Vietnamese woman," said Caputo. "Hunter looked at them, then at me with this 'Oh my God' look on his face. It turned out they had regular guys that night. They said to us, 'Please come back tomorrow night—no boyfriend tomorrow night.' "

As the two left with not just their expectations rising, "the temperature" hit "one-zero-five and rising" on the thermometer of Saigon. Even though Bing Crosby never sang "White Christmas," there would be no tomorrow night at the Green Dragon. Back at the Continental, Nick Proffitt was on the phone long-distance with the editor in chief of *Newsweek,* Ed Kosner, asserting his logic for remaining in Saigon until the absolute end. The Washington *Post* journalists had panicked, left early, and become the laughingstock for those who kept the vigil. Proffitt's argument won out, and he came down to the other correspondents gathered in the Continental Shelf and put on a mocking imitation of the high-strung New York accent of his boss.

The next day, Caputo fought back nerves as he and Proffitt were bused past scenes that looked like a soccer riot. On the tennis courts where General Westmoreland and Henry Cabot Lodge had perfected their tennis games, they boarded a Marine Sea Stallion helicopter that dodged surface-to-air missiles before landing them on the safety of the U.S.S. *Denver.* They did not know how—or if—Thompson got out. A year or so later, home in Beirut, Proffitt received confirmation that Hunter had indeed made it. A journalist he knew had come from the States and told him a tale of being at a party at the house of Dick Tuck, a correspondent who had covered the 1972 election. Proffitt said that at Tuck's, "the guy had heard an interesting tape of me making Ed Kosner sound like an asshole. It almost deep-sixed my employment with the magazine. Hunter was there, and had played it at the party. At least that time he got the tape into his recorder, the sneaky bastard!"

Tape recordings were about all anyone heard of Thompson's experience in Vietnam. He went there with another *Rolling Stone* correspondent, Laura Palmer; her stories were far more illuminating. In the few pieces that did appear, Thompson seemed primarily occupied with the availability of ice from the Continental's room service at the strange hours he would make his requests.

Some of his work was published a decade after the fall of

Saigon, a decade after a large rift opened between Thompson and Wenner. While Thompson was in Saigon, Wenner had become irritated at the lack of quality and quantity of Thompson's submissions. Wenner had cancelled all insurance policies for Hunter and his family. "He took it very personally," Alan Rinzler observed. "Hunter felt as if he had been emasculated by his inability to care for his family."

The winner of the 1975 Pulitzer Prize for editorial cartooning was Garry Trudeau. Shortly after Thompson's return from Vietnam, Trudeau, in "Doonesbury," got to the heart of the matter regarding Hunter and his family. While being interviewed on his arrival from Saigon, Raoul Duke is asked how he feels about being away so long from his wife. In response, Duke was sketched as emitting a large cloud of bubbles; in one of them is the word "wife," followed by a large question mark. The question mark was about to take on legal proportions.

20.

Gonzo

Goes

Hollywood

spen's Jerome Hotel and Bar was built by Jerome Wheeler, the founder of Macy's Department store. Its opening night, Thanksgiving of 1889, was attended by high society from around the world who partied after strapping on barrel staves and sliding down the mountain slopes. In the winter of 1975–76, the pretty people still in-

vaded the hotel for their *après* ski. At one end of the bar, under a framed "THOMPSON FOR SHERIFF" poster, Hunter Thompson sat drinking among friends. The bartender was new, a stranger. He leaned across the bar and shouted to Hunter, "Hey, Hunter! Read your book. Enjoyed it. You're a crazy fucker, aren't you?"

Under normal circumstances, Thompson might have turned churlish, but Aspen is a small town where it is tough to be a stranger for long. The bartender was Stan Dzura, and Hunter already knew his background. After football and basketball heroics during high school in Honolulu, he had quickly joined the Marines to avoid a several-thousand-dollar phone bill he had run up calling friends on the mainland. On the invitation of Stanford football coach Bill Walsh, he had visited the campus, only to inadvertently incite a minor riot that put the Sigma Chi fraternity on a year's probation when he had sex on a pool table, then stood to urinate on the band. This, and the subsequent police raid, did not go down smoothly with the Stanford faculty. Coach Walsh called Mike White, then a coach at Berkeley, and said, "He's a Cal kind of guy."

At six feet six and 240 pounds, he became such a dominant force on both the rugby and the football teams that he was a *Playboy* All-America pre-pick in the fall of 1965. He immortalized himself, and captured the school spirit of the times, when he posed for the All-America team photo on the front row of the bleachers, elbows on his knees, fists together, middle finger extended in defiant salute. The censors at the magazine either missed it or felt it a fitting tribute to the times. In the sun-drenched campuses and stadiums of the Pac-Eight Conference, his political gestures as well as his athletic abilities became legend.

A near-fatal auto accident during a rugby tour of Australia cut short a professional football career, but Dzura never seemed to let life's curve balls get him down. He wandered through life with an un-housebroken, iconoclastic buoyancy, and wound up in Aspen as therapy from a lost job and a broken relationship. Just a few nights before meeting Thompson, he had jumped off the fourth floor of a hotel into a swimming pool, and then wandered, totally naked, through one of Aspen's better eating establishments, stopping to greet startled diners along the way.

That night at the Jerome Bar, knowing full well Thompson's "propensities for pharmaceuticals," Dzura decided to extend a chemical greeting to the writer. "You have to understand the times in Aspen then," Dzura pointed out. "It was pretty much a blanket policy: alcohol, sex, rock and roll. And drugs, of course."

From behind the bar, he handed Hunter a large glass container of amyl nitrate. Hunter whiffed it. He handed it to a friend at the bar who whiffed it. The bar was quite crowded. Someone accidentally jostled Hunter; the container crashed to the floor, filling the room with a cloud of the cardiac stimulant. Dzura recalls that "the entire barroom got 'whiffed.' A group amyl-nitrate rush. It was kinda weird." Dzura interested Hunter, and the two became friends. "I guess he figured I was a kindred spirit," Dzura said.

After closing the Jerome, Dzura and Hunter would party-hop until dawn, then scream past the basalt cliffs, above the Roaring Fork River along the sinuous Route 82 toward Woody Creek. Even Dzura was cowed by Thompson's driving under the influence, stating, "I don't care how drunk I was, it was one hairy white-knuckler; going at seventy miles an hour in the pitch black, Hunter would turn off the headlights, and use the moon for guiding. If there happened to be a moon. I realized that in the cause of self-preservation, I didn't want to do this too often." While Sandy slept, Hunter would sneak in, get whatever he needed, and sneak back out. "I remember spending the whole night outside a trailer park," Dzura said. "Hunter was trying to diddle some girl, waiting for her to come home. There were four of us in the car with about three gallons of various stuff, and we were supposed to be real quiet. We got loud, obnoxious, drunk, and finally passed out. When we woke up, the whole trailer park was out there looking at us, this car filled with hung-over guys and empty bottles." Thompson enjoyed Dzura's free spirit, and even used him as a bodyguard at a Willie Nelson concert after he had been warned that the Hell's Angels were in Aspen and still after him.

Thompson's and Dzura's ideas of fun were far more the rule, rather than the exception for those years in Aspen. While Gene McGarr was visiting, an attorney friend of Hunter's and Gene's was arrested in the middle of Aspen, beating a 300-pound prostitute who had refused his advances. All the time during the fight, the man's teeth were clenched around the stem of a marijuana-filled pipe. He was summarily jailed; while Thompson and McGarr tried to persuade the sheriff to release the man to their custody, the jailed attorney tore off the toilet seat in his cell and began a thunderous racket, dragging the seat back and forth across the cell bars.

During these years, Sandy would often try and stonewall Hunter's friends from contacting him. She would always answer the phone, and provide flimsy excuses for his unavailability. More than once, friends recalled, she would be seen in the middle of the night, outside some Aspen condominium, knowing Hunter was inside with another woman, yelling, "Come out of there, you son of a bitch." Her attempts to tame the man were futile. Thompson would often horrify his friends by driving at breakneck speed around the sharp mountain curves on the wrong side of the road. He exuded a sense of either fatalism or invincibility, telling McGarr that he could see other cars coming, from the reflection of their headlights off the utility lines or trees. It seemed to work for him, but John Clancey, who also had a penchant for crazy driving, ran off a "dead man's curve." His car was left straddled atop a culvert that kept him from a 600-foot fall. One of Thompson's favorite terms, "bad craziness" seemed everywhere.

The family dynamics at Owl Farm were interesting. To some who visited during the early '70s, it seemed a picture of bucolic tranquillity, with Sandy very involved in planting and gardening, and Hunter riding the crest of literary success. Few friends from that time recall Juan and Hunter together much, as Hunter was a creature of the night. They just kept different hours. There was a shared interest in football; Dzura recalled Hunter introducing him to Juan as having been a great college football player. "He enjoyed showing off his son," Dzura recalled.

With Sandy, there was humor, yet typically with a sharp edge just below the surface. In the early '70s Sandy told a friend that she called Hunter "Baldy" because she knew Hunter was sensitive about his loss of hair, but would take it. In turn, he would call Sandy "Skinny wench" for the same reasons. Her friend recalls Sandy explaining each's tolerance, saying "We can do it because we've been through so much together and we love each other so much." But love was not enough to keep the relationship and the marriage on track.

Thompson's own free spirit was eroding his marriage, and the emotional and legal toll would, in turn, erode his ability and style as a writer. His next two books, *The Great Shark Hunt* and *The Curse of Lono,* were watersheds to a protracted, draining, running marital skirmish that lasted for two years. This was a period of personal turmoil and change, where Thompson ventured not only into divorce court, but into film, screenwriting, and—at long last—fiction. He would temporarily drop the persona of Raoul Duke, and take on a voice and targets for his writing that gave vent to the frustrations of going through a divorce that ended a marriage, for better or worse, of sixteen years.

At the time Hunter dropped the heart medicine on the floor of the Jerome Bar, his work-in-progress was a vast, 602-page collection of his life as a writer. During part of the time spent compiling, selecting, and editing, he stayed near Alan Rinzler at Berkeley's Claremont Hotel. He stayed in the Honeymoon Suite for $50 a night; he stayed there alone. Somewhat later, he spent the night before Christmas Eve alone in the *Rolling Stone* suite in New York's Sherry-Netherland Hotel, completing the Author's Note, signed "H.S.T.#1, R.I.P." It included a quote from Thompson's "favorite humorist," Joseph Conrad: "Art is long and life is short, and success is very far off." Thompson pointed out that he had just turned forty, and it was "a strange feeling to be a 40-year-old writer in this century." He felt that *The Great Shark Hunt,* and its Author's Note, was analogous to carving his own tombstone; he contemplated diving to his death out the window into the Pulitzer Fountain in front of the Plaza Hotel where, two decades before, he had been ousted from the dirty water, his bottle of Jack Daniel's broken by a New York cop.

Regardless of his established position as a writer, Thompson's financial position was still not solid. Through his neighbor and leaseholder of the Woody Creek Tavern, George Stranahan, Hunter had taken a loan using his beloved home, Owl Farm, in Woody Creek as collateral; Stranahan was also given first rights to buy the 122-acre spread at fifty-five percent of market value. In the years while his divorce proceedings were dragging on, Thompson would start to make more money than ever before, but much of it went for attorneys' fees, support for Sandy, and Juan's education. Dzura had seen things sliding with Sandy and observed that Hunter "was still a wandering spirit, but with a semi-anchor. You could tell he loved this woman, and he really loved the kid. He wanted to maintain the relationship, but he still wanted to go out and maintain his freedom. He was heavily into his errant ways." During this time, Dennis Murphy recalled many late night phone calls from Sandy, saying, "I cannot take it anymore. I just cannot."

In August, 1978, Sandy and Juan moved out of Owl Farm and into town. She lived on Francis Street and worked at the Aspen Bookstore for $780 a month. In the next year, including royalties from his past three books and an advance on *The Great Shark Hunt,* Hunter made $104,000. He still pleaded poverty. He refused to respond to Sandy's attorneys' interrogatories, dragging his feet on the divorce he had legally initiated. He changed lawyers five times (three times in one four-month period), failed to pay back federal, state, and real-estate taxes, and was $11,000 in arrears on loan payments to Stranahan. Sandy and Hunter bickered over Owl Farm, then valued at $450,000. She wanted half; Hunter wanted it all. The value of petty household objects became a prime focus; Sandy said Hunter's Penton 400 motorcycle was worth $1,000, while Hunter countered with a value of $750. She wanted the black coral necklace that Hunter had brought back from Cozumel. It had been mentioned in the article "The Great Shark Hunt," and was one of the few instances where her name made its way into his journalism. There were squabblings about the valuation of stereo and video equipment, and of gun collections; Hunter stated that he had sold the pearl-handled .38. Hunter filed for divorce on the 9th of February, 1979, and left Aspen, renting Jimmy Buffet's Waddell Avenue apartment in Key West. It would be two years to the day before the courts completed matters by awarding joint custody of Juan, and sealing financial affidavits and separation agreements.

In the mid-1970s, actor Peter Boyle had been approached by director Vernon Zimmerman with a screenplay for *Fear and Loathing in Las Vegas.* It was one of various attempts to put that book into celluloid; none was successful. Finally, in 1979, as Thompson's divorce was wandering through attorneys and the courts, a deal was made to do a full-length movie based on a collage of Hunter's life during the late '60s and early '70s. It was also the year that *The Great Shark Hunt,* Thompson's best-selling book, was released. Things seemed to be happening at once; while the divorce was proceeding, the book was released the same month filming started on *Where the Buffalo Roam.* It starred Peter Boyle as Thompson's attorney, and Bill Murray as Thompson. Murray was on "Saturday Night Live," and his first movie, *Meatballs,* was released while *Buffalo* was being shot. At the start of work on *Buffalo,* Murray was a relative unknown; during the two months of filming, *Meatballs* took off like a rocket. Murray suddenly found himself in a new bargaining position. Thompson, too, found himself in a new bargaining position when he cut his deal with Universal studios, but his difficulty was bargaining with divorce attorneys. He sold the rights to his life story for $63,000. In addition, he was paid $25,000 as "consultant": he would advise on matters, like showing Murray the traditional taping of the tape recorder to his upper arm, to capture every word of both his monologue and any conversation. (Thompson still keeps all the tapes made during his and Acosta's trip to Las Vegas at his home in Woody Creek.) He had also signed a contract with Paramount studios to assist with the making of a film about drug-running. The contract was cancelled after he had been paid $24,000, because of differing agreements over expenses, a time-honored Thompson theme.

Murray had been a huge Hunter Thompson fan for years, and had gone to seek him out in the Jerome Bar, long before the movie was shot. When Thompson first met John Belushi, he felt the actor was funnier in twenty minutes than most people were in twenty years. Of the original stars on "Saturday Night Live," Murray, Dan Aykroyd, and John Belushi openly embraced Hunter and the "New Macho" style of the late '70s. Every show was an assault mission; Aykroyd called it "Gonzo Television."

Cast as a contemporary of Thompson's in *Buffalo,* Peter Boyle was just one year older than Thompson, and fifteen years older than Murray. During the filming, Boyle imposed strict self-discipline, jogging in the early morning to keep in shape, getting adequate sleep, and not partying with the boys, in order to look as close in age to Murray as possible. He was caught somewhat by surprise when he first met Thompson, who always seemed lean and conditioned regardless of his intake. On the coffee-shop patio of Universal studios, Boyle found the forty-two-year-old Thompson finishing lunch, and sweating profusely. Hunter consumed a club sandwich with a couple of beers, and then ordered chocolate cake and a double Wild Turkey. What kind of creature do we have here? was Boyle's immediate thought. Will he do wild things?

In charge of the whole operation was producer-director Art Linson, whose background before movie involvement was as a record producer and an attorney. He was a high-energy, driving man, always carrying a heavy work load, very demanding of himself. The studios loved him, as he had produced *Car Wash,* which had made five times its production costs—a celluloid alchemy trick in Hollywood. From the actor's perspective, Boyle saw him as "a little crazy, always filled with ideas." On *Buffalo,* he teamed once again with screenwriter John Kaye; both had gone to Berkeley, and knew West Coast zaniness from the inside out. Linson and Kaye had achieved success when they produced and wrote, respectively, *American Hot Wax,* the story of Alan Freed.

Linson and Kaye had flown to Aspen earlier, to get a sense of Thompson and the movie's possibilities. They were kept active during their stay; Thompson drove them from the airport in a rental car, first smashing a van that blocked their way, then getting stopped on the short stretch of Route 82 between the airport and Woody Creek for going 70 in a 35-m.p.h. zone. The car was filled with Wild Turkey and pharmaceuticals. Kaye had never met Thompson before, and sat there thinking, Great. I've been with this guy for twenty minutes and I'm history. Much to Linson's and Kaye's amazement, the officer let Hunter continue. They ended a thoroughly Thompsonian few days sitting on the grass back at the Aspen airport, well aware that there was potential in this man's story, and trying to figure out who was more deserving of the last Valium in their possession. Linson won.

Where the Buffalo Roam was shot in Los Angeles and nearby Piru, during August and September of 1979. Murray had immediate access to the character he was playing; Hunter moved into a room underneath the swimming pool in the house Murray had rented in North Hollywood, overlooking the Universal studios. His room, part of a tastelessly constructed setup for a voyeuristic bachelor, had as its only illumination two portholes through which the underwater lights from the pool flickered.

Boyle kept pretty much to himself for the two months. He carefully studied the role of the late Oscar Zeta Acosta, the Brown Buffalo, the 300-pound Samoan attorney from *Fear and Loathing in Las Vegas*. Thompson never offered a single comment on his old friend to Boyle, who found the character fascinating in its own right: a poor Mexican-American who pulled himself up by his bootstraps, worked his way through law school, then defended the rights of his ethnic minority group. Both of Acosta's books, *The Autobiography of the Brown Buffalo* and *The Revolt of the Cockroach People*, were thoroughly scrutinized for Boyle's role. When it was released, Acosta's son Marco saw the movie and commented, "I really didn't think that character was my dad." He felt the film's lawyer seemed more like other high-profile San Francisco area criminal attorneys, specifically Tony Serra, or Mike Stepanian (who briefly represented Hunter in his divorce at that time, and was best known for his 1971 book *Pot Shots*, a "How To" manual for the first-time drug offender). Marco Acosta was puzzled over the lack of similarity, even down to the name used for the role modeled after his father. What had occurred was a play of ethnic politics.

A Chicano actors' group, Nos Otros, was protesting the filming of *Buffalo;* they did not want a non-Chicano playing a Chicano. "It blew my mind," said the thoroughly prepared Boyle, the target of all the commotion. "At the last minute, I suddenly became 'Lazlo,' a Hungarian drug lawyer."

For the duration of the filming, Thompson remained surprisingly sane and controlled. One morning, Murray came onto the set in a spirit of amazement, and told of Hunter's having broken a piece of cast-iron lawn furniture at his house. Boyle heard this and said, "How can you break cast-iron furniture?" Murray, equally puzzled, said, "I don't know either, but he did!" Boyle felt that there was this "thing" that followed Hunter around, that same sense of imminent apocalypse that Tony Lukas had felt while reporting on Hunter in Washington, D.C.

When Ralph Steadman appeared to work on the art, he accused Hunter of selling out. Thompson replied that the movie was "like a huge tit: we're supposed to fasten onto it and feed."

Much of any actor's time is spent on the set sitting around, waiting and watching. For Boyle, the single most fascinating dimension to the movie was observing Hunter watching Murray play Hunter. Never one given to introspection, and always full of ambivalence about his public persona, Thompson seemed mesmerized, as if undergoing an out-of-the-body experience. Some thought that the two characters should have been played by Dan Aykroyd and John Belushi, but everyone agreed on Murray's eerily accurate portrayal of Thompson, down to the muffled, spasmotic delivery, the poking of the cigarette holder, and the strange "Thompson Shuffle." After completing *Buffalo,* Murray returned for a fifth season of "Saturday Night Live." Murray could not get Thompson out of his system; he took to wearing sunglasses constantly, smoking with a cigarette holder, and continuing to play the role to such an extent that one of the "Saturday Night Live" writers said, "Billy was not Bill Murray. You couldn't talk to him without talking to Hunter Thompson." At times, Hunter would show up backstage on the set of "Saturday Night Live." When he did, he made many people as uneasy as when the Hell's Angels had, the year before, stormed the set after a skit had shown them singing "Johnny Angel" and wearing their "colors," which they considered bad for their image. One writer said of Thompson's appearances that while he might be a fun person to go skiing with or do drugs with, "Hunter Thompson is not the person you want working on a comedy show."

On the film set, Boyle's expectations of a bizarre eruption from Thompson did not materialize: "He was intrigued by the whole process. Writers work by themselves. For him to encounter forty people, all organized and choreographed, was simply stunning." Linson's assessment of Thompson was similar, except for the time when Thompson felt Linson owed him expense money. Thompson purchased a red pitchfork, walked into Linson's office, and stabbed it upright in the pile carpeting. He got his check. Linson felt that Thompson's real power "comes from his writing, but his behavior was classically funny. Chaplinesque, if you'd ask me. And when you cut through his craziness, he is a Southern gentleman."

Hunter took an extra $25,000 to write the narrative that Murray recites at the end of the movie. The writing was put off for weeks, then done quickly, in the early dawn hours. The film was late, over budget, and in need of some special juices. The two had equipment specially set up so that Murray could read what Thompson wrote, and have it transferred immediately to the sound track. The immediacy of capturing his thoughts in living technicolor, rather than through type or on tape, provided Thompson with an ultimate non-drug high. Craig Vetter was there when the ending of the movie was shot. In going from handwritten narrative directly to the celluloid, it was as if he had transposed himself into a land of no deadlines, no editors, no barriers to giving his thoughts an immediate life of their own, on the screen, accessible at the touch of a button. "Hunter and Murray stayed up all night working on it, having a ball," Vetter said. "I came back in the morning and Hunter was absolutely—quite literally—doing somersaults. 'Hot damn, we have done it,' he was saying. 'God-damned if this isn't IT! Oh, we've flogged the beast home with this one. We finally found a way to cut through all the editors, printers, even the typewriter. No more bullshit!'"

In the ending of the film, Murray-as-Thompson is in a replica of Owl Farm. It is a large room, with a stone fireplace roaring, strewn with photos, newspaper clippings, campaign posters, memorabilia of every nature, as it is in real life, totally devoid of a woman's touch—a teenager's room after his parents have been gone six weeks. Wearing his woman's wig, he yanks out the last page of a manuscript, pours himself and his Doberman a generous slug of Wild Turkey, toasts "To better days" to the slurping pup, briefly holds an interrupting telephone hostage with a .357 at its receiver, and then reads: "It's sad. But what's really sad is: it never got weird enough for me. I moved to the country when the boat got too crowded. Then I learned that President Nixon had been eaten by white cannibals on an island near Tijuana. For no good reason at all. Golly. You hear a lot of savage and unnatural things about people these days. But Lazlo and Nixon are both gone now. But I don't think I'm going to believe that until I can gnaw on both of their skulls with my very own teeth. Fuck those people, huh? If they're out there, I'm going to find them. And I am going to gnaw on their skulls. Because it still hasn't gotten weird enough for me.''

Only at the very end did Hunter try to let down what was left of his hair. At a party held at a Mexican restaurant, Thompson appeared with Boyle's director's chair, the name in bold letters across the back. Hunter had stolen the chair just so that he could make a presentation to Boyle. He then turned to Boyle's wife, repeatedly saying, "Do you want to see my fire-eating act? Don't you want to?" She did not.

Not many people wanted to see the movie, either. Despite Ralph Steadman's inimitable artistic splatterings and "Gonzo Calligraphy," both in the film and on promotion posters, and Neil Young singing "Where the Buffalo Roam," the film had a brief lifespan in the theater before it quietly (and with the advent of video, successfully) entered the land of the Cult Classic. Many thought it was too much of an insider's movie, and would have been better directed by Ken Russell, to capture the hallucinogenic aura of Thompson and the times. When watching it on video, many people achieve the desired effect by goosing the speed up a third, to get a true amphetamine chatter out of it.

21.

Mambo,

Dildo, Gonzo,

Lono

n a tiny tabletop in the corner of a dimly lit room, two buck-naked nineteen-year-olds are connected by a monstrous double-ended dildo. They writhe, moan, make strange pain-pleasure sounds and movements with their mouths. In a hedonic jerk of pure bestial abandon, the leg of one whacks the head of a Japanese business-

man, attired in suit and tie. He bangs his head against the mirrored wall behind him, and his glasses fly into the pitch-black void beneath the corner table where he sits, and on which the women perform. He is thus rendered momentarily incapable of watching the scene, just two dildo-lengths in front of his myopic eyes. Politely, the show slows down while he collects himself.

The two naked teens, one a thin, pale blonde, called Heather, and her accomplice in this genital theater, Zia, continue their performance. Then, in mid-act, comes conversation. Heather looks across the shoulder of Zia and asks a question she has asked a dozen times tonight, a hundred times this week. In response, the businessman's face rings up emotion after emotion, like numbers on an old-fashioned cash register: bewilderment, arousal, embarrassment are quickly followed by incredulity, disbelief, and finally—the day's end tally—numbness.

"Isn't it terrible that this is my job?" Heather squeals with delight, implying that it is a crime to have fun and get paid for it.

Getting no reply, Heather and Zia shift their emotional gears like a successful drag racer. They unplug, pack the tools of their trade in a black leatherette zipper bag, and hop to the floor, heading for the next table, the next incredulous tourist, the next show.

It is general knowledge that to get to Carnegie Hall, one turns west from Fifth Avenue on Fifty-seventh Street. To get to "the Carnegie Hall of Sex," one goes north on Polk Street in San Francisco. At the corner of O'Farrell, you arrive at the Mitchell Brothers' O'Farrell Street Theater. This was the daily commute for Hunter Thompson for months. He had business cards made up, which read: "Hunter S. Thompson Night Manager The Mitchell Brothers Theater."

In August, 1979, on the front page of *The New York Times Book Review,* William F. Buckley, Jr., had read the recently released *Shark Hunt,* and stated (under the title "Blunt Instruments") that Thompson's concept of a drug-fueled life-style was "out of Hieronymus Bosch." Buckley quoted Thompson's 1967 description of the effects of a $5 cap of LSD as sounding like "the Universal Symphony, with God singing solo and the Holy Ghost on drums." Then Buckley lowered the boom, saying, ". . . Hunter Thompson has no apparent interest in sex . . ."

This was beginning to become a common criticism of Thompson's writing, and he took Buckley's public statement personally. He went to his old San Francisco friends Jim and Artie Mitchell, "the Potentates of Porn," a $50 million enterprise begun with a 16-mm. projector and a dark closet, and began to hang out at their theater. Taking Buckley's comment as part challenge, part insult, he started a book called "Night Manager." It was never consummated, even though *Playboy* did pay for an excerpt. His stint at the theater left a lasting impression on some employees, and if this was a mid-life-career crisis with Buckley as guidance counselor, Thompson, over the next months, managed to use the experience to literary benefit.

In April, 1980, Sandy had issued a restraining order to prevent Hunter from blowing the estimated $75,000 he was to receive from the first royalty payment on *Shark Hunt;* he came up short, collecting only $20,659.58. However, Sandy's attorneys were puzzled: Hunter had deposited $154,000 after commissions with his agents at ICM, and later made $84,460.32 of bank deposits. And then there were the speaking engagements; four, at $1,400 each. Sandy's attorneys figured that was adequate income to pay her legal fee of $5,000. Hunter said no. His lawyers said the royalties on *The Great Shark Hunt* had been spent, and there were no sums available. They asked for a new trial to recalibrate financial responsibilities.

The court did not agree. They agreed that Hunter had indeed paid the $7,000 tuition for Juan to attend Massachusetts's Concord Academy (he left a month after getting there). But the court also showed that Hunter's meager $20,000 in royalties, when added to the paperback rights to *Shark,* sold for $40,000, with a like amount due in six months, seemed adequate to pay Sandy's attorneys' fees of $5,000.

Thompson replied that he had not paid because he had no cash flow, and that this was all Sandy's fault. He was "reluctant to undertake any new literary works in which the Respondent wife may declare a marital interest." However, if the divorce could be finalized, he could pay, because this "would allow him to freely create new literary properties without fear." In his plea for a new trial, he listed some interesting debts: $5,000 to Jimmy Buffet; a tab of $1,600 at the Jerome Bar (enough for 2,133 draft beers at 75 cents each); and $1,200 at the Abetone Restaurant.

Meanwhile, back at the Mitchell Brothers, Thompson was hanging out in the second-floor offices of Jim and Artie, where one can watch people watching people performing sexual acts upon other people—second-stage voyeurism. The walls of the office's "Hall of Shame" included framed photos of Hunter, and Hunter with the brothers. Most of his time there was spent using their equipment to make videos. Their composition was not of a sexual nature; they were of dune buggies slamming into one another, producing traumatizing collisions and wrecks of twisted steel and rubber. Many were sold in the downstairs video shop/boutique, where they also sold Hunter's designer T-shirts and sweatshirts. Embossed with a dancing skeleton slinging around a bottle of Chivas Regal, the shirts bore the caption "The Weird Never Die." They sold out quickly, and are now collectors' items.

"Hunter Thompson? I baby-sat him," begins the recollections of a longtime Mitchell Brothers' employee. "He is a mooch, mooch, mooch. He is malicious and destructive. He has no appreciation for other people's property. He destroys everything. He doesn't even bring his own liquor. He sits upstairs and mumbles incoherently. He doesn't do that Gonzo journalism bullshit; he is incapable. There must be someone else doing it for him.

"But you read his stuff and it's all 'ha ha—have fun with Hunter S. Thompson.' Well, let me tell you, he's got an underground cult following that takes care of him. He thinks he's above it all. They think it's fun, fun, fun with Hunter, and they put him up down the street at the Hilton. Then he comes up here, gets drunk, babbles incoherently, and destroys things. He is a sick little monster. He is nothing but an overgrown juvenile delinquent. And if he comes around here again and messes with people and destroys other people's property, someone's gonna put his lights out. For good."

With the courts and the Mitchell Brothers' employees after him, Thompson stumbled across a reprieve, and, like the offers for the Hell's Angels book, it appeared in his mailbox. In May, 1980, he was asked by the editor of *Running* magazine to take Ralph Steadman and go to Honolulu to cover the marathon to be run in December. All expenses were to be paid. Hunter's attorney pleaded with the court to delay the divorce trial, stating that "in fact, the petitioner has his first job offer and contract for work in a long time." The court allowed a continuance so that Hunter could "engage in further journalistic endeavors, all of which will generate further funds." The writer's block seemed magically dissolved; Hunter and his girlfriend, Laila Nabulsi, took off for the Honolulu Marathon, from whence sprung the seeds of *The Curse of Lono,* his first piece of fiction.

In Honolulu, Thompson spent time with a friend who had a house near the starting and finishing line; the idea was to be present to see the throngs take off, get drunk watching football on TV for two hours, then go outside and berate the finishers with shouts of "You're doomed, man, you'll never make it," "Hey, fat boy, how about a beer," *"Run,* you silly bastard," and "Lift those legs." Thompson's friend, also a friend of Stan Dzura's was John Wilbur, a Stanford ball player who had played for the Washington Redskins in the 1973 Super Bowl; Hunter loved those larger-than-life embellishments, and he had them in spades. Dzura and his wife frequented the island as well.

In the midst of Thompson, Dzura, and Wilbur, Laila seemed a shadow, a waif. By nature, she is quiet and unobtrusive. Thompson met her through his "Saturday Night Live" connections, where she worked in production. Her background is Lebanese, and those who know her claim she has some ties with the PLO; a terrorist with a terror. Her style of interaction with Thompson was supportive almost to the point of fawning. But without much of a chance to get a word in edgewise, she could easily go over-looked in the crowd: small and frail of stature, tomboyish in ap-pearance, with a voice like distant wind chimes, she was simply "there" without having a clear presence, a seemingly unessential adjunct to Thompson, like another piece of jewelry. Regardless, the two had hidden chemistry; they stayed together for about five years, beginning in 1979, when she was listed on court docu-ments as living at Owl Farm. Thompson even had Laila listed in *Curse of Lono* as "Producer."

The spirit of Thompson's first venture into fiction was damp-ened with the shooting of John Lennon, when Thompson was in Honolulu. He had planned a meeting with Bob Bone, but cancelled. Bone said that "John Lennon's shooting was what threw him off. I think that was just too much for him." It may have been the loss of Lennon, or the pall of Reagan's being elected; Thompson had to return a second time, getting stuck in foul weather on the big island of Hawaii's Kona coast, before he could begin to think about finishing *Lono.* Then again, had he quickly finished the book, its earnings could have fallen under the feared category of "marital interest."

Back in Aspen, near the close of the two-year divorce proceed-ings, Thompson pulled together an interesting strategy in an at-tempt to keep possession of some part of Owl Farm. He presented to the court a list of pre-trial witnesses and exhibits, the reason-ing being that they would testify as to Thompson's "life style." Among those listed as "witnesses" were the owner of Jerome's Bar, Mike Solheim; Salisbury Harrison, former editor of *Esquire;* Jann Wenner; George Stranahan; and Ralph Steadman. Lucky number thirteen on the list was a surprise: Thompson's nemesis,

Garry Trudeau, was to be called to "testify as to the public image of the life style of the petitioner; of the petitioner's relationship with Owl Farm in Woody Creek, Colorado; of the identification of the petitioner with Owl Farm in Woody Creek, Colorado." In addition to listing Trudeau, Thompson was to offer as an exhibit "Dunesbury [sic] comic strip . . . which referred to the petitioner and his relationship with Owl Farm." Here was more than life imitating art; it was a public display that the two were synonymous. Thompson was nurturing a valuable public image; it included his life-style, his iconoclasm, and the Owl Farm.

When he and Laila returned to Hawaii, Thompson rented a place near the water, but would seek refuge from the fans and the heat at Stan Dzura's house, higher up the mountainside. On occasion he brought Ralph Steadman; Dzura's wife was British and they all got along well. Hunter and Laila would show up with a cooler of beer, arriving early in the morning after a hard night's writing. Also, given the time zone, TV coverage of football often began at 7 A.M. "Starting at seven in the morning," Dzura recalled, "we could get in two or three football games. We both liked that. You could clearly sense that he was taking a break from all the hangers-on. He just wanted to kick back and watch football."

Thompson would appear at other times, telling stories that later appeared in *Lono* of sport fishing and of "Samoan faggots" that swarmed the port towns. But there was, in real life, no mention of the famed *Lono* character with the arm turned deep blue from fishing his Ferrari car keys out of the 747 toilet, nor of the red Ferrari itself. "Hunter rented a yellow Volkswagen convertible," Dzura asserted, adding that he surely would have seen the sports car. "When he was finishing *Lono,* he and John Wilbur came by my place in the convertible and were screaming bad names at me. They were right beneath my porch. I went outside and I peed all over them. Hunter was too drunk to figure out how to get the convertible top up, or how to unbuckle the safety belt. He got the full yellow waterfall."

After Thompson went back to the mainland, Dzura sometimes got an odd-hour call from Hunter that reinforced a sense of Thompson's fragility. "I know it's kinda strange," he said, "but I found myself wanting to be protective of Hunter. He's basically a very gentle man, but you have to expect his hundred-and-eighty-degree swings in behavior. In our discussions, as well as in his writings, you can see that he is a basically self-destructive personality. We would have talks about his death wish, and about taking better care of ourselves if we were going to live this long. But he clung so tenaciously to life, to his style of fun, that it gets difficult separating the desire to live and the desire to die. In Hunter, they seem to be closely intertwined."

Lono did appear to be cursed; it just wouldn't materialize (it finally did). Alan Rinzler was again the editor, but the publisher was now Bantam Books, a seriously business minded enterprise that was bereft of the warm, supportive understanding that had gotten Hunter's work organized and into print at Straight Arrow Press. Welcome to the '80s.

Rinzler went to Aspen several times to try and get Hunter to birth *Lono*. He would stay with Hunter at Owl Farm, working alongside him, as he had done a decade before with *Campaign Trail.* But Thompson had changed. "Toward the end of editing *Lono,"* Rinzler observed, "Hunter was just too tangential. He was preoccupied with drugs, less so with writing. Sandy was long gone, and the house looked like that of an adolescent boy if he had not grown up, but fulfilled his fantasies of being a grown-up— guns, peacocks wandering about, stuffed animals, Hemingway stuff." As if to assure himself that his old editor still had his mettle, Thompson went through a rite of initiation similar to what took place when the two first met. "Hunter kept saying this was really, really important. He had two women with him, one that he knew from his friendship with John Belushi—she had some role in 'Saturday Night Live.' The four of us went out into a shed behind his log cabin. He proceeded to set off all kinds of fireworks in the shed. The idea was that none of us could leave the room. It was an ordeal, a test, an initiation. Hunter liked to do this. Boyish stuff. But I was younger then. I kind of enjoyed it."

Rinzler waited until Thompson fell asleep one morning, then gathered up the pieces of *Lono* and took the next plane to New York. "I didn't have to break in; I was already there. I gathered everything he had. Some of it was written on brown paper bags, on the backs of envelopes. I xeroxed it in New York and sent it all back. I didn't want to steal his property, but Bantam gave me a lot of pressure to get the book done. *The Curse of Lono* has great parts to it, but it doesn't quite gel as a real good book. It is disjointed and incoherent in places. It is a real curiosity."

At the very end of *Lono,* Thompson seemed to put into work his education from the stint at the Mitchell Brothers, and to exorcise some feelings toward Sandy, now that the divorce was behind him. The book is a collection of thoughts, letters, Hawaiian cultural and historical anecdotes, joined by Steadman's renderings of it all. As in *Las Vegas,* the original quest of covering the Honolulu Marathon is quickly forgotten; it was just an excuse to get down into the tropics. For Thompson, it all came back to Gatsby; at the very end, he says, "It was like seeing The Green Light for the first time . . . I was born 1,700 years ago . . . and lived my life as King Lono . . . Until I became offended with my wife . . ." He was living out of sight of tourists in the Hawaiian City of Refuge, he told Steadman in a letter, revered by the true Hawaiians as a reincarnation of their long-lost deity. Laila would bring him food and liquor; the natives would send him women. "But they won't come into the hut—for the same reason nobody else will—so I have to sneak out at night and fuck them out there on the black rocks. I like it here. It's not a bad life."

Here was fiction, and here was sex. It seemed he had answered William Buckley, after all. And, as an added touch, if one looks closely on the horizon of the seascape splattered by Steadman at the very beginning of the book, one can see that Hunter dedicated the book "To my Mother, Virginia Ray Thompson."

22.

Shortest

Night

of the

Year

s Hunter Thompson drove from his house on Florida's Ramrod Key to dinner five miles away, the sky suddenly cracked open like a giant egg, spitting lightning and sucking up houses, boats, and vehicles with a series of rampaging tornadoes. The evening of the 21st of June, 1983, Thompson and Laila met me, the author of this

book, for dinner. I was interviewing him for the *Saturday Review.* Thompson was in a state of transition, and he took that opportunity to look both back and ahead. True to form, he appeared two days and six hours late, as if waiting until Mother Nature would light his parade. Laila had been dutiful, calling hourly to the Sugarloaf Key Lodge, the only chip of civilization closer than Key West, providing progress reports ("He's been writing the Roxanne Pulitzer piece, and he's sleeping . . . he's *still* sleeping . . .").

Studio artists have consciously changed styles with the times; Picasso moved from the "blue period" to the "rose period." Andy Warhol changed from soup cans to movie stars. Jackson Pollock changed from his psychoanalytic style to drip and splatter. Few writers have changed in the way Thompson has, with such regularity and such muscular effort, like slamming a heavy door behind him. Since 1960, when he returned from Rio in a "Kennedy, Peace Corps, patriotism frenzy," he has taken on a new persona with the advent of each decade. In 1970, it was Raoul Duke; in 1980, the character of Gene Skinner appeared for the first time, in Thompson's coverage of the Honolulu Marathon. This persona was an alleged former Air America pilot Thompson had met in Saigon. He introduces himself to the world, drinking margaritas with his creator at the Kahala Hilton bar, discussing Samoans castrating a motorist and the possibility of raping a penguin. He barks to the intimidated, eavesdropping bartender a concise summary of how Hunter felt about himself and the times: "It's all bullshit anyway. We lie for a living, but we're good people."

Sugarloaf Key was the nearest bar along the road to Key West that would run a tab for Thompson, and he arrived at their motel just after the backup generators began to thump-thumpa-thump electricity back into the system; the tornado had wiped out all conventional power.

In the room where I waited for Hunter, when the storm lashed down, the TV set had gone dead, along with all lights and airconditioning. Outside, there had been rasping sounds of deafening volume: snaps, clangs, pops, bangs, and a huge wet crunch, like the world's largest boot stomping the world's largest cockroach. Across from the Lodge on U.S. Route 1 there had been a violent flash-dance of lights and sparks from exploding gas lines, electrical wires, and power boxes. All had been whirled and blown about with the clean cruelty that can only come from a force of nature. The lights from the blue-and-white explosions had reflected off a jumbled kaleidoscope of what had been, a few minutes before, several three-bedroom houses. Then the generators began their bass-drum booming. The tornado had passed.

Outside, camper tops and aluminum boats were wrapped around concrete power poles like knots around your finger so you won't forget. Trees had been jerked out by their roots and strewn like matchsticks. Inside, the TV just sat there glowing, as if covered by a blue rhinestone paste.

Into this walked Hunter Thompson; several steps behind came Laila. "What the fuck was that?" he spat, shunning any formal introduction. He was tall, lean, and tanned, wearing tennis shoes and an aloha shirt; he looked like a balding split end for the Miami Dolphins. He strode over to the television, slopping a little beer from the Heineken bottle dangling as if an extension of his hand. He stood silently staring at the phosphorescent screen, as if its lobotomized blue eye was a source of higher power.

"Tornado" was the simple explanation given.

"Yeah. Shit, the lights were out all the way down here. Let's get some dinner."

*T*he *Curse of Lono* had been delayed in its arrival at bookstores, and Thompson had not been a visible part of the American sociological scene since the triple-witching of the beginning of his divorce, the filming of *Buffalo,* and the release of *Shark Hunt.* It had not been for lack of trying. To cover the Ali-Spinks fight in New Orleans in September, 1978, George Plimpton had approached Jann Wenner with the idea of a collaborative piece with Hunter for *Rolling Stone.* The idea was that Plimpton and Thompson would write alternating paragraphs. "It would be like a triangulation on a marine chart" was Plimpton's analogy. Wenner felt it was a sound idea, knowing how well the two had got on in Zaire, and off they had gone. All had a great time; Thompson took Jimmy Buffet up to Ali's suite to introduce the two, and he and Aspenite Mike Solheim enjoyed New Orleans thoroughly. At the fight, it was déjà vu all over again—an empty seat next to Plimpton, who never saw Hunter at all. "I guess I should have known better," chuckled Plimpton, who had to write the whole piece himself.

In 1980, with the advent of Ronald Reagan promising new beginnings, Alan Rinzler had sent Thompson to Washington to capture his rendering of "the Great Communicator." In the summer of '67, Thompson had called then Governor Reagan "the White Hope of the West . . . straight from a George Grosz painting." After paying for two weeks of room service tabs and getting no manuscript, Rinzler had pulled the plug.

Thompson needed targets. His style was furiously personal, emanating from caves that ran deep within him. When someone else suggested a target, he would balk. When he felt something that opened the floodgates to his creative streams, he could not be stopped. In the early '80s, he rang clear on the topic of divorce. He invaded Palm Beach and joined the army of journalists covering the divorce of Herbert ("Pete") and Roxanne Pulitzer, where the press indulged themselves in what appeared to be a case involving indulgence. Charges of lesbianism, ménage à trois, cocaine use, and bizarre sex partners floated across the bannerlines like confetti at a parade. It was the music that caught Hunter's ear; when the New York *Post* splashed its front page with "I SLEPT WITH A TRUMPET," Thompson took interest, telling the Palm Beach *Post,* "We *all* sleep with trumpets. The real question is, is Peter Pulitzer jealous of the trumpet?"

Thompson felt an affinity for Roxanne Pulitzer. In 1978, at a lush Aspen restaurant, a waiter had presented Roxanne Pulitzer a birthday gift: "Happy Birthday Rox" spelled out in lines of cocaine. The festivities became another splotch in the pentimento canvas that was Hunter's town. Both were good friends of Jimmy Buffet, and though Roxanne was twelve years younger, she bore a striking resemblance to Sandy Thompson. There were other tidbits that Hunter picked up along the trial where, under Florida law, all documents were left outside the courtroom in a supermarket basket, for public perusal. Hunter claimed to have uncovered a record of payment for $441,000 worth of cocaine in one year, saying, "God knows what their rich friends' bills were." Herbert Pulitzer's first attorney, Ronnie Sales, made an opening statement to the court, describing Roxanne as someone who "sleeps late in the day . . . stays out all night . . . abusing herself with drugs and alcohol."

Roxanne Pulitzer had come from a working family in upstate New York, and married the millionaire grandson of the publisher, founder of the Pulitzer Prizes, and donor of the fountain that Thompson had thought of launching himself into while finishing the Author's Note to *Shark Hunt.* In the alimony issue of the divorce's final judgment, the court referred to Roxanne's "exorbitant demands" by quoting lyrics from the country singer Jerry Reed: "She Got the Gold Mine, I Got the Shaft."

"If anyone wonders what I have been doing for the past few years," Thompson said over a dinner lit by a dim bulb powered by a generator and enough candles for a macumba exorcism, "they will get a pretty clear idea when they see this *Rolling Stone* thing on the Pulitzer trial. It will be a really shocking, dark, vicious combination of cocaine, sex, violence in cruel, rich people." The thesaurus of malevolence poured out of him as fluidly as alcohol and caffeine poured in. "The reaction will be interesting to see. I've created a new persona named Gene Skinner. I've given up Duke—he's funny. Skinner is not so funny."

Perched on a coral chunk closer to Havana than Miami, Thompson, as he drank, slowly came to life. With increased ingestion, his delivery actually changed. It began with a muffled, spasmodic monotone: staccato bursts delivered with a stiff upper lip and punctuated by noisy silences. After several hours and various chemicals, one heard a smoother expression; the inflections of surprise and laughter leached out slowly from behind his psychic armor plating. After a six-pack of Heineken's came two more bottles. He ordered and consumed two Bloody Marys, each with a side of coffee with sugar. Chemically, this does not make sense, but the waitress knew him, and much of the drink ordering was non-verbal. As the night progressed, he sucked down four tall Chivas Regals.

Thompson was a tough person to open up. It was nighttime, and he was not wearing his trademark mirrored sunglasses. He seemed quite uncomfortable. Eye contact was like the flippers on a pinball machine: *ping-a-ping*. As he consumed more, he loosened up, talked more, and alternated between rocking to his left like an autistic child and reaching straight over his head with both arms, stretching. He went back to talking about Gene Skinner and the Pulitzer trial while staring at his untouched side order of tomatoes and onions. Perhaps he ordered it as a still life.

He explained that he had first come to the Keys during winter. He kept Owl Farm after the divorce (Sandy was granted a parcel of the acreage and sold it, leaving Hunter the buildings and considerable land). But he dislikes the long Colorado winters, and especially the influx of wealthy Hollywood personalities invading his town to ski. On his first trip to the Keys, the climate was not adequately inhospitable for him to get into the proper state of mind to capture the discomforting sensibility he saw in the trial. That was why he came here during the sweltering summer. Laila laughed at his longing for a sweltering, hostile ecology; her voice tinkled like distant music. She started to make another comment, but was overpowered by Thompson, who said, "That's what I am creating now. So I'm down here living. That's why I chose this place with these savage fucking violent people—the Keys. I live in a jungle now, and it is what I want. It is a sense of cruelty in the people—a kind of brainless, predatory nature that comes from being four generations of pirates. It seems like a natural thing for me. It is decidedly not Key West, this strip of fish heads and conchs."

Thompson described his falling out with *Rolling Stone* as "getting fired on my way to the war zone. I would never write for them again. I had done that kind of journalism. It got dull." A new editor, Terry McDonell, had suggested a column. "I was trying to keep from writing a column," he said, and was pleased when the Pulitzer trial loomed on the horizon. "This goofy story on Palm Beach turned into a real monster." Thompson had just finished reading some of his own writing, saying, "I actually cracked up reading it. You should pick one up. You'll enjoy it; there is some genuinely sick stuff in it." Thompson had to call his brother Davidson in Chagrin Falls, Ohio, and tell him not to let his kids read the article. "They were just down here. I am 'Uncle Hunter' to them, and the idea that I might smoke a joint is horrifying."

The restaurant closed, and the offer was made to pick up the entire tab, including Hunter and Laila's meal; aside from the still-uneaten vegetables, the bulk was in the bar bill. At the offer, Hunter looked up, wide-eyed, grinning slyly. "Yeah? Sure!" he said, with the same sense of victory and glee in his voice that Henry Miller must have felt when his sycophants sent him his favorite corduroy pants. Thompson wanted to watch "Nightline," featuring an anti-nuclear demonstration, and a debate between a spokesperson for Berkeley's Los Alamos Research Labs and Dr. Benjamin Spock, who looked like a moth-eaten Santa. For someone immersed in creating a new persona to fit the hard edge of the 1980s, Thompson seemed curiously nostalgic.

Thompson got excited. "Hot damn! Now listen, I think we've really got something going here," he said, squeezing his glass of Wild Turkey in one hand, a smoking joint in the other, and leaning toward the TV. He was involved, and his strange, cryptic economy of emotion was finally beginning to erode. He clearly wanted to be a part of the action, especially when the screen showed the police in Los Alamos hauling away passive resisters who had tried to block the entrance to an arms repository.

Nostalgia, they say, is an exercise in grammar wherein you find the present tense and the past perfect. It was clear that Thompson's mind, triggered by the sit-in scenes in Los Alamos, was fluttering its way back through a time warp to Sproul Hall, to the Vietnam Day Committee Protest, to People's Park, to the Golden State Park Be-in, to all the nameless and forgotten causes and demonstrations he'd witnessed. There never had been and never will be another time quite like that, he thought.

"In the '60s it got contagious. Then it turned into a brushfire. It got to be fun. You looked forward to the next demonstration. Nobody does now; it's like looking forward to your next beating." "Nightline" went off, not surprisingly without resolving the nuclear-freeze question, but Thompson rolled on. "The generation then that was rebelling—against fathers, the establishment, whatever—we had the war as a focus. To me it implied the sort of message that there was a belief among the people who were rebelling that if they were indignant enough, the enemy would feel fear. There was the assumption that they could be persuaded. If the three of us went down to Mallory Square in Key West tomorrow and protested something, we'd get kicked, spit on."

He rambled on a bit, reminiscing about times with Kesey at his Parnassus Avenue apartment, of tossing a trash can under a downhill Muni bus. "I was cranked up to do something interesting. One of those buses came down the steep hill and I said 'This'll be fun' and threw the garbage can underneath it. Goddamned thing got caught, dragged the whole way down. And of course the driver couldn't stop going downhill. A hideous, screeching, ungodly sound. I still remember it. Like ripping a blackboard apart. That's a violent thing, but it doesn't hurt anybody."

The question was raised as to the origins of the signature term "Fear and Loathing." His response was as sudden as the lightning outside. "My heart! People wrote accusing me of stealing it from Kafka or [Thomas] Wolfe. It came straight out of my heart. I like words. Attention must be paid to words, and then you think after what it really means. But Fear and Loathing is a very proper and valid stance to take."

He pondered the question of his favorite book, saying he thought more in terms of paragraphs. He recited the part from *Fear and Loathing in Las Vegas* about history being hard to know, but that regardless it is "entirely reasonable to think that every now and then the energy of a whole generation comes to a head in a long fine flash, for reasons that no one really understands at the time—and which never explain, in retrospect, what actually happened. . . . We all had the momentum; we were riding the crest of a high and beautiful wave."

He sat back near quiet Laila, crossed his legs, looked out the window, and said peacefully, "That's a nice page, isn't it?"

Out the sliding glass doors at 3 A.M., he could see the jumble of headlights from what appeared to be heavy construction equipment. He suddenly came to action, saying, "Look! Look! Bulldozers! Over by the airstrip! Damn, I wonder if the tornado cut across there—it might have ripped up the Bat Tower!" He was up on his feet now, pacing and agitated. "Boy, it would be a shame if we lost the Bat Tower." The party moved, in a rented Chevette, toward headlights stabbing the black night. Hunter rode shotgun and shouted directions.

The Bat Tower was an architectural piece of craziness. It was wooden, about sixty feet high, rectangular in cross section, pointed at the top, and sat eight feet off the ground on four pylons. It looked like a launch vehicle.

Thompson had reached the unscathed tower; he was ecstatic and relieved, as if his best friend just walked away from a ten-car pileup. Now the party moved to see the real carnage, where several houses had been carried away.

The blue flashing lights of the sheriff's car illuminated the roped-off access road. Thompson urged the driver to pull over to where a policeman in a blue jumpsuit seemed to be in charge.

Pulling up, Thompson leaned over the driver and started shouting at the sheriff above the din of a couple of auxiliary generators nearby. "What the hell happened? My God, do you mean to tell me those were houses over there? Holy shit! What a terror job." He pointed out the window to the spotless concrete slabs. The sheriff made a halting attempt to respond, adding something about ". . . not only three houses, but a sailboat, a camper, and . . ."

Somehow, amid Thompson's senseless prattle and mad flailing, pointing at different parts of the wreckage, his full glass of Wild Turkey had passed under the driver's nose and slopped on the leg of the policeman's jumpsuit. The whiff of 101-proof whiskey raised his eyebrows.

The cop stuck his face in the car window. The driver hid his own cheap motel glass of whiskey by shoving it into his crotch and casually placing a hand over it. The officer's gaze was frosty. He looked at Thompson as if inspecting a smoking gun. Then he turned and left. Maybe they knew Hunter Thompson, maybe they didn't want to. Maybe drinking and driving was a distant second to cleaning up after a tornado.

Back at Sugarloaf Key Lodge, Sugar, the captive porpoise, greeted the returning party by leaping playfully out of her pool. Thompson saw her and commented, "Jesus, but she could give you a hell of a ride. Let's take our clothes off and jump in the water with her." He refrained, preferring to speak more about the Pulitzer piece, which had actually been finished for days; his recent bout had been quarreling furiously with libel lawyers. Thompson commented on the difficulties he has had over the years with lawyers; having to leave out Neil Cassady's name, and that of his San Francisco neighbor, the LSD researcher Dr. DeRupp, from *Hell's Angels*. But of the Pulitzer piece he said proudly, "I have never seen so much crazy libel put in one small package anywhere. And the lawyer put it through," he announced, but then related that this required hours of wrangling. Thompson had pulled out all the stops, going far beyond malevolence: it was a verbal torch of pure venom, aimed at anyone who dared dicker with his creativity. "I called the lawyer a butt-fucking Jew, some filthy liberal neighbor of Leonard Bernstein, some shit-eating swine, a pervert. This is the *Rolling Stone* counsel in New York."

The point was brought up that an attorney acquaintance in Palm Beach had already commented on Thompson's covering the trial. Thompson recoiled like a cornered snake. The pall of fear covered him heavily. He inquired as to specifics, but few were available. "What it means to me," Thompson said, "is that there must be some dark, dark legal implications. That the lawyers would know about it before it's out." The publication date was in two weeks; Hunter was strung tightly over this new news. An offer was made to call the attorney whom the information came from. "I would be curious," Hunter said. "I wouldn't call too much attention to it."

A call was put through to West Palm Beach attorney Joe Mincberg, who took no time at all to reassure the hyper-vigilant writer. "Everyone in town knew that Hunter was covering the trial, "Mincberg said. "He is a hard guy to blend into the woodwork, don't you know." Thompson seemed soothed by the counsel's words, and continued discussing both his current persona and his interpretation of the American Dream.

He described his work as having a clear anti-humanist spirit, and a character who was fit for the times. "It is a whole new style, and not as complete as I'd like it to be." Part of the article would have a short story built into it. "At one point, I'm trying to think of rape as seen through the eyes of a lesbian coke fiend. It's just one of these departure points that you reach every so often." He felt that it was not easy work: "I am trying to split myself. The two parts of me. One being Gene Skinner, the freak for the '80s; the other being the atavistic '60s person. Very much like Gatsby and

Nick Carraway. Two sides of the same person. It is hard work," he concluded, adding that he could be a bartender, or a fisherman, as he had found a new intrigue with his 18-foot Mako fishing boat and the labyrinth of small cays that surround him. "Writing is a hard fucking dollar," he stated. "I would love to stop writing. What else would I do? I have always looked at publishers of all sorts as people paying for my continuing education, so my books have allowed me to come down here and live and buy the boat. I would like to be able to con these people into letting me take them fishing. 'Gonzo Tours.'"

He spoke of the American public's infatuation with celebrity. "The Hinckley disease: to be on television. That is the only fucking thing, and anybody tells me different it's a lie. To me there is a great lust to be a celebrity. You see it in the freak at the World Series and football games; the guy with the color-striped Afro wig on. He could be on the cover of *People* magazine!" His personal bouts with celebrity status had been hard for him. He expressed difficulty in learning how to sign autographs. It seemed a status level toward which he had ambivalence: "Success in this country is worshipped to a point where it is a frenzied renown. You are swarmed over. Made crazy. It's hard to be gracefully successful and remain a human being. . . . You don't realize that until you've reached that point. The air! It is hard to find air anymore. It gets real difficult to breathe. There is so much clamping around you."

With a final shout to Sugar, he and Laila slalomed past randomly strewn coconuts and drove toward the east where the sun rose onto the second longest day of the year. They would wait two weeks for the issue of *Rolling Stone* to hit the stands, before the public had access to his "departure point," the "small package of crazy libel." When they did, and the magazine sold out quickly, Hunter, they found, was still a potent draw. "Roxanne Pulitzer," he wrote, "is not a beautiful woman. There is nothing especially striking about her body or facial bone structure, and at age thirty-one, she looks more like a jaded senior stewardess from Pan Am than an international sex symbol." Then Thompson changed his tune: regardless of "beauty," there was, he hinted, something to this woman Roxanne: "There is no mistaking the aura of good-humored out-front sexuality. This is clearly a woman who likes to sleep late in the morning." With a final Thompson twirl, he said that for about one thousand dollars a month, Herbert "Pete" Pulitzer ". . . had rented the Best Piece of Ass in Palm Beach for six and a half years." That was the Gonzo reporter speaking; once again he was not going on firsthand information.

"Oddly enough, I met Hunter," Roxanne Pulitzer explained. "It was at a dinner party thrown by a mutual friend in Palm Beach, Guy de La Valdene." During the trial, Roxanne Pulitzer refused to read any of the volumes of material written about her. When she attended the dinner party, the two had never met. She did not know Thompson was in town to cover the trial; it was just a random meeting, she figured, because they knew people in common. During the dinner party, Thompson managed to arrange to be seated next to her. "He was very entertaining, very nice to me during the dinner," Pulitzer said. She had known of *Fear and Loathing in Las Vegas,* but said, "I really did not know *who* he was," referring to the fact that Hunter could be both an enchanting guest or a bull in society's china shop. She felt that the dinner party was a respite from the swirling storm of the trial. "That party was refreshing for me," she noted. "Especially after being dragged through the foolishness of lesbianism and sleeping with trumpets."

The morning after the dinner party, Roxanne Pulitzer walked into a packed courthouse; there was a separate area for the army of international reporters. Strangely obvious among the throngs of journalists was her table partner from Guy de La Valdene's. "Bermuda shorts, sunglasses, the whole uniform."

When the *Rolling Stone* article appeared, Pulitzer was vehemently cautioned by her best friend, Lorraine Odasso: "She warned me not to even get *near* the article; she felt Thompson had used friends to get us together, in order to have some material to work with. Using friendships under false pretenses," she said, "is really surprising. He had only nice things to say at the party. He never interviewed me or any of the principals at the trial. I'm surprised at him."

23.

The Doctor

Makes House

Calls

s mentioned earlier, Hunter Thompson, when he was a teenager, locked himself in a closet with a newfangled machine and discovered the entertainment powers of his tape-recorded voice. Beginning in the early '70s, he found that college undergraduates would pay serious money both to see in the flesh the creator of their rebellious

dreams, and to listen to the voice that coined terms such as "greed head," "fear and loathing," "generation of swine," "gonzo," and "when the going gets weird, the weird turn pro." Always torn between needing an audience, needing total isolation, needing money, and self-proclaimed laziness, he had taken his act on the road in many different forms of disguise. He always managed to provide some brand of entertainment, never predictable, never on time. Mailer had complained that Thompson's audience was so easy to please it was "like playing tennis with no net." On the speaker's tour, there were times when Thompson did not even have to serve the ball. Show up, talk, drink, and get paid for it. He'd been in training all his life. Always quotable, always potable: at one of his first stops he was actively removed because of drunkenness.

Just before going to Africa to cover the Ali-Foreman fight, Thompson had lectured in Duke University's Page Auditorium. Thompson was given the hook because his state of inebriation was such that the Dean of Student Affairs, William Griffith, had felt there was imminent danger to Thompson, the microphone he was draped over, the podium, and the orchestra pit. For Thompson, the "lecture" was the end of a long day. He had been met at the airport by a Duke representative who offered him some hashish, a precursor to a few shots of Wild Turkey in his hotel room. The audience was kept waiting for forty-five minutes, and when he finally arrived on stage, his politics were not well received. Nixon was out of office, but Thompson opened by saying, "I'm very happy to be at the alma mater of Richard Nixon." A week later in Zaire, he explained to George Plimpton that his comment had "not exactly put them in my pocket."

The audience heated up, and began to ask direct political questions. One of them was Hunter's opinion as to whether or not Duke's president, Terry Sanford, should run for President; it was an election year. Thompson immediately recalled that Sanford had been part of a "block McGovern" movement, and told the students that Terry Sanford "was a worthless pigfucker. I didn't realize he was the president of Duke," Thompson explained later. "Not long after, I was given the hook."

When Hunter saw that he was to be physically escorted off stage, he became startled. In one of his spasmodic fits, he tossed his glass of Wild Turkey high into the air; it left a permanent Gonzo calling card on the velvet curtain. Once outside the auditorium, Thompson sat on the hood of a parked car for over an hour talking with students; this was where he would feel most comfortable—one-on-one, informally surrounded by admirers.

Was Thompson contrite about his behavior at, of all places, a university named "Duke"? "Not at all," Plimpton said. "He was worried whether he was to be paid. He wasn't clear on the details of his contract—just how long he had to talk before getting his money. He also was not perfectly clear it had been Duke." ·

Over the '70s, '80s, and into the '90s, Thompson has repeatedly gone on tour, often telling his young, impressionable audience that he does it just to pay for his drugs. He usually returns to Aspen in an indigo-blue funk; he is a sensitive creature, and it does not feel right to be yelled at and heckled by kids who were born when he was riding with the Hell's Angels. The Doctor does not like the taste of his own medicine. Sometimes, though, even a lecturing Hunter Thompson can appear to be having fun.

At New York University in the fall of 1978, the student body had the misfortune to schedule Thompson at 7:30 on a Monday night. Only modestly late, Thompson came on stage to a packed, noisy crowd, followed by his entourage. He wore a wool Pendleton shirt, and carried a stuffed handbag in one hand. In the other he held an ice-filled, sterling-silver pedestal champagne holder. Next to him on stage, he placed the champagne holder, filled with beer and a whiskey bottle. Fortified, he began the standard "lecture" format—questions from the audience. A few minutes into the Q and A, he rolled up the sleeve of his shirt, looked at his Rolex, and announced that he would have to call things to a close early: he was leaving to watch TV's Monday Night Football. If the students didn't like it, then tough. There was some muttering from the students. Thompson quickly turned that into shrieks of delight; he opened a betting window at a corner of the stage with a new member of his entourage—John Belushi. The audience went nuts. Two crazies for the price of one!

For a half hour, Thompson entertained questions on politics and the NFL, with Belushi tossing him lines to ad-lib; Thompson may be the only person ever to use that comic as a straight man. Betting was furious while Thompson rambled, speaking as if he held a mouthful of Heineken caps. The inevitable heckling began: a voice in loud tones shouting, "Thompson, you're all washed up." Immediately, Belushi stopped taking bets, ran to the microphone, and stung the audience with "Hey, kid, you are what I call a NeanderFuck." The audience somehow removed the heckler, and it all went back to baseline chaos. Insulted by a celebrity—what status!

Pondering a question tossed to him, Thompson fumbled, trying to light a cigarette. Suddenly, the entire sleeve of his Pendleton was ablaze; he had unknowingly spilled lighter fluid on it. Thompson began to make wild flapping movements, which only made the flames shoot higher. Belushi again abandoned his position at the betting window, and rushed to his friend's assistance. He picked up the champagne cooler and dumped the entire contents—beer, whiskey bottles, ice, and water—on Thompson's arm. It worked.

All the time, the kids were jeering Thompson, shouting, "Loser," "Idiot," "Washout," "We're not getting our money's worth," and, "You're a bum." Thompson fought their fire with his, both literally and figuratively. He ended the night early, as promised, with a scathing exchange of unpleasantries, then slid out the back door into a limo with Belushi, and on to his apartment to watch the game in peace.

After the release of *The Curse of Lono,* and after the November, 1983, Broadway opening of the stage version of *Doonesbury,* Thompson again took to his stage tour—personal appearances are always good for sales. At UCLA it was written into his contract that he had to give one interview; he was cagey, unapproachable, and generally himself. The next day, he would be doing the same thing at Berkeley, but the schools are a world apart. UCLA's operative motif is parties, smog, and student parking lots filled with new Porsches and BMWs. This was L.A. and this was the '80s. After a "lecture" where he was actually given, and responded to, legitimate questions, he left in a limo; he was pursued by three shirtless young men in a black convertible Porsche. Pulling up next to Thompson at a traffic light, each waved an arm at the limo: they were painted a deep blue.

Driving to the posh Westwood Marquis Hotel, someone inside the limo passed around an illicit substance. The woman who was supposed to be the recipient of Thompson's contracted interview was offered some. She declined politely, telling Hunter that "it" made her paranoid. Thompson erupted: "You mean you've got a *drug problem?"* he shrieked. "Oh God, that makes *me* paranoid." He refused to answer any questions "that require a lot of thought," claiming that he could not be spontaneous working with another journalist who was straight. (Once, in Key West, Thompson successfully propositioned a woman, only to be rejected by her after he listed the kinds and amounts of substances each would have to ingest before having sex.)

He did, however, discuss his recent coverage of the U.S. invasion of Grenada. "I went to open a casino. To buy some land and open a casino. The invasion gave me a reason to go there to write for *Rolling Stone.*" Thompson spent his time on Grenada at the St. James guest house, the fourth such place he inspected before settling for its cleanliness. There was a resident fruit bat in Room 15; that may have swayed his decision. But it hooked him up with Loren Jenkins again, and introduced him to the Trinidad-born writer V. S. Naipaul with whom he shared a mini-moke jeep, bouncing around the island, declaring that "a bunch of newsmen with baseball bats could have taken this island."

The day after UCLA, Hunter thought he was back on some kind of terra firma when he tried to speak to students at Berkeley. This was the campus whose causes he had championed so vehemently that when he wrote "The Nonstudent Left," he had been essentially barred from further writing for the *National Observer.* But that was the '60s; welcome to the '80s. Even at Cal.

"Hunter," the anonymous voice somewhere in Wheeler Auditorium yelled. "Do you think Walter Mondale would make a good scuba diver?" "Hey, Doctor Gonzo, what's your favorite drug— Tanqueray or Beefeater's?" And so it went—straight downhill for the king iconoclast at the bastion of iconoclasm. Clearly this was not what he should keep for his day job.

Into the next decade he went, making headlines and fielding flak from students. Thompson accepted an offer of $5,000 to "lecture" at Fort Lewis College, in Durango, Colorado, six weeks after the end of the Gulf War, on April 4, 1991. It was near Aspen, and he had a very good buddy who lived there: John Clancey, the lawyer who had lived at Big Sur in 1960. Through his lecture agent, Jodi Solomon Speakers Bureau, in Boston, Hunter took the offer from the college and amended the wording. He requested that there be an allowance for liquor. Specifically, he requested a twelve-pack of Beck's, a case of Heineken's, and one bottle each of Stolichnaya vodka and Chivas Regal Scotch. The request was rejected by the college: the student senate constitution prohibits purchasing of alcohol as part of such a contract. In addition, Fort Lewis College, with 4,000 students, is heavily Native American—the single ethnic group with the highest rate of alcoholism and alcohol-related deaths. It just might set a bad example, some urged. The Director of Student Activities, Dave Eppich, wanted to "do the right thing." He applied to the Liquor Authority for a special-events liquor license to allow Hunter to drink on stage. He had to buy his own, though. The Durango Liquor Authority held a public hearing, at which there were no objections. The permit cost $50, and was in effect from 9 P.M. until midnight, when Hunter's bottle would become a pumpkin.

The rationalization for getting the permit was that should Thompson get out of hand (the school researched his past college appearances, and found that such a permit was unprecedented; other schools had simply turned a blind eye; they also found that Thompson spilled or dropped his drink an average of four times an appearance), they did not want him hauled off, leaving five hundred angry students primed to riot. If Hunter's presence incited them, O.K.; if it was Hunter's absence, then there would be hell to pay, as well as his $5,000 lecture fee, plus airfare on a chartered Lear, and hotel expenses at the Red Lion Inn. College guests usually stayed at the General Palmer Hotel, but Thompson requested the Red Lion; just months before, he had been involved in a nasty "life-style bust" where he was accused of twisting the breast of a former pornography producer. Her last name was Palmer, and Hunter wanted no memories to interrupt his sleep. However, he did call the Assistant Director of Student Activities at her home at 2:30 in the morning, interrupting her sleep to make sure security was in place and all reservations were set. He also wanted her to pick him up at the airport, then to go and have a drink. She declined and sent a student.

The special city permit raised the visibility of Durango and Fort Lewis College to international proportions, as the news media picked up on the liquor-license maneuver: no one had cared when he drank illegally, but this made hot press. The school requested police protection for only the second time ever. While local editorial pages spoke of the "splendid role models of Timothy Leary and G. Gordon Liddy," who had previously addressed the students, police protection had been requested for Tamsanqua Linda, the first elected black Mayor of Port Elizabeth Township, South Africa.

When Hunter arrived, he began filming the partying students who were dancing to a band. "I've got to film these things because who knows what will happen tomorrow," Thompson said. In his other hand he carried a PowerMax; a 120,000-volt combination cattle prod and alarm whistle. "This," Thompson said, aiming the device at the audience and letting it rip, "is for anyone who wants to argue."

Introduced as "a man who has been called many things, a

maverick, a genius, the Devil's child of journalism," Thompson stode forth with hands held high, like a cocky fighter entering the ring. At his side, sitting at the small table on stage, was a mid-twenties woman, with blond hair, who acted quasi-interested throughout his talk. She was introduced by Hunter as "Gina, my interpreter . . . from Russia." For that, she kissed him on the back of the neck to loud hoots of some undergraduate emotion. A great deal of time was spent reading to the audience the special liquor permit, and discussing the implications of it to personal freedoms. Hunter monologued endlessly and repeatedly about his run-in with the porn producer Gail Palmer, and the ensuing eleven-hour search of his house that resulted in a two-month-long trial for five felony charges of drug possession and dynamite possession without a permit.

While speaking, he wore a diamond-pattern shirt out over his Levi's. His liver is distended; if he dresses this way, it does not show. The white tennis shoes and his shades were, as always, in place. Gina, silent and nurse-like, loaded his cigarette holder with a Dunhill and handed it to him. The uniform was complete. When he finally stood, after grabbing a twelve-battery flashlight to pick out someone in the dark asking a question, he did so awkwardly. He stood sideways to the crowd; his large feet were firmly planted and did not move, as if bolted down. One knee was slightly bent. His entire body was straight except for a slight forward stoop from the waist, as if he were carrying a heavy pack. When he spoke, the only part of his body to move were the fingers of his right hand, extended straight up into the air. He looked like a George Segal sculpture, with his hand a bird on a string trying to escape.

A thin man in the back row began to heckle him. Hunter went on about the liquor-permit discussion "not being a terribly edifying opening for you," and the voice boomed, "Shut up and drink." Thompson went on to other topics; the NBA, what happened to Lazlo, his thoughts on the Gulf War ("Which Gulf? Oh . . . I was thinking of The Gulf of the Doomed"), returning repeatedly to the porn film *Café Flesh.* If one were to parse out Thompson's flow of logic, it would look like a time-lapse photo of chain lightning.

Again the voice: "Fuck you. Shut up and drink. We want our money's worth. Stick it in your mouth. Mr. Thompson, what is your favorite caliber?" Finally, Hunter got the lights to be turned on after dodging the big bomb. The voice seemed to take over the room; it could no longer be ignored. It intoned, "I wanna know; I wanna know . . . Saddam Hussein and Norman Schwarzkopf—ARE

THEY GAY LOVERS? I'm curious. The *world* is curious." This was quickly followed by "Have you ever had a girl, buns up, kneeling and squealing?" Then came the question "Can you still get it up?"

This general line of questioning has plagued Thompson since before William Buckley's comments. People constantly question his sexuality, and he has a large gay following. His writing is so macho as to appeal to the far end of any continuum of sexuality, yet has never, even in *Lono*, included a real sex scene. The world *was* curious, and they let him know that night.

This time, his reaction was to turn to his table of female supporters. Another woman in her mid-twenties had mysteriously appeared moments before to describe the plot line of *Café Flesh* (sex in a post-nuclear-war world). It seemed strange, as if he could not bring himself to talk about it. Thompson appeared confused. He asked of the two women, "What were we talking about? Do we have a *Deliverance* fan here?"—referring to the movie with scenes of sodomy in the Georgia mountains. He turned to the audience. "I have no aversion to the type of question," he responded to the voice. "It is the stupid ignorance in the presentation of it."

The questions about Thompson's sexuality had another source: Hunter's younger brother, Jim. The two had never kept in close contact. In the early 1980s, Jim Thompson moved from Louisville to the Castro section of San Francisco. He worked in a health food store and was as openly gay as he was silent about being the brother of Hunter S. Thompson. He wanted to be known as his own person, and did not appreciate the attention he would receive for being the brother of the journalist.

In many ways, Jim resembled Hunter: his shuffle, his style of speech, and his fanaticism for sports. By the late '80s he had contracted AIDS. In 1989, when Hunter was in San Francisco, Jim met him at his hotel room for dinner, one of the few times they saw each other. Jim was disgusted as he watched his brother order room service and snort cocaine openly in front of the hotel staff bringing food. That was the last the two had seen of one another, but the public awareness of Jim's homosexuality, and of his dilemma with AIDS, was widespread among Hunter Thompson fans, especially on the West Coast. Thompson never has acknowledged this publicly, other than to make a brief comment while discussing government policy on Sugarloaf Key in 1983, saying that "the government has yet to spend a nickel on AIDS research."

Thompson's response to that line of questioning at Fort Lewis College was total avoidance; he launched into discussion of the necessity to fight city hall (his persona for the '90s), of his two red convertibles, and of his love of guns. Toward the end of the second hour, Thompson was seated, again inspecting the pattern in the tablecloth. The woman next to him had been staring into his eyes (from the side she could see them; besides, they were sharing the same chair). Nearing the end of the night, the time of expiration of the liquor license, she was rolling the bottle of Scotch on its side, back and forth across the table. She seemed to be making pie-crust, far removed from the hecklers' shouts of "Drink, you bastard—you're getting paid $5,000" or Hunter's retort, "If you people were a little smarter, I wouldn't have to talk so much. I am a mean fucker." The audience loved the verbal sadomasochistic beating they had paid for, and finally went unto the night a happy lot.

As usual, Hunter retired to the Red Lion with some of the more faithful and energetic; it was only midnight, and this is when the real show begins. In his hotel room, Thompson proceeded to "eat the acid" and then experienced a strange sensation of emotion: he fell in love with a two-foot-high antique wooden bureau sitting in the corner of his room. In the wee hours of the morning, he had one of his entourage phone the manager and inquire as to the cost. It was not for sale. "You don't seem to understand," the caller from Thompson's room stated, "the man wants the antique." "No" was the hotel's final statement. They had all been warned to expect possible eccentricities, and told not to allow a bar tab over a certain amount.

The next morning, Thompson, his human entourage, and several of his peacocks were seen walking across the tarmac, boarding the Lear for the flight to Aspen. One of the party carried something unwieldy. After takeoff, the employees of the Red Lion went to clean Thompson's room. The antique wooden bureau was missing. At age fifty-three, Hunter Thompson had eloped with a piece of furniture.

24.

Dessert

at the

Carpe Diem

Hotel

n a spring afternoon in 1992, Hunter Thompson rides a dark green John Deere tractor with a backhoe. He drives slowly across his front lawn. The lower end of Woody Creek valley is a broad spread in the mountains. One can see snow-topped peaks in the distance to the west. Just across the river, differing shades of green mark

where the aspen trees have filled in the lumbered pines. He is not doing anything functional with the tractor, just out cruising his yard. Astride the vehicle, he putts past the vulture-topped entry gates, by the metal bat sculpture, the stolen Aspen streetlamp near the wooden terrace with the sunset view, and a few bullet-riddled autos. He wears no hat, yet the sun is strong. A red Toyota Land Cruiser makes dust devils passing his house going uphill, toward the top of the valley. He eyes the car suspiciously until it disappears.

Within the microcosm of American culture that is Aspen and Woody Creek, Hunter S. Thompson stands as symbol, a living testimony to the sense of rugged individualism that placed this area on the map of every ecologist, lover of the arts, and Holly-wood-star watcher. This was once a renaissance town, filled with renaissance people. Some things have changed, but Hunter is not one of them.

Aspen needs Hunter Thompson. This is a town that refuses to grow up, and he is their Peter Pan. This is the town where business people in ponytails ride bicycles to work. The Mayor holds outdoor public meetings and asks attendees to bring lunch in a brown paper bag. Many full-time residents were '60s people who stumbled across an island of peace and intellect amidst a country whose culture had turned strange and hostile. Here they could listen to Albert Schweitzer speak, watch Shakespeare, and hear Mahler, or the babble of brooks and the cry of eagles.

The concept of "no growth" was a central issue of Thompson's campaign for sheriff in 1970; despite his loss of the election, much of that concept was enacted. Later, as developers invaded the place, a finite amount of land was fought over by an infinite amount of money, until many people who had come to Aspen seeking shelter had to leave because of the storm. One evening in early 1992, Sylvester Stallone went out to dinner. He was accompanied by seventeen bodyguards, and no one knew where to put them. There was talk of opening a Club for Bodyguards, and no one laughed. Houses rent for $35,000 a month, off season. The average price of a house in Aspen hovers around one million dollars; many of Hunter's era could not afford not to sell.

Hunter is still provided every opportunity to act out his aggressions toward people with more money, and against the authorities who would love to see him put in jail. His years in Aspen have annealed his spirit like a forge-hardened Toledo blade. He fights the infidels, and in his fight carries the banner of every true Aspenite.

Not surprisingly, Hunter Thompson makes good press in Aspen. And while Loren Jenkins has returned to run the Aspen *Times,* the police blotter may be the more accurate documentary of Hunter's actions. His writing since *Lono* has consisted exclusively of compilations of articles, many from the column he wrote for Will Hearst in the San Francisco *Examiner.* His last, *Songs of the Doomed,* is the only one of Thompson's books not to make the best-seller list. He calls it his "left-handed" book, an obligatory sequel in a two-book contract. He works slowly on new fiction—in 1967 he had a Random House secretary steal back his *Rum Diary* manuscript; it may appear yet.

In a 1992 *Rolling Stone* article on Clarence Thomas, Hunter's style took on a more incendiary tone, an even harder edge, appealing to the head-banging heavy metal freaks; he has found a whole new audience for his macabre visions of social commentary.

In July of 1987, he was ticketed at 5:30 in the afternoon for firing a shotgun at a golf ball on the Aspen Municipal Golf Course. Hunter practiced golf often, as he had a girlfriend whose father was a golfer; clearly this maneuver would change either their relationship or Hunter's score. In the same year, he was attacked by the American Humane Society after writing an article for the *Oregonian* magazine about the revenge of Joan Baez. A fox had killed one of Hunter's cats; he trapped the fox live, sprayed it with a mixture of glue, tar, peacock dung, and feathers, and blinded it with Mace and let it go. The *Oregonian* published an apology to readers for having run the column. Thompson said, "I could write about raping and disemboweling a human and not get this reaction." He threw a smoke bomb into a crowded Woody Creek Tavern; before they would welcome him back, he first had to post a handwritten letter of apology on the wall of the combination tavern-post office. The notice stayed on the wall for months; the citizens of Aspen love their black sheep.

In early August, 1989, Thompson felt that his microcosm of "old Aspen" was being sullied, and he'd better do something about it. Six miles up the road that snakes past Owl Farm, Floyd Watkins was building a new house. In 1985, he had driven past the property on a Tuesday, and bought it on Thursday for $330,000. In the spring of 1992, he turned down a $10 million offer. The place is nice without being ostentatious, tastefully decorated without being a museum, and the main house has yet to be built. Further, the property contains the ashes of Errol Flynn's son Kevin, and its Louis XV living room is guarded by the World

Record Musk Ox (it was killed by Floyd's son Lance; a framed triptych of photos shows him aiming his bow, hitting the target, then holding up the blood-covered horns). When the ox was shot, only the head was brought back to mount; three years after Floyd found out that it was a world record, the derrière made its way up Woody Creek to Watkins's Running Beaver Ranch.

In the sensibilities of old Aspenites, it was not the back end of an ox or the French period-piece furnishings that caught their attention; Floyd messed with the water, and in the West that is not done. Specifically, he had rerouted some of Woody Creek to feed into a series of trout ponds; he began to raise expensive trout and planned to charge the public to fish. With the locals, this went over as well as when he paid for his beers at the Woody Creek Tavern with hundred-dollar bills. Someone had defaced a sign close to the main road pointing to Watkins's place. The new version read, FAT FLOYD'S TACKY BEAVER RUN RANCH, PUBLIC FISHING WELCOME, 6 MILES.

Sixty Minutes had done a spot on Hunter. When Hunter asked Floyd to use Running Beaver for a backdrop, Floyd was puzzled but allowing. He was aware of his neighbor's difference in taste: Thompson had called his ranch "a hideous eyesore that only a madman or a werewolf would live in." Thompson had also borrowed a gun from Watkins's extensive collection, and returned it with a bottle of wine and a cryptic note that Floyd could not interpret. Was Hunter checking out the place?

So it was with some confusion as well as concern that Watkins found "Fuck you prick" handwritten in some newly poured concrete, just before he received a telephone call warning him that someone was going to either shoot up or burn down his property that night. Floyd and Lance, who was an alternate on the Olympic skeet-shooting team, hid in waiting all night. They communicated through walkie-talkies; Floyd stayed in his souped-up jeep mounted with an AR-14 semiautomatic rifle with 100-shot clips, while Lance was prepared astride a Kawasaki dirt bike, armed with a laser-scoped M-14.

At 4 A.M., a semiautomatic weapon began making beautifully arced red contrails over Floyd's house. Hunter was firing from the road with his girlfriend of the time, a University of Arizona graduate who had followed him home after a lecture. With a blast from the AR-14, and the buzzsaw rasp of a speeding Kawasaki, the Watkins-Thompson Feud entered the record books. Down the peaceful valley it sped, past Running Beaver, past Sitting Cat, and into the driveway of George Stranahan's Flying Dog Ranch, where

Hunter was hunted and cornered. The girl shouted at Stranahan's house, but to no avail. Floyd says Hunter poked him in the chest twice and said, "No trout farm. No concrete." He zapped Thompson's shooting hand with a million-candlepower light from his boat, telling the writer that if he moved he would never use his hand again and that he would also do some things to Thompson that, for legal reasons, would be best left off the record. Floyd felt that Thompson, that night, was so messed up that he did not even know his own name. Thompson apologized, offered Floyd his last beer, and invited him to come over the next day and watch an NFL game on TV with him. Floyd declined. A few days later, at the Woody Creek Tavern, Thompson asked Floyd to be his date to a party. Again Floyd declined, saying, "You're not quite my type."

Thompson gave his version of the feud to the Aspen *Times Daily* over the phone while seated at Loren Jenkins's kitchen table. Thompson denied it all, saying he was near Watkins's ranch when he came face-to-face with a giant killer porcupine. "Don't laugh," he told the reporter. "Look at Jimmy Carter. He was attacked by a killer swamp rabbit and had to beat it with his oar."

Three days later, Watkins woke up to a chain of trout ponds filled with $40,000 worth of dead fish; he hinted that Thompson had a hand in this. Thompson's quick rebuff was "Maybe I ought to poison my peacocks." At the Woody Creek Tavern, Thompson offered a $500 reward to find the poisoner, and a large glass appeared, reading "Your $ Can Put Trout Back in Floyd's Ponds." It turned out that an excess of Cutrine, a copper-based algae-control chemical, had been put in by mistake, but not before Hunter had his word. "Floyd is a trouble junkie. I am an action junkie and there's a huge difference. He is looking for trouble. I've got a sense of fun about me."

In late February of 1990, all the way across Route 70 from the Denver Airport to their rented condo in Snowmass, Gail Palmer had great fun reading out loud to her husband from *Fear and Loathing in Las Vegas.* When she was an undergraduate at Michigan State in the late 1970s, someone who knew her had recommended the book, saying, "You'd really like Hunter Thompson, because he's wild and crazy." After thirteen years as a producer in the pornography business, she married an ophthalmologist and was leading a small-town life in St. Clair, Michigan. Now, having skied three winters in the Aspen area, Palmer decided to try to meet the author who had provided her so much entertainment. This was not an uncommon motive for people lurking near the Jerome Bar, the Woody Creek Tavern, or even Owl Farm. Her decision to meet the writer was sealed when she read Thompson's piece in *Generation of Swine,* "A Clean, Ill-lighted Place"; it was about their mutual friends, the potentates of porn, the Mitchell Brothers.

Palmer was not one to skulk about Thompson's hangouts and wait to pounce. She diplomatically wrote him, telling when and where she would be in the area, and to phone if possible. Hunter did not call. His longtime companion, Ignatius Semmes Luckett III, did the phoning. He announced on the phone that it was "Semmes; I am a palindrome." Palmer paused, wondering for a moment if she knew anyone from that family; he then explained the symmetry of his name. "I knew then it would be an eclectic evening," she predicted to herself.

When Palmer met Thompson at Owl Farm, the evening of the Emmys, she said, "It was like meeting Santa for the first time when you're a little girl. He was funny, he was comical, he was endearing. There were things about him that were very attractive." Over the phone she had inquired as to his age. He shot straight: "Fifty-two." She countered: "I didn't think you were that old." His retort: "That's a hell of a thing to say to an unemployed writer."

Entering Thompson's house, she was immediately taken aback by the decor: a meat cleaver stuck in the ceiling, a machine gun mounted on a tripod with a ribbon of bullets hanging down the side.

However, she enjoyed the stay at Hunter's, meeting him and his assortment of hangers-on who'd come over to watch the Emmys. Hunter knew Bonnie Raitt when she came on the TV, as well as a former sound man for Bob Dylan. It was when Palmer turned interviewer, and launched some questions at him, that things began to disintegrate. First, she inquired why he was "hiding behind those sunglasses." Thompson, she says, answered that he was afraid of women. "I fear them" was what she heard. That led to a discussion of the value of sisters, while Hunter continued bartending, berating his friends, commenting on the Emmys, and generally moving about the cluttered living area like a man with springs in his feet. "He likes an audience," Palmer observed. "I had a million questions I wanted to ask, and he's up and he's down and all around. He likes to entertain. I bet he has people around him all the time. The people there were like followers. They would just take whatever he said to them, and some were not very nice words."

Palmer parried and thrust with the toughest of questions: "How come there's no hint of sex in your writing?" Thompson turned dramatic, she says, leaping to his feet in front of the group, acting deeply offended, arms outstretched, hands flapping like palsied birds, shouting. "I can't believe she asked that," he boomed over the Emmys. "A perfect stranger!" Thompson turned to a girl named Cat and commanded her to "get The ScrewJack Files."

Palmer had been introduced to Cat as the sister of Hunter's girlfriend, who was not in attendance. Cat had been helpful in interpreting for Palmer the speech and actions of Thompson, as if he were communicating in a foreign language. "She was his ambassador and his subtitler" was how Palmer described her role that evening.

The ScrewJack Files were dumped in Palmer's lap. It was a pile of computer paper with typing on it. She was requested to read it out loud, with proper emphasis, which she proceeded to do with gusto. "It is about a guy fucking his cat," Palmer explained. "But then the cat grows to be a two-hundred-pound beast. It was . . . like . . . perverse." For the reading, Thompson stood, rapt, nodding and rocking behind his shades like an old black man listening to New Orleans jazz, nudging people when to laugh, grunting approval of her diction and delivery. It was great for him; it was inadequate for Palmer. She related that the sexuality of many authors can be interpreted from their writing; after her reading, she was still left with questions. "Hunter hides it very well in his writing. I can't tell his sexuality at all. It is hard to believe that he makes love to his cat. . . . I don't know."

Gail remembers that Thompson was pleased with her work, announcing, "Now! There, you have sex!" He then took her on a tour of the house, she recalls vividly, that started and ended in the hot-tub room. Thompson was leaning against the wall, mumbling something about his girlfriend. She remembers him reporting that it "was a bad situation," because his girlfriend's sister was there, and that he would feel a lot better, Palmer interpreted, if she were to join him in the hot tub. "And he went on and on," Palmer said. "And I said, 'Hunter, what are you trying to tell me? Do you want me to go in the hot tub with you?' and he said, 'Yeah . . . I guess so . . . yeah . . . that'd be O.K.'" Santa seemed in a giving mood, but Palmer politely refused, asked to use the phone, and called her husband and said she'd be home in an hour. She returned to a raging monster.

Thompson was beside himself, she reports, frenzied, pacing, accusing her of calling the police. She reacted by laughing and saying to Hunter, "Paranoia'll destroy ya!" Strangely enough, it calmed the man, and they watched the end of the Emmys with no further interruptions.

The show on TV over, Palmer went to use the bathroom, and planned to call a cab for the ride back to Snowmass. In the bathroom she was joined by Cat, who explained that Hunter had had a bad week, that he really wanted Palmer to get in the hot tub, that he was harmless, that Cat would even find a bathing suit for her. Palmer explained that people often get the wrong impression of her because of her background in the pornography business; "People automatically think I am going to get crazy with them, swing from the chandeliers, and do amazing things that they only see in explicit films. That is not me. In all the thirteen years I lived in Hollywood," she told Cat, "there's not anyone who can say 'I hot-tubbed with Gail Palmer' or 'I got a blow-job from Gail Palmer.' This is how I have been able to keep my life together."

Hollywood may have been a boring place, but Woody Creek was about to go ballistic. At Owl Farm, Palmer reports, feathers began to fly. The two women came out of the bathroom, and Palmer saw Thompson go berserk when Cat told him, "She's not going to do it." Palmer reports that Thompson launched a cranberry-juice-and-vodka drink in their general direction, called her a "Goddamned dyke bitch," and then grabbed Cat by her hair, pulling her to the ground, saying, "You clean it up, bitch, you're her fucking girlfriend." Palmer tried to intervene, putting an arm between the two, saying, "Hunter, you'd better stop. You're out of control." Thompson, no Santa now, pushed her away brusquely, and spat out, "You're goddamned right I'm outta control. Where's my fucking gun? I'm gonna blow your fucking head off."

Having seen guns strewn around the house like empty beer cans, Palmer decided that was enough to call it a night. She ran outside, had Cat call her a cab, and returned to her husband a sobbing, cranberry-and-vodka-splattered mess. But this is Aspen, where help can appear in strange forms: the female cabdriver was a moonlighting therapist, specializing in battered women. She tried to convince Palmer to call the police, to seek help. Palmer steadfastly refused, and told her husband not to, as she knew her past would change the color of any proceedings; she wanted it all left behind. They decided to use the wisdom of an arbitrator, and phoned a friend in Los Angeles, explained what had happened, and felt much better after speaking with a levelheaded objective outsider. They called it a night. The man in L.A. called it a nightmare, and phoned local Pitkin County authorities, thus making Palmer a secondhand accuser.

The next morning, Palmer and her husband awoke to police calling, trying to encourage her to come down and tell her story. "They explained to me," Palmer said, "that Hunter is a loose cannon. I have a copy of this. He tape-recorded it. They said even his wife, when he was married, had been down to the police several times." Palmer refused to talk. Going outside to ski, she and her husband passed racks of newspapers for the day: PORNO QUEEN IN HOT TUB SCENE was the most poetic; THE DOCTOR IN TROUBLE AGAIN was the alternative choice.

This was one week after Valentine's Day. The trial raged on until the late spring. "I know it sounds weird," Thompson told the legion of press that picked up his every uttering, "but I am thinking of covering my own trial."

The Mitchell Brothers and their stable of porn stars arrived. They camped out in Hunter's yard. They drove back and forth along Main Street, past the courthouse, with leggy silicone vamps sitting atop the back seat of an old convertible (The Red Shark), carrying signs saying "H.S.T. WAS SET UP" and a logo for "NO KANGA-ROO COURT."

Inside the courthouse, Hunter had great freedom. He was a funny man during Palmer's questioning. She sat on the witness stand a yard from where Hunter, chin in hands, made goo-goo faces, and Groucho Marx eyebrows to her. "It was really hard to ignore him," she admitted.

When an offense was alleged, Hunter would smack his forehead loudly with his palm, saying, "Ohhh . . . What bull!" At one point, he took headache medicine from his shirt pocket, spilled the pills on the floor, searched to find and take them, saying, "Oh, good. I found them," while on all fours under the lawyers' table. When an attorney asked Palmer to describe a container that had allegedly held pharmaceuticals that night at Hunter's, she fumbled for the right words. Thompson jumped to his feet, shouting, "Wait! Wait! She doesn't have to describe it—I have it here in my pocket!" and whipped out a pill container, brandishing it around for all to see, like the long-lost murder weapon. "It was like a TV show," Palmer said, of the antics. "You can't get away with that, but they did."

The authorities also got away with overlooking the assault charge, but stormed Hunter's residence, searching for eleven hours. Nothing of final incrimination turned up—a trace of this, some sticks of dynamite—but Hunter became indignant, saying, "They've been after me a long time. The legal system has changed. This is like Germany, 1933. They want me rehabilitated. I'd be willing to go to dynamite rehab in order to learn more about dynamite."

This was the great "life-style bust," the legal airing of old Aspen versus new Aspen, Thompson's persona for the decade: fight city hall. Thompson was acquitted on the 23rd of May, 1991.

The only loud noise heard since was in April of 1992, just as fiction author John Irving was preparing to give a reading from his works-in-progress at the Wheeler Opera House. Thompson fired a red marine distress flare near a skimobiler tooling past Owl Farm. Again, his comments to the papers were eminently quotable: "I am a good citizen. I am a hero of American Literature and a champion of freedom. There were these vultures over the valley, so large—blotting out the sun. I didn't want these vultures attacking tourists, clawing their scalps off, tearing their eyeballs out. It was an attempt to help." The Aspen *Times,* which put Hunter on page 1 and John Irving on page 11, called it Flares and Loathing.

Hunter's constant abuse of his body was taking its toll. People who have known him for the duration express dismay over the cumulative deletrious effects of his life-style of narcotics intake, playing pharmaceutical roulette. A few years before the life-style bust, Thompson had gone to his Aspen physician, Dr. Morgan, who told him in unequivocal terms, "You *are* dead. And you have been for *two years!"* The Doctor had given up on Hunter and soon moved his practice, but not before Thompson sent him a personalized "Thank you." Dr. Morgan used to keep the "Thank you" in his office desk, bringing it out occasionally to make a point about the writer's humor, durability, and survival skills. It was a photo of Thompson clad only in shorts, taken at the Miami Dolphins' training camp. Hunter liked it so much he put a copy inside the dust jacket of *Generation of Swine.* It shows him about to launch a football for what seems the length of the field. He autographed it, writing "Thanks for the advice . . . H.S.T."

After a fluke meeting with an old chum from Louisville, Thompson flew home in May, 1991, for a reunion in his honor of Castlewood Athletic Club members. Hunter's brother Jim had planned a trip to Louisville that coincidentally overlapped with Hunter's. When he learned Hunter's plans, he cancelled his own arrangements. Sam Stallings learned of his old friend's arrival and, for the first time in thirty-five years, called Thompson's mother, to ask for scheduling details. When she answered, Stallings gave his name; Virginia blurted out, "What's wrong now?"

Hunter's stay was a memorable time, but for all the wrong reasons. He drank constantly, and brought his brother Davidson to the reunion, introducing him as "my bodyguard." He wore a plaid shirt, tucked out to hide his liver, and kept on his sunglasses. And he mumbled a lot, explaining to Gerald Tyrrell that he had brain damage. He also told the tale of the piece of furniture in Durango: "Sexiest little table I've ever seen," he mumbled, saying that the price—$592—was paid by another high-school friend living there. When he was videotaped giving his acceptance speech, many there felt it an embarrassment to allow him in front of a crowd of old friends in such condition. Others felt differently—that it was a good time, with good friends. It gave them all a feeling of rootedness. Thompson commented on the sense of competitiveness he had first learned during his days in the athletic club, saying that "yes, it was a gang. But we were a good gang."

In May of 1992, Thompson was inducted into the Louisville Male High Hall of Fame. He took with him for the celebration his new girlfriend, Nicole, and Juan. Thompson's son, after attending Tufts University for the academic year 1982–83, graduated from the University of Colorado (a copy of his diploma hung on the wall in the Woody Creek Tavern for years) and is a free-lance illustrator in Boulder. In a rented Lincoln Town Car, Nicole drove them first to visit with Hunter's mother, who was recovering from a knee transplant in Baptist East Hospital. Jim was in Louisville at this time, to stay and care for Virginia. He and Hunter did not meet.

At one point during their stay, Thompson made a very early morning visit to a sidewalk sale thrown by an electronics store; he had been drinking all night, and continued as he and Nicole looked over the goods. Observing this strange scene, store employees called the St. Mathews police about the tall man with the drink in his hand, wandering and mumbling incoherently in their front yard. After inquiring who had been driving the car, the police administered a breathalizer test—to Nicole. The two were then allowed to continue on, but Hunter raved about the police's imposition as he tried to buy beer at the Holiday Inn where he was staying; they informed him that at 8:30 on a Sunday morning, it was too early to sell liquor in a hotel. He went to his room to sulk.

Nicole then drove to the black-tie affair, at the new grounds of Male High. Thompson asked a friend to accompany him: Ralston Steenrod, an attorney in Louisville, who had been with Hunter the night of the incident in Cherokee Park in 1955 that landed Hunter in jail, then the Air Force.

Thompson, Nicole, Juan, and Ralston toured the campus, Hunter asking for counsel from the attorney as to what he should say in his acceptance speech. His communications were lucid at times, in need of reorienting at others. His glass of Wild Turkey was repeatedly filled from a bottle kept in the car. Often he mumbled, yet at times his speech would clear long enough to converse. Before giving his talk, Hunter and Juan collaborated on some teamwork to help his delivery; this had been needed the year before at the Castlewood reunion. Hand signals from Juan to his father were agreed on, to signal when Hunter might be going too fast, or speaking incoherently. It seemed to work.

"I was not born," Hunter began a well-prepared and obviously edited speech, "I sprang from the head of the statue in Hogan's Park . . ." His allusion was to the area near his boyhood home where for years teens have hung out, drunk beer, and smoked dope. It is Louisville's answer to Haight-Ashbury. The audience was attentive and responsive, and the group went after the ceremonies to KT's, a restaurant whose part-owner was also an old high-school friend. Thompson ate a great quantity of food, and consumed a volume of fruit juices; he is an episodic, binge-like eater, and has always believed in the prophylactic properties of vitamin C. He also drank large quantities of alcohol; but he was in Louisville, among friends.

When he left for the evening, he seemed reconciled with the past, embracing Steenrod, saying, "Well, Ralston, I guess we have come full circle."

Until the late 1970s, the movie *King of Hearts* played repeatedly in Aspen's Wheeler Opera House. The movie tells the story of a town turned over to the control of the inmates of an insane asylum, and Aspenites used to pack the Opera House and cheer with gusto. It used to be their story, but it does not play there anymore. When *King of Hearts* moved on, so did the core ethos of old Aspen: the lure of lunacy. Hunter Thompson used to be just one of the crowd in this town, but he no longer is.

In the old times, Hunter and Sandy would go to the Leather Jug in Snowmass and listen to a young folksinger. They liked him, brought him back to Owl Farm, and laced him with so much marijuana, LSD, and loud rock and roll that he panicked, and cried for someone to take him home. His name was John Denver. Just after graduating from West Point, the author Lucian Truscott was stationed at a nearby Army base. He would fill his jeep with inexpensive food and liquor at the base's PX, and spend the weekend at Hunter's talking literature, drinking beer, and watching football on TV. Henry Preston was a ski instructor in Aspen in the old days, when the Louisville Binghams had a condo there. They would invite Henry and Hunter over for a good Southern reunion—until Hunter found that the condo below was owned by Eric Sevareid, and he tossed in a smoke bomb.

The times were fun, life was simple, and little responsibility was required. When Aspen suddenly became the magnet for the quality of life that Hunter shunned, he wrote himself into a corner, while his friends from old Aspen became responsible parts of the working process. They assumed jobs, raised families, and still kept their political sensibilities. One old friend, Bob Braudis, is sheriff of Pitkin County; on his office walls are hung both his own election poster and Hunter's from 1970. Mike Solheim is deeply involved with politics, and sells real estate. Hunter speaks with them on the phone; they visit him only on occasion. Many who knew Hunter from years ago refer to the people who currently hang out at Owl Farm as, simply, "them," or as "the sycophants." Life there is an ongoing party, a fountain of youth with rock-and-roll music, where chemicals help keep the real world at a distance. There is always a swirl of people through the house, and in new relationships Hunter does not rebuild, he reloads. The cult following is endless; the party never stops.

Hunter, his myth, and his success, when coupled with the American culture's thirst for proximity to the successful, have rendered him cut off from the community for which he once stood as symbol. Surveillance cameras monitor his iron front gate, which is usually locked and covered with a No Trespassing sign. At the W. C. Tavern, the workers must be protective; they do not give directions to the multitude of strangers who come by and ask for Owl Farm. Even the W. C. Tavern, in the '90s, has become crowded with outsiders; Hunter has taken to a new tavern, Friedl's, where others do not think to look for him. For visiting friends, finding a private place to eat or drink in Aspen is difficult during low season, impossible during the busy times. When approached by strangers, Thompson usually reacts in one of two styles. When he has been up for a three-day stint, and feels on the ragged edge, he can react with paranoia, literally running away. When feeling well put together, he has a weakness for speaking with fans. Some think it a reflection of his Kentucky gentility that keeps him talking to strangers, when people such as Hunter's long-time friend Jack Nicholson shoot daggers at anyone attempting to approach. At other times, he can fail to recognize people he knows. Gail Palmer stopped at the W. C. Tavern less than a year after the trial, and had to remind Hunter who she was; Thompson was saving her a stool at the bar, thinking she was there to do an interview. Even Hollywood wants a piece of him; both Jon Peters and Don Johnson have homes in Woody Creek, an area once referred to as "backwater." Thompson will make a sortie into town; he did so in May, 1992, to the Jerome, for the wedding reception of Earl Biss, an old Aspenite, and Native American artist. As always, the unexpected became protocol, such as in October, 1989, when he tossed into the air, and fired his pistol through a copy of *Campaign Trail* at the Woody Creek Tavern wedding reception of political journalist, Dick Tuck. At the Jerome, Thompson found Biss and his bride drinking $175 a bottle champagne; he consulted the bartender and ordered a bottle that was priced at $225. The ending was preordained: Biss danced around the room showing the guests a suitcase filled with $35,000 in cash his in-laws had given the couple for a wedding present; the more expensive champagne was consumed, then Hunter, Loren Jenkins, and the Bisses ran out the front door, jumped into Thompson's red convertible and took off. Left behind was the pricey and empty bottle, the next item on Hunter's bar tab.

Thompson, always nocturnal, will often stay up for two or three days in a row. At times, he will simply watch CNN over and over, or listen to music and party with friends. He had a FAX machine installed at his mother's condo in Louisville, and keeps in close contact.

The last day of July, 1992, Thompson joined Jann Wenner, P. J. O'Rourke, and William Greider in the *Rolling Stone* Lear jet. With a camera crew, they flew to Little Rock, and interviewed Governor Clinton, while eating tamales and cheeseburgers at a low-key local eatery, Doe's Eats Place. Two hours before the scheduled gang interview, Clinton had been informed of the sudden death of his long-time friend and political fund raiser, Vic Raiser, but opted to go through with the three-hour interview and photography session—it was a cover story. Thompson was politically sharp; the questions he asked were strictly policy issues, tactical and detailed to the point of being boring to Clinton staff members. The atmosphere was relaxed, yet formal. The line of questioning from Thompson and the others was so intense in style that an aide felt the walls of the building could have collapsed around them, without their awareness or disruption. There were no shenanigans.

When he has a contract, he will spend the night writing and faxing his work to *Rolling Stone* just before the deadline. His style of work is, in George Plimpton's terms, "like stoking a locomotive." Alcohol, coffee, speed—only then does the engine of creativity begin to roll. He can become ragged toward the end of a long writing jag, and react with extremes of irritation when people drop by or call. Phone calls to his unlisted number are screened by Debra Fuller. She has worked for him for a decade and seen it all. One person who has dealt with Hunter through Debra has said of her staying powers, and her ability to manage Hunter's emotionality, "Come the apocalypse, the reptiles and Debra will make it through alive."

Hunter's isolation has increased recently; his public appearances have become more episodic. When he signed a seven-figure contract for his fiction book *Polo Is My Life,* he slowed down his pace on the lecture circuit, as he did not need the money and never enjoyed the abuse students often served up. In the spring of 1992, he failed to appear for three consecutive sell-out shows at the Strand, in Redondo Beach, California. Management does not welcome him there anymore. One of his Speakers Bureaus refused to book him anymore, because his contractual requirements for alcohol are litigiously difficult.

However, he did appear in Louisville's Kentucky Center for the Arts Whitney Hall on September 9, 1992. The occasion was a reading to raise money for a literacy program. After Tama Janowitz and local writer James Still read from their most recent works, Thompson came on stage, asking, "Can I have a drink?" To his surprise and pleasure, a fifth of Chivas had been placed beneath the table where he sat. He first took a slug directly from the bottle, then a hand appeared from backstage and offered him a glass. He then began his own reading of sorts, a bilious letter to Ted Turner complaining about the CNN polls of the Bush-Clinton race. He started his reading with, "Dear Ted, are you out of your fucking mind???"

With rare exceptions, it appears that he is withdrawing from the world around him, and it concerns those who know him well. But even for those who have observed him for decades, he remains chimerical.

If the past is prologue to the future, people who have known Hunter well from different times still have difficulty in integrating all the various aspects of his personality. Hunter Thompson was described by William F. Buckley, Jr., as "an important sociological phenomenon," but that was descriptive, not explanatory. He remains a big puzzle to some who see odd-shaped pieces of his personality that do not seem to mesh properly.

Two schools of thought pervade. One says that he has achieved the highest plateau of writing in his epistolary, personalized style about the dysfunctional world around him. Others see in him a smugness. They see him as having far exceeded anyone's expectations, including his own. He is really a hillbilly high-school dropout with a half-dozen best-selling books to his name, even a movie.

Ralston Steenrod says he sees "basically the same patterns. You get only a glimpse of the inner Hunter by reading him. The inner Hunter is perceptive, and characterized by a strong sense of justice and injustice. My impression is that this stemmed from his run-ins with authority of all kinds. Hunter was just attracted to things rebellious."

Sam Stallings says of Thompson, "He is never gonna conform. And he's gonna drink until he dies." Many from the Athenaeum hit on a similar theme. They are surprised at his level of success, given his anti-social personality that displayed itself so early and so violently. Hunter was a dropout, they agree, but he succeeded in his style of dropping out.

Alan Rinzler, midwife to so much of Thompson's creative productivity, feels the author has untapped talent. "It puzzles me as to why somebody so talented, so famous would want to kill themselves. As a therapist, I would have to go back to the family origins, some great father-son wound. He is like a smart little brat, writing graffiti, calling attention to himself. He never got past that. Maybe what puzzles me the most is why he has no insight into himself, and doesn't look at himself very deeply."

Paul Semonin is puzzled by the oxymoronic combination of great human tenderness and violence. When asked to describe this defining trait, Semonin spoke of Thompson "as surreal; he is a compassionate shark."

The tenacity of Thompson to look into society's dark side is what puzzles Mike Solheim. "Where does he get the energy to do this, to keep his nose in what is the worst part of our culture, our weakest links? It must be painful. It must hurt to articulate these issues as he does. Perhaps the humor takes off the edge."

Thompson is clearly an angry writer, in an angry land. His sense of profound outrage is a key to his success and a hallmark of the times. It can be difficult to see the depth of Thompson's bile because his humor can become so infectious as to deflect the reader's attention. His cultivated lunacy can override his eagle eye to the errors of convention. He can be seen as an entertainer, an iconoclast, a social reformer, or the ultimate con-artist who has receded into a drug fillod world, and knows nothing of reality. Thompson himself says:

> Nothing puzzles me about myself. My inability to be massively rich? I should be profoundly rich, and it all makes perfect fucking sense. It all makes an extreme kind of high-tension sense. I'm like a weird engine that runs in a lot of different ways. And you think, "He can't be sane. Nobody would put something like that together." But to me, it makes some kind of terrible sense. I'm not at all puzzled.

Underneath the main house at Owl Farm is a small room. It is rarely used. When the police searched the house in 1990, they had to force their way in, as it had been left closed for so long. Inside, the room is dark; there are no windows, no natural light at all. It is painted black. It contains a couple of stuffed owls, and the dust of years gone by. In a corner is a large desk, cluttered but unused. On the wall hangs a photo. It is of Hunter Thompson as a teen, in Louisville, around 1954. He wears Levi's, a T-shirt, and a leather jacket. He looks at the camera over his shoulder, in stern defiance. Few people have seen this photo. Few need to; they can read his works instead.

Interviews

MA	Marco Acosta	GM	Gene McGarr
RLB	Raylynn Barry	MMc	Max McGee
PB	Porter Bibb	GMcG	George McGovern
BB	Bob Bone	NM	Norman Mailer
PBo	Peter Boyle	FM	Frank Mankiewicz
ZB	Zeke Bratkowski	AM	Anne Matera
PC	Philip Caputo	JMi	Joe Mincberg
CC	Chris Cassatt	LM	Larry Mohammad
JdG	Jahn DeGroot	JM	Joseph Monin
WD	William Dorvillier	BM	Bryan Monroe
SD	Stan Dzura	DM	Dennis Murphy
WE	Col. William Evans	MM	Mike Murphy
JF	Joy Ferguson	MP	Max Palevsky
AG	Allen Ginsberg	GPa	Gail Palmer
SG	Shirley Gossett	GP	George Plimpton
NG	Norvin Green	HP	Henry Preston
MG	Minarca Gurule	RPr	Richard Price
FH	Frank Haddad	NP	Nick Proffitt
JH	Jo Hudson	RP	Roxanne Pulitzer
LJ	Loren Jenkins	CR	Cliff Ridley
WK	William Kennedy	ARi	Alan Rinzler
KK	Ken Kesey	AR	Al Romm
TK	Ted Klemens	PSc	Paul Scanlon
TL	Timothy Leary	PS	Paul Semonin
AL	Art Linson	RSe	Robert Semple
GL	George Logan	TFS	T. Floyd Smith
JL	John Lombardi	SS	Stewart Smythe
JAL	J. Anthony Lukas	MS	Mike Solheim

SSt	Sam Stallings, Jr.	GTr	Garry Trudeau
RS	Ralston Steenrod	LT	Lucien Truscott
ST	Studs Terkel	GT	Gerald Tyrrell
ET	Eustace Theodore	CV	Craig Vetter
JT	Jack Thibeau	FW	Floyd Watkins
HST	Hunter S. Thompson	POW	Peter O. Whitmer
VRT	Virginia Ray Thompson*	TW	Tom Wolfe

*all interviews done before 1 October 1991

Journal Abbreviations

APIT	*A Place in Time*. Published by the Louisville Courier-Journal and Louisville Times Company. 1989.
ADI	Ashland (Kentucky) *Daily Independent*.
AT	The Aspen (Colorado) *Times*.
BG	The Boston (Massachusetts) *Globe*.
CJR	*Columbia Journalism Review*.
DH	Durango (Colorado) *Herald*.
DMH	Durham (North Carolina) *Morning Herald*.
ECC	Eglin Air Force Base (Eglin, Florida) *Command-Courier*
GT	Glasgow (Kentucky) *Times*.
H	*Harper's*.
HT	*High Times* magazine.
LAT	Los Angeles (California) *Times*.
LC-J	Louisville (Kentucky) *Courier-Journal*.
M	*MORE* magazine.
NYT	*New York Times*.
NYTBR	*New York Times Book Review*.
P	*Pageant*.
PB	*Playboy*.
PADN	*Playground Area Daily News* (Ft. Walton Beach, FL).
ROR	*Review of Reviews*.
R	*Rogue for Men*.
RS	*Rolling Stone* magazine.
SMH	Santa Monica (California) *Herald*.
SR	*Saturday Review of Literature*.
S	*Scanlon's*
SM	*Smart* magazine.
T	*Time* magazine.

TDC	*The Daily Californian* (University of California, Berkeley).
TDD	*The Distant Drummer.*
TN	*The Nation.*
TNO	*The National Observer.*
TNY	*The New Yorker.*
UWD	University of Washington *Daily.*
USAT	*USA Today.*
VHM	*Virginia Historical Magazine.*
WAL	*Wax and Lead.*
WFMT	WFMT Radio Station, Chicago, IL.

Source Notes

City, Missouri, unpublished: Thompson Genealogy. Also: Genealogy services of Lonni Crosby, Gretna, Virginia. Also: Nottoway County, Virginia, records. Also: *Virginia Historical Magazine.* Vol. 44, 1936, 160–63.

17 In the language of the times . . . Will and Ariel Durant, *The Story of Civilization,* vol. ix, *The Age of Voltaire.* New York: Simon & Schuster, 1965.

17 Another legacy of . . , Nottoway County, Virginia, records, 174. Also: Virginia Historical Magazine, Vol. 44, 1936, 160–163.

17 In the 1920s it was . . . anonymous.

17 As recently as 1940, . . . anonymous.

18 When William Thompson made the move . . . *A History of Horse Cave.* Hart County (Kentucky) Historical Society.

18 Both names were from . . . Thomas D. Clark, *Kentucky: Land of Contrast.* New York: Harper, 1968.

18 In the 1820s when . . . ibid.

18 The name "Stockton" . . . birth records.

18 "Hunter" was the maiden name . . . ibid.

18 Pocahontas, the legendary Indian . . . Laura Purcell Robertson—*Thompson Genealogy,* 3. Hart County Historical Society.

19 Horse Cave was surveyed . . . *A History of Horse Cave.* Hart County Historical Society.

20 During the time of . . . George R. Leighton, "Louisville, Kentucky: An American Museum Piece." *Harper's.* September 1937.

20 Audubon came and painted . . . *The New Yorker,* February 25, 1991.

20 As late as 1937 . . . Leighton, "Louisville, Kentucky."

20 Hunter Thompson's paternal . . . *Kentucky Genealogy and Biography,* vol. 1, 1985–86, 98, 104.

21 John and Corrie Lee . . . interview SG-POW.

21 Their group trick . . . ibid.

22 Her zeal of preference . . . interview RB-POW.

22 Another prank . . . interview SG-POW.

22 But even this carefree . . . Glasgow *Times* (Kentucky) December 29, 1911.

22 When Jack Robert made the . . . interview AM-POW.

23 Baseball would become . . . anonymous.

23 Jack Robert Thompson . . . National Archives.

23 While thousands of doughboys . . . *A Place in Time* (a publication of The Courier-Journal and Louisville Times Co.), 1989

24 The twelve months of duty . . . National Archives.

24 When Jack Robert mustered-in . . . Andrew Turnvull, *Scott Fitzgerald, a Biography.* New York: Collier, 1962, 82; Joseph Blotner, *Faulkner, A Biography.* New York: Vintage Books, 1991, 65.

24 His wife, Garnett Sowards . . . Ashland *Daily Independent,* December 17, 1923.

25 On the heels of the Hatfield-McCoy . . . Harry Caudill, *Night Comes to the Cumberlands,* Chap. 12.

25 During Jack Robert's stay . . . ibid.

25 Garnett was dying of . . . Kentucky Bureau of Vital Statistics.

Chapter Three:
Louisville Sluggers

27 Virginia was born . . . Kentucky birth records.

27 Her father, Presley Stockton Ray . . . interview VRT-POW.

27 He decided to start . . . Louisville Chamber of Commerce, *Louisville Business Records,* 1903–1905.

27 Virginia was bright and . . . University of Michigan *Michigensian,* 1927.

27 In the history of Louisville . . . Leighton, "Louisville, Kentucky."

27 Jack Robert and Virginia moved . . . Louisville property records.

28 The Cherokee Triangle neighborhood . . . *A Place in Time,* The Courier-Journal and Louisville Times Co., 1989, 30.

28 The house at 2437 Ransdell . . . author's visit, courtesy of Rick and Fay McDonough.

29 With the move to Cherokee Triangle . . . all interviews in this section are with individuals as quoted in the text.

31 Hunter spent his first six . . . L. Hovekamp, *Wax and Lead,* vol. 1, #5, summer 1990, Louisville, Kentucky, 40.

32 "A little dictator" . . . ibid.

33 The appearance of Early Gonzo . . . courtesy of Duke Rice.

35 The youngest of . . . Commonwealth of Kentucky, Certificate of Incorporation.

36 As Hunter set off . . . anonymous.

36 During the two summers . . . interview GT-POW.

39 After a three-month stay . . . Commonwealth of Kentucky: Death Certificate.

39 The results indicated a rare . . . interview VRT-POW.

41 When Virginia was working . . . anonymous.

Chapter Four:
Very Male, Very High

45 The principal was a . . . Male High Yearbook, 1955.

45 Across the country . . . interview RS-POW.

53 There was one girlfriend . . . anonymous.

Chapter Five:
Controlling Chaos

57   Hunter, with an able . . . *Interview: Hunter Thompson,* by Ron Rosenbaum. *High Times,* September, 1977, no. 25, 36.

59   After quietly locking himself . . . interview SS-POW.

Chapter Six:
Endgame

60   On the first Saturday . . . LC-J, May 8, 1955.

61   "Young people of America . . . Athenaeum (Male High) Literary Association Yearbook, *The Spectator,* 1955.

61   "Security . . . what does this . . . ibid.

62   Hunter Thompson stood at . . . group interview with Athenaeum Literary Association members and POW.

63   Eleven days before . . . *LC-J,* May 12, 1955.

63   Steenrod, about to . . . interview RS-POW.

64   He tried to bribe . . . interview JM-POW.

65   The police brought Monin . . . interview JM-POW.

65   Officer Dotson . . . ibid.

65   Hunter's hearing took place . . . *LC-J,* June 16, 1955.

65   In the larger of . . . interview FH-POW.

66   When Judge Jull's case . . . ibid.

66   They waited briefly . . . ibid.

66   In the stillness of . . . ibid.

66   Regardless of the conflict . . . *LC-J,* June 16, 1955.

67   Jull spoke directly . . . ibid.

67   A man easily given to . . . ibid.

67   Jull barked out . . . ibid.

67   Further, Jull stated . . . June 16, 1955. *LC-J,*

67   No one was expecting . . . ibid.

67   Jull had seen enough . . . ibid.

67   Even one of the . . . interview JM-POW.

67   Years after the . . . interview FH-POW.

Chapter Seven:
Upward Mobility

71   Ironically, it was . . . interview GL-POW.

72   "You are not . . . August 18, 1955. *LC-J.*

72   It was early in . . . interview NG-POW.

73   Timothy Leary, drawing . . . interview TL-POW.

73   Brendan Behan at the . . . Goertzel & Goertzel, *Cradles of Eminence,* 225–6. Boston: Little, Brown, 1962

Chapter Eight:
The Great Blue Yonder

75 He complained in . . . interview with GL-POW and GT-POW.

76 He later reported . . . interview HP-POW.

78 In the middle of . . . interview WE-POW.

79 This sand dune on . . . Staff Sergeant Joe LaVigne, Eglin AFB.

79 The 30th of August . . . Eglin AFB *Command-Courier,* August 30, 1956.

81 The officer Logan referred . . . interview WE-POW.

82 The first touchdown . . . interviews with MMc and ZB-POW.

82 To add to his . . . *Playground Area Daily News,* Fort Walton Beach, Florida, files.

83 He had time . . . interview HP-POW.

83 The Seagull Bar . . . interview owner-POW.

84 And his behavior . . . interview HP-POW.

85 He had become . . . interview HP-POW.

86 Before leaving the . . . Eglin AFB *Command-Courier.* May 30, 1957.

88 When Thompson had received . . . interview GM-POW. Also see Robert Draper, *Rolling Stone,* especially Chap. 9, 194 ff.

Chapter Nine:
The Smoldering Hatred of a Peasant

90 Thompson steered clear . . . interview GM-POW.

91 Later, when Tyrrell . . . interview GT-POW.

91 Actually, Thompson lived . . . interview PB-POW.

92 It was man versus . . . interview GM-POW.

92 F. Scott Fitzgerald had done . . . Andrew Turnvull, *Scott Fitzgerald, A Biography,* 92. Also, 338–9 regarding Zelda Fitzgerald and her Kentucky relatives.

92 He wore his normal . . . interview TFS-POW.

94 It was in the . . . see Turnvull, 93.

94 For Thompson, a view . . . interview GM-POW.

96 Faulkner's *Winter Dreams* . . . see Harold Bloom, *Modern Critical Views: F. Scott Fitzgerald.* New York: Chelsea House Publishers, 1985. See especially the chapters by Marius Bewley and Malcolm Cowley.

97 Thompson would sit . . . interview CV-POW.

97 Sandra Dawn Conklin . . . interview GM-POW and anonymous.

98 Sandy and her date . . . interview RS-POW.

98 Hunter and Sandy began . . . anonymous.

98 One hallmark of . . . ibid.

98 Often after one . . . interview GM-POW.

100 The city pools were . . . interview GM-POW.

103 They managed to escape . . . ibid.

103 The Middletown *Daily Record* . . . interview AR-POW.

103 In Middletown . . . interview BB-POW.

103 Another of Thompson's . . . ibid.

103 He ate Chou En-lai's . . . J. Anthony Lukas, *More.*

104 The *Record* had a candy . . . interview BB-POW and AR-POW.

104 Out of a job . . . interview BB-POW.

104 In the late fall . . . interview PS-POW.

105 The relationship between . . . anonymous

105 *El Esportivo* was . . . interview WD-POW.

105 In 1992, Kennedy . . . interview WK-POW.

105 Thompson liked the . . . interview PS-POW.

105 After a game of . . . interview TK-POW.

106 The newspaper job never . . . interview PS-POW.

106 Bermuda *Royal Gazette,* July 10, 1960; courtesy of Dave Skinner and Bill Zool.

106 However, Murphy had lost . . . interview DM-POW.

106 "My editor at . . . see Peter O. Whitmer, *Aquarius Revisited.* New York: Macmillan, 1987, Chapters 9 and 10.

107 He had been delivered . . . interview with DM-POW and MM-POW.

107 Dennis and his . . . ibid.

107 Thompson had read . . . interview RS-POW.

107 After he read . . . interview GM-POW.

107 The area around Big Sur . . . see Lawrence Ferlinghetti and Nancy Peters, *Literary San Francisco.* San Francisco: City Lights Books and New York: Harper & Row, 1980.

107 An article on . . . Mildred Edie Brady, "The New Cult of Sex and Anarchy." *Harper's,* April, 1947, 312–22.

Chapter Ten:
New Cult, Old Stuff

109 Those who blazed . . . Walter Truett Anderson, *The Upstart Spring,* Reading, Mass.: Addison-Wesley, 1983, Chap. 2.

110 It is a long-standing joke . . . interview JH-POW.

110 But, in the words . . . interview RPr-POW.

110 Thompson had been hired . . . interview MM-POW.

111 Dennis Murphy, no stranger . . . interviews DM-POW and MM-POW.

111 Dennis Murphy, who knew . . . interview DM-POW.

112 *Rogue for Men* . . . W. T. Anderson, *The Upstart Spring,* 53.

112 Before the time of Henry Miller . . . ibid., 21.

113 It was life in free-form . . . interview JH-POW. Also see Henry Miller, *Big Sur and the Oranges of Hieronymus Bosch,* New York: New Directions, 1957, 30–45.

113 People are always . . . Hunter S. Thompson, "Big Sur and the Tropic of Henry Miller." in *Rogue for Men,* July 1961, 34–50.

113 The owner, Bill Fassett . . . Mary Dearborn, *The Happiest*

Man Alive: Henry Miller: a Biography, New York: Simon & Schuster, 1991, 284.

113 Miller's legacy loomed . . . ibid., Chap. 12.

114 When Allen Ginsberg wrote . . . ibid.

114 An amateur anthropologist . . . Henry Miller, BSOHB, Chapters 2 and 3; Dearborn, *The Happiest Man Alive,* Chap. 12.

114 A physicist from Berkeley . . . Henry Miller, BSOHB, Chapters 2 and 3.

115 Thompson once stopped . . . *TUS,* 47.

115 "Sandy was always . . . interview DM-POW.

116 The two men . . . interview JH-POW.

116 Joan Baez's kittens . . . interview JH-POW.

117 At Slate's she lived . . . interview JH-POW.

117 She stated she was . . . Joan Baez, *And a Voice to Sing With.* New York: Summit Books, 1987.

117 If Thompson thought . . . ibid.

118 There were the typical . . . interview JH-POW.

118 The last part of . . . interview JH-POW.

119 "The very first night . . . interview MM-POW.

119 Murphy was there . . . interviews RPr-POW and MM-POW.

119 Price had done . . . interview RPr-POW. Also see *TUS,* Chap. 2, 25–36.

120 As time went on . . . interviews JH-POW and MM-POW.

121 The following night . . . interviews RPr-POW and MM-POW.

121 Finding himself on . . . interview MM-POW.

122 Big Sur was . . . interview MM-POW.

122 "Young man," . . . interview MM-POW.

122 Mike Murphy missed . . . interview MM-POW.

Chapter Eleven:
The Monkey Who Couldn't Say No

124 Loping along in . . . interview BB-POW.

125 Out of the speeding . . . ibid.

125 Thompson apologized for . . . ibid.

125 Luckily, Hunter had . . . interview BB-POW; also see *National Observer,* December 31, 1962, 14.

125 Bone had arrived . . . interview BB-POW.

125 Hunter had reached . . . interview BB-POW; also *The National Observer,* December 31, 1962, 14.

125 Thompson did have . . . interview CR-POW.

126 Latin America was incredibly . . . *The South American Handbook*—1963. London: Travel Publications, Ltd.

126 Before leaving the . . . interview CR-POW.

126 Ridley saw something . . . ibid.

127 After visiting Barranquilla . . . The National Observer, December 31, 1962, 14.

127 His hometown paper . . . LC-J, November 11, 1962.

127   Taking a break . . . ibid.

127   "Poverty, dysentry, boredom" . . . interview CR-POW.

127   True to form . . . ibid.

128   In *The National Observer* . . . ibid, and see *TNO,* December 31, 1962, 14.

128   Despite indigence and . . . ibid.

128   He took the train . . . *TSAH,* 1963, and *TNO,* December 31, 1962, 14.

128   In Guayquil, Thompson . . . interview CR-POW; also see *TNO,* December 31, 1962, 14.

128   In Bogotá, Thompson . . . ibid.

128   To Ridley, Thompson made . . . interview CR-POW; also *TNO,* December 31, 1962.

128   More train trips . . . ibid.

129   In stumbling down . . . Hunter S. Thompson, *The Great Shark Hunt.* New York: Summit Books, 1979, 348, 352.

129   In Cali, Colombia . . . interview HST-POW.

129   It was while . . . *TNO,* December 31, 1962, 14.

129   No Orient Express . . . author's travel notes.

129   Thompson crossed the . . . *TSAH,* 1963; also *TNO,* December 31, 1962.

130   As he commented . . . interview CR-POW; also *TNO,* December 31, 1962.

130   Thompson lived in . . . interview BB-POW.

130   Soon after moving . . . ibid.

130   This was no . . . ibid.

131   It is doubtful . . . *TNO,* October 28, 1963.

131   Less than two weeks . . . *TNO,* November 11, 1963, 17.

132   Thompson wrote that . . . ibid.

132   Thompson moved out . . . interview BB-POW.

132   Bone and Thompson . . . ibid.

132   Bone recalled the . . . ibid.

132   In February of 1963 . . . *TGSH,* 362.

133   For Bone, this . . . interview BB-POW.

133   Thompson said that . . . interview HST-POW.

133   Other pressures worked . . . anonymous.

134   "He appeared at . . . interviews RSe-POW, and CR-POW.

134   "They had been married . . . State of Indiana, Clark County Document; Book Number 262, page 232, record 12287.

134   Gerald Tyrrell and . . . interview GT-POW.

134   "He got married down . . . ibid.

134   *The National Observer* began . . . see *The Great Shark Hunt,* 521, for complete *TNO* bibliography.

135   As Thompson said . . . interview HST-POW.

135   Thompson was fast . . . Pitkin County (Colorado) Court; Case #79DR13.

135   The youngest Thompson's . . . ibid.

136   The Menace is loose . . . Hunter S. Thompson, *Hell's Angels.*
New York: Ballantine, 1966, 11.

137   The Berkeley campus . . . *Aquarius Revisited,* Chap. 18.

137   Thompson wrote about . . . *TNO,* April 20, 1964.

137   He wrote about this . . . *The Nation,* September 27, 1965.

137   He portrayed the Establishment's . . . ibid.

137   The status of the . . . ibid.

137   They were like . . . ibid.

138   Thompson said of his . . . interview HST-POW.

138   Always driven by . . . *New York Times Magazine,* May 14,
1967.

138   Thompson stated that . . . interview HST-POW.

139   Thompson despised this goalless . . . *New York Times Magazine,* May 14, 1967.

139   Thompson, Sandy and Juan . . . interview GM-POW.

140   Agar flushed one . . . interview TFS-POW.

140   During the summer of . . . interview TFS-POW.

140   What made the most . . . ibid.

141   He traveled to Montana . . . interview MS-POW.

141   Thompson would make . . . interview JdG-POW.

141   The entire Thompson family . . . ibid.

141   At one point, . . . anonymous.

142   In 1965, during . . . interview MM-POW.

143   Carey McWilliams had . . . Carey McWilliams, *The Education
of Carey McWilliams.* New York: Simon and Schuster, 1979.

143   H. L. Mencken had been . . . ibid., 51.

143   In high school . . . interview SS-POW.

144   In first meeting . . . *TNO,* May 17, 1965, and *Playboy,*
November 1974, 75.

145   Hunter stated that . . . *TN,* ibid.

145   "The difference between . . . ibid.

146   The sum total of . . . *TN.,* June 14, 1965, letters to the editor.

146   "Christ!" he recalled . . . *Playboy* interview.

147   Thompson recalled the initial . . . interview HST-POW.

147   "I had an agent . . . interview HST-POW.

147   Jack Thibeau, a good friend . . . interview JT-POW.

147   "The publisher kept . . . interview HST-POW.

148   Getting a contract for . . . interview JH-POW.

149   Smackey Jack stories . . . *Hell's Angels,* 220 (with permission).

149   Thompson mentions Algren's . . . *Hell's Angels,* 199.

149   Thompson wanted permission . . . interview HST-POW.

150   "It is a sense of . . . *Hell's Angels,* 327.

150   His broad meanwhile . . . *Freewheelin' Frank, Secretary of*

the Angels, as told to Michael McClure by Frank Reynolds. Grove Press, 1967 (with permission). See 103ff.

151   On the way to . . . Thompson, *Hell's Angels,* 181.

151   At Hunter and Sandy's apartment . . . HST-ST (WFMT tape).

151   As time progressed . . . ibid.

151   To the Chinese . . . interview HST-POW.

152   For a touch of . . . correspondence TW-POW.

152   Hunter was in awe . . . HST-POW.

152   The introduction of Kesey . . . Thompson, *Hell's Angels,* 292.

152   Thompson described the . . . interview HST-POW.

152   As Jack Thibeau observed . . . interview JT-POW.

153   "I was involved in . . . interview HST-POW.

153   Thibeau, who spent . . . interview JT-POW.

153   He shined, and he . . . interview KK-POW, and see Chap. 20, Whitmer, *Aquarius Revisited.*

153   Kesey's true intention . . . ibid.

154   As the leader of . . . ibid, 184.

155   Jack Thibeau compared . . . interview JT-POW.

155   When Thompson and . . . Whitmer, *Aquarius Revisited,* 99–100, and Tom Wolfe, *The Electric Kool-Aid Acid Test.* New York: Bantam Books, 1968, Chap. 13.

157   Kesey had one way . . . Whitmer, *Aquarius Revisited,* 204.

157   Kesey had been introduced . . . ibid., 204, and *SR,* May-June 1983.

157   Thompson had been aware . . . interview HST-POW.

157   Thompson balanced . . . ibid.

158   "I just measured . . . ibid.

158   "These people who . . . ibid.

158   "In a sense, LSD . . . ibid.

158   The most "violent" incident . . . Thompson, *Hell's Angels,* 297.

159   "See what the fucking lawyers . . . interview HST-POW.

159   In his analysis . . . Thompson, *Hell's Angels,* 302.

159   It was all "ha-ha", . . . Frank Reynolds, *Freewheelin' Frank.* New York: Grove Press, 1967, 78.

160   Ginsberg, then teaching . . . Whitmer, *Aquarius Revisited,* 180–2.

160   Ginsberg, like Thompson . . . ibid.

160   Recalling the night at . . . interview AG-POW.

160   That goddamned Ginsberg . . . Thompson, *Hell's Angels,* 316.

160   Thompson commented . . . interview HST-POW.

160   Soon after the meeting . . . Thompson, *Hell's Angels,* 323.

160   However, trouble for Thompson . . . ibid., 346.

161   He got in his car . . . ibid.

161   "Every biker in the . . . interview HST-POW.

161 In Chicago, on WFMT . . . interview ST-POW, and radio station WFMT tape.

162 In Denver he met . . . interview NM-POW.

Chapter Thirteen:
Tricks of the Trade

163 The scene would ice . . . *Pageant,* 1968.

164 In his mind . . . ibid.

165 Robert Semple, who . . . interview RSe-POW.

165 Price had come up . . . HST-ST (WFMT tape, March 14, 1973).

165 Thompson was stunned . . . *Pageant,* 1968.

166 When the limo stopped . . . ibid.

166 Even as the 1968 . . . ibid.

166 He had attended . . . Hunter S. Thompson, *Fear and Loathing: On the Campaign Trail, '72.* New York: Straight Arrow Books, 1973.

166 One night in early . . . *High Times,* September 1977.

166 Thompson's first act . . . *Scanlon's,* June 1970, and Hunter S. Thompson, *The Great Shark Hunt,* 24.

167 He slung mud at . . . ibid.

167 Thompson helped the newcomer . . . ibid.

167 Steadman picked up quickly . . . ibid.

168 A sudden turn of . . . *High Times,* September 1977.

168 Within a few days . . . ibid.

168 Entitled, "The Kentucky Derby . . . *Scanlon's,* June 1970.

168 A letter came . . . *High Times,* September 1977.

169 He based his approach . . . *Rolling Stone* #67, October 1, 1970.

169 Wenner had heard . . . interview JL-POW.

169 Lombardi read the article . . . ibid.

169 . . . cheap, mean, grinning-hippie . . . *The Distant Drummer,* Summer 1967 (with permission).

170 Three years later . . . interview JL-POW.

170 "He was a bizarre . . . ibid.

171 Thompson knew the impact . . . ibid.

171 Wenner had dropped out . . . Robert Draper, *Rolling Stone Magazine—The Uncensored History.* New York: Harper Perennial, 1990; also see: Robert Sam Anson, *Gone Crazy and Back Again.* Doubleday, 1981.

171 And in 1967 . . . *The Daily Californian,* Spring 1967, Doe Library, The University of California, Berkeley.

171 In founding the first magazine . . . see Draper, *Rolling Stone Magazine,* and Anson, *Gone Crazy.*

172 During one of Thompson's . . . interview JL-POW.

172 Acosta, who would soon . . . interview MS-POW, and MA-POW.

172 When Henry Preston . . . interview HP-POW.

172 In the third week . . . Aspen *Times,* October 29, 1970, 11A.

173 Months before, Thompson had . . . interview MS-POW.

173 Bromley, as the biker . . . Aspen *Times,* October 29, 1970.

173 Along with Acosta . . . interview MS-POW.

174 Curiously, his actual intention . . . ibid.

174 When the incumbent . . . Aspen *Times,* October 29, 1970.

174 "Politics is an art . . . interview HST-POW.

175 While still at MacMillan . . . interview ARi-POW

Chapter Fourteen:
High Bouncing, Gold-Hatted Drugger

176 Fireworks marked the first . . . interview ARi-POW.

177 Rinzler's first impressions . . . ibid.

177 Underneath a banner . . . interview PS-POW.

178 "I want you to know . . . Hunter S. Thompson, *Fear & Loathing in Las Vegas.* New York: Warner Books, 1971, 6.

178 In his family life . . . interview MP-POW.

179 In real life he was . . . interview GM-POW, and MA-POW.

180 As if rehearsing . . . interview MA-POW.

180 "Basically, he was performing . . . interview MA-POW.

181 Let him list the menu . . . *FLLV,* Part 1, Chap. 6.

182 Instead, he and the . . . *FLLV,* Part 2, Chap. 3.

182 "I had to put my boots on . . . *FLLV,* 187.

183 In a moment of reflection . . . ibid., 178.

183 The American Dream . . . ibid., 191.

183 Journalism is not a . . . ibid., 200.

183 When the real-life . . . interview ARi-POW.

183 Acosta's concerns were . . . interview MA-POW.

183 The action in Las Vegas . . . interview MA-POW.

184 Further, much of the dialogue . . . ibid.

184 Not only did Thompson do . . . interview CV-POW.

184 When Scanlon read the . . . interview PSc-POW.

Chapter Fifteen:
Rock and Roll

185 Over dinner at one . . . interview ARi-POW, and *FLLV,* 184.

186 Arthur Rock had begun . . . *Time,* January 23, 1984.

186 One of his deals . . . interview MP-POW.

186 In turn, Palevsky . . . ibid.

186 After about a year . . . ibid.

186 In Palevsky's eyes . . . ibid.

187 At the end of the . . . interview FM, MP, and GMcG-POW.

187 For days, the staff . . . Draper, 232–235.

187   But Wenner was crafty . . . interview ARi-POW.

188   Thompson spoke of the . . . interview HST-POW.

188   This particular campaign . . . interview GMcG-POW.

189   Thompson used the analogy . . . *FLLV,* 380.

189   "Once *Rolling Stone* established . . . interview PB-POW.

190   Wenner's errors of enthusiasm . . . see Draper, *Rolling Stone Magazine,* and Anson, *Gone Crazy.*

190   When John Lombardi resigned . . . interview JL-POW.

190   Thompson called on his . . . interview RSe-POW.

191   For the first part . . . Timothy Crouse, *The Boys on the Bus.* New York: Ballantine Books, 1974.

191   But Thompson overlooked . . . Kenneth Lynn, *Hemingway.* New York: Simon & Schuster, 1987, 69.

191   Also, Joe Mankiewicz . . . interview FM-POW, also see Harold Bloom, ed., *Modern Critical Views—F. Scott Fitzgerald,* 59.

191   "What I thought about . . . interview FM-POW.

191   George McGovern had come . . . interview GMcG-POW.

191   McGovern said . . . ibid.

192   "I don't think he missed . . . interview PSc-POW.

192   Alan Rinzler would often . . . interview ARi-POW.

192   Even the august . . . *Columbia Journalism Review,* November 1973.

192   ". . . very hard to walk . . . Thompson, *Fear and Loathing: On the Campaign Trail,* 222.

193   In another year . . . interview CV-POW.

193   "Hunter sensed that . . . interview FM-POW.

193   McGovern concurred with . . . interview GMcG-POW.

194   McGovern went further . . . ibid.

194   Especially in the early . . . ibid.

194   McGovern won the party . . . interview ST-HST, March 14, 1973, WFMT tape.

195   Apparently Hunter made . . . interview FM-POW.

195   McGovern refers to Watergate . . . interview GMcG-POW.

195   "Hunter despised Nixon . . . ibid.

195   Mankiewicz felt that . . . interview FM-POW.

196   Timothy Crouse stated . . . Crouse, *Boys on the Bus.*

196   Crouse spoke of his . . . interview JAL-POW.

196   "He always had a beer . . . interview GMcG-POW.

196   "The man drank like . . . Thompson, *Fear and Loathing: On the Campaign Trail,* 258.

197   John Lombardi showed up . . . interview JL-POW.

197   Max Palevsky's house . . . interview MP-POW.

198   Other incidents at Woody Creek . . . ibid.

199   Palevsky looked back . . . ibid.

199   "I personally assured Ehrlichman . . . interview RSe-POW, also see Thompson, *Fear and Loathing: On the Campaign Trail,* 404.

199   In real life . . . interview AR-POW.

Chapter Sixteen:
God and Gonzo at Yale

202 Journalist Tony Lukas . . . interview JAL-POW.

202 "When I did the piece . . . ibid.

203 Around the mirror in . . . *MORE*, November 1972 (with permission).

203 "I would understand by . . . ibid.

203 Thompson began his night shift . . . ibid.

204 "It was getting real . . . interview JAL-POW.

204 "Thompson surrendered the . . . ibid.

204 Leaping up from . . . *MORE*, November 1972.

204 Lukas admitted that . . . interview JAL-POW.

205 A while after Lukas's article . . . ibid.

205 In the long run . . . ibid.

205 The staunch anti-Vietnam . . . William F. Buckley, Jr., *God and Man at Yale.* South Bend, Indiana: Regnery/Gateway, 1977, xxi

206 Eustace Theodore . . . interview ET-POW.

206 They felt as if . . . ibid.

206 It was an impossibility . . . ibid.

207 Almost paradise . . . ibid.

207 The door to the . . . ibid.

208 In his freshman year . . . *Time*, February 9, 1976.

208 Hunter Thompson was not . . . ibid.

208 As a pipesmoking . . . Boston *Globe*, March 9, 1987, 3.

209 Thompson went for . . . *HT*, September 1977.

209 Flying to the west coast . . . Universal Press Syndication—POW.

209 When Thompson began covering . . . interview *HT*, September 1977.

210 When asked about . . . correspondence GTr-POW.

210 The connective tissue . . . *Time*, February 9, 1976.

Chapter Seventeen:
To Duke or Not to Duke

212 "I have never believed . . . interview *Playboy*, November 1974 (with permission).

213 Thompson had been annoyed . . . interview CV-POW.

213 "Those were the fat . . . ibid.

214 "Hunter represented what . . . ibid.

216 The previous time . . . Whitmer, *Aquarius Revisited*, Chapters 3 and 4.

216 Hunter Thompson was sitting . . . *Playboy*, November, 1974.

216 Vetter had known . . . interview CV-POW.

217 Months before the interview . . . interview CV-POW.

218 For a while . . ., Thompson, *The Great Shark Hunt*, 486.

218　This irked George . . . interview GMcG-POW.

218　"I was giving . . . *HT,* September 1977.

219　On the West Coast . . . interview PSc-POW.

219　Scanlon had been . . . ibid.

220　Thompson and Steadman spent . . . interview GP-POW, and George Plimpton, *Shadow Box.* New York: Putnam, 1977, 254 (with permission).

Chapter Eighteen:
. . . . . As in Magic

223　"Bad Genet . . . Norman Mailer, *The Fight.* Boston: Little Brown, 1975.

223　On the flight from . . . interview GP-POW.

223　Dressed in his uniform . . . Plimpton, *Shadow Box,* 251.

224　Ernest Hemingway had been . . . Plimpton, *Shadow Box,* 259.

224　The relationship between . . . interview GP-POW.

224　"I wanted to start it . . . interview GP-POW.

224　Passing through New York . . . Plimpton, *Shadow Box,* 259–63.

225　In covering the fight . . . ibid., 259.

225　Plimpton caught many . . . ibid., 244.

225　Mailer saw the same . . . Mailer, *The Fight.*

225　"Hunter's idea . . . interview GP-POW.

226　Plimpton noted . . . ibid.

226　For getting him the tapes . . . correspondence TW-POW.

226　He said "The people . . . Thompson, *The Great Shark Hunt,* 108.

226　Plimpton said of . . . interview GP-POW.

227　"They turned away . . . Plimpton, *Shadow Box,* 253.

227　Thompson and Cardoza . . . ibid., 242–3.

227　One episode involved . . . ibid., 335–6.

228　The next day . . . interview GP-POW.

228　"This is a bad town . . . Plimpton, *Shadow Box,* 334.

229　Hunter explained that . . . ibid.

229　Thompson did in fact . . . interview HST-POW.

230　"Well, vehicular . . . Plimpton, *Shadow Box,* 336.

230　One of Thompson's last . . . ibid., 256.

230　On a wall in . . . author's research, courtesy of GP.

Chapter Nineteen:
Dinner at the Existential Café

231　Lying on his stomach . . . interview PC-POW.

232　For him, this was a . . . Philip Caputo, *Means of Escape.* New York: HarperCollins, 1991.

232   On his way to . . . interview BB-POW.

233   In a corner of the . . . interview PC-POW.

233   Caputo had expected . . . interview PC-POW.

233   Proffitt was "surprised . . . interview NP-POW.

234   Loren Jenkins had moved . . . interview LJ-POW.

234   The journalists' regular driver . . . interview PC-POW.

235   But when Proffitt . . . interview NP-POW.

236   Suddenly, the silence . . . interview PC-POW.

237   Thompson was fascinated . . . interview NP-POW.

237   The journalist caught . . . ibid.

237   For all its dangers . . . interview PC-POW.

238   They found the American . . . Caputo, *Means of Escape,*
Chap. 7.

238   Caputo had told them . . . interview PC-POW.

239   "You could measure . . . ibid.

239   Proffitt assumed his absence . . . interview NP-POW.

239   "I do not know . . . ibid.

240   After a while . . . interview PC-POW.

240   Caputo said . . . ibid.

240   When Hunter's loud cursing . . . interview NP-POW.

240   The next night . . . interview PC-POW.

241   Back at the Continental . . . interview NP-POW.

241   A year or so later . . . ibid.

241   He went there . . . *RS,* May 22, 1975.

242   "He took it very personally . . . interview ARi-POW.

Chapter Twenty:
Gonzo Goes Hollywood

244   The bartender was . . . ibid.

244   At six feet six . . . *"Playboy All-America Pre-season Team,"
Playboy,* September 1965.

244   Just a few nights . . . interview SD-POW.

244   That night at the Jerome . . . ibid.

245   Even Dzura was cowed . . . ibid.

245   While Gene McGarr . . . interview GM-POW.

245   During these years . . . ibid.

246   The family dynamics . . . anonymous.

246   There was a shared . . . interview SD-POW.

246   With Sandy, there was . . . anonymous.

247   He stayed in the Honeymoon . . . interview ARi-POW.

247   Somewhat later . . . Thompson, *The Great Shark Hunt,* 17–
18.

247   He felt that . . . ibid., and interview HST-POW.

247   Through his neighbor . . . Pitkin County (Colorado) Records,
Case #79DR13.

247   Dzura had seen things . . . interview SD-POW.

247   During this time . . . interview DM-POW.

247   In August 1978 . . . Pitkin County Records.

248   In the mid-1970's . . . interview PBo-POW.

248   He sold the rights . . . Pitkin County Records.

248   (Thompson still keeps . . . interview MA-POW.

249   Murray had been . . . interview PBo-POW.

249   Of the original stars . . . Doug Hill and Jeff Weingrad, *Saturday Night, A Backstage History of Saturday Night Live*. New York: Beach Tree Books, 1986, Chap. 20.

249   Cast as a contemporary . . . interview PBo-POW.

249   Linson and Kaye . . . "The Best of Hollyweird," *Playboy*, June 1980, 143.

250   Murray had immediate . . . interview PBo-POW.

250   Boyle kept pretty much . . . ibid.

250   When it was released . . . interview MA-POW.

250   A Chicano actors' group . . . interview PBo-POW.

251   One morning, Murray . . . ibid.

251   When Ralph Steadman appeared . . . "The Best of Hollyweird," *Playboy*.

251   For Boyle, the single . . . interview PBo-POW.

251   After completing Buffalo . . . Hill and Weingrad, *Saturday Night Live*, 350-1.

251   When he did . . . ibid., 229.

251   One writer said . . . ibid., 351.

251   On the film set . . . interview PBo-POW.

251   Linson's assessment of . . . interview AL-POW.

252   Hunter took an extra . . . Pitkin County Records.

252   The writing was put off . . . "The Best of Hollyweird," *Playboy*.

252   Craig Vetter was there . . . interview CV-POW.

252   In the ending . . . movie, *Where the Buffalo Roam*.

253   Only at the very end . . . interview PBo-POW.

Chapter Twenty-one:
Mambo, Dildo, Gonzo, Lono

254   On a tiny table top . . . author's research.

255   In August 1979 . . . NYTBR, 5 August 1979.

256   In April 1980, Sandy . . . Pitkin County Records.

256   The court did not agree . . . ibid.

256   Thompson replied . . . ibid.

256   Meanwhile, back at . . . author's research.

257   "Hunter Thompson? I baby-sat . . . ibid.

257   In May 1980, . . . Hunter S. Thompson, *Curse of Lono*. New York: Bantam, 1983, 8-10.

257   Hunter's attorney pleaded . . . Pitkin County Records.

257   In Honolulu, Thompson spent . . . Thompson, *Curse of Lono*, 61.

258   By nature, she is quiet . . . author's research.

258 Thompson even had Laila . . . Thompsom, *Curse of Lono*, 4.

258 The spirit of Thompson's . . . interview BB-POW.

258 Back in Aspen . . . Pitkin County Records.

259 When he and Laila . . . interview SD-POW.

260 Alan Rinzler was again . . . interview ARi-POW.

260 Rinzler went to Aspen . . . ibid.

261 For Thompson, it all . . . Thompson, *Curse of Lono*, 154–5.

261 And, at an added . . . ibid., 4.

Chapter Twenty-two:
Shortest Night of the Year

263 I was interviewing . . . *SR,* January–February, 1984, 18.

263 True to form . . . all author's research, including interview HST-POW, unless otherwise noted.

263 He introduces himself to . . . Thompson, *Curse of Lono*, 39.

264 To cover the Ali-Spinks . . . interview GP-POW.

264 In 1980, with the . . . interview ARi-POW.

265 It was the music . . . Roxanne Pulitzer, *The Prize Pulitzer*. New York: Ballantine Books, 1987, 204.

265 Herbert Pulitzer's first attorney . . . ibid., 185.

265 In the alimony issue . . . ibid., 265.

266 He kept Owl Farm . . . Pitkin County Records.

He had used . . . Thompson, *Hell's Angels*, 78.

270 A call was put through . . . interview JMi-POW.

271 "Roxanne Pulitzer . . . *RS,* July 1983.

272 "Oddly enough . . . interview RP-POW.

Chapter Twenty-three:
The Doctor Makes House Calls

274 Thompson was given the hook . . . Durham *Morning Herald,* October 24, 1974.

274 He had been met . . . Plimpton, *Shadow Box,* 251.

274 A week later . . . interview GP-POW.

275 Was Thompson contrite . . . ibid.

275 At New York University . . . interview JT-POW.

276 After the release of . . . *New York Times,* Arts and Leisure Section, November 13, 1983.

276 At UCLA it was written . . . Elaine Warren, in Santa Monica *Herald,* February 27, 1984, B-1.

276 (Once in Key West . . . anonymous.

277 Thompson spent his time . . . Los Angeles *Times,* November 21, 1983.

277 But it hooked him . . . *Time,* December 5, 1983, 50.

277 The day after UCLA . . . *USA Today,* February 28, 1983.

277 Thompson accepted an offer . . . interview MG-POW.

278 However, he did call . . . ibid.

278 While local editorial pages . . . Durango *Herald,* March 20, March 31, and April 5, 1991.

278 When Hunter arrived . . . video of HST at Fort Lewis College.

280 The questions about . . . anonymous.

280 In many ways . . . ibid.

281 In his hotel room . . . interview GT-POW.

281 In the wee hours . . . interview RLB-POW.

Chapter Twenty-four:
Dessert at the Carpe Diem Hotel

282 On a spring afternoon . . . author's research.

284 In 1985, he had . . . interview FW-POW.

284 The place is nice . . . author's research.

285 In the sensibilities of . . . Aspen *Times,* August 5, 1989.

285 The new version . . . Ted Conover, *Whiteout.* New York: Random House, 1991, 105–9.

285 *60 Minutes* had done . . . interview FW-POW.

285 So it was with some . . . ibid.

286 Thompson gave his version . . . Loren Jenkins, *SM,* January-February, 1990, 39.

286 In late February of 1990 . . . interview GPa-POW; also see *High Times,* August 1990, and *Rolling Stone,* June 28, and July 12, 1991.

The newspapers . . . Aspen *Times,* April 6, 1992.

291 Hunter's constant abuse . . . interview MS-POW.

291 Hunter's brother, Jim . . . anonymous.

292 Sam Stallings learned . . . interview SSt-POW.

292 Hunter's stay was a . . . interview GT-POW.

292 In May of 1992 . . . interview RS-POW.

292 Jim was in . . . anonymous.

292 At one point during . . . anonymous.

293 In the old times . . . interview MS-POW.

294 Just after graduating from . . . interview LT-POW.

294 Henry Preston was a . . . interview HP-POW.

294 One old friend . . . author's research.

295 At the Jerome . . . interview CC-POW.

295 Two hours before . . . Clinton-Gore Headquarters-POW.

296 The line of questioning from . . . ibid.

296 In the spring of 1992 . . . author's research.

296 However, he did appear . . . interview LM-POW.

297 Hunter Thompson was described . . . *NYBTR,* August 5, 1979.

Bibliography

Acosta, Oscar Zeta. *The Revolt of the Cockroach People.* New York: Vintage 1989.

——. *The Autobiography of a Brown Buffalo.* New York: Vintage 1989

Anderson, William Truett. *The Upstart Spring.* Reading, Mass.: Addison-Wesley, 1983.

Anson, Robert Sam. *Gone Crazy and Back Again.* New York: Doubleday, 1981.

Baez, Joan. *And a Voice to Sing With.* New York: Summit Books, 1987.

Bloom, Harold. *Modern Critical Views: F. Scott Fitzgerald.* New York: Chelsea House, 1985.

Blotner, Joseph. *Faulkner, a Biography.* New York: Vintage Books, 1991.

Buckley, William F., Jr. *God and Man at Yale.* South Bend, Ind.: Regnery/Gateway, 1977.

Caputo, Philip. *Means of Escape.* New York: HarperCollins, 1991.

Caudill, Harry. *Night Comes to the Cumberlands.* Boston: Little, Brown, 1962.

Conover, Ted. *Whiteout.* New York: Random House, 1991.

Crouse, Timothy. *The Boys on the Bus.* New York: Ballantine Books, 1986.

Dearborn, Mary. *The Happiest Man Alive.* Henry Miller, a Biography. New York: Simon & Schuster, 1991.

Draper, Robert. *Rolling Stone Magazine—The Uncensored History.* New York: Harper Perennial, 1990.

Durant, Will, and Ariel Durant. *The Age of Voltaire.* New York: Simon & Schuster, 1965.

Ferlinghetti, Lawrence, and Nancy Peters. *Literary San Francisco.* San Francisco: City Lights Books, 1980.

Goertzel & Goertzel. *Cradles of Eminence.* Boston: Little, Brown, 1962.

Hill, Doug, and Jeff Weingrad. *Saturday Night: A Backstage History of Saturday Night Live.* Beach Tree Books, 1986.

Lynn, Kenneth. *Hemingway.* New York: Simon & Schuster, 1987.

McClure, Michael. *Freewheelin' Frank, Secretary of The Angels.* New York: Grove Press, 1987.

McWilliams, Carey. *The Education of Carey McWilliams.* New York: Simon & Schuster, 1979.

Mailer, Norman. *The Fight.* Boston: Little, Brown, 1975.

Miller, Henry. *Big Sur and the Oranges of Hieronymus Bosch.* New York: New Directions, 1957.

Plimpton, George. *Shadow Box.* New York: Putnam, 1975.

Pulitzer, Roxanne. *The Prize Pulitzer.* New York: Ballantine Books, 1987.

The South American Handbook—1963. London: Travel Publications, Ltd.

Thompson, Hunter S. *Curse of Lono.* New York: Bantam Books, 1983.

———. *Fear & Loathing in Las Vegas.* New York: Warner Books, 1971.

———. *The Great Shark Hunt.* New York: Summit Books, 1979.

———. *Hell's Angels.* New York: Ballantine, 1966.

Turnvull, Andrew. *Scott Fitzgerald, a Biography.* New York: Collier, 1962.

Whitmer, Peter O., *Aquarius Revisited.* New York: Macmillan, 1987.

Wolfe, Tom. *The Electric Kool-Aid Acid Test.* New York: Bantam Books, 1968.

Index

Rice, Grantland, 165
Ridley, Clifford, 126–30
Rinzler, Alan, 174–75, 183, 189,
    192, 196, 200, 219, 242,
    247, 260, 264–65, 297;
    Thompson as perceived by,
    176–77; Thompson's contract
    and, 187–88
Robbins, Tom, 89, 177
Robinson, Jackie, 33
Rock, Arthur, 185–86, 187
Rogers, Isaiah, 20
Rogue for Men, 112, 113, 115,
    116, 121, 122
Rojas Pinilla, Gustavo, 128
Rolling Stone, 14, 91, 92, 169,
    170, 173, 176, 184, 186,
    187, 188–92, 196, 197, 198,
    202, 209, 210, 218, 219,
    226, 232, 238, 241, 247,
    264, 266, 267, 270, 271,
    272, 277, 284, 295, 296;
    Thompson's first piece for,
    171–72
Rolling Stones, 203
Romm, Al, 103, 104
Roosevelt, Nicholas, 113
Rum Diary (Thompson), 106,
    115, 126, 132
Running, 257
Rupp, Adolph, 38, 80
Russell, Ken, 253
Ruwe, Nick, 166

Sales, Ronnie, 265
Salter, Jim, 166
Sanders, Harlan, 61
Sandpiper, The (film), 142
Sanford, Terry, 274
San Francisco *Chronicle*, 153
San Francisco *Examiner*, 145,
    284
San Juan *Star*, 172
"Saturday Night Live," 248, 249,
    251, 258, 260
Saturday Review, 263
Savage Lucy, 182
Savio, Mario, 171
Scanlon, Paul, 184, 192, 219
Scanlon's, 166, 168
ScrewJack Files, 288

"Security" (Thompson), 61–62
Seiler, Robert, 63
Semonin, Paul, 90–91, 92, 94,
    98, 104–7, 134–35, 140, 297
Semple, Bob, 134, 190, 199, 203,
    205
Sergeant, The (Murphy), 106,
    107, 112, 115
Serra, Tony, 250
Sevareid, Eric, 294
Shadow Box (Plimpton), 230
Shelley, Burton, 49–50, 57, 58
Shockley, William, 186
Shriver, Sargent, 195
Sinclair, Upton, 107
Singular Man, A (Donleavy),
    131–32
"Sixty Minutes," 285
Smith, Bill, 29, 48, 49
Smith, T. Floyd, 31, 32, 47, 50,
    57, 90, 92–93, 94, 115, 140
Smythe, Stewart, 50–51, 59, 62,
    68
Snepp, Frank, 233
Snow, Hank, 77
Snyder, Gary, 136
Solheim, Mike, 172, 173, 258,
    264, 294, 297
Sometimes a Great Notion
    (Kesey), 155
Songs of the Doomed (Thompson),
    284
Sound and the Fury, The
    (Faulkner), 93
Southern Cross, 219–20
Southern Star, 33–34
Spectator, 46, 55, 61, 79
Spock, Benjamin, 267
Sports Illustrated, 181, 224
Stalin, Joseph, 103
Stallings, Sam, Jr., 8, 42, 51–52,
    53, 54, 57, 62, 70, 75, 292,
    297; Cherokee Park incident
    and, 63–66
Stallings, Sam, Sr., 43, 64,
    65–67
Stallone, Sylvester, 283
Starr, Bart, 82
Steadman, Ralph, 166–68, 179,
    219, 220–21, 223, 257, 258,
    259, 261